MACMILLAN / McGRAW-HILL

LANGUAGE ARTS TODAY

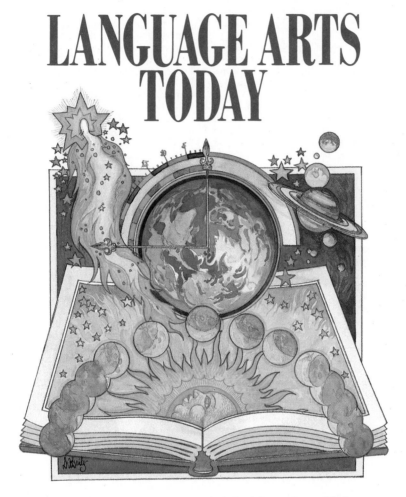

Great literature is an inspiration. Roy A. Gallant's *Private Lives of the Stars*
inspired artist Don Daily to create the illustration on the cover of your book.
The selection begins on page 476. We hope that you enjoy the selection and
the illustration!

SENIOR AUTHORS

ANN McCALLUM   WILLIAM STRONG   TINA THOBURN   PEGGY WILLIAMS

Literature Consultant   Joan Glazer

Macmillan / McGraw-Hill School Publishing Company
New York   Chicago   Columbus

ACKNOWLEDGMENTS

The publisher gratefully acknowledges permission to reprint the following copyrighted material:

Beyond the Divide by Kathryn Lasky. Copyright © 1983 by Kathryn Lasky. Reprinted by permission of Macmillan Publishing Company and reprinted and recorded by permission of Sheldon Fogelman.

"The Cat Who Thought She Was a Dog and the Dog Who Thought He Was a Cat" from *Naftali the Storyteller and His Horse, Sus and Other Stories* by Isaac Bashevis Singer. Text copyright © 1973, 1976 by Isaac Bashevis Singer. All rights reserved. Reprinted by permission of Farrar, Straus and Giroux, Inc.

I Know Why the Caged Bird Sings by Maya Angelou. Copyright © 1969 by Maya Angelou. Reprinted and recorded by permission of Random House, Inc.

Private Lives of the Stars by Roy A. Gallant. Copyright © 1986 by Roy A. Gallant. Reprinted with permission of Macmillan Publishing Company.

"Rising Above the Obstacles" by Joan Ackermann-Blount. Copyright © 1984 by Joan Ackermann-Blount. Originally appeared in *Sports Illustrated*, January 16, 1984. Photographs by Mark Perstein/Sports Illustrated.

Sam Ellis's Island by Beatrice Siegel. Copyright © 1985 by Beatrice Siegel. Reprinted with permission of Four Winds Press, an imprint of Macmillan Publishing Company.

"Tackle the Big Jobs" was originally titled "When Does Education Stop?" and is from *A Michener Miscellany: 1950-1970* by James A. Michener. Copyright © 1973 by James Michener. Originally published in *Reader's Digest*. Reprinted and recorded by permission of the William Morris Agency, Inc. on behalf of the author.

Poems, Brief Quotations, and Excerpts
"The Base Stealer" by Robert Francis. Copyright © 1960 by Robert Francis. Reprinted by permission of Wesleyan University Press.

"Night Thought of a Tortoise" from *The Flattered Flying Fish and Other Poems* by E. V. Rieu. Copyright © 1962 by E. V. Rieu. Reprinted by permission of Associated Book Publishers PLC.

Brief quotation by Beatrice Siegel is from the March 1983 *Junior Literary Guild* catalog. Reprinted by permission of the author.

Haiku by Soin is from *An Introduction to Haiku*, edited by Harold G. Henderson. Copyright © 1958 by Harold G. Henderson. Reprinted by permission of Doubleday, a division of Bantam, Doubleday, Dell Publishing Group, Inc.

Excerpt from "Jewels" from *Small Poems* by Valerie Worth. Copyright © 1972 by Valerie Worth. Reprinted by permission of Farrar, Straus and Giroux, Inc.

"Mountain Wind" by Barbara Kunz Loots is used by permission of Barbara Kunz Loots.

Excerpt from "The Song of the Settlers" and full poem from *A Mirror for the Sky* by Jessamyn West. Copyright 1947, 1975 by Jessamyn West. First published in *The New Yorker*. Reprinted by permission of Harcourt Brace Jovanovich, Inc. and Russell & Volkening, Inc.

Haiku by Shiki is from *More Cricket Songs*, Japanese Haiku translated by Harry Behn. Copyright © 1971 by Harry Behn. All rights reserved. Reprinted by permission of Marian Reiner.

(Acknowledgments continued on page 603.)

Cover Design: Barnett-Brandt Design
Cover Illustration: Don Daily

Macmillan/McGraw-Hill School Division
10 Union Square East
New York, New York 10003

Printed in the United States of America

ISBN: 0-02-244118-2
9 8 7 6 5 4

MACMILLAN/McGRAW-HILL

LANGUAGE ARTS TODAY

C O N T E N T S
THEME: *TREASURES*

AWARD WINNING
SELECTION

THEME: *REFLECTIONS*

AWARD WINNING
SELECTION

THEME: *LEGACIES*

THEME: *ACHIEVEMENTS*

THEME: *IMPRESSIONS*

AWARD WINNING
SELECTION

THEME: *PERSPECTIVES*

THEME: *GALAXIES*

WRITER'S REFERENCE

I'm here to answer some questions about writing, writer to writer, you might say. Ready? Let's begin!

How can I
get ideas
for writing?

This book can really help you there. There's great literature between these covers. I noticed that after reading a good story, biography, or poem, I wanted to respond. Sometimes I wanted to write about the same topic or in a similar style. Sometimes I wanted to write a journal entry.

Writers
are readers,
and readers
are writers!

I know that sometimes, no matter how hard I try, the ideas won't come. Reading a story doesn't work. Talking with my friends doesn't help. Then, I take a look at the **PICTURES** SEEING LIKE A WRITER section in this book, and presto! Ideas start to flow. The pictures turn up the volume on my imagination.

IMAGINE

What will I write about today?

Writers observe, and observers can find lots of ideas for writing.

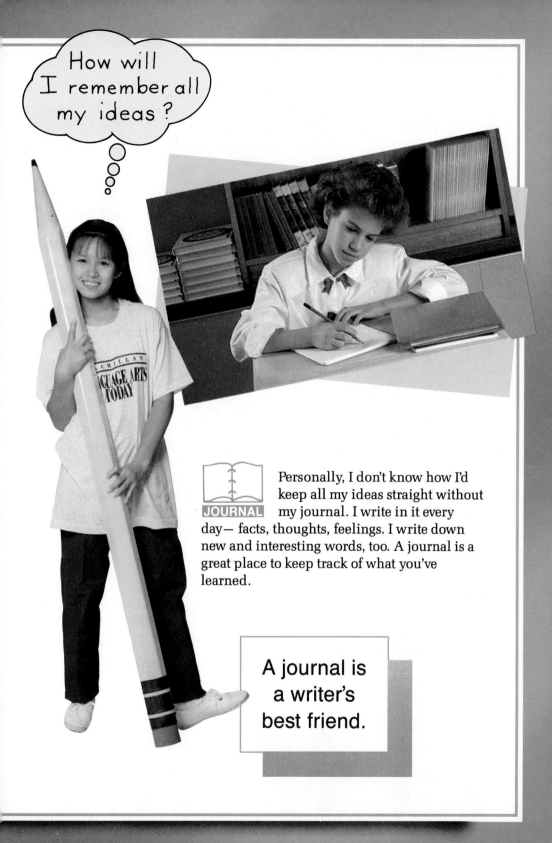

How will I remember all my ideas?

Personally, I don't know how I'd keep all my ideas straight without my journal. I write in it every day— facts, thoughts, feelings. I write down new and interesting words, too. A journal is a great place to keep track of what you've learned.

A journal is a writer's best friend.

How does working with a group help?

Writing doesn't have to be something that you do alone. I get lots of ideas when I work with my classmates. During group writing, we write and conference together. When it's time to write on my own, I'm all warmed up and ready to go.

Writing together builds confidence; conferences get the ideas flowing.

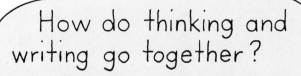

How do thinking and writing go together?

I really give my brain a workout when I write. I can't help it. To write, you have to think about many things: sequence; main idea; cause and effect; and likenesses and differences.

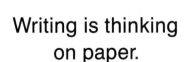

Writing is thinking on paper.

What is the writing process, and how will it help me?

Writing isn't something that just happens 1-2-3. It takes time to write. The writing process allows me the time I need.

Prewrite

At this stage I can get ideas and plan my writing. I need to think about my purpose and audience. Graphic organizers can really help here.

born Oakland, Ca. — 1934

— 1940

studied nursing — 1951
met Granddad, married April 10 — 1953
moved to Portland — 1956
Sarah (Mom) born — 1960
moved to Virginia — 1966
retired from nursing — 1970
bike trip in France — 1971
Jaime born — 1977
— 1980
trip to India — 1982
— 1990

Write a First Draft

This is the stage when I overcome the "blank paper blues." I don't let small mistakes hold me up. I like this stage because I finally get to *see* what I think. I guess that's what it means to be a writer.

MACMILLAN
LANGUAGE ARTS
TODAY

> Don't tell anyone, but I feel most like a writer when I revise. It's such a thrill to be in control!

| **Revise** | Before I revise, I take some  **TIME-OUT** . I need to let my writing settle a bit. Then I read my writing to myself and to a friend. I then take pencil in hand and go to it. I add, take out, move around, and combine some sentences. I even go back to prewriting for more ideas. |

| **Proofread** | During this stage, I fix all my grammar, spelling, capitalization, and punctuation mistakes. I proofread for one error at a time. (Take my advice. Learn the proofreading marks. You can use them to make changes simply and easily.) |

| **Publish** | I knew I was an author when I saw the word "publish." Publishing can mean reading your writing to friends or taking it home to show your family— anything that involves sharing your writing with your audience. |

1

Sentences

In this unit you will learn about kinds of sentences. By using different kinds of sentences in your writing, you can express your thoughts in a variety of ways. Sentence variety helps to make your writing interesting for your audience.

Discuss Read the poem on the opposite page. Why are words like jewels?

Creative Expression The unit theme is *Treasures*. What do you treasure? Write about something that is of value to you. You might want to write a poem or a letter to a friend. Write your thoughts in your journal.

THEME: *TREASURES*

In words, in books,
Jewels blaze and stream
Out of heaped chests
Or soft, spilled bags:

Diamonds, sharp stars
Polished emerald tears,
Amethysts, rubies, opals
Spreading fire-surfaced pools . . .

—Valerie Worth, from "Jewels"

1 KINDS OF SENTENCES

A sentence is a group of words that expresses a complete thought.

Different kinds of sentences serve different purposes. The punctuation mark used at the end of a sentence depends on the kind of sentence it is. All sentences begin with a capital letter.

Declarative Sentence		Exclamatory Sentence	
Purpose:	makes a statement	**Purpose:**	expresses strong feeling
Example:	We looked for treasure.	**Example:**	I found it!
End mark:	period	**End mark:**	exclamation mark
Interrogative Sentence		**Imperative Sentence**	
Purpose:	asks a question	**Purpose:**	commands or requests
Example:	Did you dig deep?	**Example:**	Look at this pirate chest. Please help me lift it.
End mark:	question mark	**End mark:**	period

Be sure to use the correct punctuation at the end of your sentences. These marks tell your reader what kind of thought you are expressing.

Guided Practice

Tell what kind of sentence each is.

Example: Help me dig.   *imperative*

1. Can we find the treasure?
2. It is buried here.
3. Give me a shovel.
4. How exciting the search is!
5. Where is the map?

 THINK

- How can I use different kinds of sentences to improve my writing?

REMEMBER

- A **declarative sentence** makes a statement.
- An **interrogative sentence** asks a question.
- An **exclamatory sentence** expresses strong feeling.
- An **imperative sentence** makes a command or request.

More Practice

A. Identify the kind of sentence each is. Write **declarative, interrogative, exclamatory,** or **imperative**.

Example: Do you know where the treasure is?
interrogative

6. We planned a treasure hunt.
7. What an adventure it would be!
8. Would it succeed?
9. Listen to the story.
10. We had a map.
11. How old the map looked!
12. Did the map give an accurate picture of the site?

B. Add the correct capitalization and end punctuation to each sentence and then write what kind of sentence it is.

Example: look at the map carefully
Look at the map carefully. imperative

13. we followed the map
14. it took us to a cave
15. what a scary place the cave was
16. please go through that narrow passage
17. can you squeeze through it
18. you made it
19. what joy we felt
20. whose long-lost treasure had we discovered

Extra Practice, page 24

WRITING APPLICATION A Personal Narrative

Think of an experience in your life in which you found something that you valued. Write a brief story of this event. Exchange your narrative with a classmate and identify the kinds of sentences.

---

2 COMPLETE SUBJECTS AND COMPLETE PREDICATES

Every sentence needs two parts to express a complete thought. The **complete subject** names what or whom the sentence is about. The **complete predicate** expresses what action the subject does. Sometimes it describes what the subject is or is like.

COMPLETE SUBJECT	COMPLETE PREDICATE
I	read *Treasure Island*.
Robert Louis Stevenson	wrote the book.
Some wonderful characters	appear in the book.

In interrogative sentences the complete subject usually comes after part of the complete predicate.

Did you **read** the part about the Black Spot?

In imperative sentences the complete subject, *you*, is often not stated.

(You) Read the chapter about Ben Gunn.

Guided Practice

Identify the complete subject and complete predicate in each sentence.

Example: The action begins at night.
    The action   *complete subject*
    begins at night.   *complete predicate*

1. My name is Jim Hawkins.
2. Billy Bones died at our Admiral Benbow Inn.
3. I found a map among his belongings.
4. Did the map show the location of a buried treasure?
5. Read *Treasure Island* for the answer.

 THINK

■ How can I identify the complete subject and the complete predicate in a sentence?

REMEMBER

- The **complete subject** of a sentence includes all the words that tell whom or what the sentence is about.
- The **complete predicate** of a sentence includes all the words that tell what the subject does or is.

More Practice

A. Write each sentence. Underline the complete subject once and the complete predicate twice. Write **(You)** to identify the complete subject of an imperative sentence.

Example: My mother trusted Squire Trelawney.

   <u>My mother</u> <u>trusted Squire Trelawney.</u>

6. This gentleman bought a ship for our voyage.
7. He hired Long John Silver as the ship's cook.
8. Long John Silver plotted a mutiny by the crew.
9. I told my friends about Silver's plot.
10. Guess the results.
11. Did Captain Smollett send all the members ashore?
12. The loyal members occupied a stockade.

B. Write each sentence. Draw a line between the complete subject and the complete predicate. If necessary, reorder the words.

Example: The hostile pirates left the ship.

   The hostile pirates | left the ship.

13. Silver's pirates attacked the fort repeatedly.
14. The sly Silver asked for a talk with the loyal men.
15. The peg-legged villain wanted the treasure map.
16. I sneaked away from the fort.
17. Get the ship to a safe anchor in the harbor.
18. Dr. Livesey gave the map to the pirates.
19. Had Ben Gunn moved the treasure?
20. Imagine the end of the story.

Extra Practice, page 25

WRITING APPLICATION A Summary

Write a short summary of an adventure book that you enjoyed. Exchange sentences with a classmate and identify the complete subjects and complete predicates in each other's work.

3 SIMPLE SUBJECTS AND SIMPLE PREDICATES

As you know, the complete subject consists of all the words in the subject. The complete predicate consists of all the words in the predicate. In the complete subject the main word is called the **simple subject.** In the complete predicate the main word is called the **simple predicate.**

SIMPLE SUBJECTS	SIMPLE PREDICATES

My beautiful **ruby** **shines** like a star.

The smooth **surface** **reflects** the light.

In an interrogative sentence, the simple predicate is usually divided by the complete subject.

Did you **start** your rock collection?

In an imperative sentence, the simple predicate is usually the first word. *You* is the simple subject.

(You) **Give** me that hammer.

In sentences that begin with *There is, There are, Here is,* and *Here are,* the complete subject follows the complete predicate.

There **are** many **kinds** of rocks.

Guided Practice

Identify the simple subject and the simple predicate in each.

Example: Our club goes on outings.
club simple subject   goes simple predicate

1. My best friend specializes in gemstones.
2. There are many such treasures in the earth.
3. Do these large gemstones cost a great deal?
4. Our rock hound club has sometimes found them.
5. Put those gemstones in the display case.

THINK

- How do I identify the simple subject and the simple predicate in a sentence?

REMEMBER

- The **simple subject** is the main word or words in the complete subject.
- The **simple predicate** is the main word or words in the complete predicate.

More Practice

Write each sentence. Then underline the simple subject once and the simple predicate twice.

Example: Water washes some precious stones to the surface.

Water <u>washes</u> some precious stones to the surface.

6. Some rock hounds collect many minerals.
7. The members of our club like jewels best.
8. The colors of gemstones are very pure.
9. Do stonecutters study their trade for years?
10. Here is a book about gemstones from our library.
11. Hold these uncut diamonds in your hand.
12. Large diamonds have been found in Arkansas.
13. Most gemstones come from mines.
14. Can a good jeweler appraise my jewels?
15. Our collection of gemstones is priceless.
16. Visit a treasure of jewels in the Tower of London.
17. Only color distinguishes a sapphire from a ruby.
18. Both stones are forms of corundum.
19. There are some man-made gems.
20. Look at these synthetic rubies.

Extra Practice, page 26

WRITING APPLICATION A Journal Entry

COOPERATIVE LEARNING

Form small groups and write an imaginary journal account about how the group discovered a diamond mine. Make your account funny or exciting. Exchange papers with another group. Identify the simple subjects and simple predicates in their work.

4 COMPOUND SUBJECTS AND COMPOUND PREDICATES

You have seen that a sentence has a subject and a predicate. Sometimes two or more **simple subjects** share the same predicate. This kind of subject is called a **compound subject.**

Sutter and **Marshall** farmed quietly at Sutter's Mill.

They and their **neighbors** tilled the soil.

Other sentences may have one subject that has two or more simple predicates. This kind of predicate is called a **compound predicate.**

Marshall **saw** yellow metal and **wondered** about it.

He **took** it to town and **learned** the good news.

Compound subjects and compound predicates may be joined by *and, but, or, either . . . or, neither . . . nor, both . . . and,* and *not only . . . but also.*

Some **miners** and **merchants** made great fortunes.

Neither **Sutter** nor **Marshall** profited from the gold.

Guided Practice

Tell whether each sentence has a compound subject or a compound predicate.

Example: Rumors and facts about gold spread quickly.
compound subject

1. Sutter's workers searched the area and found gold.
2. Miners collected their nuggets and took them to assayers in San Francisco.
3. Both men and women invaded the gold fields.
4. News of gold not only reached the East but also caught the ear of President Polk.
5. The president made a speech about the discovery and started a rush for gold.
6. Both decent folks and rascals joined the gold rush.
7. Some merchants not only sold goods but also overcharged for them.

 THINK

■ How do I decide if a sentence has a compound subject or a compound predicate?

1. Sutters workers searched the area and found gold.
compound predicate

2. Miners collected their nugets and took them to assayers in
in San Francisco. Compound predicate.

3. Both men and women invaded the feilds.
compound subject.

13. Men with machines worked the mines and found treasure.

       compound predicate

14. California and San Francisco flourished

    compound subject

15. Both Businessmen and bankers charged very high prices.

    compound subject

16. Bankers and politicians invested the gold.

    compound subject

18. Many prospectors quit and became farmers.

compound predicate

19. Other prospectors either returned home or sought new mines.

compound predicate

20. Some towns were deserted and became ghost towns.

compound predicate

5. The president made a speech about the discovery and started a rush for gold. - compound $predicate.

6. Both decent folks and rascals joined the gold rush. - compound subject.

7. Some merchants not only sold goods but also overcharged for them. - compound predicate.

8. compound predicate   panned, dug
9. compound predicate   overran, abused
10. compound predicate   struck, became
11. compound subject   companies, engineers
12. compound predicate   surveyed, analyzed

REMEMBER

- A **compound subject** is two or more simple subjects with the same predicate.
- A **compound predicate** is two or more simple predicates with the same subject.

More Practice

A. Write whether each sentence contains a **compound subject** or a **compound predicate.** Then write the simple subjects or the simple predicates in each compound.

Example: Ships and stagecoaches took adventurers west.
compound subject ships, stagecoaches

  8. The men either panned in streams or dug in the earth.
  9. Some miners overran farms and abused livestock.
10. Only a few struck pay dirt and became wealthy.
11. Mining companies and engineers joined the race.
12. Geologists surveyed the fields and analyzed them.

B. Write each sentence. Underline the complete subject once and the complete predicate twice. Then write whether it has a **compound subject** or a **compound predicate.**

Example: Both hardships and failure defeated miners.
Both hardships and failure defeated miners.
compound subject

13. Men with machines worked the mines and found treasure.
14. California and San Francisco flourished.
15. Both businessmen and bankers charged very high prices.
16. Bankers and politicians invested the gold.
17. The nation won the rewards and became rich.
18. Many prospectors quit and became farmers.
19. Other prospectors either returned home or sought new mines.
20. Some towns were deserted and became ghost towns.

Extra Practice, page 27

WRITING APPLICATION A Newspaper Article

Write a brief newspaper account of your discovery of a gold mine, complete with a headline. Exchange articles with a classmate and identify the compound subjects and compound predicates in each other's work.

5 COMPOUND SENTENCES

Many of the sentences you use are **simple sentences.** A simple sentence has one complete subject and one complete predicate. A simple sentence may contain a compound subject or a compound predicate or both.

> I wanted a vacation.

> Tom and I wanted and planned a vacation.

A **compound sentence** is formed when you join together two or more simple sentences. A compound sentence contains two or more complete subjects and two or more complete predicates.

> I **wanted** a vacation , and **Carol wanted** a study tour.

When you form a compound sentence, you usually join the two simple sentences with a conjunction such as *and, but,* or *or.* Use a comma before the conjunction in a compound sentence.

The two simple sentences within a compound sentence can also be joined by a semicolon.

> I reasoned with her; she would not budge.

Guided Practice

Tell whether each sentence is simple or compound.

Example: The Great Barrier Reef is the world's largest reef.
simple sentence

1. Will Tom come with us, or will he stay at home?
2. We would see Australia's Great Barrier Reef.
3. Tom could meet us in Australia, and we could explore the reef.
4. The reef is one of the world's natural treasures.
5. Carol planned the trip, and I made the budget.
6. We flew to Australia, and Tom met our plane.
7. I rented diving gear, but Carol had her own.

 **THINK**

- How can I decide if a sentence is simple or compound?

REMEMBER

- A **simple sentence** has one complete subject and one complete predicate.
- A **compound sentence** contains two or more simple sentences.

More Practice

A. Write whether each sentence is **simple** or **compound.**

Example: Tom could join us, but he could not travel with us.
compound sentence

8. Tom told us all about the Great Barrier Reef.
9. A barrier reef is a long chain of coral rock.
10. Coral rock is made by animals, but its colors come from algae.
11. Coral animals secrete lime, and rock forms.
12. The Great Barrier Reef is about 1,250 miles long.

B. Write each sentence. Underline each complete subject once and each complete predicate twice. Then identify each sentence as **simple** or **compound.**

Example: Underwater exploration is very hazardous.

Underwater exploration is very hazardous. *simple*

13. Tom wore his swim fins, and he walked awkwardly.
14. I jumped into the water, but Carol fell in.
15. Would we see great things, or would we see nothing?
16. I shut my eyes, but I soon opened them.
17. The reef displayed magnificent treasures.
18. Many fish swam nearby, and seaweeds drifted in the currents.
19. I enjoyed the bright fish, but I preferred the coral rocks.
20. Some creatures destroy coral, but the reef is still beautiful.

Extra Practice, page 28

WRITING APPLICATION A Description

Write a short description of a treasure from nature. Exchange papers with a classmate and identify the simple and compound sentences in each other's work.

6 CORRECTING FRAGMENTS AND RUN-ON SENTENCES

A complete sentence must have a subject and a predicate. When the subject or the predicate is missing, the result is a **sentence fragment.** A fragment does not express a complete thought. Correct a fragment by adding the missing part.

SENTENCE FRAGMENT: The great Thomas Jefferson.

COMPLETE SENTENCE: The great Thomas Jefferson designed his home.

Do not run sentences together without using the correct punctuation. This kind of error is called a **run-on sentence.**

RUN-ON SENTENCE: Jefferson built his home on a hilltop he called his home Monticello.

How to Correct a Run-on Sentence

■ Make two simple sentences.

Jefferson built his home on a hilltop. He called it Monticello.

■ Make a compound sentence by using a comma and a conjunction.

Jefferson built his home on a hilltop, **and** he called it Monticello.

■ Make a compound sentence by using a semicolon.

Jefferson built his home on a hilltop; he called it Monticello.

Guided Practice

Tell if the words form a sentence, a fragment, or a run-on.

Example: Visited the Blue Ridge Parkway.   *fragment*

1. We vacationed in Virginia I saw Monticello.
2. Many clever features of the house.
3. A compass on the ceiling registers the wind direction.
4. Works through a weathervane on the roof.

 THINK

■ How can I correct sentence fragments and run-on sentences?

REMEMBER

- A **sentence fragment** is a group of words that is only part of a sentence.
- A **run-on sentence** joins together two or more sentences that should be written separately.

More Practice

A. Identify each group of words as a **sentence,** a **fragment,** or a **run-on.**

Example: Multitudes of flowers in the gardens. *fragment*

5. The dome room was empty its purpose is unknown.
6. We walked across the lawn the trees were stately.
7. Stored ice blocks from the frozen river.
8. The kitchen was a good distance from the house.
9. In case of fire, was not near the house.
10. I looked at the clock the machinery was interesting.
11. Clock weights marked the days of the week along a wall.
12. Sat down in the lovely little tea room.

B. Write each item, correcting fragments and run-ons.

Example: A guide showed us the house she was very knowledgeable.
A guide showed us the house; she was very knowledgeable.

13. One of the earliest parquet floors in America.
14. Crowded with natural history specimens.
15. The chess set may have been carved in Africa.
16. Several thousand books.
17. Dad and Jefferson shared an interest they both liked silver.
18. Mom liked the serving table in the dining room.
19. I spotted the music stand it held music for five musicians.
20. The guide opened some panels they hid the dumbwaiters.

Extra Practice, page 29
Practice Plus, pages 30–31

WRITING APPLICATION A Magazine Article

Write a short feature article for a magazine about an interesting place that you have visited. Exchange papers with a classmate. Check each other's work for fragments and run-on sentences.

7 MECHANICS: Punctuating Sentences

Punctuation marks help make the meaning of a sentence clear. Use end marks to signal the end of a sentence.

Type of Sentence	End Mark	Example
Declarative	period	In Japan talented people are called treasures.
Imperative	period	Look at these photographs.
Interrogative	question mark	Have you visited Japan?
Exclamatory	exclamation mark	What wonderful pottery I saw!

Join the parts of a compound sentence in one of two ways.

Punctuation	When to Use	Example
Comma (,)	with conjunction (*and, or, but*)	Other people made the pottery, and she painted it.
Semicolon (;)	without conjunction	Other people made the pottery; she painted it.

Guided Practice

Tell what punctuation is needed in the following sentences.

Example: Are these artists called treasures   *question mark*

1. Some artists are treasures and they are respected by everyone
2. Who are these people
3. Give me a list of them
4. They are great artists the government honors them
5. Their talents are many one skill is not superior
6. We saw several living national treasures
7. Did they all work in pottery
8. Tell me about the actor at the Kabuki Theater

 THINK

■ How can I decide what punctuation marks to use in sentences?

REMEMBER

- Use a **period** to end a declarative or an imperative sentence. Use a **question mark** to end an interrogative sentence. Use an **exclamation mark** to end an exclamatory sentence.
- Use a **comma** before the conjunction in a compound sentence or join the parts with a semicolon.

More Practice

A. Write each sentence. Add the correct punctuation.

Example: Tell me about the crafts you saw
Tell me about the crafts you saw.

  9. What a magnificent performance he gave
 10. His costume was embroidered with gold thread
 11. Some Japanese paper caught my eye
 12. It was beautifully colored and the texture was fine
 13. Look at this beautiful woodblock print
 14. Artists must preserve a folkcraft tradition but they must also make a contribution to the art
 15. Much of the pottery is simple but elegant

B. Add the correct punctuation. Explain your answers.

Example: Where did you see the paper and did you buy any
Where did you see the paper, and did you buy any? compound sentence, interrogative

 16. Did you see the weaver or did you watch the swordmaker
 17. The bamboo was supple and the weaver's hands flew
 18. Japanese swords are very fine collectors seek them
 19. What strength the swordmaker had
 20. The steel was folded many times the sword-maker beat it thin each time and the sword had many layers

Extra Practice, page 32

WRITING APPLICATION A Biographical Sketch

Write a short biography about someone you know. Then exchange papers with a classmate. Check each other's work for correct punctuation.

GRAMMAR

8 VOCABULARY BUILDING: Words in Context

When you come across an unfamiliar word while reading, you sometimes can figure out its general meaning right away. That is because you know the meaning of all the words that are used with it. These surrounding words are called the **context,** and the context often contains clues that give you an idea of what the unfamiliar word means.

> Dad chartered a **schooner,** and we sailed out of the harbor and headed for the open seas. Because the wind was against us, we **tacked** in a zigzag course.

Though you may not know the meaning of *schooner,* other words in the sentence—*chartered, sailed out of the harbor,* and *headed for the open seas*—all suggest that a schooner is some kind of ship. If you check the word in a dictionary, you will find that a schooner is a sailing vessel with two masts rigged fore and aft.

Can you guess the meaning of the verb *tack,* used above? If you study the sentence, you can tell it means "to maneuver a sailing ship into the wind by taking a zigzag course."

Guided Practice

Tell the meaning of each underlined word by using context clues. Use a dictionary to check your work.

Example: The <u>corsairs</u> robbed the ship's treasure.   *pirates*

1. We would search the ocean floor for valuable <u>plunder</u> from a sunken pirate ship.
2. To discourage curious and distracting visitors, we had to keep a <u>vigil</u>, night and day.
3. Rough waters were a <u>vexation</u> to our able sailors, but they sailed steadily forward.
4. I paused <u>momentarily</u> but soon dived into the dark waters.
5. My sister checked her watch and <u>verified</u> my time under water.
6. The fish were a <u>shimmering</u> display of gold and blue.

 THINK

- What clues within a sentence can help me to know the meaning of an unfamiliar word?

REMEMBER

- The **context**—the words and phrases used with or near an unfamiliar term—may contain clues to the meaning of the term.

More Practice

Write the meaning of each underlined word. Use context clues to help you. Then use a dictionary to check your work.

Example: Mammals cannot <u>submerge</u> for long because they need air.   *submerge—to sink out of sight by going beneath the surface of a liquid*

7. There was no sign of the <u>timbered</u> hull; all wooden parts of the sunken ship had rotted away.
8. The divers knew how to <u>wield</u> their underwater picks.
9. Careful practice added to our <u>competency</u> with the equipment.
10. Only metal, glass, and marble are <u>durable</u> in water.
11. We had to be careful with our digging, for it is wrong to <u>tamper</u> recklessly with a historical site.
12. We did not want to <u>obliterate</u> the site completely, so we left some landmarks untouched.
13. <u>Artifacts</u> of metal and glass were our first finds.
14. We had to remove the <u>encrustation</u> covering the metal pieces before it dried and hardened.
15. Each coin <u>depicted</u> the profile of a Spanish king.
16. Buried glass becomes <u>iridescent</u>, like the colors in bubbles.
17. There was much <u>exultation</u> aboard when we joyfully realized we had actually found a pirate chest.
18. I needed a <u>respite</u> because I was very tired from diving.
19. Dad's <u>crucial</u> business sent us sailing back home.
20. We scrubbed down the ship until it was <u>immaculate</u>.

Extra Practice, page 33

WRITING APPLICATION A Descriptive Paragraph

With a partner, write about a familiar object. Describe how it looks or how it is used. Then substitute the word *blank* for the name of the object. Read your work to your classmates and let them identify the "blank" from the context.

GRAMMAR

GRAMMAR —AND WRITING CONNECTION

Combining Sentences

Good writers use descriptive words to create a clear picture for their readers. Often you can combine details from a number of sentences into a single sentence.

> SEPARATE: My baby-sitting job was a challenge. The job was my **strangest.** The job was my **longest.**

> COMBINED: My **strangest** and **longest** baby-sitting job was a challenge.

You can sometimes use a comma in place of *and.*

> SEPARATE: The baby started to cry. The baby was **cute.** The baby was **loud.**

> COMBINED: The **cute, loud** baby started to cry.

You can sometimes tell more about the main action in the new sentence.

> SEPARATE: My friend tickled the baby. My friend is **funny.** My friend's tickle was **gentle.**

> COMBINED: My **funny** friend tickled the baby **gently.**

Working Together

COOPERATIVE LEARNING

With your classmates talk about each group of sentences. Then decide how you would combine them into a single sentence.

Example: The baby was quiet. The baby slept.
The baby slept quietly.

1. I have a newspaper route. The route is tricky. The route is long.
2. A dog was in front of one house. The dog was huge. The dog was nasty.
3. The newspaper boy walked past the dog. The newspaper boy was scared. He was alert. His walk was soft.

Revising Sentences

Here is some dialogue from a student play. Help make the dialogue more interesting by combining each group of separate sentences into one sentence.

4. Felicia: I distributed community leaflets last summer. The leaflets were important. Their distribution was careful.

5. Albert: I helped Felicia with the distribution. The distribution was daily. My help was frequent.

6. Sandra: This past summer I had a job as a junior counselor. The job was difficult. The job was enjoyable.

7. Pete: My friend and I sold popcorn. My friend is brainy. My friend is tall.

8. Jessica: During the winter holidays I knitted a sweater. The winter holidays were long. The winter holidays were cold. The knitting was slow.

9. Rafael: My friends chipped in for a bike. The bike is sleek. The bike is speedy. The chipping in was cheerful.

10. Felicia: We all learned about the value of work. The work was hard. The work was exact. The learning was quick.

WRITER AT WORK

Think about a job you have had—or would like to have. Write a paragraph in which you tell what you did (or would do) on the job.

When you revise, work with a partner to find sentences to combine. Experiment with adjectives and adverbs to include in the combined sentences.

UNIT CHECKUP

LESSON

Kinds of Sentences (page 2)   Write each sentence, using the correct punctuation and capitalization. Then label each as **declarative, interrogative, imperative,** or **exclamatory.**

1. i sailed with Jason
2. look for the golden fleece
3. did Medea give Jason a charm
4. what magic the charm possessed

LESSON

Complete Subjects and Complete Predicates (page 4)   Write each sentence. Underline each complete subject once and each complete predicate twice.

5. The story of Jason is my favorite myth.
6. It may contain a bit of truth.
7. The myth may tell of a real expedition.
8. I learned more about Jason in Greece last summer.

LESSON

Simple Subjects and Simple Predicates (page 6)   Underline the simple subject once and the simple predicate twice.

9. My best friend collects baseball cards.
10. His large collection will be put on display.
11. The hundreds of cards are his greatest treasure.
12. My gift should please him immensely.

LESSON

Compound Subjects and Compound Predicates (page 8) Write each sentence. Underline each compound subject once and each compound predicate twice.

13. My aunt and uncle took me to San Francisco.
14. I rode the cable cars and visited Chinatown.
15. Alcatraz and Angel Island are both visible.
16. We went to Fisherman's Wharf and ate lunch.

LESSON

Compound Sentences (page 10)   Write each sentence. Underline the complete subjects once and the complete predicates twice. Label each sentence as **simple** or **compound.**

17. I am Midas, and Bacchus gave me the golden touch.
18. Could I touch food, or would it turn to gold?
19. I liked my power at first, but I later hated it.
20. I finally asked for a release from my power.

LESSON 6

Correcting Fragments and Run-on Sentences (page 12)
Read each group of words. Then write whether the words are
a **sentence,** a **sentence fragment,** or a **run-on sentence.**

21. Shaker artifacts have a simple grace.
22. Works of pure design.
23. I saw the exhibit of Shaker objects every object was a lovely treasure.
24. Boxes with beautiful workmanship.

LESSON 7

Mechanics: Punctuating Sentences (page 14)   Write each sentence. Correct the punctuation.

25. Superman is a great comic-strip character?
26. Will you come to a Superman movie with me.
27. Superman movies are fun I never miss one!
28. What a wonderful Superman movie this one is.

LESSON 8

Vocabulary Building: Words in Context (page 16)   Write each sentence. Then draw a line under the context clues that help explain the meaning of the underlined word. Define that word after the sentence.

29. Corn was indigenous to America, but now it is grown throughout the world.
30. Native Americans domesticated the wild plant in their gardens long before Europeans came to America.
31. The plant has been cultivated for so long that it never reverts to its original form.
32. Because of this, it is necessary that man nurture the plant to keep it from extinction.
33. Corn is used as fodder for cattle; other livestock eat it also.

Writing Application: Writing Sentences (pages 2–3, 12–15)
The following paragraph contains 10 errors, including sentence fragments, run-on sentences, and errors in punctuation. Rewrite the paragraph correctly.

34.–43.   Petroleum was known in ancient times it was used in mortar and on boat hulls! Rarely burned in lamps. Native Americans used it as medicine and they made paint from it. One of its first commercial uses was in streetlamps kerosene soon was used in lamps? Replaced whale oil. Petroleum was little used until the invention of the combustion engine and then it became a major resource. Today as fuel, dye, lubrication, and synthetics. Petroleum moves the modern world?

Putting Ideas into Your Head

An idiom is an expression with a special meaning that cannot be understood from the meaning of the individual words in it. *To nose about,* for example, means "to pry." Below are some idioms that use the names of parts of the head. Complete each one. Then explain what the idiom means. Then use the idiom in a sentence.

IDIOM	WORD BANK
1. To lose ___	nose
2. To have an ___ for	tongue
3. To pay through the ___	ear
4. To lend an ___	face
5. To hold one's ___	eye

Now try to think of more such expressions on your own.

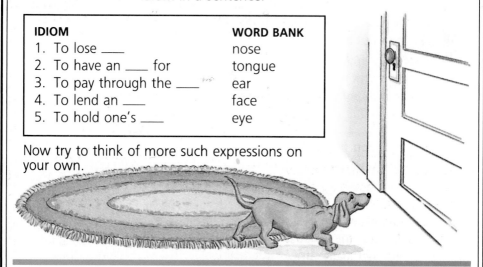

Trailing Sentences

Play this game on the chalkboard or on paper as a group or as a class. Choose someone to write a sentence. The next person must then write another sentence beginning with the last word in the first sentence. This continues until everyone has taken a turn. When everyone has written a sentence, then classify each sentence as declarative, interrogative, exclamatory, or imperative.

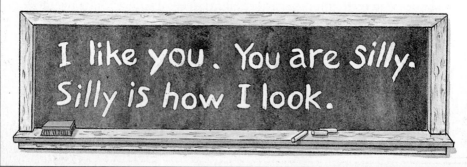

I like you. You are silly. Silly is how I look.

Dealing with Dialogue

In everyday, informal conversation, the number of words in sentences is kept to a minimum. "Hi" really means "Hello, how are you?" With a partner, write ten sentences of dialogue each. Try to "say" as much as possible in as few words as possible. When you both finish, read your dialogue to the class. The class should rate each conversation on a scale from one to ten, making the winners the pair who say the most in the fewest words. Try to make your dialogues funny.

SPINNING YARNS

Play this game with the whole class. Appoint a committee to fill a cardboard box with a variety of items, such as a key ring, an airline schedule, a can of soup, a broken toy, a post card, an empty toothpaste tube. The odder the items are, the better. Then have a student choose three objects from the box. He or she must then make up a sentence that begins a story that includes each of the items from the box. Each member of the class in turn should choose an item and add a sentence to the story. When all the items are included, try to bring the story to a reasonable ending.

Locating Treasures

As a group, think of yourselves as modern-day pirates. Then think of a treasure and where it might be hidden. Draw a map showing how to reach the treasure. Put in the necessary physical features—terrain, landmarks, buildings, and so on—and label anything that needs it. Be sure to add a compass rose in order to show directions. Decorate the borders of your map with objects included in the treasure.

Again as a group, write out step-by-step directions for finding the treasure. In your directions include declarative, interrogative, imperative, and exclamatory sentences. Make some sentences simple and make some of them compound. When you decide on the final form, write out the directions in a piratical manner and display them with the map.

EXTRA PRACTICE

Three levels of practice

Kinds of Sentences (page 2)

LEVEL

A. Write each sentence. Then write **declarative, interrogative, imperative,** or **exclamatory** after each.

1. A scavenger hunt is like a treasure hunt.
2. Can I find all the things on this list?
3. The list is very long.
4. What a challenge this will be!
5. Find a rug beater.
6. Etta and I are partners.
7. Will we win a prize at the end of the hunt?
8. Start at the beginning.
9. Where will we find a pretzel bender?

LEVEL

B. Write each sentence, adding the correct punctuation at the end. Then write whether the sentence is **declarative, interrogative, imperative,** or **exclamatory.**

10. We looked in our attic
11. What a lot of junk we have
12. Is that a rug beater over there
13. Look in that trunk
14. Move that old baby buggy
15. Is this a rug beater
16. What is next on the list
17. What fun this is

LEVEL

C. Complete each sentence, adding the correct punctuation at the end. Then write whether the sentence is **declarative, interrogative, imperative,** or **exclamatory.**

18. Look for a _____
19. My baby brother has _____
20. Will he let us _____
21. What a great time we are _____
22. We have found _____ on the list
23. The prize is _____
24. What a wonderful prize _____
25. Who won the _____

EXTRA PRACTICE

Three levels of practice

Complete Subjects and Complete Predicates (page 4)

LEVEL

A. Identify the underlined words as a complete subject or as a complete predicate.

1. Heinrich Schliemann is my name.
2. I read the *Iliad* in my childhood.
3. The stories of the ancient Greeks captured my imagination.
4. I could be the discoverer of ancient Troy!
5. King Priam was very real to me.
6. The events of the Trojan War thrilled me.
7. Historians considered the events as fiction.
8. The discovery of Troy became my goal.
9. Did Homer base his stories on a real event?

LEVEL

B. Write each sentence. Then underline the complete subject once and the complete predicate twice.

10. My youth was full of poverty and adventure.
11. A family friend got me a job in Amsterdam.
12. A good deal of luck came my way.
13. Hard work in Russia and America enhanced my fortune.
14. My retirement from business occurred at the age of forty-one.
15. Archaeological studies claimed my attention from then on.
16. The site of Troy became an obsession.
17. I formed an expedition.

LEVEL

C. Write whether each group of words could be the complete subject or the complete predicate of a sentence. Then write a complete sentence using the words.

18. many ancient cities
19. is one of those buried cities
20. offer a key to past civilizations
21. groups of archaeologists
22. many beautiful objects
23. are displayed in museums throughout the world
24. everyday items
25. is increased through archaeology

GRAMMAR

EXTRA PRACTICE: Lesson 2   **25**

EXTRA PRACTICE

Three levels of practice

Simple Subjects and Simple Predicates (page 6)

LEVEL
A. Read each sentence. Then write the simple subject and simple predicate of each one.

1. This colorful book contains my photographs.
2. Each photograph in it records a treasured memory.
3. Hand me that roll of film, please.
4. These black-and-white pictures are some of my early shots.
5. Such beautiful scenery should have been in color.
6. The whole sequence was taken in the Rocky Mountains.
7. Look at the snow-capped peaks.
8. Have you been to the Rockies?
9. There are many wonderful sights of natural beauty.

LEVEL
B. Write each sentence. Then underline the simple subject once and the simple predicate twice.

10. Photographic portraits are a speciality of mine.
11. Many families in this town ask for my pictures.
12. My best clients often want pictures as mementos.
13. Most families save their favorite photographs.
14. Future generations will have a family record.
15. Shoot a picture of the whole family reunion.
16. There are some tintypes in this album.
17. Have you ever seen a tintype before?

LEVEL
C. Write each sentence. Underline the complete subject once and the complete predicate twice. Then write the simple subject and the simple predicate.

18. Did I take that picture?
19. I climbed to the top of the hill.
20. The steep hill gave me a broad view of the scenery.
21. The beauty came partly from the expert development.
22. Precise development of film is an art.
23. My pride in this picture is very great.
24. Look at the composition.
25. There is a true skill to photography.

EHTRA PRACTICE

Three levels of practice

Compound Subjects and Compound Predicates (page 8)

LEVEL
A. Write each sentence. Then write whether the sentence has a **compound subject** or a **compound predicate.**

1. Entertainment and history await tourists to gold country.
2. Both old hotels and Victorian mansions have survived.
3. My family and I toured the gold country.
4. We flew to San Francisco and then rented a car.
5. We started at Chinese Camp and followed Route 49.
6. The highway winds and dips through the countryside.
7. Many Chinese people either lived or worked at Chinese Camp.
8. Trees of heaven were planted and form a lush canopy.

LEVEL
B. Write each sentence. Underline each complete subject once and complete predicate twice. Write whether the sentence has a **compound subject** or a **compound predicate.**

9. Our family rented a claim for a day and panned for gold.
10. Pans and instructions came with the rental fee.
11. We rocked the pans slowly and poured off the top layer.
12. The sand and dirt wash away easily.
13. Gold is heavy and settles to the bottom of the pan.
14. Neither Dad's pan nor my pan collected any gold.

LEVEL
C. Write each sentence. Underline the complete subject once and the complete predicate twice. Then write the conjunction that joins the compound subject or predicate.

15. Not only some gold dust but also a few particles finally settled in my pan.
16. I cashed in my hard-won treasure and bought a nugget.
17. Columbia is a state park and features many restored Gold Rush buildings.
18. The park at Coloma has a replica of Sutter's sawmill but was not open on the day of our visit.
19. The Gold Rush Museum and other exhibits at Fiddletown showed the prospector's way of life.
20. We could look for antiques or go white-water rafting next.

EXTRA PRACTICE

Three levels of practice

Compound Sentences (page 10)

LEVEL

A. Write each sentence. Identify each as **simple** or **compound.**

1. I went to the Morgan Library, and Jeff met me there.
2. The library is a treasure-house of books in New York.
3. This quiet place is in the center of a noisy city.
4. Would I be bored, or would I enjoy the books?
5. Jeff knew he would enjoy his visit, and he did.
6. The library had an exhibit of early printed books.
7. Early printing is beautiful; it resembles medieval script.
8. We saw several books with unusual bindings.
9. The library is now one of my favorite places in New York.

LEVEL

B. Write each sentence. Underline each complete subject once and each complete predicate twice. Then identify each sentence as **simple** or **compound.**

10. The place is a library, but only scholars may use the books.
11. The exhibits are free, and many people see them.
12. Sometimes books are shown, and sometimes art is displayed.
13. There is also a large collection of music manuscripts.
14. Mozart wrote in tiny script, and Beethoven made blots.
15. I have seen drawings by da Vinci and by Michelangelo.
16. Jeff loved some portraits, but I preferred some old books.
17. The exhibits change every three or four months.

LEVEL

C. Write each sentence. Identify each one as **simple** or **compound.** Then add a closely related sentence to each simple sentence, to turn it into a compound sentence.

18. J. P. Morgan was a wealthy banker, and he collected books.
19. The library building was once Morgan's home.
20. His study is furnished with books and lovely objects.
21. Secret stairways lead up to the upper level of books, but the public is not permitted to climb them.
22. The library shop has delightful things for sale.
23. Jeff bought a teddy bear, and I bought a rubber stamp.
24. There are reproductions of old books and cards.
25. I love all the treasures in the Morgan Library.

EXTRA PRACTICE

Three levels of practice

Correcting Fragments and Run-on Sentences (page 12)

LEVEL

A. Write whether the words form a **sentence,** a **sentence fragment,** or a **run-on sentence.**

1. This garden looks great now it was once an overgrown jungle.
2. I worked on the restoration of the garden.
3. All the beautiful flowers.
4. Preserve historic treasures.
5. The boxwoods had become two stories high we cut them back.
6. This garden is next to a fine historic house.
7. The garden is really two gardens.
8. One is a kitchen garden it supplied vegetables for the family.
9. A pretty English flower garden.
10. A brick pathway leads through it.

LEVEL

B. Write each group of words, correcting the sentence fragments and run-on sentences. Write **correct** next to any group of words that is a sentence.

11. Old menus from the family's records told me about the vegetables in the original garden.
12. Offered glimpses of the original contents of the garden.
13. A special place for herbs.
14. Grew many different kinds of roses.
15. I roam happily through the garden it makes me feel serene.
16. I believe in restoring treasured houses and gardens.
17. Definitely had a green thumb.
18. The garden is open to the public it can be seen on the Historic Garden Tour in April.
19. I am proud of my contribution to the garden.
20. A treasure from the past.

LEVEL

C. Rewrite the paragraph, correcting sentence fragments and run-on sentences.

21.–25. A kind of football was played in ancient Greece and Rome, the game survived through the Middle Ages. In England, two forms. One was a kicking game, in the other, called rugby football, the players carry the ball. In the United States grew from rugby football. Here, the kicking game called soccer.

PRACTICE + PLUS

Three levels of additional practice for a difficult skill

Correcting Fragments and Run-on Sentences (page 12)

LEVEL
A. Write whether the words form a **sentence,** a **sentence fragment,** or a **run-on sentence.**

1. Thousands of children have read about Winnie-the-Pooh, he was a wonderful teddy bear.
2. A treasured toy of Christopher Robin.
3. Christopher Robin was a character in the Pooh books, he was based on the author's son.
4. The author's name was Alan Alexander Milne.
5. The animals in the Pooh books were the real toys of Christopher Milne.
6. The Pooh stories originally were bedtime stories, later A. A. Milne wrote them down.
7. The real Pooh and the actual other stuffed animals.
8. First brought the stuffed animals to the United States from England in 1947.
9. They toured the United States in an exhibit.
10. Crowds of children visited their favorite characters, they came from everywhere.
11. The first Pooh book appeared in 1924.
12. Popular in England and America.
13. The books have been translated into twenty different languages, children all over the world treasure them.
14. Some of the stories were translated into Latin.
15. Christopher Milne is now a retired bookseller in England, his toys are over 65 years old.
16. Pooh and his friends Tigger, Piglet, Eeyore, and Kanga.
17. Stayed in a New York publishing house for forty years.
18. The publishing house arranged a surprise.
19. Donated the toys to the Central Children's Room of the New York Public Library.
20. They occupy a climate-controlled case in the library, now all children can treasure them.

PRACTICE + PLUS

LEVEL

B. Write each group of words, correcting the sentence fragments and run-on sentences. Write **correct** next to any word group that is a complete sentence.

21. Many people collect things as a hobby.
22. Coins and stamps are traditional things for collections they can be bought through clubs and catalogs.
23. More unusual things like old phonographs and stereoscopes.
24. Visits flea markets and antique stores.
25. My mother has a huge collection of salt and pepper shakers.
26. Old photographs from albums in junk stores.
27. Fountain pens are a popular collectors' item.
28. Dolls of many lands and many materials.
29. Some dolls are very rare they command a very high price.
30. Baseball cards are popular with young collectors.
31. Comic books from the 1940s and 1950s.
32. Wealthy people collect jewelry and paintings vintage automobiles are also popular with the rich.
33. Fortunately, collectors are not always rich.
34. Satisfaction in the collection, not its value.
35. Interest in folk art is high.
36. Weather vanes, wooden toys, and mail boxes.
37. Watches and clocks make interesting collections.
38. People repair and restore.
39. Quality and not quantity of the collection.
40. About the past and how people lived.

LEVEL

C. Rewrite the paragraph, correcting fragments and run-ons.

41.–50. Calendars are systems for reckoning time most calendars are based on cycles in nature. The cycle of the sun and the cycle of the moon. Harmonize solar and lunar time. Years cannot be divided into perfect numbers of solar days or lunar months. Leap year is a way of adjusting the imperfections of our calendar one day is added to February every four years. Julius Caesar is responsible for the calendar as we know it today, it was modified by Pope Gregory XIII. In 1582. Called the Gregorian calendar. England used the Julian calendar until 1752 England found itself eleven days behind the Continent. The science of chronology is now very exact. Fractions of a second. Modern times truly on time.

GRAMMAR

Three levels of practice

Mechanics: Punctuating Sentences (page 14)

LEVEL

A. Write each sentence. Then write the name of the punctuation mark that belongs at the end of each sentence.

1. I saw an exhibit about the history of writing systems
2. What an achievement an alphabet is
3. Who developed a writing system first
4. The Sumerians developed the first writing system
5. They wrote with sticks on tablets
6. How funny the marks look
7. Their system was not an alphabet
8. Tell me about Egyptian hieroglyphics
9. Can we read them

LEVEL

B. Write each sentence, correcting the punctuation.

10. How beautiful the Egyptian hieroglyphics are?
11. The pictures are beautifully simple!
12. What does that mean.
13. Each character represented a syllable or a word, one letter for each sound had not yet been invented?
14. The Phoenicians came close to a full alphabet; but they did not have letters for vowels!
15. Look at the Phoenician inscriptions over there?
16. Our alphabet is influenced by Phoenician letters?
17. The Phoenicians were traders, their culture was widespread!

LEVEL

C. Write each sentence, adding punctuation marks where they are needed.

18. How strange the Greek alphabet looks
19. The Greeks invented letters for vowel sounds they created the first full alphabet
20. The Romans based their alphabet on the Greek writing system but they changed the order of some letters
21. Where did the English alphabet come from
22. The English alphabet is based on the Roman system
23. Did English once have more letters
24. Give me that book about alphabets
25. What a wonderful treasure an alphabet is

EXTRA PRACTICE

Three levels of practice

Vocabulary Building: Words in Context (page 16)

LEVEL

A. Write each sentence. Then, using context clues, write what each underlined word means.

1. My name is Howard Carter, and I am an <u>Egyptologist</u> who studies the culture of ancient Egypt.
2. I was sure that the tomb of Tutankhamen existed, although other experts were <u>skeptical</u>.
3. I <u>excavated</u> in various places before digging at a place I had once overlooked.
4. Lord Carnarvon, my sponsor, wanted to <u>relinquish</u> our right to dig and give up the project.
5. I <u>beseeched</u> him for one more season, and he finally agreed.

LEVEL

B. Write each sentence. Then underline the words in the context that help you understand the word in dark type.

6. Finding the tomb **intact** was unlikely because grave robbers had stolen from most of the tombs.
7. On the the fourth day of our final attempt, my diggers **unearthed** some stairs.
8. The stairs gave us **access** to a sealed door.
9. After opening the door, we **traversed** a long aisle that led to another sealed door.
10. I bored a hole in the door and put a candle through it to **illuminate** the room inside.

LEVEL

C. Write each sentence. Underline the words in the context that add to your understanding of the word in bold type. Then, using context clues, write the meaning of the word.

11. A **treasure-trove** of valuable objects was piled in a heap.
12. Everyone **exulted** when I told them the good news.
13. The objects inside were **resplendent** with gold overlaid with precious jewels.
14. King Tutankhamen's tomb held the richest **cache** of priceless objects ever found in Egypt.
15. The appreciative public has given me great **acclaim** for my achievement.

UNIT 2

Writing Personal Narratives

Read the quotation and look at the picture on the opposite page. Talk with your classmates about the quotation. What things do you think are possible for you?

In a personal narrative, a writer tells about a memorable event—an event that was in some way important to the writer.

Focus A personal narrative tells about an important event in your life.

What event would you like to write about? On the following pages you will find a narrative by Maya Angelou. In it, she tells of an event that was important in her life. You will find some photographs, too. The narrative or the photographs may give you some ideas for writing.

I believe all things are possible for a human being, and I don't think there's anything in the world I can't do.

—Maya Angelou

LITERATURE

Reading Like a Writer

Is there an experience in your life that you treasure? Is there someone who has helped you in a special way? Is there someone who has helped you bring out your confidence?

Although Marguerite is a strong reader, her teachers report that she has trouble speaking in class. Building on the girl's interest in reading, Mrs. Flowers helps boost Marguerite's confidence in speaking. She introduces Marguerite to many new ideas about language, including the beauty of recited poetry.

As you read the selection, look for details the author uses to help you see and feel the changes Marguerite experiences.

from

I Know Why the Caged Bird Sings

by Maya Angelou

There was a little path beside the rocky road, and Mrs. Flowers walked in front swinging her arms and picking her way over the stones.

She said, without turning her head, to me, "I hear you're doing very good school work, Marguerite, but that it's all written. The teachers report that they have trouble getting you to talk in class." We passed the triangular farm on our left and the path widened to allow us to walk together. I hung back in the separate unasked and unanswerable questions.

"Come and walk along with me, Marguerite." I couldn't have refused even if I wanted to. She pronounced my name so nicely. Or more correctly, she spoke each word with such clarity that I was certain a foreigner who didn't understand English could have understood her.

"Now no one is going to make you talk—possibly no one can. But bear in mind, language is man's way of communicating with his fellow man, and it is language alone which separates him from the lower animals." That was a totally new idea to me, and I would need time to think about it.

"Your grandmother says you read a lot. Every chance you get. That's good, but not good enough. Words mean more than what is set down on paper. It takes the human voice to infuse them with the shades of deeper meaning."

I memorized the part about the human voice infusing words. It seemed so valid and poetic.

She said she was going to give me some books and that I not only must read them, I must read them aloud. She suggested that I try to make a sentence sound in as many different ways as possible.

"I'll accept no excuse if you return a book to me that has been badly handled." My imagination boggled at the punishment I would deserve if in fact I did abuse a book of Mrs. Flowers's. Death would be too kind and brief.

The odors in the house surprised me. Somehow I had never connected Mrs. Flowers with food or eating or any other common experience of common people. There must have been an outhouse, too, but my mind never recorded it.

The sweet scent of vanilla had met us as she opened the door.

"I made tea cookies this morning. You see, I had planned to invite you for cookies and lemonade so we could have this little chat. The lemonade is in the icebox."

It followed that Mrs. Flowers would have ice on an ordinary day, when most families in our town bought ice late on Saturdays only a few times during the summer to be used in the wooden ice-cream freezers.

She took the bags from me and disappeared through the kitchen door. I looked around the room that I had never in my wildest fantasies imagined I would see. Browned photographs leered or threatened from the walls, and the white, freshly done curtains pushed against themselves and against the wind. I wanted to gobble up the room entire and take it to Bailey, who would help me analyze and enjoy it.[1]

"Have a seat, Marguerite. Over there by the table." She carried a platter covered with a tea towel. Although she warned that she hadn't tried her hand at baking sweets for some time, I was certain that like everything else about her the cookies would be perfect.

They were flat round wafers, slightly browned on the edges and butter-yellow in the center. With the cold lemonade they were sufficient for childhood's lifelong diet. Remembering my manners, I took nice little lady-like bites off the edges. She said she had made them expressly for me and that she had a few in the kitchen that I could take home to my brother. So I jammed one whole cake in my mouth, and the rough crumbs scratched the insides of my jaws, and if I hadn't had to swallow, it would have been a dream come true.

As I ate, she began the first of what we later called "my lessons in living." She said that I must always be intolerant of ignorance but understanding of illiteracy. That some people, unable to go to school, were more educated and even more intelligent than college professors. She encouraged me to listen carefully to what country people called mother wit. That in those homely sayings was couched the collective wisdom of generations.

When I finished the cookies, she brushed off the table and brought a thick, small book from the bookcase. I had read *A Tale of Two Cities* and found it up to my standards as a romantic novel. She opened the first page, and I heard poetry for the first time in my life.

"It was the best of times and the worst of times . . . ." Her

1. Supporting details help make the narrative vivid.

voice slid in and curved down through and over the words. She
was nearly singing. I wanted to look at the pages. Were they the
same that I had read? Or were there notes, music, lined on the
pages, as in a hymn book? Her sounds began cascading gently. I
knew from listening to a thousand preachers that she was near-
ing the end of her reading, and I hadn't really heard, heard to
understand, a single word.

"How do you like that?"

It occurred to me that she expected a response. The sweet
vanilla flavor was still on my tongue, and her reading was a
wonder in my ears. I had to speak.

I said, "Yes, ma'am." It was the least I could do, but it was
the most also.

"There's one more thing. Take this book of poems and memorize one for me. Next time you pay me a visit, I want you to
recite."

I have tried often to search behind the sophistication of years
for the enchantment I so easily found in those gifts. The essence

escapes, but its aura remains. To be allowed, no, invited, into the private lives of strangers, and to share their joys and fears, was a chance to exchange the Southern bitter wormwood for a cup of mead with Beowulf or a hot cup of tea and milk with Oliver Twist. When I said aloud, "It is a far, far better thing that I do, than I have ever done . . . " tears of love filled my eyes at my selflessness.

On that first day, I ran down the hill and into the road (few cars ever came along it) and had the good sense to stop running before I reached the store.

I was liked, and what a difference it made. I was respected not as Mrs. Henderson's grandchild or Bailey's sister but for just being Marguerite Johnson.

Childhood's logic never asks to be proved (all conclusions are absolute). I didn't question why Mrs. Flowers had singled me out for attention, nor did it occur to me that Momma might have asked her to give me a little talking to. All I cared about was that she had made tea cookies for *me* and read to *me* from her favorite book. It was enough to prove that she liked me.[2]

2. The conclusion expresses the main idea of the narrative.

Thinking Like a Reader

1. Why do you think Marguerite's visit with Mrs. Flowers made such a strong and lasting impression on the young girl?
2. Mrs. Flowers caused Marguerite to reconsider her attitude towards speech and the sound of words. Who has had an effect on the way you think about something?

Write your responses in your journal.

Thinking Like a Writer

3. How does the author use details that appeal to the reader's senses? What effect does this have?
4. The author uses dialogue frequently. What effect does this have?
5. Think of an experience that had an effect on your way of thinking about something. How would you begin writing about this?

Write your responses in your journal.

LITERATURE

Brainstorm *Vocabulary*

In *I Know Why the Caged Bird Sings* Maya Angelou tells about the power of language while exercising it. She chooses words that make her writing precise and powerful. Such words as *infuse*, *leered*, *cascading*, and *aura* are vivid and interesting words. As a way to help make your writing more vivid and interesting, start a personal vocabulary list in your journal. Organize this list in a manner that is most useful to you. As you read and hear words that capture your interest, add them to your list. Use these words in your writing to make your work precise and powerful.

Talk It Over Swap Stories

Maya Angelou's name is a pen name. The author grew up as Marguerite Johnson. This fact lets the reader know that the author of *I Know Why the Caged Bird Sings* is recalling an incident that happened to her during her childhood. Everyone has personal stories to tell, whether from the distant past or as recent as something that happened today. These are stories to be treasured, and they can be shared with others. As a class group, take turns telling about a personal experience that was important to you.

Quick Write *Impressions*

Try writing about one of your experiences. Imagine your words being flashed before a crowd on a large teleprompter (words displayed electronically across a screen). For example, if you were recalling your birthday party, these words might flash across the teleprompter.

I held my breath. I counted thirteen candles. Oh, there's another candle for next year! I was supposed to make a wish—I wish I could think of something to say! My six-year-old sister was looking at me—strangely. I finally made my wish (but I made it to myself). There was laughter and applause (from my sis, too). The tension was broken at last.

Idea Corner *The Time I . . .*

List some writing topic ideas beginning with the words, "The Time I. . . ." For example, such topics might include "The Time I Finally Faced My Dentist," "The Time the Computer Went Haywire," and "The Time I Lost My Ring and Found a Friend." You may want to extend your ideas by making drawings of the places where the incidents happened or writing a page of dialogue that could have taken place during the incident.

PICTURES 📷 *SEEING LIKE A WRITER*

Finding Ideas for Writing

Look at the pictures. Think about what you see. What ideas for writing a personal narrative do the pictures give you? Write your ideas in your journal.

Emerald crystals

Gold bars from a sunken Spanish treasure ship

The Constitution of the United States of America

ornia redwoods

1 GROUP WRITING: A PERSONAL NARRATIVE

COOPERATIVE
LEARNING

A personal narrative tells about a specific incident that happened to the writer. This incident involves a series of events that took place within a specific period of time. What makes the writing of a personal narrative clear and effective?

- Good Beginning Sentence
- Supporting Details
- Order of Details

The **purpose** of writing a personal narrative is to inform or to entertain, or a combination of these goals. When you write, also think about who your **audience** is. Are you writing to inform a friend, a classmate, a family member, or a variety of readers?

Beginning Sentence and Supporting Details

Notice the beginning sentence in the paragraph below.

> The day I became a "whale" was the highlight of last summer. My journey started in the early morning when I tested Lake Ozomo's water with my toe. The water was cold, and the air was foggy. I could barely see the other side of the lake, a mile away! A few minutes later I lunged into the water. I did the crawl, then switched to the breast stroke and alternated between the two. The minutes seemed to crawl along, too. There were times when I wanted to hang onto the boat that was always there beside me. I guess a feeling of pride kept me afloat. Tired and cold as I was, I swam for an hour until I reached land on the other side of the lake. Cheers from my fellow campers greeted me. I was a whale at last!

A good **beginning sentence** gives the reader an overall idea of what to expect in the narrative. It should immediately catch the interest of the reader. All of the **supporting**

details in the paragraph should tell more about the beginning sentence. In a personal narrative the supporting details are usually related actions or events. You should aim to select those details that vividly capture the experience you want to relate. Look back at the preceding paragraph.

- What are the main details?
- How do the details support the beginning sentence?

Guided Practice: Writing a Beginning Sentence

As a class, use the list below to help you think about an incident that would be interesting to write about together—perhaps an experience shared by all. Explore some ideas with your classmates. Then write a beginning sentence.

school trip	sports event	music concert
assembly program	class election	skating party

Example: The bus trip to Adventure Park was an adventure in itself.

Order of Details

The supporting sentences in a personal narrative are often expressed in **chronological order.** Chronological order presents the details of an incident in the order in which they actually happened. Relating the events in time order helps the reader understand what is happening and wonder what will happen next.

The action in a personal narrative should build to an effective ending. The last sentence may reemphasize, summarize, or restate in a different way the paragraph's beginning sentence.

Transition words and phrases used in a personal narrative help clarify how details are related in time. Examples of transition words include *later, next, eventually, finally, first, last, now, soon, then,* and *meanwhile.*

In the paragraph that tells about becoming a whale, chronological order helps you visualize the events as they unfold. Look back at the paragraph.

- Which words help you see the events in the beginning of the incident? Which help you see the middle and ending?
- Which transition words help clarify the order of events?

Guided Practice: Ordering Details

Recall the beginning sentence about the incident that the class chose to write about. As a class, make a chart like the one below. Think about the events that might make up the beginning, middle, and ending of your incident. Write these events in your chart. For example:

Beginning	Middle	Ending
late start	lights went out for a minute	teacher told about park

Putting a Personal Narrative Together

With your classmates, think about your topic. Decide if it is suitable for your purpose and audience. Then take a look at your Beginning-Middle-Ending charts to see what chronological order details you might wish to include.

Here is how one student made some choices about the bus trip. Notice the time order of the details that are checked.

Beginning	Middle	Ending
✔late start	saw billboards	teacher told about park
trip chaperoned	✔lights went out for a minute	✔driver finally sang, too
principal did not come	kids began singing	reached destination
	Jenny got sick	

Guided Practice: Writing a Personal Narrative

Now write your personal narrative. Write your beginning sentence and then add at least three sentences from your chart. Be sure that details in these supporting sentences are in chronological order. Be sure that they support your beginning sentence. When possible, use transition words that clarify how events are related in time. Be sure that you have an effective ending. Check to see if you have properly indented your paragraph.

Share your work with someone from your audience. Ask if he or she thinks your personal narrative is clearly and effectively written.

Checklist A Personal Narrative

To help you remember the important elements of a personal narrative, use a checklist when you write. Copy the checklist below. Keep it in your writing folder.

CHECKLIST

- Choose a purpose.
- Choose an audience.
- Write a good beginning sentence.
- Arrange supporting details in chronological order.
    Beginning
    Middle
    Ending
- Write a good ending sentence.

2 THINKING AND WRITING: General and Specific

Writing a personal narrative is like writing a story—a story that happened to you. You choose your topic and then support that topic with details. Sometimes the details a writer chooses to tell the story are too general. For example, such words as *nice* or statements such as "the trip was wonderful" are so general that they have little meaning.

As you write, think about each word you choose. Ask yourself if the words you use express exactly what you want to say. For example, *animal* is a general term. *Dog* is a specific animal. *Dalmatian*, however, is even more specific. Compare these examples of general and specific words.

General	Specific	More Specific
food	meat	pork chop
plant	flower	daisy
go	hurry	rush
seat	chair	armchair

Compare the messages sent by two people who were visiting the same place at the same time.

Here I am. Nice place. Weather good. Saw some ships. Food good. I like it here. I'm having a great time.	Arrived on Tuesday. San Francisco is breathtaking. Days are sunny. Visited the harbor. The seafood is delicious. Rapture!

Thinking Like a Writer

- Which words are too general?
- Which words describe the writer's impressions?

It is important for the writer to notice the difference between writing that is general and writing that is specific. In this case, the message on the left is too general and will not really help the reader to share the visit to San Francisco.

When you write a personal narrative, you will have to search for ways to make your images, ideas, words, and sentences as specific as possible.

THINKING APPLICATION General and Specific

COOPERATIVE
LEARNING

Each of the writers named below is planning to write a personal narrative. Help each writer to decide which details to include. Write the details in your notebook. Then, with a partner, compare and explain your choices.

1. Gloria's paragraph tells about the Mother's Day dinner she prepared. She wants to convey the idea that she did it all by herself. Which details should she include?

   - ordered the main dish
   - lots of people were at dinner
   - picked up 12-pound butterball turkey
   - got some presents for Mom
   - a total of 16 family and friends came
   - picked up red carnation at Flores's Flower Shop
   - peeled the potatoes

2. John's narrative tells about a personal incident he treasures, his stint as a disk jockey at a local school dance. He wants to show that the evening went very smoothly except for one jarring incident. Which specific details should he include?

   - one of the dancers said, "This is the best dance yet!"
   - played different kinds of records
   - something bad happened
   - needle got stuck in groove, played over and over
   - spun 42 records, from slow dance ballads to novelty rock 'n' roll
   - someone enjoyed himself
   - played my favorite song

3. Alicia's narrative tells about her experience on a quiet beach. She wants to show how she treasures the little—but important—things in life. What specific details should she include?

   - the hot sun glistened on tanned swimmers
   - played with aquamarine coral shells and wondered at their creation
   - the thing with the bird was nice
   - nursed a bird with a broken wing back to health
   - weather OK
   - ate a banana
   - "listened" to a seashell

3 INDEPENDENT WRITING: A Personal Narrative

Prewrite: Step 1

Now you are ready to begin writing a personal narrative of your own. Your first concerns are your purpose for writing and who your audience will be. Then you are ready to choose your subject, an incident from your life. Prewriting techniques will help you find an idea from your treasure chest of experiences.

Mark, a student your age, wanted to write a narrative for his classmates. He chose a topic by brainstorming. In **brainstorming**, the writer lists any thoughts—words, phrases, or questions—that immediately come to mind.

Choosing a Topic

> trip to Atlanta
> championship hockey game – too close to it still?
> ✓ performing in a play
> joining computer club — ok, but only school play
> made up with Marla   which one?

Mark liked the third incident on his list best. Since his **audience** was his classmates, he narrowed the topic to performing in a school play. His **purpose** for writing would be to inform his readers about how he performed in the play.

Exploring Ideas: Freewriting Strategy

Mark decided he would do some freewriting to generate more ideas. In **freewriting,** a writer keeps pen or pencil in constant motion for a specified time so that thoughts and feelings flow freely. Before beginning to write, Mark closed his eyes and pictured the performances of the play to recall more details.

Here is what he wrote:

> School play ... which one? How about the first one. Oh, do
> I remember that one! It was a musical—Guys and Dolls.
> But there's so much that happened. Okay, I'll write about
> how I tried out for it and rehearsals and those three
> wonderful performances. I was scared. It was the first
> musical I had ever been in. I had a math test that day and
> was late for tryouts. Then I forgot part of my monologue.

Mark thought that he had some good ideas. As he looked
at his freewriting, he realized that his topic, performing in
the play, was too broad. There was too much to write
about the performances. He decided to limit his topic to au-
ditioning for the play. He decided to freewrite about the
try-outs.

> My first musical—Guys and Dolls. Late for tryouts. I was
> scared. Almost didn't get the part because I sang off-key.
> Then I forgot part of my monologue ... Mr. Harris gave me
> a second chance.

Thinking Like a Writer
- What did Mark add to his freewriting?
- What did he decide to delete?
- Why do you think he deleted that part?

YOUR TURN

JOURNAL

Think of a personal incident you would like to write about.
Use **Pictures** or your journal for ideas.
- Make a list of incidents that happened to you.
- Choose the one you want to write about the most.
- Narrow your topic if necessary.

Do some freewriting. Think about your purpose for writing
and your intended **audience**. You may want to do some
additional brainstorming. Remember, you can add to or delete from your brainstorming notes at any time.

Write a First Draft: Step 2

Mark knows what a personal narrative will include. To be sure that he does not forget anything, Mark made a planning checklist. Look at his checklist below.

Mark is now ready to write his first draft.

Mark's First Draft

> Trying out for the school musical took work that was hard. I walked to the Auditorium after school, there were butterflies in my stomach. Because I was nervous First, I did alot of preparing at home. For a hole week, I studied the script, Guys and Dolls. The show is a musical. I prepared a song. I was late because of a math test, and there was a line when I got to the tryout. The line was long. I sang off-key! Then it was time for my monologue, a speech from another play. I was so nervous, I forgot some lines. Mr. Harris the director asked me to do an improvisation. I had to pantomime drinking milk. That's right. The next day I read the bulletin board. I found out I got the part of Nathan Detroit. I still glow when I think back how I tried out for my first musical.

While Mark was writing his first draft, he was not concerned with writing perfectly. He was more interested in putting his ideas down on paper. He knew he could correct grammatical details later.

Planning Checklist
- Think about purpose.
- Choose an audience.
- Write a good beginning sentence.
- Arrange supporting details in chronological order.
  Beginning
  Middle
  Ending
- Write a good ending sentence.

YOUR TURN

Write your first draft. As you prepare to write, ask yourself these questions:

- What is my purpose for writing? What does my audience need to know?
- What is the main idea? How can I best express it with a clear beginning sentence and specific details?

TIME-OUT You might want to take some time out before you revise. That way you will be able to revise your writing with a fresh eye.

Revise: Step 3

After he finished his first draft, Mark read it over to himself. He wondered if his personal narrative would entertain his audience, his classmates. He decided to ask a classmate to read his work and make suggestions for improvement.

Are you sure the actions are presented in the right order?

I'll check that. Thanks for the pointer.

Mark took a long look at his beginning sentence. He realized that hard work was not what he wanted to write about. He again considered his purpose, to entertain, and realized that he had not stated his overall idea clearly.

Mark then looked back at his planning checklist. He decided to make a copy of the checklist to help him as he revised his work. He made a check mark on the list to remind him to think through the order of the actions. He also made a check mark to help him remember to rework the beginning sentence.

Mark then began revising his personal narrative. At this stage Mark concentrated on the important points that he had included on his checklist. He asked himself several questions. Was his beginning sentence strong? Were the actions arranged in chronological order? Mark did not correct errors in spelling or punctuation at this stage. He knew he could correct these errors later.

Mark carefully made changes on his first draft, adding some details and moving or taking out others. Look at Mark's revised draft on the next page.

Revising Checklist
- Think about purpose.
- Choose an audience.
- ✔ Write a good beginning sentence.
- ✔ Arrange supporting details in chronological order.
  Beginning
  Middle
  Ending
- Write a good ending sentence.

W R I T I N G

PROCESS

Trying out for the school musical ~~took work that~~ *was truly trying.*
~~was hard.~~ I walked to the Auditorium after school, there
were butterflies in my stomach. Because I was nervous

First, I did alot of preparing at home. For a hole week, I

studied the script, Guys and Dolls. The show is a musical. I *so*

prepared a song. ~~I was late because of a math test, and~~ *long*

there was a line when I got to the tryout. ~~The line was~~
~~long.~~ I sang off-key! Then it was time for my monologue, a

speech from another play. I was so nervous, I forgot some

lines. Mr. Harris the director asked me to do an improvis- *I drank it like a cat.*

ation. I had to pantomime drinking milk. That's right. The *and*

next day I read the bulletin board. I found out I got the

part of Nathan Detroit. I still glow when I think back how

I tried out for my first musical.

Thinking Like a Writer

WISE
WORD
CHOICE

- Which sentence did Mark move? Why did he move it?
- Which sentences did he combine? How did combining
  them make his work more effective?
- What details did he take out? Why did he take them out?

YOUR TURN

Read your revised draft. Ask yourself these questions.

- How can I improve the beginning sentence?
- What details can I add to strengthen the beginning? the
  middle? the ending?
- Which words can I change to be more specific?
- Which sentences could I combine?

If you wish, ask a friend to read your paragraph and make
suggestions. Then revise your paragraph.

Proofread: Step 4

Now that Mark had revised his work, it was time to proofread it. He knew that proofreading meant correcting errors in grammar, spelling, punctuation, and capitalization. To help him remember what to look for as he proofread, Mark decided to make a proofreading checklist. He also referred to the list of special marks used in proofreading.

Look at how Mark made corrections on his draft after he proofread it.

Part of Mark's Proofread Draft

> Trying out for the school musical ~~took work that~~ *was truly trying.* ~~was hard.~~ I walked to the Auditorium after school there were butterflies in my stomach. Because I was nervous, First, I did (alot) *a lot* of preparing at home. For a (hole) *whole* week I studied the script, Guys and Dolls. The show is a musical, I *so* prepared a song. ~~I was late because of a math test, and~~ there was a *long* line when I got to the tryout. ~~The line was long.~~ I sang off-key! Then it was time for my monologue, a speech from another play.

YOUR TURN

Proofreading Practice

Practice your proofreading skills. First find the errors and then write the paragraph with corrections on a separate sheet of paper.

> Thanksgiving is my favorit holiday. We always go to Grandmas' house, the dinner is always delicious. Their is always a fire in the fire place. We allways pop popcorn. Games with my cousins. Each year thanksgiving is better than the last

Proofreading Checklist
- Did I indent my paragraph?
- Did I spell all words correctly?
- What punctuation errors do I need to correct?
- What capitalization errors do I need to correct?
- What sentence fragments or run-on sentences do I need to correct?

Applying Your Proofreading Skills

Now proofread your personal narrative. Read your checklist again. Review both **The Grammar Connection** and **The Mechanics Connection.**

THE GRAMMAR CONNECTION

Remember these rules about sentence fragments and run-on sentences:

■ A **sentence fragment** can be made into a complete sentence by adding a subject part, a predicate part, or both.

The neighbors. (fragment)
Gave us a kitten. (fragment)
The neighbors gave us a kitten. (complete sentence)

■ Avoid a **run-on sentence** by separating ideas into two sentences, by forming a compound sentence, or by adding a semicolon.

Run-on: Meg loved Muffin she had named the kitten well.

Correction: Meg loved Muffin. She had named the kitten well.

or: Meg loved Muffin, and she had named the kitten well.

or: Meg loved Muffin; she had named the kitten well.

Check your personal narrative. Read your work to be sure that you have avoided writing sentence fragments and run-on sentences.

THE MECHANICS CONNECTION

Proofreading Marks
Indent ¶
Add ∧
Add a comma ⋏
Add quotation marks ⌄⌄
Add a period ⊙
Take out ℐ
Capitalize ≡
Lower-case letter /
Reverse the order ∿

Remember to end your sentences with periods, question marks, or exclamation marks.

■ **Declarative:** She wrote about Thanksgiving.

■ **Imperative:** You read it.
Read it.
Please read it.

■ **Interrogative:** Did you like it?

■ **Exclamatory:** How funny it was!

Check your personal narrative. Have you used end marks correctly?

Publish: Step 5

Mark looked forward to sharing his personal narrative with his classmates. He made a clean, final copy of his work and posted it on the class bulletin board. He also posted a photograph of himself as Nathan Detroit in *Guys and Dolls.* He was pleased that several of his classmates asked him questions about trying out for an upcoming school play.

YOUR TURN

Make a clean, final copy of your personal narrative. You, of course, should share your personal narrative with the audience that you had in mind when you wrote it. Think of some other ways to share your work. You might want to use one of the ideas that you find in the **Sharing Suggestions** box below.

SHARING SUGGESTIONS

Create a magazine called *Personal Treasures.* Illustrate your personal narratives.	Read your narrative to a group of interested people at a home for senior citizens.	Turn your personal narrative into a brief play and make an audio-tape of it.

4 SPEAKING AND LISTENING: Telling About an Incident

How many times a day do you hear a conversation begin with something like, "You'll never guess what happened to me"? Everyone enjoys telling a personal story. Now that you have written a personal narrative, you can use what you know to present a personal narrative as a short talk to an interested audience.

To tell a story effectively you need to do a bit of planning. You must consider your purpose. The purpose of most narratives is to entertain the listener. Will your audience find your story entertaining? In what ways could you draw out the humor in your story?

You must also consider your audience. Will your story interest them? What details must your audience know to appreciate your story?

First of all, you will want to prepare a note card to use as a guide during your talk. It is not a good idea to write out your talk on the card. Too much time would be spent reading your material instead of speaking directly to your audience. Your note card should include only the main points.

For example, look at this note card:

Notes: Moss Gathers a Rolling Stone — Personal Narrative
1. *Jay and I lost in woods*
2. *heading north back to cabin*
3. *went in circles*
4. *remembered moss grew on north side of trees*
5. *found moss, headed to cabin*
6. *great sense of joy and relief*

Notice that the notes present what happened in chronological order. What other important details are included?

Would the notes have been clearer if they had been arranged under the topics Beginning, Middle, and Ending?

The following guidelines will help you when you are telling about something that happened to you.

WRITING EXTENSION

> **SPEAKING GUIDELINES: Telling About an Incident**
>
> 1. Practice your talk, using a note card.
> 2. Remember your main purpose—to inform or to entertain.
> 3. Open with a clear and interesting beginning sentence; close with an effective concluding sentence. Include specific details that are presented clearly in chronological order.
> 4. Look at your listeners as you speak.
> 5. Speak your words clearly so they can be heard and understood. Emphasize important details with your voice and with gestures.

- Why are a good beginning sentence and a good ending sentence important when telling a personal narrative?
- Why is chronological order important when telling a personal narrative?

SPEAKING APPLICATION Telling About an Incident

Prepare a note card to use in presenting a short talk about an incident from your life that has left an impression on you. Use the speaking guidelines to help you practice. Your classmates will use these guidelines as they listen.

> **LISTENING GUIDELINES: An Incident**
>
> 1. Listen for a good beginning sentence.
> 2. Listen for the sequence of events.
> 3. Listen for a good ending sentence.

THE CURRICULUM CONNECTION

Writing About Social Studies

A large part of social studies is concerned with the many fascinating happenings of the past. An important way we learn about these past events is through primary sources. **Primary sources** include eyewitness accounts written by the men and women who actually were involved in the historical events. Their words—recorded in journals, letters, and autobiographies— provide a treasure house of information.

Maps, dates, charts, and documents are all important in social studies, but they are only important because they reflect the lives of real people. How do people govern themselves? How do they handle their resources? How do groups relate to each other? These are the kinds of questions that social studies tries to answer.

By studying how people interact in groups, social scientists help us understand ourselves as individuals. The true stories of human life they uncover are not only instructive but can often be more fascinating than any fictional narrative.

ACTIVITIES

Make a Time Line

Design a poster-size time line showing scenes from an incident in history. Illustrate the time line with drawings of the people involved. Draw some thought balloons for the historical figures and have them say something about their accomplishments. Post the time line on the bulletin board.

Letters from the Past

Choose someone from history who you believe has made an important contribution. Imagine being that person and write a letter that tells what contribution you made. You and your classmates may want to read or act out your letters in a program called "People Who Made History Happen."

Respond to Literature

The following personal narrative is taken from *We*, an auto-biography by Charles A. Lindbergh. Lindbergh was the first person to make a solo airplane flight between North America and Europe. After reading the selection, write a response. For example, your response might be a letter of congratulations to Lindbergh, a poem expressing how you would feel flying all alone for over thirty-three hours, or an imagined dialogue between you and Lindbergh taking place in the cockpit.

The Lone Eagle Arrives in Paris

Lindbergh recalls the landing of his monoplane, *The Spirit of St. Louis*, near Paris on May 21, 1927:

I flew low over the field once, then circled around into the wind and landed. After the plane stopped rolling, I turned it around and started to taxi back to the lights. The entire field ahead, however, was covered with thousands of people all running toward my ship . . . .

I cut the switch to keep the propeller from killing someone. Speaking was impossible; no words could be heard in the uproar . . . .

I started to climb out of the cockpit, but as soon as one foot appeared through the door, I was dragged the rest of the way without any assistance on my part.

UNIT CHECKUP

LESSON

Group Writing: A Personal Narrative (page 44)   Rewrite the following paragraph on a separate sheet of paper. Arrange the events in chronological order, adding transition words where they are needed.

I arrived at the newspaper office a little late. I hastily filled out the form. A secretary gave me a form to fill out. I was shown into the office of Mr. Adams, the circulation manager. He was a pleasant man. He told me about the responsibilities of a newspaper route and asked me several questions. I will never forget the day I interviewed for my first job. He looked at the form that I had completed and let out a laugh. Mr. Adams said that this would make me the oldest newspaper carrier in the world. I got the job anyway. He saw that I had written 1990 in the space on the form that asked for my age.

LESSON

Thinking: General and Specific (page 48)   Imagine that you took some notes for writing a personal narrative about the time you entered an ice-skating contest. Which general notes would you eliminate? Which specific details would you keep?

nervous before I began my routine—ice conditions bad—three hundred people cheered and clapped—made a nice move—cut a sharp figure eight—audience appreciated—ice chipped in three spots—skating music was played—skated to music of 1812 Overture

LESSON

Writing a Personal Narrative (page 50)   Imagine that you are a famous author. You are about to go on a national television show to promote your latest book, *My Treasured Moments*. Write a personal narrative that describes a treasured moment in your life that you would like to share with the television audience.

LESSON
4

Speaking and Listening: Telling About an Incident (page 58)   Write a brief paragraph in which you explain why using chronological order is important when you are telling a personal narrative.

Writing personal narratives about treasured experiences in your life gives you the opportunity to share them with others. Famous people often share their personal experiences on television when they appear on programs known generally as "talk shows." Imagine that you have been asked to appear on a television talk show. How would you prepare for your appearance? What purpose could your appearance have? What personal experiences would you share? Would these be interesting for a television audience?

Use the picture below as the basis for a discussion with your classmates about the place of personal narratives in everyday life. How do they provide entertainment? How do they teach us?

Organize a classroom talk show. Choose people to be guests, hosts, and announcers. You will also need a director to be in charge of the presentation.

- Organize a group to make up a product to be the sponsor. Write and act out some commercials.
- Organize a group to be in charge of the set for the program. This group would also be in charge of lights and props.
- Have someone make a recording of your program.
- Share your talk show with another class or with the school.

UNIT

3

Nouns

In Unit 3 you will learn about nouns. Nouns are words that name people, places, things, or ideas. When you write, you can make your meaning clearer if you use nouns that are exact.

JOURNAL

Discuss Read the poem on the opposite page. What mood does the poem convey?

Creative Expression The unit theme is *Reflections*. A reflection can be an image that you see of yourself in a mirror, or it can be a quiet thought that you have. Write about a time when you reflected about something important. Write your thoughts in your journal.

THEME: *REFLECTIONS*

When I was young,
every day was as a beginning
of some new thing,
and every evening ended
with the glow of the next day's dawn.

—Eskimo

1 KINDS OF NOUNS

A noun names a person, place, thing, or idea.

Every day the busy world around you is filled with different people, places, things, and ideas. The words you use to name these people and things are called nouns.

Nouns may name general or specific things. A **common noun** is the general name of a person, place, thing, or idea. A **proper noun** is the name of a particular person, place, thing, or idea. A proper noun always begins with a capital letter.

Common Nouns	state	author	team	song
Proper Nouns	New York	Willa Cather	Royals	"Dixie"

A **concrete noun** names something that you can see or touch. An **abstract noun** names something that cannot be seen or touched, such as an idea, emotion, quality, or condition.

Concrete Nouns	author	village	book	horse	saddle
Abstract Nouns	cleverness	joy	fear	wisdom	humor

Guided Practice

Identify each noun and tell whether it is common or proper.
Example: Sleepy Hollow was a rural village.
Sleepy Hollow proper village common

1. A well-written story brings pleasure to the reader.
2. Washington Irving had a talent for description.
3. "The Legend of Sleepy Hollow" is set in New York.
4. Sleepy Hollow was near the Hudson River.
5. Irving created humor and suspense in the story.
6. The author drew a fanciful picture of rural life.
7. Generations of Americans have loved this tale.

 ## THINK

■ How do I decide whether a noun is common or proper?

REMEMBER

- A **common noun** names any person, place, thing, or idea. A **proper noun** names a particular person, place, thing, or idea.
- A **concrete noun** names something that can be seen or touched. An **abstract noun** names something that cannot be seen or touched.

More Practice

A. Make a list of nouns from each sentence. Next to each noun write whether it is a **common noun** or a **proper noun**.

Example: Ichabod Crane was a schoolteacher.
Ichabod Crane proper   schoolteacher common

   8. The students in Sleepy Hollow teased Crane.
   9. With marriage in mind, Ichabod courted Katarina Van Tassel.
10. Katarina was the beautiful daughter of a wealthy farmer.
11. Another suitor for Katarina was Brom Bones.
12. Brom was a man with a fondness for mischief.
13. Ichabod had many weaknesses.

B. Write each sentence. Draw one line under each concrete noun and two lines under each abstract noun.

Example: One reason for their interest in Katarina was her wealth.
One reason for their interest in Katarina was her wealth.

14. Supposedly, a headless horseman haunted the area.
15. The legend contrasts with the peacefulness of the valley.
16. Ichabod started toward his home on a horse.
17. A strange rider stalked Ichabod along the trail.
18. Terror gripped the schoolteacher and the horse.
19. At the bridge Ichabod thought his safety was sure.
20. Later, a hat and a smashed pumpkin were found.

A·LEGEND·OF
SLEEPY·HOLLOW
BY·WASHINGTON·IRVING
ILLUSTRATED·BY
ARTHUR·RACKHAM

Extra Practice, page 88

WRITING APPLICATION A Journal Entry

Write a journal entry describing a joke someone played on you. When you complete this, draw one line under each common noun and two lines under each proper noun.

2 SINGULAR AND PLURAL NOUNS

A noun shows **number;** it is either singular or plural. You use singular nouns to name one person, place, thing, or idea. You use plural nouns to name more than one.

Singular Nouns	To Form Plural	Examples
most singular nouns	add *s*	cow boy road cows boys roads
nouns ending with **s, ss, x, z, ch, sh**	add *es*	box waltz ash boxes waltzes ashes
nouns ending with a **consonant and y**	change the *y* to *i* and add *es*	sky city lady skies cities ladies
nouns ending with a **vowel and o**	add *s*	radio studio rodeo radios studios rodeos
nouns ending with a **consonant and o**	generally add *s* but sometimes *es*	piano cello tomato pianos cellos tomatoes
some nouns ending with a **consonant and o**	add either *s* or *es*	volcanoes or volcanos mottoes or mottos
nouns ending with **ff, f,** or **fe**	most add **s,** some change **f** to **v,** add **es**	cuff roof life cuffs roofs lives
some irregular nouns	change their spelling	woman tooth foot women teeth feet
a few irregular nouns	keep the same spelling	moose bison deer species corps series

Guided Practice

Tell the plural form of each noun.

Example: potato *potatoes*

  1. glass   **2.** horse   **3.** piano   **4.** arch

 THINK

- How do I decide when to add *s* or *es* to form a plural noun?

REMEMBER

- A **singular noun** is a word that names one person, place, thing, or idea. A **plural noun** is a word that names more than one person, place, thing, or idea.
- To form the plural of most nouns, add *s* or *es*.

More Practice

A. Write the plural form of each noun.

Example: shelf *shelves*

5. Ross	**8.** echo	**11.** mystery	**14.** tooth
6. ally	**9.** Latino	**12.** hunch	**15.** cuff
7. mirror	**10.** flash	**13.** journey	**16.** cafe

B. Write each sentence, changing each singular noun in parentheses to a plural noun.

Example: (Writer) can carry (reader) to many (place).
Writers can carry readers to many places.

17. Printed (page) can transport us to real or imaginary (land), to foreign (country) or distant (planet).
18. (Locale) can range from peaceful (valley) to bustling (city).
19. (Story) tell about (princess), (cowboy), and (explorer).
20. In describing (character), writers explore various (personality) and (idea).
21. Many people enjoy reading about the daring (adventure) of extraordinary (hero) and (heroine).
22. Other people prefer reading (story) about (problem).
23. (Sketch) and (narrative) about (individual) and (family) help us form (view) about our own (life).
24. (Fantasy) for young children often feature small (creature), such as (elf) and (dwarf).
25. Even animals—such as (deer), (mouse), (goose), and (donkey)—may play (role) in these (drama).

Extra Practice, page 89

WRITING APPLICATION A Friendly Letter

Imagine that you are visiting an animal preserve in Africa or a large zoo. Write a letter to a friend describing the animals you see. Then exchange papers with a classmate and underline each singular noun once and each plural noun twice.

3 POSSESSIVE NOUNS

You often use special forms of nouns to show who owns or possesses something. These nouns are called **possessive nouns** and contain an apostrophe (**'**). Both singular and plural nouns have possessive forms.

A **captain's** duty includes protecting his **sailors'** lives.

To form the possessive of a singular noun, add *'s*.

bee	fox	soprano	sister	Tyrone	Jones
bee's	fox's	soprano's	sister's	Tyrone's	Jones's

For plural nouns ending in *s*, first write the plural form and then add an apostrophe.

bees	foxes	sopranos	sisters	Tyrones	Joneses
bees'	foxes'	sopranos'	sisters'	Tyrones'	Joneses'

For plural nouns that do not end in *s*, add an apostrophe and *s*.

mice	deer	children	men	geese	oxen
mice's	deer's	children's	men's	geese's	oxen's

Remember that apostrophes are used to form the possessive, not to form the plural.

The **writers** held a monthly meeting. (plural noun)
The **writer's** typewriter was broken. (singular possessive)
The **writers'** agent sold their stories. (plural possessive)

Guided Practice

Write each possessive noun and tell if it is singular or plural.

Example: The reader's interest is strong.   *reader's singular*

1. "The Open Boat" is based on Stephen Crane's experiences.
2. The captain's efforts could not save the ship.
3. Passengers' fates were at the mercy of the angry sea.
4. The crewmen's attempts at rescue were useless.
5. Each danger is reflected vividly in the author's account.

THINK

- How do I decide where to place an apostrophe when forming possessive nouns?

REMEMBER

- To form the possessive of a singular noun, add *'s.*
- To form the possessive of a plural noun that ends in *s*, add only an apostrophe. When a plural noun does not end in *s*, add *'s.*

More Practice

A. Write the possessive noun in each sentence. Then write whether it is a **singular possessive** or a **plural possessive.**

Example: The author's skill is immediately apparent.
author's   singular possessive

  6. Stephen Crane's job was as a newspaper writer.
  7. On Captain Malloy's orders, four men entered a lifeboat.
  8. Each man's turn at the oars was long and hard.
  9. The captain's coat became their sail.
10. The victims' spirits rose when they saw land.
11. Observers' signals from shore encouraged the men.
12. As night fell, the voyagers' hopes for aid dimmed.
13. The writer's style reflects the desperate struggle.

B. Change each underlined word to a possessive noun.

Example: The men in the boat saw fishermen signals.
The men in the boat saw fishermen's signals.

14. The captain injuries limited his activity.
15. Crane watched a shark fin in the water.
16. Each man fatigue grew more intense.
17. At dawn their rescuers boats were not in sight.
18. A huge wave tossed Crane body over the empty boat.
19. Higgens bravery and strength impressed Crane.
20. Ashore, the survivors relief was mixed with sadness.

Extra Practice, page 90

WRITING APPLICATION A Journal Entry

Imagine that you are stranded at sea. Suddenly you see sharks circling. Write a brief journal entry describing this event and your reactions. Exchange papers with a classmate and circle the possessive nouns in each other's work.

4 COLLECTIVE NOUNS

You know that a noun is a word that names a person, place, thing, or idea. **Collective nouns,** however, name a group made up of individual persons or things.

> **Common Collective Nouns**
>
> group   crowd   club   flock   audience   orchestra   band
> crew   army   class herd   committee   family   swarm

Because a collective noun names one group, its meaning can be singular. When the group is acting as a unit, use a singular verb.

> The **club** *sponsors* the contest. (one group, singular)
> The **committee** *selects* the winner. (one group, singular)

When the individuals within the group are thought of as acting separately, the meaning of the collective noun is plural. Use a plural verb.

> The **committee** *review* each story. (individuals, plural)
> The **jury** *disagree* about the issue. (individuals, plural)

Guided Practice

Read the sentences. Identify each collective noun and tell whether the meaning is singular or plural.

Example: The group sings folk music.
        group   singular

1. The band plays softly.
2. One group surrounds the winners.
3. The winner's family is delighted.
4. The family speak about their reactions.
5. Then the audience hears a narrative poem.
6. An adventurous group has sailed from England.
7. During the journey, the crew handles the boat well.
8. Later, a landing party reaches the foreign shore.

 THINK

- How do I know when to use a singular or plural verb with a collective noun?

REMEMBER

- A **collective noun** is a noun that names a group of people or things.
- A collective noun is singular in meaning when it refers to the group as a unit. A collective noun is plural in meaning when it refers to the individual members of the group.

More Practice

A. Write each collective noun and tell whether it is **singular** or **plural** in meaning.

Example: The club agree about the trip. *club plural*

 9. The band move off in different directions.
10. Unknown to the English, a native tribe lives nearby.
11. A family discuss the strangers who approach the village.
12. A delegation speaks with the English.

B. Write each sentence. Draw one line under each collective noun. Draw two lines under the verb and write whether the collective noun is used in the **singular** or **plural.**

Example: Our class discuss stories of the American West.
Our <u>class</u> <u>discuss</u> stories of the American West.
plural

13. A great number of individualists have appeared in the American West.
14. A new crop of authors write of their experiences.
15. A group of stories were written about the mining camps.
16. A great pair of Western writers are Mark Twain and Bret Harte.
17. The eager public always enjoys reading wild tales.
18. A legendary gang were the American cowboys.
19. During the Civil War, cattle were often untended.
20. When the war was over, an army of cowboys was needed to round up the maverick cattle.

Extra Practice, page 91

WRITING APPLICATION A Narrative Paragraph

Write a brief paragraph about a group activity you have enjoyed. Exchange papers with a classmate and circle the collective nouns in each other's work.

5 APPOSITIVES

A noun placed after another noun to identify it or add information about it is called an **appositive.** An appositive often directly follows the noun it identifies.

> An American writer, **Edgar Allan Poe,** helped develop the short story.

Other words sometimes accompany an appositive.

> Poe, **the creator of the detective story,** introduced new ideas.
> The author, **the son of actors,** was an orphan as a young child.

Appositives often supply information that is not essential to understanding a sentence. When you leave out the appositive or appositive phrase, the meaning of the sentence does not change. Use commas to set off this kind of appositive. Sometimes, however, an appositive is needed to clearly identify the noun with which it appears. In such instances, the appositive is essential and is not set off by commas.

> ESSENTIAL: The poet **Poe** uses strong rhythms and strange images.
> NOT ESSENTIAL: "The Gold Bug," **a story by Poe,** explores logic.

Guided Practice

Name each appositive. Tell which noun the appositive identifies.

Example: Poe, a poet, uses language well. *a poet   Poe*

1. Often people in a story face a dilemma, an unpleasant choice.
2. The main character, perhaps an inspector, seeks a solution.
3. The conflict, a battle between choices, is important.
4. Personality, an unpredictable trait, may be a clue.
5. The story "The Gold Bug" is suspenseful.
6. "The Gold Bug," a famous story by Poe, has a wonderful plot.
7. "The Gold Bug" centers on the discovery of a bug, a beetle.

 THINK

- How do I decide if I should use a comma with an appositive?

REMEMBER

■ An **appositive** is a word or group of words that follows a noun and identifies or explains it.

More Practice

Write each sentence. Draw one line under each appositive. Draw two lines under the noun that the appositive identifies. Add commas where necessary.

Example: The setting a swampy area is vital to the story.
The setting, a swampy area, is vital to the story.

8. The main character William Legrand believes the bug will lead to buried treasure.
9. Legrand lives on Sullivan's Island a lonely place off the coast of South Carolina.
10. His only companion is his elderly servant Jupiter.
11. Legrand's friend a man from Charleston visits the island.
12. Legrand's preoccupation his one focus is on the gold bug.
13. The friend joins a secret mission a visit to the mainland.
14. The friend is filled with dread a terrible fear about Legrand's sanity.
15. The search the hunt for treasure seems doomed.
16. Legrand seems possessed by demons evil spirits.
17. The treasure a pirate's booty is uncovered.
18. The treasure was buried by the infamous pirate Captain Kidd.
19. The answer to the mystery was a cipher a code of numbers and symbols written on parchment.
20. Legrand used thought powerful logic and found the treasure.

Extra Practice, page 92

WRITING APPLICATION A Summary

Write a brief summary of a mystery story you have read or have seen on television, describing the setting, the characters, and the plot. Exchange your summary with a classmate and identify the appositive nouns and phrases in each other's work.

COOPERATIVE LEARNING

6 MECHANICS: Capitalizing Proper Nouns

A **proper noun** names a particular person, place, thing, or idea. Proper nouns always begin with a capital letter. Use the following rules as a guide for capitalizing proper nouns.

1. Capitalize a person's name, including initials and titles and the abbreviations *Jr.* and *Sr.*

   Sir Arthur Conan Doyle   Samuel L. Clemens

2. Capitalize words that show family relationships when used as titles or as substitutes for a person's name.

   Do you know Grandmother Jones?

3. Capitalize names of specific places, such as cities, states, countries, continents, and special regions.

   Yuma   Utah   Mexico   the West

4. Capitalize the names of oceans, lakes, mountains, and other specific geographical features.

   Pacific Ocean   Rocky Mountains

5. Capitalize the specific names of buildings, bridges, monuments, streets, and highways.

   Chrysler Building   Bay Bridge   Market Street

6. Capitalize the names of written works, such as books, stories, poems, magazines, and newspapers.

   Incredible Tales   "Rain"   *Miami Herald*

Guided Practice

Read each sentence. Tell which underlined words are proper nouns and should be capitalized.

Example: Irving served as a <u>diplomat</u> to <u>spain</u>.
      Spain

1. America's first notable <u>writer</u> was <u>washington irving</u>.
2. Born in <u>new york</u>, he was the youngest <u>son</u> in a large family.
3. Irving wrote for a <u>newspaper</u>, the <u>morning chronicle</u>.
4. He also wrote essays for a <u>magazine</u> called <u>salmagundi</u>.

 THINK

■ How do I decide which nouns I should capitalize?

REMEMBER

- Always capitalize a proper noun, the name of a particular person, place, thing, or idea.

More Practice

A. Write the proper nouns from each sentence, using correct capitalization.

Example: Europeans learned about america through irving.
Europeans   America   Irving

5. Irving traveled to england and later to spain.
6. A friend, sir walter scott, helped him in europe.
7. Irving's best stories and reflections are in *the sketch book.*
8. One story is set in the catskill mountains during the 1700s.
9. The mountains are just west of the hudson river.
10. henry hudson's men supposedly revisited the area every twenty years.
11. "Rip van winkle" is the story of a man who meets these spirits.
12. Irving also described london and westminster abbey.

B. Rewrite each sentence and use correct capitalization.

Example: Nathaniel hawthorne was born in salem, massachusetts.
Nathaniel Hawthorne was born in Salem, Massachusetts.

13. Hawthorne worked as a clerk in boston for a time.
14. Many of his stories were accounts of new england.
15. In *the wonder book,* he retold myths from classical greece.
16. One of his admirers was president franklin pierce.
17. Also from new england was harriet beecher stowe.
18. Harriet stowe is best known for *uncle tom's cabin.*
19. However, mrs. stowe knew little about the south.
20. She based her book on a brief time spent in ohio.

Extra Practice, page 93

WRITING APPLICATION A Description

Think of a person or place that has impressed you. Write a brief description giving your impressions. Exchange papers with a classmate and check each other's work for correct capitalization.

7 MECHANICS: Forming Possessive Nouns

Apostrophes are used with nouns to show ownership or possession. You form the possessive of a singular noun by adding an apostrophe and an *s*.

> My little **brother's** storybook is well used.
> **Timmy's** fingers have worn the pages.

You form the possessive of plural nouns that end in *s* by adding only an apostrophe.

> The **authors'** stories had been told many times.
> The **narrators'** words were carefully written down.

You form the possessive of plural nouns that do not end in *s* by adding an apostrophe and an *s*.

> Simple **people's** tales were saved for the future.
> Folk tales appeal to **children's** imaginations.

When two or more people possess something together, add the possessive ending after the last named.

> **Jack and Carol's** report was about the Grimm brothers.
> **Jack's and Carol's** reports were both about folk tales.

Guided Practice

Tell whether the underlined word is the possessive form of a singular or a plural noun.

Example: Snow White won the dwarfs' love.
plural noun

1. The Grimms' search for folk tales took many years.
2. Katherina Viehmann's memory was phenomenal.
3. The storyteller's eyes sparkled as she told tales.
4. Roosters' speech, tailors' cleverness, and geese's trickery are featured in several stories.
5. The Grimm brothers' collection included them all.
6. Viehmann's stories were recited slowly.
7. The folklorists' pens took down every word.

 THINK

- Where do I place the apostrophe when I write a possessive noun?

REMEMBER

- Form the possessive of a singular noun by adding 's.
- Form the possessive of a plural noun that ends in s by adding an apostrophe.
- Form the possessive of a plural noun that does not end in s by adding 's.

More Practice

A. Write each sentence. Draw one line under each singular possessive noun. Draw two lines under each plural possessive noun.

Example: Today the storytellers' words would be on tape.
Today the <u>storytellers'</u> words would be on tape.

  8. Viehmann's repertory included such famous stories as "The Goose Girl."
  9. Dorothea Wild's foremost story is "Hansel and Gretel."
10. Dorothea's nurse had taught her many tales.
11. The nurse's store of tales included "Little Red-Cap."
12. It was from such sources that the Grimms' collection grew.
13. Much of a folk tale's effect depends on specific words.

B. Rewrite each sentence, changing each word in parentheses to a possessive noun.

Example: The (tales) sources were humble.
The tales' sources were humble.

14. The (brothers) serious regard for their sources was unique.
15. Other (collectors) stories were freely rewritten.
16. The Grimms set down the (tellers) own speech.
17. The first volume of the tales was published in the winter of (Napoleon) retreat from Moscow.
18. (Jacob) preciseness was stricter than (Wilhelm).
19. Selecting the tales was left to (Wilhelm) excellent judgment.
20. (Jacob and Wilhelm) German dictionary is an important work.

Extra Practice, Practice Plus, pages 94–96

WRITING APPLICATION A Summary

Briefly retell a favorite tale. Then exchange papers with a classmate. Check for the correct use of apostrophes in possessive nouns in each other's papers.

8 VOCABULARY BUILDING: How Language Changes

English is constantly changing as new words are added to its vocabulary. Here are some of the ways in which new words are formed and enter the language.

English owes much of its richness to **borrowed words,** which come from other languages.

dentist (from French)   toboggan (from Algonquian)

Clipped words are words that are shortened by having a part cut off from the beginning, from the end, or from both.

gym (from *gymnasium*)   flu (from *influenza*)

Compound words are formed by joining two words into a single term. A compound word often has a meaning different from that of its separate parts. There are three kinds of compounds: open (two words), closed (one word), and hyphenated.

OPEN COMPOUND	CLOSED COMPOUND	HYPHENATED COMPOUND
fire engine	blueprint	by-product

If parts of two words are combined into one term, the result is called a **blend word.**

motel (blend of *motor* and *hotel*)

Guided Practice

A. Tell whether each compound word is open, closed, or hyphenated.

Example: dog biscuit   *open*

1. railroad
2. mix-up
3. circuit breaker
4. voting machine

B. Tell the origin of each word by looking in a dictionary.

Example: peninsula   *Latin*

5. myth
6. corral
7. squash (noun)
8. squash (verb)

 THINK

■ How do new words enter the English language?

REMEMBER

- A **borrowed word** comes from another language.
- A **clipped word** has been shortened from a longer word.
- A **compound word** is made up of two or more words.
- A **blend word** is one in which two words have been telescoped into one.

More Practice

A. Look up each word in a dictionary and write it properly as an open, closed, or hyphenated compound.

Example: easy going   *easygoing*

9. heavy duty
10. space ship
11. paper weight
12. jump suit
13. out and out

B. Write each word and look it up in a dictionary. Beside each word, write its origin.

Example: broccoli   *Italian*

14. kimono
15. freckle
16. sofa
17. ballet

C. Draw four columns headed **borrowed, clipped, compound, blend.** Look up the history of the following words in a dictionary and write each in the appropriate column.

Example: route   *borrowed*

18. rodeo
19. headlight
20. cafe
21. sphere
22. polka
23. smog
24. bike
25. math

Extra Practice, page 97

COOPERATIVE
LEARNING

WRITING APPLICATION A Story

Look in a dictionary for the names of the people and places behind these words: *zeppelin, pasteurize, guppy, meander,* and *jeans.* Write a funny short story using the people as characters and the places as settings for your story. Make the story as fantastic and silly as you please.

GRAMMAR —AND— WRITING CONNECTION

Combining Sentences

Sometimes you can combine short sentences by adding a noun that identifies another noun.

> **SEPARATE:** Life with my cat is full of surprises. My cat's name is Snoozy.
>
> **COMBINED:** Life with my cat **Snoozy** is full of surprises.

You need to use commas if the noun you add gives extra, nonessential information.

> **SEPARATE:** Snoozy is afraid of thunder. Snoozy is my gray cat.
>
> **COMBINED:** Snoozy, **my gray cat,** is afraid of thunder.

You can also combine sentences by adding words that show possession.

> **SEPARATE:** Snoozy has a friend. Her name is Lolly. Lolly is a French poodle.
>
> **COMBINED:** **Snoozy's** friend **Lolly** is a French poodle.

Working Together

COOPERATIVE
LEARNING

With your classmates talk about these groups of sentences. Then tell how you would combine them into a single sentence.

Example: Snoozy has courage. This courage fails during rain-storms.   *Snoozy's courage fails during rainstorms.*

1. When it thunders, Snoozy has a hiding place. The hiding place is his basket.
2. Snoozy has a toy. It is a gray rubber mouse. It is called Mousey.
3. During the rain Snoozy hides under the couch. The couch is a hiding place big enough for Mousey and him.

Revising Sentences

One student decided to write a story about people and their pets. Help him revise sentences from his story by combining each group of sentences into a single sentence.

4. Alex has a tiny turtle. Her name is Trendy. She is a box turtle.
5. Martha has an aunt. Her name is Mrs. Amato. She bought a sleek Siamese cat.
6. My pet was a birthday gift. My pet is a little gerbil.
7. Do you know my friend? His name is Reuben.
8. Janet's horse lives on a farm. The horse is a gorgeous mare.
9. You should see my rabbit eat lettuce. My rabbit is a furry delight.
10. Jackie has a frog. His name is Legs. He is a terrific hopper.
11. Legs hops. His hops span an impressive distance.
12. Legs has a girlfriend. She is called Ms. Frog. She can jump farther than Legs.

WRITER AT WORK

Think about the importance of animals in daily life. Write a short story based on a real or fantasy experience with an animal. Revise your work with a partner and find sentences to combine. Experiment with using both appositives and possessives when you combine sentences.

UNIT CHECKUP

Kinds of Nouns (page 66)   Write each sentence. Draw one line under common nouns, two lines under proper nouns.

1. O. Henry was the name used by William Sydney Porter.
2. Porter wrote nearly three hundred stories.
3. In New York, the author watched people pass his window.
4. The writer imagined adventures for these people.
5. The stories of O. Henry are favorites of my friend Tom.

LESSON
Singular and Plural Nouns (page 68)   Write the plural form.

6. arch   **7.** piano   **8.** lily   **9.** Charles   **10.** self

LESSON
Possessive Nouns (page 70)   Write the following sentences. Draw one line under each singular possessive noun and two lines under each plural possessive noun.

11. O. Henry's characters are a delight.
12. Jane admires the young women's search for a career.
13. Tom is amused by the hoboes' boastful ways.
14. The stories tell of the characters' ambitions.
15. The writer's trademark is the unexpected ending.

LESSON
4
Collective Nouns (page 72)   Write each sentence. Draw one line under each collective noun. After the sentence, write whether the collective noun is singular or plural in meaning.

16. A familiar trio are the chief locations in Henry's stories.
17. One group of locations is in cattle country.
18. A couple are set in Central America and are very funny.
19. An audience listens to a story of life in the big city.
20. A jury selects "The Last Leaf" as its favorite story.

LESSON
Appositives (page 74)   Write each sentence. Draw one line under each appositive noun or phrase. Draw two lines under the noun to which the appositive refers.

21. He wrote about the Gentle Riders, a parody of the Rough Riders.
22. The Central American country Anchuria is a satire of politics.
23. One target, "tainted money," criticizes bad business methods.
24. One event in Porter's life, a prison term, affected him deeply.
25. A painful emotion, shame, made him tolerant of underdogs.

LESSON 6

Mechanics: Capitalizing Proper Nouns (page 76)   Rewrite each sentence, using correct capitalization.

26. William sydney porter was born in greensboro, north carolina, in 1862.

27. At nineteen he moved to texas for his health, and the west was the locale for some of his best stories.

28. He took the pen name o. henry from the name of orrin henry, a prison guard.

29. In new york city, the writer lived near madison square, in the heart of manhattan.

30. The sales of his second book, *the fourth million*, assured his popularity as a writer.

LESSON 7

Mechanics: Forming Possessive Nouns (page 78)   Rewrite each sentence, changing each word in parentheses to a possessive noun.

31. (Birds) nests vary in size and construction.

32. An (eagle) nest is an untidy pile of sticks.

33. A nest shaped like a tiny, neat cup reflects the (hummingbird) size.

34. (Geese) nests are hidden away on the ground.

35. (Woodpeckers) young are raised in hollow trees.

LESSON 8

Vocabulary Building: How Language Changes (page 80) Write each word and identify it as **borrowed, clipped, compound,** or a **blend.** If it is a compound word, write whether it is **closed, open,** or **hyphenated.**

36. videotape   39. smog

37. croissant   40. piano stool

38. lab

Writing Application: Noun Usage (pages 66–78)   The following paragraph contains 10 errors, including the formation of plural nouns and possessive nouns, the use of collective nouns and appositives, and the capitalization of proper nouns. Rewrite the paragraph correctly.

41.–50.   Our glee club a volunteer group presented a program of Holiday songs for the residentes and staff of the Crestview nursing Home. The audience were ready for us, but we were not ready for them. Their face's glowed with appreciation. The club announce that it was our best concert. The staff reply that it was the best program in Crestviews' history. Our singer's reward was the best reward happy faces.

Four of a Kind

Divide the class into two teams. Each team makes a list of categories of nouns, such as fruits, breeds of dogs, countries of Asia, rivers, basketball teams, and so on. The first player names a category. The first player on the opposite team must name four objects in that category. If the player cannot name four objects, the next player on the first team names another category for the second player on the opposite side. Any player who answers correctly earns the chance to challenge the opposite team. Every object named earns one point.

Animal Young

The young of animals sometimes have special names that are equivalent to the familiar *calf*, *cub*, or *pup*. Copy the numbered nouns below. Then match each lettered name of a young animal with the name of its parent.

1. goose
2. horse
3. frog
4. kangaroo
5. swan

a. colt
b. cygnet
c. joey
d. gosling
e. pollywog or tadpole

Common and Proper

Form two teams. Each team should compile a list of twenty common nouns. The members of one team should then take turns calling out a common noun. Any member of the opposite team should instantly reply with a proper noun that falls into the category of the common noun. For example, someone on the first team calls out "horse." Someone on the second team could immediately reply with "Black Beauty" or "Secretariat." When the first team has exhausted its list of common nouns, then the second team should call out from its list. Have someone keep time and score.

CREATIVE EXPRESSION

Late Starting Dawn

It's late starting dawn that breathes my vision,
inhales and exhales the sound of waking birds
And pokes ten miles of cold gray sky at a deer
standing alone in a meadow.

—Richard Brautigan

TRY IT OUT!

In this lyric poem, the poet calls up strong images, or "pictures," to the mind of the reader. He also uses personification, giving human qualities to nonliving things. Write two or more sentences that use personification, showing how an object might be human in form, actions, or feelings. Then try writing your ideas in the form of a poem with strong images.

EXTRA PRACTICE

Three levels of practice

Kinds of Nouns (page 66)

LEVEL

A. Write each sentence. Then draw a line under each noun.

1. Glass is made of ordinary materials.
2. Sand is the main ingredient of glass.
3. Ashes make the glass melt at a fairly low temperature.
4. Lime protects the glass from damage by moisture.
5. Color is added to glass by various substances.
6. Nature creates glass, too.
7. Obsidian is a product of volcanic action.
8. The great heat of a volcano melts sand into glass.
9. Quartz is another natural creation.

LEVEL

B. Write the following sentences. Draw one line under each common noun and two lines under each proper noun.

10. The Phoenicians may have invented glass.
11. The Romans credited the invention to sailors from Phoenicia.
12. The Romans were in error about the origin of glass.
13. Glass was invented in the Middle East over 3,500 years ago.
14. The date was earlier than the era of the Phoenicians.
15. The Romans made important developments in glassmaking.
16. Glassmakers made elegant new styles during the height of the Islamic empire.
17. In Italy the craft reached new heights in Venice during the Renaissance.

LEVEL

C. Write the following sentences. Draw one line under each concrete noun and two lines under each abstract noun.

18. The qualifications of a glassmaker require experience as well as talent.
19. Workers must have skill, patience, and control.
20. In ancient times glass was a rare luxury.
21. Ancient peoples regarded glass with wonder.
22. Folk tales tell of mountains and slippers of glass.
23. Mirrors and windowpanes inspired awe.
24. Craftsmen guarded secrets about ingredients for glass.
25. Now glass has many familiar uses in everyday life.

EXTRA PRACTICE

Three levels of practice

Singular and Plural Nouns (page 68)

LEVEL

A. Write the following words. After each word, write whether its plural requires *s* or *es*.

1. book   **4.** clock
2. wish   **5.** lunch
3. lens   **6.** match

LEVEL

B. Write the following words. After each word, write its plural form.

7. chimney   **10.** domino
8. mouse   **11.** airman
9. supply   **12.** thief

LEVEL

C. Rewrite each sentence, changing each singular noun in parentheses to a plural noun.

13. In these (hutch) is my collection of glass (animal).
14. These (bronco) and (pony) are placed near the (ox).
15. I have some (monkey) and (kangaroo) on these (shelf).
16. Here are some (rhino) and (hippo) and two (giraffe).
17. These little (dormouse) are (favorite) of mine.
18. The (pig) are in these (sty) near the (marsh).
19. Several (bird) appear in my (display).
20. Here are (flamingo), (thrush), and (cardinal).
21. The (puppy) belong to the two (beagle).
22. My (animal) include the (armadillo) and the (buffalo).
23. The (duck) are only (decoy).
24. Some tiny (mosquito), three (butterfly), and two (daddy-longlegs) are all insects.
25. The only (thing) I haven't shown are the (fox) and the (wolf).

EXTRA PRACTICE

Three levels of practice

Possessive Nouns (page 70)

LEVEL
A. Write whether the underlined word is the possessive form of a singular or plural noun.

1. Many things in my <u>parents'</u> house are made of glass.
2. <u>Janie's</u> goblet is empty.
3. The water in the <u>girls'</u> aquarium needs changing.
4. Sam filled <u>Mother's</u> mason jars with pickles.
5. Put the cream puffs on <u>Grandmother's</u> cake plate.
6. Someday this will be the <u>Marshes'</u> milk-glass vase.

LEVEL
B. Write each sentence. Draw one line under each singular possessive noun and two lines under each plural possessive noun.

7. Put the scraps in the dogs' bowls.
8. Harris's paperweight collection is marvelous.
9. Etta could see the children's bottles on the shelf.
10. We welcomed Dad's purchase of some light bulbs.
11. The Dickenses' chandelier fell and broke.
12. The women's glass pitchers are collector's items.

LEVEL
C. Rewrite each sentence, changing each word in parentheses to a possessive noun.

13. We washed the headlights on (Charles) car.
14. (Stella) measuring cup was inaccurately marked.
15. We all cherish my (great-aunt) cut-glass pickle dish.
16. There were no glass windows in the (horses) stable.
17. My (nieces) beakers are used with their chemistry set.
18. The (men) casseroles were delicious.
19. The TV screen in (Mom) workroom is dusty.
20. We fill the (cat) bowl before dinner.
21. The (boys) microscope rests in a place of honor.
22. (Carlos) collection of slides is large and varied.
23. The (neighbors) front window was broken.
24. (Bill and Tad) marble collection often shows up in the strangest places.
25. The thermometer in (Dad) workshop registered zero.

EXTRA PRACTICE

G
R
A
M
M
A
R

Three levels of practice

Collective Nouns (page 72)

LEVEL
A. Write the following sentences. Draw a line under each collective noun.

1. A flock of sightseers is entering the museum.
2. A group look at the varied collection of glass on display.
3. The largest bunch finds the display interesting.
4. The rest are not enthusiastic.
5. A jury has disagreed about the exhibit.
6. A band of tourists is crowding the lobby.
7. That beautiful group of bowls is my favorite item.
8. A family purchased the bowls for this exhibit.
9. The public is attending the exhibit.

LEVEL
B. Write the following sentences. Draw a line under each collective noun. After each sentence write whether the meaning is singular or plural.

10. A majority of the exhibit items are located here.
11. A number is displayed on the lower level.
12. The remainder have been set up in the annex.
13. A troop of guards is in charge of security.
14. The board of directors is having a reception next Friday.
15. The staff explains the exhibit to tourists.
16. The guild of glassmakers is sponsoring the show.
17. A local corporation finances the exhibitions.

LEVEL
C. Write each sentence. Draw one line under each collective noun. Draw two lines under the verb that shows whether the noun is singular or plural in the sentence.

18. A committee of glassmakers greet the guests.
19. A string quartet is playing during the reception.
20. The ensemble practices their parts separately.
21. A party of important people attends.
22. A crowd of onlookers has gathered outside.
23. The audience comment as notable people arrive.
24. A team of television reporters film the celebrities.
25. The police force controls the crowd.

EXTRA PRACTICE

Three levels of practice

Appositives (page 74)

LEVEL

A. Write each sentence. Underline each appositive.

1. Shakespeare wrote about a game of marbles, Cherry Pit.
2. Marbles were also mentioned by the Roman poet Ovid.
3. A rainy-day form of marbles, Persian, is played indoors.
4. The game of marbles, Ringer, is played in tournaments.
5. Marbles, a children's game, is not as popular as it once was.
6. Pete and I, great fans of marbles, regret the decline of interest in the game.
7. Pete gave me a taw, his best shooter.
8. I have a collection of mibs, the target marbles.
9. Pete's steelies, steel ball-bearings, are not interesting to me.
10. His aggies, marbles of agate stones, are colorful.

LEVEL

B. Write each sentence. Draw one line under each appositive. Draw two lines under the noun that the appositive identifies.

11. I have some crockies, marbles of fired clay.
12. My favorites are my glassies, glass marbles of many colors.
13. Lutz glassies, marbles with a swirl and gold bands inside, are greatly prized by collectors.
14. They are named for Nicholas Lutz, a great glassblower.
15. Lutz marbles, a misnomer, were imports from Germany.
16. Pete has some sulphides, clear marbles with a figure inside.
17. I saw the newest innovation, marbles as works of art.
18. Josh Simpson's marbles, spectacular creations, are not toys.

LEVEL

C. Use the information given in each item to write a sentence, each containing an appositive.

19. Robin Hood (a legendary English outlaw)
20. his chief archer (Little John)
21. Sherwood Forest (hideout)
22. spies (Friar Tuck and Maid Marian)
23. corrupt officer (the Sheriff of Nottingham)
24. King John (greedy ruler)
25. ballads (songs that tell stories)

GRAMMAR

EXTRA PRACTICE

Three levels of practice
Mechanics: Capitalizing Proper Nouns (page 76)

LEVEL

A. Write each proper noun, using correct capitalization.

1. james p. fox, jr.
2. mediterranean sea
3. george washington bridge
4. uncle al
5. richardson, texas
6. *old yeller*
7. appalachian mountains
8. *our town*
9. park boulevard
10. lake superior

LEVEL

B. Write each sentence. Capitalize each proper noun.

11. Last summer uncle alex bought me a kaleidoscope.
12. My grandmother had a kaleidoscope, too.
13. The kaleidoscope was invented in 1819 by sir david brewster.
14. Within three months, stores in paris and london had sold 200,000 of brewster's kaleidoscopes.
15. Kaleidoscopes are again popular in the united states.
16. Artists like carolyn bennet make kaleidoscopes.
17. Bennett's studio is in media, pennsylvania.
18. I found an article about kaleidoscopes in *scientific american*.
19. Judith karelitz builds kaleidoscopes that use polarized light.
20. Her kaleidoscopes are sold at the museum of modern art in new york and at the smithsonian institution.

LEVEL

C. Write a proper noun that fits each of the following descriptions. You may make up these words. Then write a sentence using each proper noun.

21. the name of your local newspaper
22. the name of your physician
23. a street in your town that is named after a kind of tree
24. the title of your favorite book or story
25. the name of a lake, river, or mountain range that is near you

EXTRA PRACTICE

Three levels of practice

Mechanics: Forming Possessive Nouns (page 78)

LEVEL

A. Write each sentence. Then write whether the underlined word is the possessive form of a **singular noun** or a **plural noun.**

1. Washington Irving first wrote for his <u>brother's</u> newspaper.
2. <u>Irving's</u> friend Sir Walter Scott helped his career in Europe.
3. The <u>writer's</u> best collection of work is *The Sketch Book.*
4. <u>Readers'</u> favorites include the story "Rip Van Winkle."
5. Here Irving told of <u>Rip Van Winkle's</u> long nap.
6. Many <u>Europeans'</u> impressions of America were from Irving.
7. Irving became <u>America's</u> leading man of letters.

LEVEL

B. Write each sentence. Draw one line under each singular possessive noun. Draw two lines under each plural possessive noun.

8. Sarah Orne Jewett's novels and stories reflect her native Maine.
9. Farmers' and fishermen's lives impressed young Sarah.
10. Her family's library provided much of her early education.
11. The writer's career began in her youth.
12. Some stories appeared in the nation's popular magazines.
13. The stories capture New Englanders' characteristics.
14. Jewett was a strong influence on Willa Cather's writing.

LEVEL

C. Write each sentence, changing each word in parentheses to a possessive noun.

15. Mark (Twain) real name was Samuel Langhorne Clemens.
16. He took his pen name from (leadsmen) calls on riverboats.
17. For two fathoms, a (leadsman) call was "mark twain."
18. (Clemens) childhood home was Hannibal, Missouri.
19. Hannibal was the model for Tom Sawyer and "Huck" (Finn) home town.
20. Clemens learned the (printer) trade and worked in the East.
21. He returned to Hannibal and took a (pilot) job.
22. River (pilots) responsibilities are great.
23. The (author) experiences inspired *Life on the Mississippi.*
24. The Civil War interrupted the (writer) career on the river.
25. He followed many (Americans) paths to the West.

PRACTICE + PLUS

Three levels of additional practice for a difficult skill

Mechanics: Forming Possessive Nouns (page 78)

LEVEL

A. Write each sentence. After it, write whether the underlined word is the possessive form of a **singular noun** or a **plural noun.**

1. The Greens' veterinary clinic is on Mill Road.
2. They care for our family's pets.
3. Last week there was a sore on our cat's paw.
4. Bouncer's limp became noticeable.
5. He hissed at the other pets' attentions.
6. The children's job was to hold Bouncer during the trip.
7. Dad's experience with the cat in the car had been unhappy.
8. Bouncer almost connected with the assistant's finger.
9. Dr. Green examined Bouncer's foot.
10. Dr. Green's methods are very gentle.
11. His wife's manner is equally soothing.
12. He applied some lotion to the animal's skin.
13. The doctor's treatment was successful.
14. Mom's job was to apply more lotion.
15. The cat's job was licking off the lotion.
16. Dr. Green also treated Mark and Sam's pets.
17. The dogs' ears had become infected.

LEVEL

B. Rewrite each sentence, changing each word in parentheses to a possessive noun.

18. Summer is the time for our (family) vacation.
19. Everyone in the family decides on each (summer) trip.
20. The (member) votes must all agree finally on one place.
21. Each (person) wishes are carefully considered.
22. (California) national parks were our current destination.
23. We would all go in (Dad and Mom) car.
24. Ms. Gomez had planned several (family) routes.
25. (Ms. Gomez) many trips there made her an expert.

26. We visited two of the (state) national parks.
27. All of the (park) camping facilities were pleasant.
28. We all appreciated the (rangers) courtesy.
29. The (trail) clear markers kept everyone safe.
30. We took these pictures with (Mom) camera.
31. Tonight we will show the slides at (Polly) house.

C. Rewrite each word group as another group that includes a possessive noun.

Example: the books that the Carters have
         the Carters' books

32. the stable for the horse
33. the capital of the state
34. the stories Mark Twain wrote
35. the clocks my brother owns
36. the trip that our cousins took
37. the appointment Mrs. Pearl made
38. the building where your sisters work
39. the barks of the dogs
40. the car Mark and Celia drive
41. the detailed lecture of the professor
42. the new computer that Sally owns
43. the house where my grandparents live
44. the playground for the children
45. the house of the neighbors
46. the friend of my uncle
47. the birthday of my sister
48. the bicycle belonging to the twins
49. the front yard of my aunt and uncle
50. a present for a friend

EXTRA PRACTICE

GRAMMAR

Three levels of practice

Vocabulary Building: How Language Changes (page 80)

LEVEL
A. Write each word. After each word, write whether it is an **open,** a **closed,** or a **hyphenated** compound.

1. cable car
2. armchair
3. comic strip
4. deep-freeze
5. jet engine
6. handcuff
7. meatball
8. lamppost
9. degree-day
10. runner-up

LEVEL
B. Draw lines down a piece of paper to make four columns. Head the columns **borrowed, clipped, compound, blend.** Then classify each word in its appropriate column.

11. polio
12. yogurt
13. ferryboat
14. mike
15. cliché
16. beanbag
17. sandwich
18. bull's-eye
19. electrocute
20. umbrella
21. magnet
22. lifeboat
23. senate
24. boxcar
25. taxi
26. smuggle
27. phone
28. sitcom
29. loot
30. bus

LEVEL
C. Write each word. Then look it up in a dictionary that contains word histories. Beside each word, write its origin.

31. bus
32. chortle
33. rodeo
34. jackal
35. shampoo
36. solar
37. exam
38. bungalow
39. muscle
40. poncho
41. motorcade
42. magic
43. sauna
44. saxophone
45. plaid
46. photo
47. attic
48. parka
49. poodle
50. skate

MAINTENANCE

UNIT 1: SENTENCES

Kinds of Sentences (page 2)
Write each sentence. Then write whether each sentence is **declarative, imperative, interrogative,** or **exclamatory.**

1. The magnolia trees are in bloom.
2. Have you seen them?
3. How beautiful they are!
4. Look at them tomorrow.
5. The petals have fallen to the ground.

Complete Subjects and Complete Predicates (page 4)
Write each sentence. Underline the complete subject once and the complete predicate twice.

6. The archer inserted an arrow into the bow.
7. He pulled the bowstring back toward his face.
8. The arrow hurtled swiftly toward the target.
9. The point of the arrow struck the target with great force.
10. Did the skillful archer hit the target in the center?

Simple Subjects and Simple Predicates (page 6)   Write each sentence. Underline the simple subject once and the simple predicate twice.

11. Several hikers climbed the side of the crater.
12. There was a volcanic explosion recently.
13. The upper part of the mountain had collapsed inward.
14. Did the party of hikers realize the danger?
15. Look at the smoke arising from the volcano.

Compound Sentences (page 10)   Write each sentence. Underline each complete subject once and each complete predicate twice. Then identify each sentence as **simple** or **compound.**

16. I wanted eggplant for lunch, but Liza wanted broccoli.
17. Liza chose the groceries, and I paid for them.
18. Neither of us could look at another carrot.
19. Liza cooked the broccoli, and I made a cheese sauce.
20. Broccoli was a good choice for lunch after all.

Correcting Fragments and Run-on Sentences (page 12)
Identify and correct each sentence fragment and run-on sentence. Write **correct** next to any group of words that is a sentence.

21. I heard the broadcast, the story was scary.

22. Filled with details of the catastrophe.
23. The sound effects gave me the creeps.
24. Few really good horror stories.
25. Radio drama is exciting, my imagination runs wild.

Words in Context (page 16)

Write each sentence. Underline the words that help show the meaning of each word in dark type. Then, using the context clues, write what that word means.

26. The Foleys will restore their **dilapidated** summer house to its original condition.
27. They will **dismantle** the sagging eaves piece by piece.
28. The **façade** will be more visible when the front porch has been removed.
29. **Demolition** of historic structures destroys an important part of our heritage.
30. More old buildings will be saved now that the **preservation** of fine structures is encouraged.

UNIT 3: NOUNS

Kinds of Nouns (page 66)

Write each sentence. Underline each common noun once and each proper noun twice. Make a list of common nouns that are abstract.

31. Tintagel is the reputed birthplace of King Arthur.
32. In the town of Tintagel is a rocky hill by the sea.
33. Ruins of an ancient castle can be seen on the hill.
34. The enchanter Merlin supposedly haunts a cave below the hill.
35. To anthropologists the legends have some basis in fact.

Singular and Plural Nouns

(page 68)   Write the plural form of each noun.

36. address
37. holiday
38. tax
39. ship
40. scarf
41. radio
42. lily
43. brush

Possessive Nouns (page 70)

Write each word. After each one write its possessive form.

44. alto
45. boys
46. thieves
47. Diazes
48. oxen
49. boss
50. family
51. men

Collective Nouns (page 72)

Write each sentence. Underline the collective nouns in each. Then write whether they are **singular** or **plural** in use.

52. Our band rehearses each Saturday afternoon.
53. The group discuss the music before they play.
54. Our audience are the neighbors near the garage.
55. This family does not appreciate our efforts

UNIT

4

Writing Stories

Read the quotation by Isaac Bashevis Singer on the opposite page. Why do you suppose that Singer believes that time, men, and animals do not vanish in stories?

When you write a story, your words can capture the interest of your audience. If your audience remembers your words, your stories do not vanish.

Focus A story contains an introduction, conflict, and a resolution. The characters in a story move the action along.

What do you imagine would make a good story? On the following pages you will find a story and some interesting photographs. You can use them to find ideas for your own writing.

In stories time does not vanish. Neither do men and animals. For the writer and his readers all creatures go on living forever.

—Isaac Bashevis Singer

AWARD
WINNING
SELECTION

Do you think that a glance in a mirror could change your life? Try to imagine the effect a mirror could have on someone who had never seen one.

Jan Skiba is a poor peasant who lives with his family and their pets in a one-room hut. One day a peddler visits the family and sells them a mirror. None of the members of the family had ever seen themselves in a mirror. Can a mirror ever reflect the real person?

As you read the story, look for the details that the writer uses to help you understand the story's characters and their world.

The Cat Who Thought She Was a Dog and The Dog Who Thought He Was a Cat

by Isaac Bashevis Singer

Once there was a poor peasant, Jan Skiba by name. He lived with his wife and three daughters in a one-room hut with a straw roof, far from the village. The house had a bed, a bench bed, and a stove, but no mirror. A mirror was a luxury for a poor peasant. And why would a peasant need a mirror? Peasants aren't curious about their appearance.

But this peasant did have a dog and a cat in his hut. The dog was named Burek and the cat Kot. They had both been born within the same week. As little food as the peasant had for himself and his family, he still wouldn't let his dog and cat go hungry. Since the dog had never seen another dog and the cat had never seen another cat and they saw only each other, the dog thought he was a cat, and the cat thought she was a dog. True, they were far from being alike by nature. The dog barked, and the cat meowed. The dog chased rabbits, and the cat lurked after mice. But must all creatures be exactly like their own kind? The peasant's children weren't exactly alike either. Burek and Kot lived on good terms, often ate from the same dish, and tried to mimic each other. When Burek barked, Kot tried to bark along, and when Kot meowed, Burek tried to meow, too. Kot occasionally chased rabbits, and Burek made an effort to catch a mouse.[1]

The peddlers who bought groats, chickens, eggs, honey, calves, and whatever was available from the peasants in the village never came to Jan Skiba's poor hut. They knew that Jan was so poor he had nothing to sell. But one day a peddler happened to stray there. When he came inside and began to lay out his wares, Jan Skiba's wife and daughters were bedazzled by all the pretty doodads. From his sack the peddler drew yellow beads, false pearls, tin earrings, rings, brooches, colored kerchiefs, garters, and other such trinkets. But what enthralled the women of the house most was a mirror set in a wooden frame. They asked the peddler its price, and he said a half-gulden, which was a lot of money for poor peasants. After a while, Jan Skiba's wife, Marianna, made a proposition to the peddler. She would pay him five groshen a month for the mirror. The peddler hesitated a moment. The mirror took up too much space in his sack, and there was always the danger it might break. He, therefore, decided to go along, took the first payment of five groshen from Marianna, and left the mirror

1. Singer quickly establishes characters and setting.

with the family. He visited the region often, and he knew the Skibas to be honest people. He would gradually get his money back and a profit besides.

The mirror created a commotion in the hut.[2] Until then Marianna and the children had seldom seen themselves. Before they had the mirror, they had only seen their reflections in the barrel of water that stood by the door. Now they could see themselves clearly, and they began to find defects in their faces, defects they had never noticed before. Marianna was pretty, but she had a tooth missing in front, and she felt this made her ugly. One daughter discovered that her nose was too snub and too broad; a second that her chin was too narrow and too long; a third that her face was sprinkled with freckles. Jan Skiba, too, caught a glimpse of himself in the mirror and grew displeased by his thick lips and his teeth, which protruded like a buck's. That day, the women of the house became so absorbed in the mirror they didn't cook supper, didn't make up the bed, and neglected all the other household tasks. Marianna had heard of a dentist in the big city who could replace a missing tooth, but such things were expensive. The girls tried to console each other that they were pretty enough and that they would find suitors, but they no longer felt as jolly as before. They had been afflicted with the vanity of city girls. The one with the broad nose kept trying to pinch it together with her fingers to make it narrower; the one with the too-long chin pushed it up with her

2. The conflict begins.

fist to make it shorter; the one with the freckles wondered if there was a salve in the city that could remove freckles. But where would the money come from for the fare to the city? And what about the money to buy this salve? For the first time the Skiba family deeply felt its poverty and envied the rich.

But the human members of the household were not the only ones affected. The dog and the cat also grew disturbed by the mirror. The hut was low, and the mirror had been hung just above a bench. The first time the cat sprang up on the bench and saw her image in the mirror, she became terribly perplexed. She had never before seen such a creature. Kot's whiskers bristled, she began to meow at her reflection and raised a paw to it, but the other creature meowed back and raised her paw, too. Soon the dog jumped up on the bench, and when he saw the other dog, he became wild with rage and shock. He barked at the other dog and showed him his teeth, but the other barked back and bared his fangs, too. So great was the distress of Burek and Kot that for the first time in their lives they turned on each other. Burek took a bite out of Kot's throat, and Kot hissed and spat at him and clawed his muzzle. They both started to bleed, and the sight of blood aroused them so that they nearly killed or crippled each other. The members of the household barely managed to separate them. Because a dog is stronger than a cat, Burek had to be tied outside, and he howled all day and all night. In their anguish, both the dog and the cat stopped eating.

When Jan Skiba saw the disruption the mirror had created in his household, he decided a mirror wasn't what his family needed. "Why look at yourself," he said, "when you can see and admire the sky, the sun, the moon, the stars, and the earth, with all its forests, meadows, rivers, and plants?"[3] He took the mirror down from the wall and put it away in the woodshed. When the peddler came for his monthly installment, Jan Skiba gave him back the mirror and in its stead bought kerchiefs and slippers for the women. After the mirror disappeared, Burek and Kot returned to normal. Again Burek thought he was a cat, and Kot was sure she was a dog. Despite all the defects the girls had found in themselves, they made good marriages. The village priest heard what had happened at Jan Skiba's house and he said, "A glass mirror shows only the skin of the body. The real image of a person is in his willingness to help himself and his family and, as far as possible, all those he comes in contact with. This kind of mirror reveals the very soul of the person."

3. Dialogue is rare in a story mainly about a cat and a dog.

Thinking Like a Reader

1. How did the mirror change the lives of the Skiba family?
2. Describe an experience that changed your perception of yourself.

Write your responses in your journal.

Thinking Like a Writer

3. In what kind of order did the writer relate the events in the story?
4. What would the story be like if the end were told at the beginning?
5. If you were writing a story about characters who changed perceptions of themselves, what events might lead up to this change? What events might follow this change?

Write your responses in your journal.

Brainstorm *Vocabulary*

In "The Cat Who Thought She Was a Dog and the Dog Who Thought He Was a Cat," author I. B. Singer writes a straightforward story in a straightforward manner. Simplicity, however, can be tricky. Each word must be "just the right word." For example, consider the precision of such words as *bedazzled*, *perplexed*, and *anguish*. Reread the story and make a list of words that are "just the right word." Check their meaning in a dictionary. If you think that you can use these words in your writing, add them to your personal vocabulary list.

Talk It Over *Create Dialogue*

When the characters in a story speak directly to each other, their conversation is called **dialogue.** Perhaps because two of his main characters are animals, I. B. Singer uses dialogue only twice in his story. The first time is when Skiba reflects on the problems caused by the mirror, and the second time is near the ending, when the priest issues his words of wisdom. Neither of these statements is addressed to anyone in particular. With partners, find other places in the story where dialogue might be appropriate. Then make up the dialogue for these scenes.

Quick Write *Write a Blurb*

Write a short summary, or blurb, for the story you have just read as if you were writing an advertisement for the movie based on that story. If you prefer, write a summary for the jacket of a book that contains the story. For example, imagine that you are advertising a movie based on "Cinderella."

> Coming Soon! See the gripping story of the girl enslaved by her wicked stepmother. How does she find outside help? Will she go to the ball? Will the Prince fall in love? Hurry to your local theater for the answers.

Write your blurb or ad on a separate piece of paper. Then make an illustration for the book or movie.

Idea Corner
Think of Situations

In your journal write lists of ideas for a story of your own. You might write short descriptions of places that would make an interesting setting, such as "the park after a baseball game" or "inside a spaceship." You might write a list of characters that interest you, such as "the nervous waitress" or "the school bully." Also, you might write brief summaries of situations that could be made into good stories, such as "A girl travels back in time to meet her grandmother as a child."

PICTURES

SEEING LIKE A WRITER

Finding Ideas for Writing

Look at the pictures. Think about what you see. What ideas
for writing a short story do the pictures give you? Write
your ideas in your journal.

Baseball game at New York's Shea Stadium

Below: City building reflected in windows

1 GROUP WRITING: A SHORT STORY

COOPERATIVE
LEARNING

Narratives tell stories. A **short story** tells about imaginary people and events. The **purpose** of a story is usually to entertain an **audience**. Most stories have these elements.

- Plot
- Characters and Setting
- Dialogue

Plot

The **plot** is what people most often remember when they think of a story, but it is only the skeleton that supports the body. The plot is what happens, the action, the connected or related series of events. If the events are not related, there is no plot. For example, compare these series of events.

Rainy day, electricity off: Dorrie is at home alone. She hears a mysterious noise. She reads a magazine. She finds an old recipe book. Dorrie talks to her grandmother on the telephone. She prepares dinner for her family on the gas stove. The electricity comes on.	Championship baseball game, bottom half of the ninth inning, score tied: Carl comes to bat. He makes two strikes because the glare from the sun makes it difficult to see the ball. Cloud covers the sun. Carl hits a home run. Carl's team wins the championship.

The left-hand column contains a series of events; the right-hand column contains a plot—the events are related.

Often the plot revolves around a central problem called the **conflict.** The conflict is a struggle between opposing forces or a problem between people that needs to be solved.

Every story has suspense of some kind, or else the reader would lose interest. The suspense is the unanswered question suggested by the conflict. At some point there is usually a high point, or **climax.** The climax is the event that leads to the **resolution,** or the solution to the problem.

Guided Practice: Charting a Plot

As a group, discuss a plot for an original story. Then write your own summary of the plot, focusing on the conflict, the climax, and the resolution. Share your summary. Then, as a group, fill in a plot chart with ideas for the group story.

Characters and Setting

The people involved in a story are called **characters.** Most stories contain one **main character** around whom the story revolves and who has the conflict that provides the direction of the plot. In the story about Carl's baseball triumph, Carl is the main character. The other team members or the spectators, for example, would be **secondary characters.**

When you write stories, you can create vivid and individual characters in several ways.

1. Describe each character's physical appearance.

Carl's small freckled face became even smaller as he squinted into the sun's glare.

2. Use conversations, or *dialogue*, between characters.

"I did it! I did it! I actually did it!" Carl shouted.

3. Give descriptions of what the characters think and feel.

Carl felt the blood rush to his head as the joy of not letting his team down surged through his body.

4. Give details of the characters' behavior.

Carl picked up the bat and slowly rolled it between his palms as if he were communicating with the wood.

Where and when a story takes place is called the **setting.** The setting for the story about the baseball game is important. It is obviously a baseball field, but a baseball field where the sun can create a blinding glare. The setting of a story can both establish the mood and forecast the conflict, plot, and underlying meaning of the story. Sometimes the setting is not very specific or serves merely as a background.

Guided Practice: Creating Characters and Setting

As a class, list the characters and setting of a story that everyone has read. Each person should write a description of a character or the setting. Character descriptions should include details of appearance, behavior, and thoughts. Descriptions of setting should include location, weather, and time.

Dialogue

Dialogue is what the characters of a story say to each other. The words that a character uses and the tone in which the words are said can often reveal more about a character than direct description. Dialogue can also be used to advance the plot and to reveal the characters' relationships. Dialogue can also add interest and humor to a story.

When you write dialogue, what the character says must appear in quotation marks. Each time the speaker changes, you must begin a new paragraph.

> As Carl's right foot landed firmly on home plate, he could see Coach's smiling face towering above the gleeful faces of his teammates. "Hey, Coach, I did it! I broke the tie!"
>
> "You certainly did! They still haven't found that ball," laughed Coach as he extended his hand to Carl's.
>
> "And it was all due to a cloud," Carl laughed, "one measly little cloud. It must have been cloud nine."

Guided Practice: Writing Dialogue

As a class, discuss the climax of the story you have been writing. Assign a character to each member of the group and improvise some possible dialogue between the characters. Write down the results, being sure to punctuate the dialogue correctly.

Putting a Short Story Together

With your classmates you have discussed the plot of a story. You have also described the characters and the setting and even written some dialogue for the climax of the story. Before you begin writing your story, think about how you want to put the story together. With your group, make a list of events for the story and put them in chronological order.

EVENTS FOR THE SHORT STORY

  Beginning (includes conflict)

  Climax

  Resolution

  Ending

Guided Practice: Writing a Short Story

Write several beginnings for your story. The beginning should establish the main character, perhaps some secondary characters, the setting (time and place), and should set up the conflict. Decide which beginning best suits your purpose and audience. Then follow your plot outline. Include dialogue to bring your characters to life. Make the ending strong, keeping in mind the purpose of your story.

Share the story with your family or friends. Ask for their reactions to see if you accomplished your purpose.

Checklist A Short Story

When you write a story of your own, keep in mind what you have learned so far. Look at the checklist below. Add any other points you want to remember. Keep a copy of the checklist in your writing folder so that you can refer to it.

CHECKLIST

- Determine purpose and audience.
- Develop a plot.
    - Create a conflict.
    - Establish a climax.
    - Include a resolution.
- Develop characters.
- Introduce a setting.
- Use dialogue.
- _____

2 THINKING AND WRITING: Point of View

A story may be thought of as a journey taken by the main character, either a literal journey such as an adventure, or an emotional journey during which the character changes. The reader experiences this journey through the eyes of the storyteller's, or narrator's, *point of view.*

The words **point of view** literally mean the point or angle from which a story is viewed or seen. Since who is telling the story greatly affects how the story will be understood, choosing a point of view is an important decision you will make as a writer.

Different types of point of view produce different effects. Which point of view you choose will depend on the type of effect you want to create.

1. **First Person:** The narrator tells the story by using the first-person pronouns *I* and *we.* The "I" is often directly involved in the story and may even be the main character. Writing in the first person usually creates immediate sympathy for the narrator. The first-person point of view is limited, however. The "I" narrator can tell the reader only what happens to him or her or what he or she knows about.

   Example: As soon as I picked up the bat, I saw that the glare was against me. I rolled the bat between my palms. There was nothing I could do but try my best. I squinted at the pitcher as he began his move.

2. **Third Person Limited:** The narrator tells the story through the eyes of a character, but the character is referred to using the third-person pronouns *he* or *she.* As in the first-person point of view, the third-person point of view is limited to what this character experiences, witnesses, and feels.

   Example: Carl picked up the bat. He rolled it mysteriously between his palms. He then took his place beside home plate. He seemed to have tension in his whole body as he squinted out toward the pitcher.

3. **Third Person Omniscient:** The narrator who uses the omniscient point of view also writes in the third person. However, since *omniscient* means "all-knowing," the omniscient author sees, hears, and knows everything. The omniscient narrator can do such things as describe the thoughts and feelings of any of the characters, describe what is happening at two or more places at once, and look into the future.

Example: Carl lifted the bat and looked out toward the pitcher. His heart skipped a beat when he realized he could not really see the pitcher clearly.

    The pitcher knew that he had Carl at a disadvantage. This thought pleased him as he drew back to pitch the ball.

Thinking Like a Writer

- How would you rewrite the passage in the *Example* above using the first-person point of view?
- How do different points of view create different effects in stories?

THINKING APPLICATION Understanding Point of View

COOPERATIVE LEARNING

Each of the writers named below is planning to write a story. Help each writer decide from which point of view to write the story. You may want to discuss your thinking with other students. In your discussion explain your choices to each other. When you have decided, write a beginning for each of the stories using the point of view you think will be most effective.

1. Janice wants to write a mystery that involves a young girl who discovers a briefcase filled with money in her gym locker. During the course of the story, the girl is accused of having stolen the money.

2. Miranda's story is about a lonely little boy who discovers a secret passageway in his grandmother's house. Inside the passageway is a magic trunk. Miranda is not sure about the exact nature of the magic.

3. Carmine wants to write a science-fiction story that takes place in an underground city in the year A.D. 3000. Because of a computer error, his main character has just been made mayor even though he is only twelve.

3 INDEPENDENT WRITING: A Short Story

Prewrite: Step 1

By now you know how a story is structured. Now you are ready to write your own. Amy, a student your age, wanted to write a story to entertain her classmates. This is how she chose a topic for the story.

Choosing a Topic

Amy brainstormed a list of situations that might make an interesting story. She found her ideas in events that happened to people she knows, from news stories, and from her imagination.

Amy reflected on her list and combined some of her ideas. She decided to write about a boy whose family moved from a small town to a big city. She focused on the elements of her story by making notes in the form of a chart.

Exploring Ideas: Story Outline

Main Character	Jason—13, athletic, popular. Grew up in small town, knows little about cities.
Conflict	Jason's father gets a job in Chicago. Jason does not want to go (afraid he will not make new friends).
Resolution	In his new home, Jason meets another soccer player. (This takes time—develop ending clearly.)

Before beginning to write her story, Amy organized her ideas into an outline, adding more details and carefully planning her plot.

Outline for Exploring a Story Idea

I. Beginning

   A. Introduce the main character. Parents? Sister?

   B. Describe the setting and the central problem.
      Should the story begin in the car? In town?

   C. Present the first event of the plot—the new job.
      Introduce conflict—Jason upset.

II. Middle

   A. Describe sequence of events.
      Pack up the house. Say good-bye to friends.
      Drive to new home. Or should they fly?
      See city for the first time—reactions?
      Arrive at new apartment—explore his feelings?

   B. Describe the problem the character faces.
      Jason reflects on his fears and his old home—
      playing soccer below the orchard.

III. End

   A. Present the final event of the plot.
      Jason sees a boy with a soccer ball.

   B. Describe the main character's reaction.
      Jason is hopeful and asks about soccer.

Thinking Like a Writer

- Where could Amy describe her characters and setting?
- Which situations can she best develop through dialogue?
- Why would the third-person limited point of view be the most effective point of view for her to use?

YOUR TURN

Follow these steps to plan a story you would like to write.

- Make a list of ideas. Use **Pictures** or your journal for help.
- In a story chart, develop your ideas for characters, setting, conflict, and resolution.
- Make an outline that maps the progression of your story.
- Think about your purpose and audience.

JOURNAL

Write a First Draft: Step 2

Amy knew what a short story should include. In addition to her outline, she had made a checklist of ideas to keep in mind as she wrote her first draft.

Amy knew where in the story she would describe the characters and setting. She had selected situations she could develop through dialogue. She had the characterization in mind and had chosen to use the third-person limited point of view. Amy was now ready to write her first draft.

Part of Amy's First Draft

> Jason was thirteen years old. He had lived in Pine Grove all his life. he liked it there. Because he had many friends who liked the same things he did like sports especially soccer. He lived at 212 North Elm Street.
> Jason's mother was very excited. One day Jason's father came home with good news. His father had gotten a promotion. As head of his department. Except not in Pine Grove. The company was moving him to chicago. Jennifer didn't really care. She was his sister. She was little.
> Jasons Father noticed that Jason didn't look so happy. "What's the matter, sport? Don't you think Chicagoans like soccer? Jason was embarrassed. "I'm not that dumb!" I shouted. what's wrong with Pine Grove?"

Planning Checklist
- Determine purpose and audience.
- Develop a plot.
  Create a conflict.
  Establish a climax.
  Include a resolution.
- Choose a point of view.
- Introduce a setting.
- Develop characters.
- Use dialogue.

While Amy was writing her first draft, she was interested primarily in putting her ideas down on paper. She would correct errors in spelling, grammar, and punctuation later.

YOUR TURN

Write a first draft. As you write, ask yourself these questions.
- What will my audience want to know?
- How can I make my characters more interesting?
- How can I strengthen the presentation of the problem?

TIME-OUT You might want to take some time out before you revise. That way you will be able to revise your writing with a fresh eye.

Revise: Step 3

After she finished her first draft, Amy read her story over to herself. Then she shared the story with a classmate because she wanted a reaction to her work. She also wanted some suggestions for improvement.

This is great, but I want to know more about Jason.

Thanks. I'll be sure to add more details about him.

Amy wrote down her classmate's suggestion so she would remember it when she revised. Then Amy looked back at her planning checklist. She realized that she had overlooked another point—in one part of the story she had switched the point of view. She checked off both points on what was now her revising checklist. This would help her remember to make these changes when she revised the first draft of her short story.

Amy decided that it would be wise to review the checklist further. Were the events in her plot related? Could she improve the settings by adding more detail? Did her dialogue reveal anything about the characters and their relationships? Amy made changes in her story, but she did not concern herself with spelling and punctuation. She knew that she could do that later.

Amy also remembered that her purpose in writing was primarily to entertain. She also wanted to show that unexpected changes in life are not always as bad as they seem to be at first. She thought that her audience, her classmates, would be receptive to both purposes.

Now Amy was ready to begin revising her story.

Revising Checklist
- Determine purpose and audience.
- Develop a plot. Create a conflict. Establish a climax. Include a resolution.
✔ Choose a point of view
- Introduce a setting.
✔ Develop characters.
- Use dialogue.

Part of Amy's Revised Draft

Jason was thirteen years old. *and large for his age.* He had lived in Pine
Grove all his life. he liked it there. Because he had many
friends who liked the same things he did like sports *e*
especially soccer. ~~He lived at 212 North Elm Street.~~ *e*
(Jason's mother was very excited.) One day Jasons' father
came home with good news. His father had gotten a
promotion. As head of his department. ~~Except not in Pine~~
~~Grove. The company was moving him to~~ *in* chicago. Jennifer
Jason's little sister
didn't really care. ~~She was his sister. She was little~~ *e*
very
Jasons Father noticed that Jason didn't look ~~so~~ *e*
happy. "What's the matter, sport? Don't you think
Chicagoans like soccer? Jason was embarrased. "I'm not
he
that dumb!" ~~I~~ shouted. what's wrong with Pine Grove?"

Thinking Like a Writer

WISE
WORD
CHOICE

- Which sentences did Amy delete? Why did she do this?
- Which sentence did she move? Why did she move it?
- Why should she divide both paragraphs in two?
- Which sentences did she combine? How does combining
  them improve the paragraph?

YOUR TURN

Read your first draft and ask yourself these questions.
- How can I improve the beginning? the ending?
- How can I possibly make my characters and setting more
  interesting?
- Where can I use dialogue to best effect?
- Which sentences can I combine to vary my sentences?

Ask a friend to read your story and make suggestions. Then
revise your story.

Proofread: Step 4

Amy knew that now that she had her ideas in good order, the time had come to proofread her story. She carefully checked her work for correct spelling, punctuation, and capitalization. She had prepared a proofreading checklist, and she used proofreading marks to indicate her corrections.

> ## PROOFREADING CHECKLIST
>
> - Did I indent all new paragraphs, including dialogue?
> - Did I spell all words correctly?
> - Which punctuation errors do I need to correct?
> - Which capitalization errors do I need to correct?
> - Have I formed possessive nouns correctly?

Part of Amy's Proofread Draft

> Jason was thirteen years old, *and large for his age.* He had lived in Pine Grove all his life. he liked it there, Because he had many friends who liked the same things he did like sports especially (socer.) He lived at 212 North Elm Street. (Jason's mother was very excited.) One day Jasons father came home with good news.

YOUR TURN

Proofreading Practice

Below is a paragraph that you can use to practice your proofreading skills. Find the errors. Then write the paragraph correctly on a separate sheet of paper.

> Jasons face brightened as they entered the new apartment. He walked to the window and looked out on a strech of green park "Wow, look at that, he announced. Look at all the green."

Applying Your Proofreading Skills

Now proofread your story. Refer to the checklist and review **The Grammar Connection** and **The Mechanics Connection** below. Use proofreading symbols to mark corrections.

THE GRAMMAR CONNECTION

Remember these rules about possessive nouns.

- To form the possessive of a singular noun, add **'s.**
- To form the possessive of a plural noun that ends in *s*, add only an apostrophe (**'**). To form the possessive of a plural noun that does not end in *s*, add **'s.**
  They passed the **children's** school and their **aunt's** house.
  Jason's sister cried as the **neighbors'** dogs chased the car.

Check your story. Have you formed possessive nouns correctly?

THE MECHANICS CONNECTION

Remember these rules about using quotation marks when you write dialogue.

- Use quotation marks before and after a direct quotation.
- Use a comma or commas to set off expressions such as *she said* from the quotation.
- Place commas and periods inside closing quotation marks.
- Place question marks and exclamation marks inside the quotation marks when they apply only to the quotation itself.
  "We are moving to Chicago," said Jason's father.
  "But why," asked Jason, "are we moving so far away?"

Check your story. Have you punctuated the dialogue correctly?

Proofreading Marks
Indent ¶
Add ∧
Add a comma ⋏
Add quotation marks ⌄⌄
Add a period ⊙
Take out ⌁
Capitalize ≡
Lower-case letter /
Reverse the order ∩

Publish: Step 5

After she finished proofreading her story, Amy gave the story a title, "Winning Moves." She thought it expressed the point she was trying to make. Then she typed the story and posted it on the class bulletin board. Several people in her class asked her questions about her story. One classmate asked if her family had ever made a similar move. Amy said that the story was imagined. She said that she enjoyed writing about experiences different from her own.

YOUR TURN

Make a final copy of your short story. If your school has typewriters or word processors, you might inquire about using them for your final copy. Think of a way to share your story. You might find some ideas in the **Sharing Suggestions** box below. Remember to give your story a title.

SHARING SUGGESTIONS

Enter your story in a short story contest or present it for publication in your community newspaper.	Make a tape recording of your story. Assign each character to a different reader. Have one voice read all non-dialogue sections of the story.	With your class publish an anthology of the stories your class has written. Include illustrations, a table of contents, and an "About the Authors" section.

4 SPEAKING AND LISTENING: Having a Class Discussion

Now you have analyzed the elements of a short story and seen how plot, characters, setting, point of view, and dialogue all contribute to the final effect of a story. You can use what you know about writing short stories in discussions of other stories you have read or will be reading.

After you read a story, it is a good idea to write down questions that you would like to discuss about the story, especially if you are going to lead the discussion. Since you hope to involve as many members of the group as possible, your questions should inspire answers. Questions that can be answered with one word are not useful for encouraging discussion. Be careful not to let one person dominate the discussion. If there are misunderstandings, be sure to stop and clarify ideas before going further. A good discussion can bring out new ideas about a story, and everyone will learn something new in an enjoyable manner.

Formal and Informal Discussions

You have probably already participated in many formal discussions. A formal discussion is conducted by a leader who poses questions and calls on speakers. If you have something to say in a formal discussion, you are expected to raise your hand and wait to be called on before you speak.

An informal discussion has fewer rules. If there is a leader, this person plays a less dominant role. When participants wish to speak, they start when the previous speaker has finished. Of course, even in an informal discussion, only one person should speak at a time. No matter what kind of discussion is being held, however, being a good listener is always important.

SPEAKING GUIDELINES: A Class Discussion

1. Stay on the subject.
2. Speak in a strong, clear voice.
3. Look at all of the participants, not just at the leader.
4. Try not to repeat what other speakers have already said.
5. Refer to the contributions of other speakers.
6. Support your ideas by reading aloud from the story being discussed.

- What is the difference between a formal and an informal discussion?
- Why should you quote the story being discussed?

SPEAKING APPLICATION: A Class Discussion

As a group, agree upon a story that you would all like to read or one you have already enjoyed reading. Each member of the group should have read the same story. Then prepare a list of questions that could be used by the leader of an informal discussion of the story. Take turns leading the group discussion. Refer to the speaking guidelines before you begin the discussion.

Remember that you are still participating in the discussion even when you are not speaking. Your classmates will be using the following guidelines as they participate in the discussion.

LISTENING GUIDELINES: A Class Discussion

1. Listen to each speaker's opinion.
2. Reflect on your reaction to each opinion offered.
3. Take notes about important points being made.
4. Ask questions if a point is unclear.

THE CURRICULUM CONNECTION

Writing About Literature

One of the joys of reading a good book is sharing your pleasure with other people. Writing a book report—or giving it orally—allows you to share the book with others. It also encourages you to think about your own reactions to the book.

<table>
<tr>
<td></td>
<td>Johnny Tremain</td>
</tr>
<tr>
<td>Introduction:
title, author</td>
<td>Johnny Tremain, by Esther Forbes, is a novel set in an important period of American history. Both the story and the background seem to come to life.</td>
</tr>
<tr>
<td>Body:
main
characters,
setting,
plot</td>
<td>Johnny Tremain is a teenage boy who lives in Boston during the early days of the American Revolution. Johnny is a clever young orphan who is an apprentice to a silversmith. Due to an injury to his hand, Johnny can no longer study to be a craftsman. While looking for a new job, he becomes caught up in the company of such Revolutionary patriots as Paul Revere, Samuel Adams, and John Hancock. Johnny becomes a link in the actions that lead to the Boston Tea Party and the battles of Lexington and Concord. During the course of these adventures, Johnny makes both friends and enemies as he searches for his place in the world. His character changes from being a bossy know-it-all to that of a young man of strong actions and sound judgment.</td>
</tr>
<tr>
<td>Conclusion:
your opinion,
reasons</td>
<td>I enjoyed Johnny Tremain for several reasons. I liked the person I read about; the author made the character of Johnny Tremain very real. The story itself was interesting, and I thought the way history came to life was very exciting.</td>
</tr>
</table>

Writing a Book Report

A book report is a way for you to let others know about a book you have read. A good book report will help others decide whether they want to read the book or not.

A book report should contain the following information.

1. The **title** and the **author**
2. The **introduction** should include
   - whether the book is fiction or nonfiction
   - an opening sentence that will capture your reader's attention
3. The **body** should include
   - information about the setting and main characters
   - a summary of the plot that informs your readers about the problems the characters face, but without revealing the whole story
4. The **conclusion** should include
   - your opinion of the book—what you liked and did not like
   - reasons for your opinion
   - your recommendation to others

ACTIVITIES

Oral Book Report

Using the book report on *Johnny Tremain* as a model, make notes for an oral report about a book that you have read. When you deliver your report, be sure to follow the guidelines you have studied about speaking effectively.

Respond in Writing

Look at the cover illustration for *Johnny Tremain* above. How has the artist attempted to reflect the subject matter of the novel? Is he successful? What do the drawings in the background tell you about the story? What does Johnny's stance tell you about him? Write your responses in your journal.

UNIT CHECKUP

LESSON

Group Writing: A Short Story (page 110)   Read this familiar rhyme. On a separate sheet of paper, analyze it as if it were a short story. List the setting, the characters, and each event in the plot. Then write a paragraph explaining why this rhyme is or is not successful as a short story. Finally, write several sentences of dialogue and insert them into the rhyme at an appropriate place.

> Humpty Dumpty sat on the wall,
> Humpty Dumpty had a great fall.
> All the king's horses and all the king's men
> Couldn't put Humpty together again!

LESSON
2

Thinking: Point of View (page 114)   A story must be written with a point of view. Write an opening paragraph about each situation described below. Use the point of view indicated.

Situation 1: A girl who is carrying a heavy book bag boards a bus. She walks to the one unoccupied seat, but before she can sit down, another person takes the seat. (first-person point of view)

Situation 2: A student is taking a report to the principal's office when he smells burning wood. He sees smoke coming from under the door of the closet where cleaning supplies are kept. He knows immediately what to do. He races to the fire alarm outside the principal's office. (third-person limited point of view)

Situation 3: The captains of two rival basketball teams meet face to face in the locker room after a tense game. (third-person omniscient point of view)

LESSON

Writing a Short Story (page 116)   To entertain an audience of your classmates, write the opening paragraph or paragraphs of a short story that begins with this sentence: I knew I couldn't stop now. Be sure to use the steps of the writing process as you develop your work.

LESSON

Speaking and Listening: A Class Discussion (page 124) Write a brief paragraph explaining the differences between a formal and an informal discussion.

THEME PROJECT *ONE-ACT PLAY*

Perhaps you have noticed that the stories you wrote are expressions of your concerns and interests. When you discussed the stories you read and wrote with your classmates, you may have discovered new and varied reflections of your experiences.

Look at the photograph below of a scene from *Fiddler on the Roof*. The plot for this full-length musical is based on several related short stories. With the class, discuss who the characters in the photograph might be. What is happening? What might they be discussing? Where are they? In what period of time is the play set?

A one-act play is similar to a short story. Both forms are brief and focus on one central plot and a limited number of characters.

- Select a favorite short story from the stories shared in class.
- Rewrite the story as a one-act play. This means that everything is expressed by means of dialogue.
- Give a dramatic reading of the finished play.
- Insert appropriate songs and create a one-act musical.
- When your one-act play is polished, perform it on stage in full production for another class or for the whole school.

5

Verbs

In this unit you will learn about verbs. Verbs add life and action to your writing. By choosing the most vivid verbs to use in your writing, you can keep your audience interested in what you have to say.

Discuss Read the poem by Jessamyn West. Why might the poet think that "freedom is a hard-bought thing"?

Creative Expression The unit theme is *Legacies*. A legacy is something that is passed on from generation to generation. Think of a legacy that is important to you. Write an explanation that tells why it is important. Write your thoughts in your journal.

THEME: *LEGACIES*

Freedom is a hard-bought thing—
A gift no man can give.
For some, a way of dying,
For most, a way to live.

—Jessamyn West,
from "Song of the Settlers"

1 ACTION VERBS

An action verb is a word that expresses action.

Your everyday actions help to shape the world around you. When you speak or write, these actions are expressed by verbs. If a word tells what a subject does, it is an **action verb.**

The main word in the predicate of a sentence is a verb. Note the action verbs in the sentences below.

> Thomas Jefferson **wrote** the Declaration of Independence. Jefferson **chose** the words carefully.

Some action verbs express physical action.

> Delegates **debated** the text for three days.
> Benjamin Franklin **made** some changes in the document.

Other action verbs express mental or emotional activity.

> Delegates **realized** the importance of their acts.
> Many of them **feared** the consequences.
> These brave men **hoped** for the best.

Guided Practice

Identify the action verb in each sentence.

Example: The delegates believed in their mission.
            believed

1. Sue read carefully about the Continental Congress.
2. The convention met in Philadel-phia, Pennsylvania.
3. One by one the delegates signed the document.
4. Some members regarded the document with caution.
5. John Hancock, however, wrote his name in large letters.
6. This gesture gave confidence to reluctant delegates.

 THINK

■ How can I recognize an action verb?

REMEMBER

- An **action verb** is a word that expresses a physical or mental action.

More Practice

A. Write the action verb in each sentence.

Example: This document proclaimed America's freedom.
proclaimed

7. Benjamin Franklin changed some of the wording.
8. He thought of the truths as "self-evident."
9. Originally Jefferson wrote "sacred and undeniable."
10. The Congress blamed George III for slavery in America.
11. The delegates later rejected this idea.
12. The Declaration contained many radical ideas.
13. The document declared the people's right to revolution.
14. The Declaration of Independence still inspires people throughout the world.

B. Write each sentence and underline the action verb. Then write whether the verb expresses a **physical** or **mental** action.

Example: Many colonists wanted representation in England.
Many colonists <u>*wanted*</u> *representation in England.* mental

15. The colonists challenged England many times before their open rebellion.
16. With the Declaration of Independence, however, they announced a new nation.
17. Compromise no longer satisfied the colonists.
18. The colonists then fought for their freedom.
19. Farmers raised their guns at Lexington and Concord.
20. These patriots believed in their new nation.

Extra Practice, page 164

WRITING APPLICATION A Narrative Paragraph

COOPERATIVE LEARNING

Think of the action verbs that could express your actions during the school day. Write a paragraph describing how you spend a typical day at school, from the time you arrive until the time you leave. Exchange papers with a classmate and identify the action verbs in each other's work.

2 DIRECT OBJECTS, TRANSITIVE AND INTRANSITIVE VERBS

You know that every sentence has a subject and a predicate. In some sentences the predicate is a single action verb.

The clerk **wrote.** Then the clerk **called.**

The predicate of a sentence can also contain a **direct object,** which is a noun or pronoun that receives the action of the verb. The direct object answers the question *whom?* or *what?* after an action verb.

The clerk *wrote* the **message.**   (what?)

Then the clerk *called* the **sheriff.**   (whom?)

The sheriff *contacted* the **mayor.**   (noun)

The mayor *notified* **me.**   (pronoun)

The direct object of a verb may be compound.

The mayor *met* the **sheriff** and his **deputy.**

An action verb that has a direct object is called a **transitive verb.** An action verb that does not have a direct object is called an **intransitive verb.** Many verbs can be either transitive or intransitive.

TRANSITIVE: They *returned* the message.
INTRANSITIVE: I *returned.*

Guided Practice

Tell whether the verb in each sentence is transitive or intransitive.

Example: Samuel Morse invented a code for the telegraph.
transitive

1. Rhonda and Greg learned the code.
2. They interpreted the dots and dashes.
3. Morse's code allowed instant communication.
4. Words traveled quickly over great distances.
5. Soon wires on poles dotted the landscape.

 THINK

■ How can I tell whether a verb is transitive or intransitive?

REMEMBER

- A **direct object** is a noun or pronoun that receives the action of the verb. It answers the question *whom?* or *what?*
- A **transitive verb** has a direct object. An **intransitive verb** does not have a direct object.

More Practice

A. Write the verb in each sentence and whether it is **transitive** or **intransitive.**

Example: Chemical batteries caused a revolution in communications. *caused transitive*

6. The development of batteries opened the way for telegraphy.
7. Telegraphs sent messages electrically.
8. Several people invented versions of the telegraph.
9. Samuel Morse developed the telegraph in the United States.
10. Morse painted for his livelihood.
11. However, scientific matters always interested him.
12. One day in 1832, he seized an idea from a conversation.
13. He then experimented with electricity.

B. Write each sentence. Draw one line under the verb and two lines under any direct objects. Label the verb **transitive** or **intransitive.**

Example: A wire carried a message by means of electricity.
A wire *carried* a *message* by means of electricity.
transitive

14. Morse's discoveries produced further ideas.
15. Morse spent twelve years on this project.
16. Congress financed this telegraph line.
17. The line ran between Baltimore, MD, and Washington, DC.
18. A revolution in communications began on May 22, 1884.
19. On that day Morse sent the first words by wire.
20. The message spanned a distance of thirty-seven miles.

Extra Practice, page 165

WRITING APPLICATION Directions

Write directions explaining how to do something that you enjoy doing. Exchange papers with a classmate and identify the direct objects in each other's work.

3 INDIRECT OBJECTS

Direct objects receive the action of a verb. An **indirect object** is a noun or pronoun in the predicate that answers the question *to whom? for whom? to what?* or *for what?* after an action verb.

indirect   direct
object   object

Ms. King gave our **class** a **demonstration.**

A sentence may contain a compound indirect object.

She also showed the **students** and the **principal** a videotape.

A sentence that contains an indirect object always contains a direct object. To help you tell them apart, remember that an indirect object always comes before a direct object.

In addition, you can often rewrite the sentence by using the preposition *to* or *for* before the indirect object without changing the meaning.

Ms. King showed **us** a songbook.
Ms. King showed a songbook **to us.**

Guided Practice

Tell whether the underlined word is a direct object or an indirect object.

Example: Ms. King teaches <u>us</u> music.   *indirect object*

1. We are learning <u>songs</u> from musical comedies.
2. Ms. King plays <u>us</u> the melodies first.
3. Then she teaches the <u>sopranos</u> their parts.
4. She taught the <u>class</u> a song from *Cats.*
5. This song gives <u>everyone</u> great pleasure.
6. America gave the <u>musical</u> a new shape.
7. Early musicals offered <u>audiences</u> plays with songs.
8. Often the songs simply interrupted the <u>play</u>.

?! THINK

- How can I tell the difference between a direct object and an indirect object?

REMEMBER

- An **indirect object** is a noun or pronoun in the predicate that answers the question *to whom? for whom? to what?* or *for what?* after an action verb.

More Practice

A. Write the indirect object in each sentence. If the sentence does not contain an indirect object, write **none.**

Example: Critics give *Oklahoma!* credit as the first unified musical.   *Oklahoma!*

 9. The songs strengthened the plot and the characterization.
10. Oscar Hammerstein wrote singers strong lyrics.
11. Richard Rodgers gave the lyrics wonderful melodies.
12. Even the dances told viewers some of the story.
13. *Oklahoma!* gave the public a new kind of musical.

B. Rewrite each sentence so that the underlined phrase becomes an indirect object. Then identify each direct object and indirect object.

Example: Ms. King played some songs <u>for the class</u>.
         Ms. King played the class some songs.
         songs direct object   class indirect object

14. She told the story of *Oklahoma!* <u>to us.</u>
15. Then she gave the lyrics <u>to the best singers.</u>
16. Ms. King allowed after-school rehearsals <u>for our group.</u>
17. We sang some of the songs <u>for the principal.</u>
18. The principal offered an assembly performance <u>to our troupe.</u>
19. We gave a modest production of *Oklahoma!* <u>for the whole</u> school.
20. Now we must find a thank-you gift <u>for Ms. King.</u>

Extra Practice, page 166

WRITTEN APPLICATION A Personal Narrative

Write a personal narrative about an experience you have had while working with others. Focus on what you accomplished that you could not have achieved on your own. Exchange narratives with a classmate. Identify the indirect objects in each other's work.

4 LINKING VERBS

You use a **linking verb** when you want to tell what the subject of a sentence is or is like. Linking verbs do not express action.

Anita **is** a patent attorney.
She **was** a law student for several years.

A **linking verb** connects the subject with a noun or an adjective in the predicate. A noun that follows a linking verb and tells what the subject is, is called a **predicate noun.**

Patents are **copyrights** for inventions.

An adjective that follows a linking verb and describes the subject is called a **predicate adjective.**

Patents are **numerous.**

The forms of the verb *be*—including *is, am, are, was,* and *were*—are linking verbs. Verbs such as *seem, feel,* and *grow* are often used as linking verbs. Many of these verbs may also be used as action verbs. They are action verbs in sentences in which the subject is performing an action.

ACTION VERB: Carl **felt** the fabric.
LINKING VERB: The fabric **felt** smooth and soft.

ACTION VERB: Farmers **grow** corn.
LINKING VERB: Corn **grows** tall.

Guided Practice

Identify the linking verb. Tell if the underlined word is a **predicate noun** or a **predicate adjective.**

Example: Sandy is a <u>student</u> of history.   *is predicate noun*

1. Sandy is <u>curious</u> about the U.S. Patent Office.
2. Its history appeared <u>rich</u> in incidents.
3. Congress became a <u>supporter</u> of patents in 1790.
4. The Secretaries of War and State were <u>overseers</u>.
5. The Attorney General also was a board <u>member</u>.

 THINK

■ How can I tell the difference between a linking verb and an action verb?

REMEMBER

- A **linking verb** links the subject of a sentence with a noun or adjective in the predicate.
- A **predicate noun** tells who or what the subject is. A **predicate adjective** tells what the subject is like.

More Practice

A. Write the linking verb in each sentence. Label the underlined word as a **predicate noun** or a **predicate adjective**.

Example: Some applications were <u>foolish</u>.
       were   predicate adjective

6. Some people falsely became <u>owners</u> of patents.
7. The true inventors were <u>angry</u>.
8. A more exacting system was <u>necessary</u>.
9. In 1836 the Patent Office became a <u>reality</u>.
10. An examination system seemed <u>appropriate</u>.
11. Many citizens became <u>owners</u> of patents.

B. Write each sentence. Draw one line under the linking verb. Draw two lines under the **predicate adjective** or **predicate noun** and label it.

Example: Machines were common objects for patents.
     Machines <u>were</u> common <u>objects</u> for patents.
     predicate noun

12. The development of many inventions was simultaneous.
13. In this case, patents seem unfair.
14. For example, Cruikshank and the Strongs were competitors.
15. In 1875 these two parties became eager for the same patent.
16. Their ant repellents seemed similar.
17. The Commissioner was not sure of either party.
18. Cruikshank felt discouraged.
19. However, the Strongs were persistent.
20. The patent eventually became their property.

Extra Practice, page 167

WRITING APPLICATION A Story

Write a brief story about an inventor. What new idea does the inventor have? Exchange papers with a classmate and identify the linking verbs in each other's work.

5 MAKING SUBJECTS AND VERBS AGREE

A verb must agree in number with its subject. When the subject is singular, use the singular form of the verb. When the subject is plural, use the plural form of the verb. Notice that the present tense of the singular form of the verb usually ends in *s* or *es*.

Singular	Plural
A *bicycle* **provides** exercise.	*Bicycles* **provide** recreation, too.
She **is** a cyclist.	*They* **are** cyclists, too.
Exercise **creates** benefits.	*Exercises* **create** good effects.

Sometimes a helping verb or the main verb comes before the subject, or the verb is separated from the subject. In these cases, make sure the verb agrees with the subject.

Interrogative sentences	**Does** *exercise* **appeal** to you?
	Do *exercises* **bore** you?
Sentences beginning with *There is/are* or *Here is/are*	There **is** a bicycle *shop* near here.
	There **are** many *bicycles* for sale.
Intervening phrases	The *bicycle* with stripes **is** costly.
	The *bicycles* at the shop **are** new.

Guided Practice

Choose the correct form of the verb for each sentence.

Example: The bicycle (has, have) a colorful history.   *has*

1. Bicycles (is, are) products of the 1800s.
2. (Do, does) early bicycles look strange to you?
3. They (was, were) mainly wooden and very fragile.
4. A metal bike of today (have, has) great advantages.
5. There (is, are) many models from which to choose.

 THINK

- How do I decide whether to use the singular or plural form of a verb with the subject of a sentence?

REMEMBER

- Use the singular form of a verb with a singular subject and the plural form of a verb with a plural subject.
- Make sure the verb agrees with the subject when a helping verb or the main verb comes before the subject or when the verb is separated from the subject by other words.

More Practice

A. Write the correct form of the verb.

Example: Europeans (claim, claims) the invention of the bicycle. *claim*

6. There (is, are) many bicycle races there today.
7. An 1820 bicycle (move, moves) very slowly.
8. Modern bicycles (travel, travels) much faster.
9. Early bicycles (have, has) interesting names.
10. One of these names (is, are) "hobbyhorse."
11. The "hobbyhorse" (has, have) no pedals.
12. The rider's feet (touch, touches) the ground.

B. Write each sentence, using the correct form of the verb.

Example: An antique bicycle from the 1800s (is, are) rare.
An antique bicycle from the 1800s is rare.

13. (Do, Does) early bicycles appear silly today?
14. One model from 1870 (is, are) the "penny farthing."
15. There (is, are) a small back wheel on this bike.
16. The front wheel (is, are) very large.
17. Many early models (possess, possesses) no chain.
18. These two-wheelers (move, moves) awkwardly.
19. Gears (give, gives) efficiency and speed to modern racing bicycles.
20. Lightweight metals (add, adds) to their speed and strength.

Extra Practice, Practice Plus, pages 168–169

WRITING APPLICATION A Persuasive Paragraph

Write a paragraph recommending an activity that can benefit you in a variety of ways. Exchange your recommendation with a classmate and check for subject-verb agreement in each other's work.

6 PRESENT, PAST, AND FUTURE TENSES

You change the form of a verb to show *when* an action takes place. The time of the action expressed by a verb is known as its **tense.**

Use the **present tense** of a verb to express an action that is happening now or that happens repeatedly.

Use the **past tense** of a verb to express an action that happened in the past. Add *ed* to most verbs to form the past tense.

Use the **future tense** of a verb to express action that will happen in the future. Add the helping verb *will* or *shall.*

	Singular	Plural
Present Tense	I work. You work. He, she, it works.	We work. You work. They work.
Past Tense	I worked. You worked. He, she, it worked.	We worked. You worked. They worked.
Future Tense	I will (shall) work. You will work. He, she, it will work.	We will (shall) work. You will work. They will work.

Guided Practice

Identify the tense of the underlined verb.

Example: Eli Whitney <u>patented</u> the cotton gin.   *past tense*

1. Catherine Littlefield Greene <u>helped</u> Whitney.
2. She usually <u>receives</u> little credit for her aid.
3. Whitney <u>visited</u> the Greenes' farm outside Savannah, Georgia.
4. Mrs. Greene <u>made</u> suggestions for the cotton gin.
5. Historians <u>will disagree</u> about the importance of her ideas.
6. Mrs. Greene <u>realized</u> the need for the machine.

 THINK

■ How can I tell what the tense of a verb is?

REMEMBER

More Practice

A. Write the verb in each sentence. Then write whether the verb is in the **present, past,** or **future** tense.

Example: Perhaps Mrs. Greene even designed the gin.
   designed   past

7. People will remember her for the wire combs.
8. Today cotton gins still use wire combs.
9. Mrs. Greene also publicized the cotton gin.
10. The patent holds only Whitney's name, however,
11. Even today women often remain in the background.
12. Surely, women will receive more recognition in the future.

B. Write each sentence, using the correct tense of the verb in parentheses. Then write whether the verb is in the **present, past,** or **future** tense.

Example: A patent (protect) an idea in future years.
   A patent will protect an idea in future years.   future

13. Today a successful patent (bring) wealth.
14. In the past most inventors (earn) little money.
15. They often (patent) their inventions too late.
16. They later (sue) without success.
17. Even then this process (be) expensive.
18. This type of carelessness still (happen) today.
19. Perhaps inventors (know) better in the future.
20. Meanwhile, a patent (guard) the new ideas.

Extra Practice, page 170

WRITING APPLICATION An Explanation

Think of an invention that you find very useful. Write about how it affects your life. Exchange compositions with a classmate and identify the verb tenses in each other's work.

GRAMMAR

7 VERB PHRASES

Verbs have four basic forms called **principal parts.** All tenses of a verb can be formed from these principal parts.

Present	Present Participle	Past	Past Participle
enjoy	(is) enjoying	enjoyed	(has) enjoyed
laugh	(is) laughing	laughed	(has) laughed

Often a principal part of a verb is used with a **helping verb** to form a **verb phrase.** In a verb phrase the word that names the main action is called the **main verb.**

    helping verb main verb
People *have* **practiced** various crafts for centuries.
My uncle *is* **interested** in cabinetry.

Common Helping Verbs		
am, is, are	has, have, had	can, could
be, been	do, does, did	might, may, must
was, were	will, shall	should, would

Sometimes a verb phrase is interrupted by other words.

    Are you **studying** crafts?   I **have** always **liked** them.

Guided Practice

Identify the verb phrase in each sentence. Then identify the main verb and the helping verb.

Example: We have visited many craft fairs. *have visited*
             visited main verb   have helping verb

1. Many communities are promoting new craft shops.
2. These outlets could encourage local craftsmanship.
3. Crafts have also received new respect from art critics.
4. Art galleries are exhibiting crafts more and more.
5. In the past, crafts were not considered seriously.

 THINK

■ How can I tell which word in a verb phrase is the main verb?

REMEMBER

■ Every verb has four **principal parts:** the present, the present participle, the past, and the past participle.

■ A **verb phrase** consists of a **main verb** and its **helping verbs.**

More Practice

A. Write the verb phrase in each sentence. Then label the **main verb** and the **helping verb.**

Example: Until recently, handicrafts were not respected.
    were respected   *respected*   *main verb*
                were   *helping verb*

6. Today, people do appreciate more the skills of the past.
7. This new interest has focused attention on handicrafts.
8. For example, people are collecting such things as hooked rugs.
9. Art critics are now writing about pottery and other crafts.
10. New definitions of art have evolved.
11. Many old objects were preserved for sentimental reasons.
12. Often no one could remember the names of the makers.

B. Write each sentence and underline the verb phrase. Identify and label the participle **present** or **past.**

Example: Once people had made quilts only for beds.
    Once people had made quilts only for beds.
    made   past participle

13. In the past, people had used baskets as containers.
14. Now these same baskets are functioning as decorations.
15. The art of the quilt is re-emerging.
16. Old quilts have provided wonderful patterns.
17. Quilters are developing new patterns as well.
18. Some quilters are using old recipes for vegetable dyes.
19. These dyes were also used for baskets and thread.
20. Mother had created yellow from onion skins.

Extra Practice, page 171

WRITING APPLICATION A "How-to" Paragraph

Write a "how-to" paragraph about a manual skill that you know well. Explain how you practice the skill. Exchange your paragraph with a classmate. Underline the verb phrases in each other's work.

COOPERATIVE
LEARNING

8 PRESENT AND PAST PROGRESSIVE

You have learned that the present tense of a verb expresses an action that is happening now. You also learned that the past tense of a verb expresses an action that has already happened.

PRESENT TENSE: Josh **practices** dance every afternoon.

PAST TENSE: Last year he **studied** in a large class.

Progressive forms of verbs express action in progress. They show that an action is continuing in the present or was continuing in the past. Progressive forms are verb phrases consisting of a form of the verb *be* as a helping verb used with the present participle of a verb. Note how the helping verbs determine the tense.

	Singular	Plural
Present Progressive Form	I **am dancing.** You **are dancing.** He, she, it **is dancing.**	We **are dancing.** You **are dancing.** They **are dancing.**
Past Progressive Form	I **was dancing.** You **were dancing.** He, she, it **was dancing.**	We **were dancing.** You **were dancing.** They **were dancing.**

Guided Practice

Identify the verb phrase in each sentence. Identify the progressive form as **present** or **past.**

Example: The students are studying classical ballet.
                  are studying   present

1. Lou is dancing in the school recital.
2. He was studying ballet at age ten.
3. The school is preparing boys for careers in ballet.
4. Years ago few boys were learning serious dance.
5. Now ballet is becoming more popular.

 THINK

- How can I tell if a verb is in the present tense or the present progressive form?

REMEMBER

- The **present progressive** form of a verb expresses action that is happening now.
- The **past progressive** form of a verb expresses action that was continuing for some time in the past.

More Practice

A. Write the verb phrase in each sentence. Then write whether it is in the **present progressive** or **past progressive.**

Example: Many students are dancing in *The Nutcracker.*
are dancing   present progressive

   6. Oona was rehearsing yesterday.
   7. Her class was practicing the party scene.
   8. Today they are fitting her for a costume.
   9. Last year she and Leo were performing together.
  10. Leo is now reading a book about George Balanchine.
  11. His ballets are still delighting audiences.

B. Write each sentence, using the form of the verb given in parentheses.

Example: Leo (prepare) for a new role.   (present progressive)
Leo is preparing for a new role.

  12. Students in his class (practice) daily.
       (present progressive)
  13. Last year Leo (begin) work with weights.
       (past progressive)
  14. Now he (lift) his weight.   (present progressive)
  15. Yesterday he (use) a machine.   (past progressive)
  16. Dancers (attend) his gym.   (past progressive)
  17. A coach (observe) Leo's class.   (past progressive)
  18. Visitors (admire) their agility.   (past progressive)
  19. Leo (accomplish) his goals.   (present progressive)
  20. Such students (give) new life to dance.   (present progressive)

Extra Practice, page 172

WRITING APPLICATION A Comedy Skit

Write a comedy skit with a partner. Use present and past progressive forms of verbs. Present your skit to the class. Ask a volunteer to record the progressive forms you use.

9 PERFECT TENSES

You know that the present participle is used to form the progressive forms of verbs. To form the perfect tenses, you use the past participle of the verb.

The **perfect tenses** of a verb consist of a form of *have* used as a helping verb and the past participle of the main verb.

The **present perfect tense** of a verb expresses action that happened at an indefinite time in the past. It also names an action that started in the past and that is still happening in the present.

> Throughout history people **have valued** freedom.
> Our nation **has protected** our freedoms.

The **past perfect tense** of a verb expresses an action that happened before another past action or event happened.

> Freedom of speech **had flourished** long before the Revolutionary War.

The **future perfect tense** of a verb expresses an action that will be completed before another action or event in the future.

> Demand for this right **will have increased** during my lifetime.

Guided Practice

Identify the verb phrase in each sentence. Then tell whether the phrase is in the present perfect, past perfect, or future perfect tense.

Example: Freedom of speech has become a basic right.
> *has become   present perfect*

1. Our Constitution has protected freedom of speech since 1791.
2. This had been one of the goals of the Revolutionary War.
3. By the year 2000 this liberty will have faced new tests.
4. In times of unrest, certain laws had limited certain freedoms.
5. Some governments have forbidden free speech.
6. The history of free speech has been dramatic.

?! THINK

- How do I decide when to use the perfect tenses?

- The **present perfect tense** is formed by using *has* or *have* with the past participle.
- The **past perfect tense** is formed by using *had* with the past participle.
- The **future perfect tense** is formed by using *will have* or *shall have* with the past participle.

More Practice

A. Write the verb phrase in each sentence. Then write whether it is in the **present perfect, past perfect,** or **future perfect** tense.

Example: Kim had studied about liberty earlier.
　　　　　had studied　past perfect

7. Has she learned about the history of freedom of speech?
8. This freedom will have required constant protection.
9. Our struggles have involved religious freedom as well.
10. By the 1700s people had accepted liberty as a right.
11. Thomas Jefferson had written often of these freedoms.

B. Write each sentence, using the tense of the verb given in parentheses.

Example: Mrs. Chu (explain) freedom of speech. (past perfect)
　　　　　Mrs. Chu had explained freedom of speech.

12. The students (discuss) various concepts of freedom. (past perfect)
13. Eric said, "My grandparents (lose) this right in another country." (past perfect)
14. Ms. Chu announced, "We (study) more about this before the year ends." (future perfect)
15. We all (realize) the importance of free speech. (present perfect)

Extra Practice, page 173

WRITING APPLICATION A Biographical Sketch

Write a sketch about a person who has influenced you. Exchange papers with a classmate, and identify perfect tenses in each other's work.

G R A M M A R

10 IRREGULAR VERBS

You have learned that the past tense and the past participle of most verbs are formed by adding *ed* to the verb. Irregular verbs, however, do not follow this rule. The chart given below shows the forms for some commonly used irregular verbs.

Verb	Past	Past Participle
be	was	(*have, has,* or *had*) been
do	did	(*have, has,* or *had*) done
have	had	(*have, has,* or *had*) had
come	came	(*have, has,* or *had*) come
run	ran	(*have, has,* or *had*) run
bring	brought	(*have, has,* or *had*) brought
buy	bought	(*have, has,* or *had*) bought
catch	caught	(*have, has,* or *had*) caught
feel	felt	(*have, has,* or *had*) felt
hold	held	(*have, has,* or *had*) held
leave	left	(*have, has,* or *had*) left
lend	lent	(*have, has,* or *had*) lent
make	made	(*have, has,* or *had*) made
say	said	(*have, has,* or *had*) said
sit	sat	(*have, has,* or *had*) sat
swing	swung	(*have, has,* or *had*) swung
teach	taught	(*have, has,* or *had*) taught
think	thought	(*have, has,* or *had*) thought
burst	burst	(*have, has,* or *had*) burst
set	set	(*have, has,* or *had*) set

Guided Practice

Name the past tense and the past participle for each verb.

Example: buy   *bought bought*

1. bring	**3.** lend	**5.** set	**7.** sit	**9.** do
2. burst	**4.** catch	**6.** be	**8.** say	**10.** swing

 THINK

■ How are irregular verbs different from other verbs?

REMEMBER

- The principal parts of irregular verbs are formed in various ways. To learn the forms, it is necessary to memorize them.

More Practice

A. Write each sentence, using the past tense or the past participle of the verb given in parentheses.

Example: Jane Addams (be) an American social worker.
Jane Addams was an American social worker.

11. She had (feel) the need for a settlement house in Chicago.
12. Jane Addams (make) Hull House a reality in 1889.
13. Here she (teach) self-help to the poor and ignorant.
14. Jane Addams (run) the settlement house well.
15. She (have) the cooperation of her neighbors.
16. The problems of the poor had (burst) into her life.
17. Friends had (lend) Addams the money for the project.
18. A great effort had (make) it work.

B. Write each sentence, using the correct past tense or past participle of the verb given in parentheses. Then write whether you used the **past tense** or the **past participle.**

Example: Hull House had ____ helpful to many people. (be)
Hull House had been helpful to many people.
past participle

19. Assistants ____ unskilled people practical crafts. (teach)
20. Addams ____ strong moral beliefs. (hold)
21. She once had ____ no to a large gift of money. (say)
22. The donor ____ his employees without mercy. (drive)
23. Jane Addams had ____ of this injustice. (think)
24. She ____ pressure on the legislature for reforms. (bring)
25. Addams had ____ the public's attention. (catch)

Extra Practice, page 174

WRITING APPLICATION An Editorial

COOPERATIVE
LEARNING

Working either alone or with a partner, write an editorial about something in your community that you would like to have changed. Suggest actions that could improve the situation. Exchange papers with a classmate or pair of classmates and check the use of irregular verbs in each other's work.

MORE IRREGULAR VERBS

You have seen that irregular verbs do not follow one pattern. Their forms must be used carefully.

Study this chart for the forms of other commonly used irregular verbs.

Verb	Past	Past Participle
blow	blew	(*have, has,* or *had*) blown
break	broke	(*have, has,* or *had*) broken
choose	chose	(*have, has,* or *had*) chosen
draw	drew	(*have, has,* or *had*) drawn
drive	drove	(*have, has,* or *had*) driven
eat	ate	(*have, has,* or *had*) eaten
fly	flew	(*have, has,* or *had*) flown
freeze	froze	(*have, has,* or *had*) frozen
give	gave	(*have, has,* or *had*) given
go	went	(*have, has,* or *had*) gone
grow	grew	(*have, has,* or *had*) grown
ride	rode	(*have, has,* or *had*) ridden
speak	spoke	(*have, has,* or *had*) spoken
tear	tore	(*have, has,* or *had*) torn
wear	wore	(*have, has,* or *had*) worn
drink	drank	(*have, has,* or *had*) drunk
sing	sang	(*have, has,* or *had*) sung
sink	sank	(*have, has,* or *had*) sunk
spring	sprang	(*have, has,* or *had*) sprung
swim	swam	(*have, has,* or *had*) swum

Guided Practice

Name the past tense and past participle for each of the following irregular verbs.

Example: sink   *sank sunk*

1. swim
2. ride
3. sing
4. fly
5. tear
6. sink
7. spring
8. freeze
9. speak
10. wear

THINK

- How can I remember the forms of irregular verbs?

REMEMBER

- Use the helping verb *have* or *has* with the past participle to form the present perfect tense. Use *had* with the past participle to form the past perfect tense.
- Do not use helping verbs to form the past tense.

More Practice

A. Write each sentence, using the past tense or the past participle of the verb given in parentheses.

Example: Modern inventions have (give) us many benefits.
    Modern inventions have given us many benefits.

11. For centuries people had (draw) water from wells.
12. They (go) to the wells several times each day.
13. In the 1800s pumps had (give) people water inside homes.
14. By 1900 most people (drink) water that flowed from a tap.
15. Today we feel helpless if the water pipes have (break).
16. Once people had (eat) fresh meat only after they caught it.
17. If anything (freeze) food, it was winter weather.
18. Then mechanical refrigeration (give) us manufactured ice.

B. Write each sentence, using either the past tense or the past participle of the verb given in parentheses. Write whether you used the **past tense** or the **past participle.**

Example: Horses _____ wagons loaded with ice.   (draw)
    Horses drew wagons loaded with ice.   past tense

19. The iceman _____ from house to house delivering large blocks of ice.   (go)
20. Many people had _____ iceboxes for storage.   (choose)
21. Since 1945 refrigerators have _____ in popularity.   (grow)
22. The public _____ the gas stove a cautious reception.   (give)
23. Some gas stoves had _____ up, and people were wary.   (blow)
24. New inventions have _____ old ways into obscurity.   (drive)
25. Everyday life has _____ easier as a result.   (grow)

Extra Practice, page 175

WRITING APPLICATION A Persuasive Paragraph

Write a paragraph in which you argue that life in the modern world is either better or worse than life in the past. Exchange papers with a classmate. Check the use of irregular verbs in each other's work.

12 MECHANICS: Using Commas to Separate Parts of a Sentence

Commas help you to understand the meaning of a sentence. A comma often signals a pause.

Uses for Commas	Examples
To separate three or more items in a series	Concord Bridge, Lexington, and Paul Revere's house are sites of interest. We arrived, toured, and then ate. The day was long, busy, and delightful.
To show a pause after an introductory word or phrase	Yes, I have seen many historic sites. By the way, Boston is my hometown. Oh, you have been there?
To set off a noun of direct address	Tim, did you visit the *Constitution?* Yes, Bob, it is a famous frigate.
To set off a phrase that interrupts flow of thought	Boston is, I believe, a beautiful city. It has, however, grown greatly.
To set off the word *too* when it means "also"	We visited the USS *Constitution,* too. You, too, can see it.

Guided Practice

Tell where a comma or commas should be used in each sentence.

Example: Do you enjoy historical places Ellen?
          comma before Ellen

1. Philadelphia is I think my favorite historical city.
2. Joe have you considered a trip to Yorktown?
3. Yes I may go next summer.
4. Newport Boston and Valley Forge are on my list.
5. I went during the summers of 1985 1987 and 1988.

 THINK

- How do I decide when to use commas in my writing?

REMEMBER

- Use commas to separate items in a series.
- Use commas to set off introductory words, nouns of direct address, words or phrases that interrupt the flow of thought, and *too* used to mean "also."

More Practice

A. Write each sentence and add the missing commas. Write **correct** if the sentence needs no corrections.

Example: Tamara you are going I believe on a trip.
Tamara, you are going, I believe, on a trip.

  6. Yes we will visit places I am eager to see.
  7. We will visit Asheville Winchester and New Orleans.
  8. Nicholas do you know who was born in each place?
  9. No I don't Tamara but please tell me.
 10. They are the birthplaces of Thomas Wolfe Willa Cather and Lillian Hellman.
 11. New York too has many sites of literary interest.
 12. Yes Wolfe Cather and Hellman all lived there too.

B. Write each sentence. Add commas where they are needed.

Example: New York is hot humid and crowded in the summer.
New York is hot, humid, and crowded in the summer.

 13. North Carolina Virginia and Louisiana are hotter.
 14. Trains cars and planes by the way will be costly.
 15. Perhaps Tamara you should visit just one city.
 16. New Orleans is famous you know for food.
 17. Crayfish shrimp and redfish are fresh and cheap.
 18. Ragtime blues and jazz flowered there Joe.
 19. Yes Tamara I will eat look and listen there too.
 20. New Orleans I believe was originally French.

Extra Practice, page 176

WRITING APPLICATION A Letter

Write a letter explaining why your reader should visit your favorite city. Exchange papers with a classmate. Check each other's work for the correct use of commas.

13 VOCABULARY BUILDING: Word Choice

Using words that are precise and vivid can strengthen your writing and speaking in several ways.

1. **Make your word choices specific and exact.**

> VAGUE: A lot of people lived all over the place.
> SPECIFIC: Tribes of Indians inhabited North America.

> VAGUE: The hunter walked as the buffalo stayed in the grass.
> SPECIFIC: The hunter stalked as the buffalo browsed.

2. **Eliminate wordiness.**

One exact noun can replace a string of adjectives. A vivid verb can be stronger than a weak verb accompanied by an adverb.

> WORDY: A large, upright rock made him completely invisible.
> CONCISE: A boulder concealed him.

Use the Thesaurus at the back of this book to help you select precise words.

3. **Choose words for their sound.**

Onomatopoeia is the use of a word that imitates sounds associated with the word.

> The browsing buffalo **chomped** the grass.

Alliteration is the use of words that repeat the same sound.

> The **h**unter **h**unched **h**imself behind the rocks.

Guided Practice

For each vague word, write two words that are more exact or vivid.

Example: big   *huge   enormous*

1. walk
2. smart
3. sadly
4. jump
5. funny
6. nice
7. car
8. music

 THINK

■ How can the careful choice of words improve my writing?

REMEMBER

- Use words that are specific and vivid.
- Use exact nouns and verbs to avoid wordiness.
- Use words for their sounds.

More Practice

A. Write the word or words from the parentheses that are more vivid or exact.

Example: Jen (saw, discovered) Indian artifacts near her house. *discovered*

  9. She proudly (had, presented) them at school.
 10. Indians must have lived (in this area, somewhere around).
 11. Ty (researched, found out about) the history of local Indians.
 12. One book pictured (big, ornate wooden shafts; totem poles).
 13. Jen immediately (liked, was fascinated by) these.
 14. They were (put up, erected) in honor of dead chiefs.
 15. The poles stood near (the place where the chief was buried, the chief's grave).
 16. The poles pictured a tribe's (most important events, history).
 17. The tribe could (know, learn) about its past.

B. Write the sentence, replacing the underlined word or words with a more precise word from the Word Bank.

Example: The Indians used small boats made from hollowed logs. *dugouts*

 18. Men did most of the traditional dances.
 19. These were presented during elaborate, customary rituals.
 20. Part of a woman's work was making baskets.
 21. The men primarily looked for fish and animals.
 22. They believed in the being born again of the soul.
 23. Jan has feelings of admiration for the Indian ways.
 24.–25. Jan believes their way of life should be kept going.

Extra Practice, page 177

WRITING APPLICATION A Description

Write a description of your most prized possession. Explain why it is so valuable to you. Exchange papers with a classmate. Determine whether your classmate's writing could be improved by using more vivid or exact words.

WORD BANK
- hunted
- rebirth
- respect
- ceremonies
- performed
- preserved
- weaving
- customs
- dugouts

VOCABULARY: Word Choice   **157**

GRAMMAR
—AND
WRITING
CONNECTION

Combining Sentences

When you write explanations, you may want to show how ideas in two separate sentences are related. Combining sentences can help you make your writing more varied.

> SEPARATE: We offer you this honor. You deserve to be president.
>
> COMBINED: We offer you this honor **because you deserve to be president.**
>
> or
>
> **Because you deserve to be president,** we offer you this honor.

Notice that a comma follows the adverb clause that begins a sentence. When you combine sentences with adverb clauses, show the relationship between ideas by using such connecting words as *after, although, because, before, even though, until,* and *when.*

Working Together

COOPERATIVE
LEARNING

With a group of your classmates, discuss how you would combine each pair of sentences below by using an adverb clause. Join the sentences with such words as *after, although, because, before, even though, since, until,* and *when.*

Example: You vote for me. You will vote for excellence.
When you vote for me, you will vote for excellence.

1. I will run for class president.
   I am qualified for the office.
2. I will run.
   Some students may not vote for me.
3. You have voted for me.
   You will not regret your choice.

Revising Sentences

Here are some campaign statements made by Alex and Shana, who are running for class president. Help them combine each of the following pairs of sentences into one sentence.

4. Alex: A vote for me is a vote for you. I care about you.

5. Shana: He will promise you the moon. His feet are not on the ground.

6. Alex: The vote is a precious right. You make your choice.

7. Shana: I will work hard for you. I am elected.

8. Alex: Vote for me. I am the better choice.

9. Shana: I am confident of the result. The choice is yours.

10. Alex: Vote for one of us. It is up to you.

11. Shana: My opponent is honest. I am the better choice.

12. Alex: You make up your mind. Consider my qualifications.

WRITER AT WORK

Think about the benefits and disadvantages that have resulted from the growth of our nation. Write a paragraph explaining how these results have affected you. Then revise your work with a partner. Find pairs of sentences that would be more interesting if they were combined.

UNIT CHECKUP

LESSON 1 **Action Verbs** (page 132)   Write each sentence. Underline the action verb, labeling it **physical** or **mental.**

1. Immigrants often bring their native foods with them.
2. Thus, people in the United States enjoy many unusual foods.
3. Americans recognize the foreign origins of many foods.
4. For example, Germans invented the hamburger.
5. A vendor at the 1904 St. Louis Fair added the bun.

LESSONS 2-3 **Direct Objects** (page 134), **Indirect Objects** (page 136)   Write each sentence and underline the verb. Label any **direct object** or **indirect object.**

6. Russian sailors brought Tartar steaks to Hamburg.
7. German cooks grilled this raw meat.
8. Germany also gave us the frankfurter.
9. Immigrant Germans brought Americans these foods.
10. The English invented sandwiches.

LESSONS 4-5 **Linking Verbs** (page 138), **Making Subjects and Verbs Agree** (page 140)   Write each sentence, using the correct form of the verb given in parentheses. Then draw one line under each linking verb and write whether it is followed by a **predicate noun** or by a **predicate adjective.**

11. There (is, are) a wide variety of fruits and vegetables from other countries.
12. The cantaloupe (grow, grows) from Italian stock.
13. Cantaloupes (become, becomes) ripe in midsummer.
14. (Is, Are) they yellow inside?
15. The kiwi fruit (originate, originates) in New Zealand.

LESSON 6 **Present, Past, and Future Tenses** (page 142)   Write each sentence, underlining the verb. Then write whether the verb is in the **present tense, past tense,** or **future tense.**

16. George Crum, an Indian chief, invented the potato chip.
17. He worked as a chef in Saratoga Springs, New York, in 1853.
18. Often inventions will develop from unusual requests.
19. A customer of Crum's asked for very thin fried potatoes.
20. People eat millions of pounds of potato chips each year.

LESSONS 7-9 Verb Phrases (page 144), **Present and Past Progressive** (page 146), **Perfect Tenses** (page 148)   Rewrite each sentence by changing the verb to the tense or form given in parentheses. Underline the verb phrase.

21. Italians introduce many foods to our menu.   (present perfect)
22. Pasta, however, came to Italy from China.   (past perfect)
23. Americans often invent pasta recipes.   (present progressive)
24. Actually, meatballs originated here.   (past perfect)
25. Many foods improved in the new land.   (past progressive)

LESSONS 10-11 Irregular Verbs I (page 150), **Irregular Verbs II** (page 152)   Write the past and past participle for each verb.

26. speak
27. go
28. catch
29. swim
30. burst
31. fly

LESSON 12 Mechanics:Using Commas to Separate Parts of a Sentence (page 154)   Write each sentence, inserting needed commas.

32. Native Americans first ate corn potatoes and yams.
33. Bagels blintzes and bialys are from Eastern Europe.
34. Corn I believe is a New World food too.
35. Italians I am told introduced eggplants.
36. Sheila what is your favorite food?

LESSON 13 Vocabulary Building: Word Choice (page 156)   Write each sentence, replacing the underlined words with words that are more specific and vivid.

37. Will you <u>fix</u> bread this weekend?
38. The bread <u>has</u> whole-wheat flour.
39. I love the smell of the <u>ingredients all mixed together</u>.
40. I hope the <u>outside of the loaf</u> is crisp.

Writing Application: Verb Usage (pages 132–152)   The following paragraph contains 10 errors in subject-verb agreement, use of tenses, and forms of irregular verbs. Rewrite the paragraph correctly.

41.–50.   Log cabins is not distinctly American. In centuries past, Scandinavians construct log houses. Swedes first builded them in America. From the beginning, the structure adapts well to the new country. There was reasons for their popularity. Few tools was necessary for their construction, and trees growed almost everywhere. Many settlers build a cabin in a few days. Has you ever seen a log cabin? Yes, many people built them today.

Each team makes a list of songs with an action verb in the title or in the first line of the lyrics. Then, in turn, each team sings the first line of a song and wins a point if the opposing team cannot identify the verb. The last team to run out of songs wins five extra points. Here is an example of a verb tune: "God Bless America." Bonus points can be awarded for the identification of the tense of the verb in each song.

Verb Tunes

Action Headlines

As the editor of *Historical Highlights,* write the headlines for three fascinating historical or current events. When writing your headlines, use colorful action verbs that describe the events. For example: ALEXANDER SUBDUES PERSIAN EMPIRE!

DON'T JUST SAY *GO*, SAY *AMBLE*

With a partner or in a small group, list as many vivid verbs as you can that express the action of one of these more general verbs: *do, go, say,* and *walk.* After you have compiled your list, play "Verb Charade" by asking each member of the class to act out a version of the verb *walk.*

THE DAILY HEADLINE

EXTRA! EXTRA! EXTRA! EXTRA!

CREATIVE EXPRESSION

The Base Stealer

Poised between going on and back, pulled
Both ways taut like a tightrope-walker,
Fingertips pointing the opposites,
Now bouncing tiptoe like a dropped ball
Or a kid skipping rope, come on, come on,
Running a scattering of steps sidewise,
How he teeters, skitters, tingles, teases,
Taunts them, hovers like an ecstatic bird,
He's only flirting, crowd him, crowd him,
Delicate, delicate, delicate, delicate—now!

—Robert Francis

Try It Out!

"The Base Stealer" is written in free verse; that is, its language is based on everyday speech patterns. The poet uses strong similes, making comparisons between two things by using the word *like* or *as*. Write a free-verse poem of your own that includes a simile. Listen to the speech around you for inspiration.

EXTRA PRACTICE

Three levels of practice

Action Verbs (page 132)

A. Write each sentence. Underline each action verb.

1. Music plays an important role in many lives.
2. Today, records, tapes, and radios make music universal.
3. Almost every household possesses a phonograph.
4. Nothing, however, replaces the pleasure of live performance.
5. Some people judge others by their taste in music.
6. Different generations enjoy different sounds.
7. Anita plays music with strong rhythm.
8. Ruth prefers classical music to rock.
9. Paco likes salsa, and Jason chooses jazz.

LEVEL

B. Write each sentence. Underline each action verb.

10. Music had a different role in the past.
11. Not too long ago, people knew only live performances.
12. Families often held concerts at home.
13. Everyone in the family played an instrument.
14. At parties guests often played the piano or sang.
15. At square dances a friend or neighbor fiddled.
16. Composers wrote music specially for one performance.
17. Today, we often hear the same song twice in an hour.

LEVEL

C. Write each sentence. Underline each action verb. Write whether each verb shows a **mental** or a **physical** action.

18. Thomas Edison made the first phonograph in the 1870s.
19. Radio brought music to our homes.
20. In other ways technology limits our appreciation.
21. For example, radio schedules required a standard length.
22. Listeners recall a repeated melody.
23. We memorize both words and music.
24. Some songwriters produce two versions of one song.
25. Often we remember the singer, not the composer.

EXTRA PRACTICE

Three levels of practice

Direct Objects, Transitive and Intransitive Verbs (page 134)

LEVEL

A. Write each sentence. Underline the direct object.

1. Fiction writers often use their own lives as material.
2. Other writers invent the details for their fiction.
3. Stephen Crane never fought a war.
4. Yet, he wrote *The Red Badge of Courage.*
5. This novel describes a soldier's life during the Civil War.
6. The soldier learns a bitter lesson.
7. The novel brought international fame to Crane.
8. Louisa May Alcott wrote books about her life.
9. However, she also chose subjects unfamiliar to her.

LEVEL

B. Write each sentence. Underline each verb once and each direct object twice. Label each verb **transitive** or **intransitive.**

10. Alcott's most popular books describe a romanticized life.
11. Her biography reveals a harder existence.
12. She lived in Massachusetts for most of her life.
13. Alcott set many of her novels there.
14. Her father educated his children at home.
15. In *Jo's Boys*, Jo March starts her own school.
16. Louisa May Alcott held other jobs, too.
17. For most of her life, however, she lived from her writing.

LEVEL

C. Write each sentence. If it contains a direct object, draw an arrow from the verb to the object.

18. Alcott held several jobs as a young woman.
19. She wrote about this in *Work: A Story of Experience.*
20. During the Civil War she joined the effort.
21. She volunteered her service as a nurse.
22. While in Georgetown, she contracted typhoid.
23. Because of typhoid she lost her hair and teeth.
24. Yet, we remember Alcott for her optimistic books.
25. Her readers rarely read her gothic tales.

EXTRA PRACTICE

Three levels of practice

Indirect Objects (page 136)

LEVEL

A. Identify the underlined word as a **direct object** or an **indirect object.**

1. The United States observes many <u>holidays</u>.
2. Congress approves official <u>holidays</u>.
3. Traditions give <u>us</u> other holidays.
4. Ground Hog Day gives <u>people</u> much amusement.
5. Everyone enjoys this annual <u>custom</u>.
6. Science disproves the <u>accuracy</u> of the ground hog.
7. Schoolchildren plant <u>trees</u> on Arbor Day.
8. This custom gives <u>them</u> an awareness of nature.
9. Congress does not recognize <u>Arbor Day</u> officially.

LEVEL

B. Write each sentence, underlining any indirect object.

10. Mrs. Cho gave us a demonstration of holiday crafts.
11. Elise made her little sister a basket for May Day.
12. Mrs. Cho showed the class many kinds of baskets.
13. She gave Lou one with a built-in handle.
14. Mrs. Cho also brought us recipes for holiday foods.
15. Linda requested her candy recipe.
16. Mrs. Cho gave her a sugarless recipe for fruit leather.
17. We should write Mrs. Cho a thank-you note.

LEVEL

C. Write each sentence. Label each **direct object** and **indirect object.**

18. Anna Jarvis created Mother's Day in 1907.
19. She suggested a holiday for all mothers.
20. She told influential friends her idea.
21. The House of Representatives passed a resolution.
22. However, the Senate caused the resolution trouble.
23. Anna Jarvis wrote many people letters.
24. Newspapers gave her idea support.
25. In 1914 President Wilson granted mothers their day.

EXTRA PRACTICE

Three levels of practice

Linking Verbs (page 138)

LEVEL

A. Write the linking verbs in each sentence.

1. Modern schools are very different from schools of the past.
2. The differences are evident in the buildings themselves.
3. Early schools were usually one-room buildings.
4. Sixty children of different ages were together.
5. The teacher often was very young, too.
6. Tables were desks, and backless benches were seats.
7. Today one-room schools are quite rare.
8. A one-room school in Cliff City, Maine, is successful.
9. One student is sometimes the only person in a grade.

LEVEL

B. Write each sentence, underlining the linking verb. Label all **predicate nouns** and **adjectives.**

10. A one-room school house is not cost-effective.
11. It often appears educationally sound.
12. One possible strength is the monitor system.
13. An older student becomes the teacher of a younger one.
14. Student tutors are common in larger schools, too.
15. For the tutors, the experience becomes a reward.
16. Over 800 one-room schools were active in 1988.
17. A one-room school appears limited in some ways.
18. For example, science labs or gyms are rare.

LEVEL

C. For each verb write a sentence about modern schools. Identify any **predicate nouns** and **predicate adjectives** in your sentence.

19. be
20. appear
21. become
22. seem
23. look
24. feel
25. smell

EXTRA PRACTICE

Three levels of practice

Making Subjects and Verbs Agree (page 140)

LEVEL

A. Write the correct verb given in parentheses.

1. Ostriches (is, are) the largest living birds.
2. Some males (weighs, weigh) over 300 pounds.
3. A full-grown ostrich (stands, stand) eight feet high.
4. Ostriches (do, does) not fly.
5. They (has, have) long necks and legs.
6. They (appear, appears) stately and dignified.
7. Their diet (is, are) mainly vegetables.
8. Some ostriches really (do, does) put their head in the sand.

LEVEL

B. Write each sentence, using the correct present-tense form of the verb given in parentheses.

9. Owls ____ also interesting birds.   (be)
10. They ____ for much of the day.   (sleep)
11. At night they ____.   (hunt)
12. The silent flight of an owl ____ it an advantage.   (give)
13. The wings ____ of very soft feathers.   (consist)
14. An owl also ____ powerful eyes and ears.   (have)
15. An owl ____ well in the dark.   (see)
16. Owls ____ widely in size.   (vary)
17. Many different species ____ in North America.   (live)

LEVEL

C. Rewrite each sentence and correct any errors in subject-verb agreement. If a sentence is correct, write **correct.**

18. Most owls like to hunt mice.
19. Owls occasionally eat squirrels.
20. Owls appear on some ancient Greek coins.
21. The bird were a symbol of Athena, the goddess of wisdom.
22. A bird watcher rarely sees owls in the wild.
23. Their hooting sounds is eerie.
24. Larger birds do not generally attacks owls.
25. An owl are well equipped by nature for self-defense.

PRACTICE + PLUS

Three levels of additional practice for a difficult skill

Making Subjects and Verbs Agree (page 140)

LEVEL

A. Write the correct form of the verb given in parentheses.

1. Do movies (influence, influences) American life greatly?
2. Some movies (is, are) famous for setting styles.
3. Many people (think, thinks) of movies as entertainment.
4. Other moviegoers (see, sees) films as art.
5. Films actually (combine, combines) art with science.
6. Critics (agree, agrees) about the influence of the theater.
7. Early movies (was, were) often films of plays.
8. Thus, the contributions of literature to movies (is, are) evident.
9. Many filmmakers (was, were) also scientists.

LEVEL

B. Write each sentence, using the correct present-tense form of the verb given in parentheses.

10. Many people ____ on one movie.   (work)
11. A star actor ____ the largest audiences.   (attract)
12. Some actors ____ their own movies.   (direct)
13. There ____ others who also produce movies.   (be)
14. The producer ____ the film's production.   (organize)
15. Does he or she ____ the other artists, too?   (hire)
16. A large studio ____ great control.   (have)
17. Now smaller companies ____ many movies.   (make)

LEVEL

C. Rewrite each sentence by changing the subject and verb from the singular to the plural form.

18. Film has uses other than entertainment.
19. A scientist employs film for many purposes.
20. For example, stop-motion film speeds any slow movement.
21. A restaurant trains cooks by means of movies.
22. A manager of a business finds cartoons useful.
23. A familiar cartoon character plays a role.
24. A tense situation is more pleasant in a cartoon.
25. The viewer learns more quickly this way.

EXTRA PRACTICE

Three levels of practice

Present, Past, and Future Tenses (page 142)

LEVEL

A. Identify the tense of the underlined verb.

1. Labor organizations <u>existed</u> in colonial America.
2. These organizations <u>functioned</u> more or less as craft guilds.
3. In 1862 Judge Lemuel Shaw <u>ruled</u> in favor of formal unions.
4. Laws strictly <u>limit</u> the power of these unions.
5. Unions <u>will remain</u> controversial.
6. Some people <u>accuse</u> unions of controlling wages.
7. Factory workers once <u>worked</u> from dawn to dusk.
8. Organized workers <u>use</u> the strike as a method.
9. A strike <u>will pressure</u> the settlement of issues.

LEVEL

B. Write each sentence, underlining the verb. Then label the verb **present tense, past tense,** or **future tense.**

10. Elizabeth Gurley Flynn was a labor organizer.
11. At the age of sixteen, she addressed her first audience.
12. People will remember her for her hard work.
13. However, her fame as an orator will last also.
14. She received a *New York Times* award for one of her essays.
15. Flynn recorded her life in *Rebel Girl.*
16. This autobiography appeared in 1955.
17. Bookstores still stock copies of this popular book.

LEVEL

C. Rewrite each sentence, using the verb tense given in parentheses.

18. Labor organizers travel widely.   (past)
19. In one year an organizer worked in many states.   (present)
20. Organizers joined strikes throughout the country.   (present)
21. Sometimes a strike lasted for a long time.   (present)
22. The Lawrence strike continues for three months.   (past)
23. The organizers help strikers with publicity.   (past)
24. These textile workers received enormous sympathy.   (future)
25. Some of their children moved elsewhere.   (future)

EXTRA PRACTICE

Three levels of practice

Verb Phrases (page 144)

LEVEL

A. Write the verb phrase in each sentence.

1. Many travelers have visited the Grand Canyon.
2. It has been called one of the world's natural wonders.
3. Geologists are always studying its formations.
4. Explorers have established a network of trails.
5. It was named a national park in 1919.
6. Millions of tourists have visited the park.
7. How many people could explore it thoroughly?
8. No one person can exhaust its possibilities.
9. The Colorado River has carved this great canyon.

LEVEL

B. Write each sentence. Draw one line under the helping verb and two lines under the main verb.

10. A protection bill for the Grand Canyon was introduced in Congress in 1882.
11. By 1892 Congress had created forest preserves.
12. In 1901 a railroad was built near the Grand Canyon.
13. The railroad would bring many tourists to the area.
14. Civilization had come to the canyon.
15. President Theodore Roosevelt had visited the area in 1903.
16. Soon he would create the Grand Canyon National Monument.
17. The nation has preserved the wilderness areas.

LEVEL

C. Write each sentence. Underline the verb phrase. Label each participle as a **present participle** or a **past participle.**

18. Kay has visited the Grand Canyon several times.
19. Usually she has camped there in the summer.
20. The temperature has reached a high of 110 degrees.
21. She had never hiked in such heat.
22. This year she is planning a trip for March.
23. Her friend Jim is staying at the Phantom Ranch.
24. President Theodore Roosevelt had stayed there also.
25. A photograph of Roosevelt is hanging in a place of honor.

EXTRA PRACTICE

Three levels of practice

Present and Past Progressive (page 146)

LEVEL

A. Write the progressive form found in each sentence.

1. Carlos is studying the history of dodgeball.
2. Native Indians were playing the game of dodgeball long ago.
3. Carlos's classmates are researching other sports.
4. They are also learning different versions of each sport.
5. Last week they were playing dodgeball in the gym.
6. Mr. Kim was teaching them the rules.
7. For Indian dodgeball they were using a bat.
8. Luke was complaining about this odd practice.
9. Most students were ignoring his complaints.

LEVEL

B. Write each sentence and underline the verb phrase. Then label each verb as **present progressive** or **past progressive.**

10. Mr. Kim was losing patience.
11. Luke is always complaining!
12. Emma was standing in the middle of the gym.
13. Emma was using the bat.
14. Before long she was hitting well.
15. Soon the entire class was participating.
16. Now they are planning a dodgeball league.
17. They are forming an after-school sports club.

LEVEL

C. Write each sentence, using the form of the verb given in parentheses.

18. They (learn) several other Native American games. (present progressive)
19. For example, they (juggle) sticks. (present progressive)
20. Chinook Indians (handle) seven at a time. (past progressive)
21. Fred (experience) difficulty coping with two sticks. (present progressive)
22. Yesterday the class (bowl). (past progressive)
23. They (use) corncob targets as pins. (past progressive)
24. Who (learn) lacrosse? (present progressive)
25. Jill and Lyn (practice) the sport each morning before class. (present progressive)

EXTRA PRACTICE

Three levels of practice

Perfect Tenses (page 148)

LEVEL

A. Write the tense of the verb in each sentence.

1. Theater has maintained its popularity in the United States.
2. Forecasters had feared competition from movies.
3. However, live performances have remained popular.
4. Many regional theaters have developed around the country.
5. Once Broadway had produced most of the new plays.
6. Now other regions have presented important plays.
7. Chicago and Los Angeles have hosted many premieres.
8. Louisville has long held a festival of new plays.
9. This festival had once concentrated on one-act plays.

LEVEL

B. Write the verb phrase from each sentence. Identify the verb phrase as **present perfect** or **past perfect.**

10. The education of theater professionals has changed.
11. Once actors had trained on the job.
12. Small theaters had hired inexperienced actors.
13. They then had learned their craft from the seasoned actors.
14. This apprenticeship system has disappeared.
15. Daria has always wanted a career in theater.
16. She had acted in every elementary school play.
17. Often she had designed the costumes as well.

LEVEL

C. Write each sentence, using the correct perfect tense of the verb in parentheses.

18. Daria recently ____ to college. (apply)
19. She ____ on a career as a costume designer. (decide)
20. Ms. Jory once ____ as an actress in New York. (work)
21. For the last ten years Ms. Jory ____ in our town. (live)
22. Our English teacher ____ Ms. Jory to our class. (invite)
23. Since January we ____ theater games. (play)
24. Often we ____ whole scenes. (improvise)
25. We already ____ several one-act plays. (study)

EXTRA PRACTICE

Three levels of practice

Irregular Verbs I (page 150)

A. Write the correct form of the verb given in parentheses.

1. Immigration has ____ the United States unique. (make)
2. Native Americans probably had ____ from Asia. (come)
3. The new land has ____ challenges for all. (hold)
4. People have ____ their native lands for many reasons. (leave)
5. Some were ____ out of their homelands by war. (run)
6. Others ____ for reasons of religion. (leave)
7. All ____ the new land would grant them freedom. (think)
8. Many groups of immigrants have ____ different hopes. (have)
9. Before 1882 immigration ____ without restriction. (be)

B. Write the sentence, using the past tense or the past participle of the verb given in parentheses.

10. In 1924 quotas were ____ by the 1890 population. (set)
11. By 1965 this quota system had ____ its course. (run)
12. Congress has ____ the quotas 270,000 each year. (make)
13. Immigration has ____ to this limit. (hold)
14. Parents of legal immigrants have ____ here. (come)
15. Most early immigrants had ____ Europe. (leave)
16. Now most have ____ the journey from Asia or from Latin America. (make)
17. Our society has ____ the change. (feel)

C. Rewrite each sentence by changing the verb in the past tense to a verb phrase using the past participle. You may want to change the word order in some sentences.

18. The United States held promise to many in the 1800s.
19. Immigrants left home with little knowledge of the new land.
20. Perhaps a relative brought wondrous tales to them.
21. A parent lent them money for passage.
22. The immigrants usually sat in the worst part of the ship.
23. They often prepared their own food during the voyage.
24. Some spoke only a few words of English.
25. They made their food and strength last two weeks.

EXTRA PRACTICE

Three levels of practice

Irregular Verbs II (page 152)

LEVEL

A. Write the correct form of the verb in parentheses.

1. Our class has ____ to the library for research. (go)
2. Holly has ____ her topic, changes in travel. (choose)
3. In the past, fortunate people ____ horses. (ride)
4. Most vehicles had also been ____ by horses. (draw)
5. In cities horses were ____ to pull trolleys. (drive)
6. Stagecoaches ____ between cities. (go)
7. Soon, overland travel ____ very expensive. (grow)
8. In the 1800s mass transportation ____ to new life. (spring)
9. Steam ____ rise to a revolution in transportation. (give)

LEVEL

B. Write the sentence, using the past tense or the past participle of the verb in parentheses. Write whether you used the **past tense** or the **past participle.**

10. Travel by water had ____ a much cheaper alternative. (give)
11. New canals, however, ____ rivers and lakes together. (draw)
12. Goods ____ cheaply from place to place. (go)
13. The length and number of canals ____ greatly. (grow)
14. Sailing ships were ____ from place to place. (blow)
15. Canal boats were not ____ by the wind. (drive)
16. In 1807 steamboats ____ new force to water travel. (give)
17. By 1820 steamboats had ____ in popularity. (grow)

LEVEL

C. Rewrite each sentence by changing the verb in the past tense to a verb phrase using the past participle. You may want to change the word order in some sentences.

18. Steam also drove early trains and automobiles.
19. Some railroads grew with the encouragement of Congress.
20. Congress gave the railroads vast tracts of public land.
21. By 1869 the rails went from coast to coast.
22. The railroads drew new settlers to the western territories.
23. Railroads broke all records for transcontinental speed.
24. Holly chose a topic about truly great changes.
25. Holly's report drew a vivid picture of these changes.

EXTRA PRACTICE

Three levels of practice

Mechanics: Using Commas to Separate Parts of a Sentence (page 154)

LEVEL

A. Write each sentence and add the missing commas.

1. Robert is studying changes in cities towns and farms.
2. "Dad was life better in the old days?"
3. "Modern conveniences Robert are a blessing."
4. Travel health and housing have all improved.
5. Work education and sanitation are also better.
6. Books of Twain Wilder and Alcott romanticized life.
7. Farm life however was lonely difficult and isolated.
8. Cities were crowded noisy and smelly.
9. Streets smelled of coal of manure and of garbage.

LEVEL

B. Write each sentence. Add commas where they are needed. Write **correct** if the sentence is correctly punctuated.

10. Women worked hard in the home too.
11. Laundry cooking and cleaning were difficult.
12. Laundry was washed then dried and finally ironed.
13. Soap powders believe it or not were not used before 1900.
14. Soap was shaved from cakes and then boiled.
15. A whole day was devoted to baking washing or ironing.
16. Only wealthy people as you know had servants.
17. On the other hand bread tomatoes and milk tasted better.

LEVEL

C. Write each sentence. Correct all punctuation mistakes.

18. Peaches strawberries, and plums were once seasonal treats.
19. Well now you can buy them in any season.
20. Industrialized farming makes food tasteless too.
21. Sanitation, waste disposal and pollution are still a problem.
22. Change I believe has produced many problems.
23. Species of birds, fish and mammals are now extinct.
24. Cities rivers and lakes are polluted by industries.
25. Our forests my friend, are not being replanted.

EXTRA PRACTICE

Three levels of practice

Vocabulary Building: Word Choice (page 156)

LEVEL

A. For each sentence write the word or words that are more vivid or precise.

1. Life in the American West was shaped by (pioneers, people).
2. Some kept (records of their daily lives, diaries).
3. Others wrote their (autobiographies, stories of their lives).
4. These helped (people who study the past, historians).
5. Willa Cather wrote (fictional books, novels) about pioneers.
6. Although she grew up in Nebraska, her (family, people) came from Virginia.
7. After college, Cather (went, migrated) to the East Coast.
8. However, her (best liked, good) books are about the West.
9. Many people (see, imagine) the West as Cather described it.

LEVEL

B. Rewrite each sentence by replacing the underlined word or words with a more precise word.

10. Cather thought the prairies were pretty.
11. She liked the hard-working settlers.
12. Many settlers were people who came from other countries.
13. Cather portrayed the tough life on the prairies.
14. She also told about the determination of the settlers.
15. *My Antonia* is probably Cather's nicest book.
16. It is the good story of an immigrant girl on a farm.
17. Many readers like *Death Comes for the Archbishop*.
18. Cather got the Pulitzer Prize for fiction in 1923.

LEVEL

C. Write each sentence. Fill in the blank with a vivid or precise word.

19. Pioneer life was very ____ .
20. The settlers were ____ .
21. They often dealt with ____ conditions.
22. Sometimes, their crops would not ____ .
23. Yet, the pioneers ____ the land.
24. Most of them ____ on their farms.
25. How fortunate for America that the settlers were so ____ .

UNIT

6

Writing Explanations

In the quotation on the opposite page, Beatrice Siegel explains what stimulated her desire to write. What reason does she give? What other reasons can you think of for wanting to write?

When you write an explanation, your purpose is generally to inform your audience. To be sure that your explanation is clear, you will want to organize your information in a logical, step-by-step way.

Focus An explanation can convey information about how to do something. The purpose of an explanation is to inform.

What would you like to explain? On the following pages you will find an explanation of an aspect of life during a particular period in the United States. You will also find some photographs. You can use the explanation or the photographs to find ideas for your own writing.

THEME: *LEGACIES*

My desire to write was stimulated by a wish to communicate the simple facts of history and of people's lives.

—Beatrice Siegel

Have you ever traveled to a strange, new place or faced a new way of doing things? What would it be like to move to a different country?

For millions of immigrants coming into the United States, the federal immigration center on Ellis Island in New York Harbor was the first stop. Many immigrants were anxious about what lay ahead for them in America. They also had great hopes for opportunities to improve their lives.

As you read the selection, look for specific details showing what steps immigrants had to go through on Ellis Island.

from

Sam Ellis's Island

by Beatrice Siegel

Renovations to Ellis Island had not yet been completed when it opened as an immigration center. Workers had put in long, hard hours for two years to make major changes. Sam Ellis's Island was expanded, reshaped, and replanted. Its original 3.3 acres was doubled. Ships from foreign ports had poured their ballast into cribs for landfill dug around the island. Ellis Island became the most international piece of land on earth as well as a receiving center for people from around the world.

Workmen had also dredged a twelve-foot channel for docks and slips. Old stone and brick buildings were converted into dormitories and storage bins. New structures included a large two-story central building, a hospital, a boiler room, laundry and electric plants, artesian wells, and cisterns. It took an additional five years before the last workers had finished their jobs. All the new construction was made of wood. On June 15, 1897, the buildings were declared completed, and the last of the workmen wrapped up their tools and left.

That night a fire broke out a little past midnight in the tower of the main hall. The roof collapsed, and flames shot through the new wooden buildings. Everything was gutted, every structure, and all the Castle Garden records were burned. A few stone buildings, remnants of older days, tumbled in the heat of the flames.

Fireboats, police patrols, and all available craft swiftly made their way to the island. They safely evacuated the two to three hundred staff and immigrants lodged there. Many of the immigrants were detainees, but a few had been hospitalized for serious illnesses.

The flames, visible for miles around, lighted up the harbor. From the Battery, where Sam Ellis had once stood and looked across the Hudson to his little island, throngs of onlookers now watched the sparks shoot out of the river.

For days acrid smells hung over the headlands of New Jersey. Ellis Island was a charred, gloomy ruin. Here and there stood a stone wall, a bulwark of Fort Gibson days.

Not only buildings and records lay buried in the ruins; the spirit of Sam Ellis's tiny island was gone. But fire wasn't the only culprit. People had intervened in the natural life of the island, changing its ecology. For many years the Hudson River had been a dumping ground, filled with debris from large cities.

Its ecology, too, had changed. Ellis Island was no longer a shelter for sea birds. Its rich beds of oysters and shellfish had been destroyed. But despite years of landfill and construction, the island lay forever low in the water, its original contours still visible. Now Ellis Island would have a new image. Brick, stone, and ironwork buildings would reflect the power and force of the United States in the industrial age.

Ellis Island had registered close to a million and a half immigrants during the five and a half years prior to the fire. While immigrants were temporarily processed at the Barge Office on the Battery after the fire, elaborate blueprints were drawn up for a new federal immigration center.

Again the island was stretched into a new shape. In 1897 it was a 10-acre site. In 1934 it had been extended to 27.54 acres. Instead of one island there were now three islands connected to each other at first by bridges, then by landfill.

No matter how much Ellis Island expanded, its facilities remained inadequate to handle the restless influx of millions. Word had spread into the rural backwaters and urban alleys of the world that the United States was the land of opportunity. And people came in a huge procession that changed the face of Europe and created new forces in the United States.

The largest wave of immigration, between 1892 and 1924, brought seventeen million through Ellis Island. The number peaked after 1901. They came mostly from Southern and Eastern Europe—Poles, Italians, Russian Jews, Rumanians, Hungarians, Turks, and Greeks. They had made their way to European ports, to Hamburg, Piraeus, Marseilles, and Naples, crowding into the steerage of oceangoing vessels for the hard crossing. In the year 1907 alone, more than one million three hundred thousand aliens arrived. On a single day, April 17, 1907, eleven thousand awaited their turn to be processed.

Like people before them, most came to escape hard lives. They left behind poverty, the army, religious persecution, hunger, and despair. What did they have to lose? A spirit of optimism lighted their minds with dreams, giving them courage to face an unknown world.

Their ships took them through the Narrows and dropped anchor in Upper New York Bay. The first sight to greet them was the Statue of Liberty. Hidden in its shadow was Ellis Island, its flat expanse protected by a seawall. After quarantine inspection, steerage passengers were placed in barges and ferried to the island. They remained crowded together for hours on these open, flat boats, protected neither from hot sun nor freezing cold. They were an exhausted, bewildered mass of people, gripped by fear. Would they pass the examinations? Would the doctor notice a lame leg, an inflamed eye? Would they be shipped back?

From their barges at the quay, immigrants faced an enormous central building called the Registry Hall. Made of brick and limestone, with arched doorways and a huge dome over its two stories, it looked as if built for eternity. Four turreted pinnacles arising from its corners gave the building height and visibility. Within, three enormous crystal and brass fixtures hung from the domed ceiling. Both ceiling and floor were tiled.

The first floor held the waiting room, baggage facilities, transportation offices, money changers, post office, and restaurant. On the second floor were the registration and examination rooms, and administration offices. Other buildings included a chapel, hospital, dormitories, child-care centers, powerhouses, and bathhouses. New facilities were added as the need increased. In all, thirty-three structures covered Ellis Island. It also had its own ferry slip.[1]

Whether Ellis Island was six acres or twenty-seven, procedures did not much vary. Each immigrant was tagged with two numbers. These told inspectors the page and line on the ship's list, called manifest sheets, where the immigrant's name could be found. Slowly lines of people walked across the quay and into the Great Hall for examinations, which took place night and day. From the first days, laughter and tears echoed through the vaulted building. People shouted and cried in forty different languages. For each language an interpreter was standing by.

After dropping off their baggage on the first floor (which many feared to do), arrivals formed lines leading up the center staircase. On the second floor medical personnel examined them for a wide spectrum of diseases ranging from poor eyesight to mental illness. Although experienced doctors could give only brief examinations to the endless lines of aliens, they quickly spotted deformities, skin diseases, and other telltale symptoms. They were on the alert for trachoma, an infectious eye disease that could lead to blindness. Here, the dreaded eye examinations took place. Using a metal instrument, doctors turned eyelids inside out, often a painful procedure.

When there was doubt, physicians put a chalk mark on the immigrant's back or shoulder. The letter *E* meant eyestrain; *H* signified heart disease; *X* stood for mental defects; *L* for lameness. Those detained were directed to wired detention centers. Families cried out in horror when a relative was isolated in one

1. The buildings on Ellis Island are presented in order of importance.

of these cages. About two percent, or about a quarter of a million aliens, were ultimately returned to their countries of origin.

When illnesses were curable, immigrants were directed to dormitories or hospitals, or they were sent to bathhouses to have lice removed. Many were angered by the implication that they had arrived carrying these parasites. They claimed they picked up lice on Ellis Island when forced to sleep on filthy benches and floors because of the overcrowding. Immigrants like Mary Zuk, who arrived in 1912, told their side of the story. "Ellis Island was lousy. Lousy. Bugs all over," she said. Others resented the "humiliating physical, mental, and moral examinations." They were "pushed around, literally pushed," many complained.

The vast majority, about eighty percent, faced another hurdle after they passed the medical examinations. They were directed through passageways into long aisles to be questioned by legal inspectors. In two minutes, officials behind large desks shot a list of thirty questions at each immigrant, checking answers against the ship's manifest. Steamship companies were required to register immigrants' vital facts before they sold tickets.

Inspectors asked: name, birthplace, age, who paid for passage, plans for jobs and housing, family or sponsors. "Are you an anarchist? Are you a polygamist? Do you have a criminal record?"

Those who gave unsatisfactory answers were pulled from the line, chalk-marked *SI*, and held for further questioning by the Board of Special Inquiry.

Finally, for millions there were "landing cards." Fears and anxieties fled. Clutching the precious cards, they fell into the waiting arms of families and friends. Or social agency staffs took them in charge. They were ferried the mile across the Hudson to New York City or a few hundred feet to the New Jersey shore. Thus millions began their lives in another country.[2]

They told and retold their stories, and handed them down to their children. They kept the words alive—Ellis Island. It meant America.

2. The examination process is described in chronological order of events.

Thinking Like a Reader
1. What were the steps in the immigration process on Ellis Island?
2. For what reasons might you want to move to another country or another part of this country?

Write your responses in your journal.

Thinking Like a Writer
3. What order does the writer use in presenting the history of Ellis Island? How does this order help the writer present information clearly?
4. What details does the author use to contrast the feelings of immigrants before, during, and after their arrival at Ellis Island?
5. Imagine that you are one of the immigrants on Ellis Island. Write at least three observations as you go through the entry process.

Write your responses in your journal.

Brainstorm *Vocabulary*

Sam Ellis's Island contains many words related to construction and to shipping. Such words as *cistern, bulwark, turreted pinnacles,* and *vaulted* all come from the vocabulary of construction, or building. Words such as *ballast, steerage,* and *quay* come from ships and shipping. Each specialized activity has its own vocabulary. What activity that you know has a special vocabulary? Create a personal vocabulary list for a special activity by writing its words and phrases in your journal. Compare your list with that of a classmate. Be sure to remember that you can use these words in your writing.

Talk It Over *Explain a Process*

Sam Ellis's Island explains the steps in the immigration process. Imagine that you have been asked to explain an activity you know well to someone who is new to it. You might explain how to change a bicycle tire, how to operate a piece of audio-visual equipment, or how to go through the cafeteria line efficiently. If you think that it would be useful, make notes in your journal listing the steps of the activity you have chosen. Then explain your activity to a partner. Refer to your notes if necessary. After practicing with your partner, you may choose to present your explanation to a larger group or to the whole class.

Quick Write *Commercials*

Write a brief commercial message explaining how to take advantage of an activity in your school or in your community. For example, if you wanted to tell interested parties how they might try out for the local theater group, you could write the following:

Are you interested in joining an interesting theater group? The Glendale Little Theater holds meetings every Thursday night at eight o'clock at the County Recreation Center in Glendale. Would-be actors and technicians are welcome. Auditions will be arranged.

Keep your commercial short and to the point, but include all the necessary information.

Idea Corner *Think of Topics*

Sam Ellis's Island tells how immigrants were received when they first arrived in the United States. The author explained a process that people went through. Explanatory writing can often explain how something works or is done. In your journal begin a list of possible topics for explaining a process. As you think of further possible topics for explaining a process, add them to your list. Keep your list as a source of ideas for composition topics.

PICTURES  *SEEING LIKE A WRITER*

Finding Ideas for Writing
Look at the pictures. Think about what you see. What ideas
about writing an explanation do the pictures give you?
Write your ideas in your journal.

Above: Antique car and period costume

Below: Boston's Beac

views—real and with a stereoscope

at work on a historic house

1 GROUP WRITING: AN EXPLANATORY PARAGRAPH

COOPERATIVE LEARNING

An explanation presents facts to inform an audience. The **purpose** of explanatory writing may be to explain how something works or how to perform an activity. An effective explanation contains several elements that help your **audience** understand the facts clearly.

- Topic Sentence
- Supporting Details
- Transition Words
- Concluding Sentence

Topic Sentence

The selection below explains how the Pony Express worked. As you read the explanation, notice the underlined sentence.

> <u>The Pony Express was established to move mail more quickly than was possible by stagecoach.</u> It followed a route from St. Joseph, Missouri, across mountains and deserts to Sacramento, California, over 1,200 miles away. Along the route were one hundred ninety stations with horses and keepers. A rider would take a sack of mail, jump on his horse, and ride as fast as possible to the next station, fifteen miles away. There, a keeper was waiting with a fresh horse. The first sack of mail left St. Joseph on April 3, 1860, and reached its destination in ten days, more than a week faster than ever before. Later, riders went even faster. The Pony Express operated until October 1861, when telegraph lines to California made it unnecessary. It was a short but glorious chapter in the history of the Old West.

The underlined sentence contains the main idea of the paragraph. This kind of sentence is called a **topic sentence.** A topic sentence often is placed at the beginning of a paragraph, but it may also be placed in the middle or at the end. The writer must decide where to place the topic sentence for best effect.

Guided Practice: Writing a Topic Sentence

As a class, choose one of the topics from the list below, or think of one on which everybody agrees. You may wish to look through your journal for ideas. Narrow the topic, if necessary, and explore your ideas with your classmates. Then, write a good topic sentence for your explanatory paragraph.

how to grow tomatoes   how a simple camera works
how to train a dog   how to make a compass
how to make a terrarium   how a baseball bat is made

Supporting Details and Transition Words

The **supporting details** in an explanation provide information that develops or supports the topic sentence in the paragraph. Supporting details in explanatory writing may be facts, examples, reasons, or steps in a process.

The supporting details in explanations are arranged in a logical order. Information can be given in **chronological order,** or time order, as in the sample paragraph. Facts may also be presented in **order of importance,** where the most important facts or steps are presented first and less important ones after that. Facts may also be arranged to show a **comparison.** For a paragraph that explains how to do something or how something works, however, chronological order is the most clear and direct, and easiest for the reader to follow.

Transition words and phrases help to show readers how ideas in an explanation are connected. Carefully selected transition words can guide the reader from one fact, step, or comparison to the next, presenting the writer's thoughts in a clear manner. In the sample paragraph on page 190, the transition words are *there* and *later.*

Guided Practice: Listing Details

With your classmates, list supporting details that explain the topic sentence that you composed together. Arrange the details in chronological order. Make sure you have not left out any important facts that your audience will need to know in order to understand your explanation. Use transition words to connect ideas.

Concluding Sentence

An explanatory paragraph often ends with a **concluding sentence.** The concluding sentence may

1. summarize the information given in the paragraph;
2. restate the topic sentence in different words; or
3. leave the audience with an important point to consider.

In the explanatory paragraph about the Pony Express, the concluding sentence leaves the audience with an important idea to consider.

Guided Practice: Writing a Concluding Sentence

As a class, decide on an effective concluding sentence for the explanation you are composing. Discuss several before you agree on the one that you think is the most effective.

Putting an Explanatory Paragraph Together

With your class you have explored ideas for an explanation, written a topic sentence, listed supporting details, and arranged the details in a logical order. You have also thought about appropriate transition words and a concluding sentence for your explanation.

Guided Practice: Writing an Explanation

Now write your explanation. Look at your topic sentence to make sure that it states the main idea of your explanation. Add any missing details that you think your audience will need to know in order to understand your explanation. Eliminate facts that do not support your topic. Add transition words to connect your ideas and guide your reader. Then decide whether the purpose of the concluding sentence that you wrote earlier is suitable. When you are satisfied that the concluding sentence is effective, add it to your paragraph.

Share your explanation with a friend. Ask if your friend was able to follow your explanation and if he or she found it informative.

Checklist An Explanatory Paragraph

When you write an explanation, keep a checklist of the important points that you need to remember. A sample checklist is shown below. Copy it and add any other points you want to remember. Keep it in your writing folder and refer to it as you write your explanation.

CHECKLIST

- Remember purpose and audience.
- Include a topic sentence.
- Provide supporting details.
- Arrange details in a logical order.
- Use transition words.
- Write an effective concluding sentence.
- _____

2 THINKING AND WRITING: Comparing and Contrasting

Explanations often tell how something works or how something is done. Sometimes you can explain something most clearly by comparing and contrasting it with a related subject. When you **compare** two things, you show their similarities. When you **contrast** two things, you show their differences.

One student was interested in learning to play the clarinet. Since he knew something about the related topic of playing the recorder, he decided to write an explanation showing the similarities and differences between the two instruments. After brainstorming for ideas, he organized the information in a chart.

	Similarities	Differences
Type:	woodwind instrument	
Method:	blow through mouth-piece, place fingers over holes or keys	—recorder: whistle-type mouthpiece, 8 holes, no keys —clarinet: reed in mouthpiece, 17 keys
Tone:	mellow	
Uses:		—recorder: early music, folk music —clarinet: band, pop, orchestra, classical

Thinking Like a Writer

■ What similarities are listed? What differences?

■ Why would making a chart like this be helpful when you write an explanation?

When you compare and contrast in an explanation, there are different ways you can arrange your information. You can present all the details about one subject first and then give all the facts about the other subject. Another way is to explain the similarities or differences point by point, alternating between the two subjects.

Notice how the writer used the point-by-point method in the following explanation.

> The recorder and the clarinet are both woodwind instruments with mellow tone, but there are significant differences between them. Both are tubes that are played by blowing into a mouthpiece. Notes are changed by covering holes in the tube. The recorder's mouthpiece is a simple, whistle type, however, while the clarinet's mouthpiece contains a reed that causes the air to vibrate in the tube. The recorder player closes the eight holes in the tube by placing fingers directly over them. The clarinet's seventeen keys give the clarinet player a wider range of notes. Finally, the clarinet player has more options for play—both classical and popular music in bands and orchestras. Recorder players are limited to playing simple music, mainly early music and folk music.

THINKING APPLICATION Comparing and Contrasting

COOPERATIVE LEARNING

Think through the exercises below, using what you know about comparing and contrasting. You may want to discuss your ideas with a group of classmates.

1. Decide which pairs of topics listed below would be appropriate to compare and contrast in an explanation.
   a. plants at sea level and at 10,000 feet
   b. porpoises and dolphins
   c. field hockey and ice hockey
   d. the trumpet and the violin
   e. Japan and California

2. Choose the sentences below that could be used in an explanation that compares.
   a. California and New York both contain major seaports.
   b. California and New York are our country's two most populous states.
   c. California is on the West Coast; New York is on the East Coast.
   d. Each state contains both large cities and rural areas.
   e. Parts of California have much summerlike weather; parts of New York have very severe winters.

3 INDEPENDENT WRITING: An Explanation

Prewrite: Step 1

You have learned the basic elements for writing effective explanations. Now you are ready to choose a topic for writing an explanation of your own. Abby, a student your age, chose a topic in this way.

Choosing a Topic

Abby's first step was to make a list of subjects that interested her and needed explanation. She looked in her journal for ideas.

space satellites
✓ farming
earthquakes
ocean travel

Abby liked the second item on her list best, but she felt it was too broad. She decided to narrow her topic and compare and contrast two periods in farming, before and after the all-purpose tractor. She thought that members of her class would be a good **audience.** Her **purpose** would be to present a clear and informative explanation.

Abby then went to the library and did some research on her subject. She made the following notes.

farming before the tractor	farming after the tractor
small family farms	large tracts of land
horse power	huge farming machinery
hand labor, few machines	harvest by machine
produced enough to feed family, sold small amount	specialized crops for market could farm larger area with fewer people

Exploring Ideas: Charting Strategy

Abby thought that she had some good ideas but needed to organize her information. She made the following chart and added some new information to complete it.

	Similarities	Differences
Purpose:	produce food	—early farming: mostly for personal use, some sales —modern farm: mostly commercial
Size:		—early farm: small —modern farm: large
Methods:		—early farm: horse and plow, manual —modern farm: huge machines, including tractors
Requirements:	love of nature, physical strength	—modern farming: understanding of business, chemistry, agriculture, mechanics

Thinking Like a Writer

- How did Abby organize her notes?
- What similarities does she list? What differences?
- What details did she add? Why?

YOUR TURN

Think of two subjects to compare and contrast in an explanation. Use **Pictures** or your journal to help you find ideas. Follow these steps.

JOURNAL

- Write a list of ideas.
- Choose two subjects that can be compared and contrasted in a brief explanation. Your subjects should not be so different that they are unrelated.
- Narrow your topic, if necessary.
- Think about your purpose and audience.

Explore your ideas in a comparison and contrast chart. You can add to or delete from your chart at any time.

WRITING PROCESS

Write a First Draft: Step 2

Abby prepared a planning checklist to use as she wrote her explanation. Then she began to think about how she could use her comparison and contrast chart. She decided to explain the similarities and differences on a point-by-point basis, alternating between the two subjects. She knew that transition words would be important to her explanation.

Abby wrote her first draft without stopping to make corrections. She knew she could make changes later.

Abby's First Draft

Early farmers relied on horses to draw the plow and other simple farm machines. today on the other hand huge machines performs almost every phaze of farm work. One of these machines is a tractor. I've seen one on a farm. Early farms was small, family farms. People raised a variety of crops for their own use and sold only what was left over.

After the invention of the tractor, Farmers could plant more land, and they began to plant one crop and to sell most of what they raised. Both early farmers and modren ones has shared a love of growing things; but today's farmers must also be businesspeople mechanics chemists and agricultural specialists.

Planning Checklist
- Remember purpose and audience.
- Include a topic sentence.
- Arrange details in a logical order in paragraphs.
- Use transition words.
- Write an effective concluding sentence.

YOUR TURN

Write the first draft of your explanation. As you write, ask yourself the following questions.

- What does my audience need to know in order for me to accomplish my purpose?
- How clearly does my topic sentence state my main idea?
- How can I best organize the details in my explanation?
- How well do the transition words connect my ideas?

TIME-OUT You might want to take some time out before you revise. In that way you will be able to revise your writing with a fresh eye.

Revise: Step 3

After she finished her first draft, Abby read it over to herself to see if there were any improvements she wanted to make. Then she shared her draft with a classmate and asked for suggestions about how she might make it a better explanation.

> Your explanation is interesting, Abby, but I wasn't sure what your topic was at the beginning.

> Thanks. I'll have to add a topic sentence.

After Abby met with her friend, she looked again at her planning checklist. She realized that she had also forgotten to include an effective concluding sentence. She placed a check mark next to both points to remind herself to make the changes in her first draft.

Abby began revising her first draft. Besides making the changes she marked on her checklist, she thought about other possible improvements. What details could she add to make her explanation clearer? What words could she change to be more precise? Was her decision to alternate back and forth between subjects the correct choice? Did she use transition words effectively?

As she revised her draft, Abby thought more about her **purpose** and **audience.** She decided that her comparisons and contrasts made her point and that her language was suitable for her audience.

Abby reworked her first draft. She added a topic sentence and concluding sentence. She changed some words and sentences. Look on the next page to see the corrections that Abby made.

Revising Checklist
- Remember purpose and audience.
- ✔ Include a topic sentence.
- Provide supporting details.
- Arrange details in a logical order.
- Use transition words.
- ✔ Write an effective concluding sentence.

Abby's Revised Draft

Farming today is very different from the family farm of a century ago.

Early farmers relied on horses to draw the plow and other simple farm machines. today on the other hand huge machines performs almost every phaze of farm work. One of these machines is a tractor. I've seen one on a farm. Early farms was small, family farms.

where

People raised a variety of crops for their own use and sold only what was left over.

After the invention of the tractor, Farmers could plant more land, and they began to plant one crop and to sell most of what *specialize in* they raised. Both early farmers and modren ones has shared a love of growing things; but today's farmers must also be businesspeople mechanics chemists and agricultural specialists.

Advances in science and engineering have greatly changed the way America produces food.

Thinking Like a Writer

WISE
WORD
CHOICE

- What did Abby add to the beginning of her explanation? Why?
- Do you think the concluding sentence she added is effective? Why?
- What sentences did she combine? Why do you think she combined them?

YOUR TURN

Read your first draft carefully and make any necessary revisions. Ask yourself these questions, or ask a classmate to give you suggestions.

- How will adding or changing the topic sentence improve my explanation?
- What details do I need to add or rearrange to make my writing clearer?
- How can I improve my concluding sentence?
- What sentences can I combine to avoid repeating words?

Proofread: Step 4

After Abby revised her first draft, she knew that she still had to proofread her writing.

Part of Abby's Proofread Draft

¶ Farming today is very different from the family farm of a century ago.

Early farmers relied on horses to draw the plow and other simple

farm machines. today on the other hand huge machines performs

almost every ~~phaze~~ *phase* of farm work. ~~One of these machines is a tractor.~~

~~I've seen one on a farm.~~ Early farms was *were* small, family farms,

where People raised a variety of crops for their own use and sold only

what was left over.

After the invention of the tractor, Farmers could plant more

land, and they began to ~~plant~~ *specialize in* one crop and to sell most of what

they raised. Both early farmers and modren ones has *have* shared a

love of growing things; but today's farmers must also be

businesspeople mechanics chemists and agricultural specialists.

Advances in science and engineering have greatly changed the way America produces food.

YOUR TURN

Proofreading Practice

Proofread the following paragraph. Then write the paragraph, making all the necessary corrections.

My friends and I celebrates the Fourth of july in different

ways. I quietly recall the value of our precious freedoms,

but my friends prefer parades and waving flags. However,

we all get together in spite of differences and have an

picnic and enjoy the freedom of celebration

Proofreading Checklist
- Did I indent each paragraph?
- Did I spell all words correctly?
- Did I use capital letters correctly?
- Did I use commas and other punctuation marks correctly?
- Do subjects and verbs agree in all sentences?

Applying Your Proofreading Skills

Proofread the explanation you have written. Review your proofreading checklist and **The Grammar Connection** and **The Mechanics Connection** below. Use the proofreading marks to make changes.

THE GRAMMAR CONNECTION

Remember these rules about making subjects and verbs agree.

- A singular subject takes the singular form of a verb; a plural subject takes the plural form of a verb.
- The singular form of most verbs in the present tense ends in *s* or *es*.

Drought **causes** crop failure.
Crops **grow** poorly in dry weather.

Check your explanation. Do your subjects and verbs agree?

Proofreading Marks
Indent ¶
Add ∧
Add a comma ⋏
Add quotation marks ⩔ ⩔
Add a period ⊙
Take out ⌇
Capitalize ≡
Lower-case letter /
Reverse the order ∿

THE MECHANICS CONNECTION

Remember these rules about using commas.

- Use commas to separate words or phrases in a series.
- Use commas to set off introductory words, nouns of direct address, and interrupting words or phrases.

The weather was dry, sunny, and windy.
Yes, Sherman, farming is risky. It is, on the other hand, necessary and important work.

Review your writing. Have you used commas correctly?

Publish: Step 5

Abby made a neat, final copy of her writing by typing it on her mother's word processor. Then she printed further copies for the members of her class. She also submitted a copy of her work to the school newspaper, which publishes student writing about varied subjects of interest in each issue. Abby also realized that the students in her social studies class might enjoy hearing her paper. She received permission to use it as a social studies report.

YOUR TURN

Make a neat, final copy of your explanation. Then decide on a good way to share your writing. The **Sharing Suggestions** box below may give you some ideas.

SHARING SUGGESTIONS

Illustrate your explanation with drawings, diagrams, or photographs and share it with a younger class in your school.	With your classmates, create a file of explanations. Organize your file alphabetically and create a subject index to help others use it.	Read your explanation to an interested friend or family member.

4 SPEAKING AND LISTENING: Giving Instructions

Perhaps you have had to give someone directions to a particular place or for operating a piece of equipment. Writing instructions and giving them orally involve many of the same steps.

First, you must consider your purpose and audience. Think about the information your audience will need to know to follow your instructions. Then, review the steps involved in your instructions. You may wish to write down notes to make sure you have included all the necessary information. One student's notes are shown below.

TOPIC: How to Make Candles

AUDIENCE: Group of Classmates

— Melt old candles of similar colors or paraffin wax in a coffee can set in boiling water.

— Weight two ends of cotton string and place them over a wooden spoon.

— Cool the wax slightly and remove any dirt or old wicks.

— Color the wax with crayon shavings.

— Dip the string in and out of the wax until candles are desired thickness.

■ Why is it important to arrange the steps in the right order in a set of instructions?

■ How should the writer rearrange the notes shown above?

SPEAKING GUIDELINES: Giving Instructions

1. Remember that your purpose is to give clear information.
2. State your topic in the first sentence.
3. Consider what your specific audience will need to know.
4. Plan the steps in your instructions. Arrange the steps in the right order.
5. Use transition words such as *first*, *after*, *before*, and *next* to help your audience see each step.
6. Speak in a clear, audible voice. Look at your listeners.

The student who made the notes about making candles organized her notes and used them in giving the following talk. She chose to write out her complete talk, but this step was unnecessary. She could have given much the same report from her notes.

How to Make Candles

With a few simple materials, you can make candles the way American colonists did, by dipping. First, prepare the wax. You can use old candle ends or paraffin wax from the supermarket. Melt the wax carefully in a coffee can set in boiling water. Then let it cool slightly and remove any dirt or old wicks. At this point, you can add color to your wax with crayon shavings. Then carefully reheat the wax.

Weight both ends of a piece of cotton string with anything small and heavy, like metal buttons. This will be your wick. Let the ends dangle over the bowl of a wooden spoon. Dip the wick into the wax and remove it to let it cool. The weights should keep your candles straight. Repeat this procedure until your candles are the thickness you want. When the wax is hard, cut the string in half. You will have two colonial candles.

SPEAKING APPLICATION Giving Instructions

Using your classmates as an audience, prepare a set of instructions about how to do or make something. Use the speaking guidelines above to help you plan and deliver your talk. Your classmates will be using the guidelines below as they listen to your instructions.

LISTENING GUIDELINES: Instructions

1. Listen for each step in the instructions.
2. Listen for the order of each step.
3. Take notes to help you to remember information.
4. Ask questions if the instructions are unclear.
5. Repeat the instructions to yourself or to the speaker to make sure you have understood them.

Writing About Science

Science is concerned with understanding how and why things work. An important part of a scientist's job is to explain, sometimes by comparing or contrasting new discoveries to something more familiar. Scientists share their findings with other scientists by means of scientific journals and through talks at scientific conferences. The general public hears about their work through science reporting in newspapers and magazines.

There are two main categories of science: *pure* and *applied*. People who study **pure science** experiment to find out how things work. These are the dedicated men and women who spend long hours seeking answers in hospitals, laboratories, observatories, and libraries. The men and women who study **applied science** examine the ways in which scientific discoveries can be practically applied. They are responsible for finding uses for discoveries ranging from "miracle" glues to "miracle" drugs. Together, scientists have brought many important discoveries to modern life.

ACTIVITIES

Make a Diagram

Review a favorite science experiment you have read about or have performed. Imagine that you are a scientist and create a diagram that explains how to perform the experiment. Then show your diagram to a partner to see if your work is clear.

Write a Hypothesis

A hypothesis is a possible explanation to a scientific problem. A hypothesis can be tested by means of experiments. Think of an aspect of nature that arouses your curiosity—for example, the causes of eclipses, hurricanes, or rainbows. Write a paragraph that explains the possible cause and effects of this phenomenon. Then do some research to see if your hypothesis was correct. Revise your paragraph to include the facts you discover

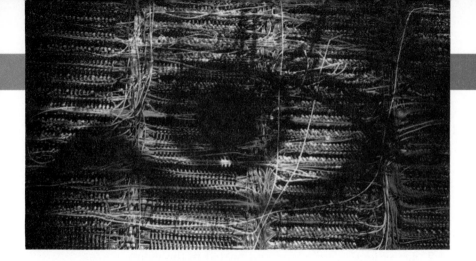

Respond to Literature

Computers may seem to think faster and better than human beings; but, in fact, they are not nearly as complex as the human brain. Computer scientists continually search for ways to create computers that "think" as people do. Science writer T.A. Heppenheimer explains why this task is so difficult.

Cells and Circuits

... The brain consists of billions of neurons, or nerve cells, each one connected to thousands of others in a complex network. Individual neurons are simple and expendable; the net's the thing that gives the brain its zing. Or as one scientist puts it: "The brain has this wonderful property— you can go through and shoot out every tenth neuron and never miss them. That's a property computers just don't have; if you break a single wire you're in trouble."

A conventional computer is not like the brain at all. Its main components are typically a single central processor and a main memory. The processor consists of an array of simple transistor circuits that perform the electronic equivalent of elementary logic operations. In sharp contrast to the neuron, each logic circuit receives inputs from only two or three other circuits and usually sends its output to only one other circuit. But with enough of these elements the processor can do arithmetic. And that is what it does best, one step at a time, following detailed commands that it fetches one-by-one from the memory; the commands are the program. If you were to shoot out even one logic circuit, the whole sequence of calculations would probably go awry.

UNIT CHECKUP

LESSON 1

Group Writing: An Explanatory Paragraph (page 190)
Imagine that you are planning to explain glassmaking in colonial times. You wish to explain how glassmaking was done and the skills it required. Write a topic sentence. Then decide which of the following details you would use in your explanation. Write those details on a separate piece of paper.

1. Glass was used in the colonies and exported to England.
2. Ingredients were mixed and heated to the melting point.
3. Melted glass was gathered onto the end of a blowpipe.
4. The first glassworks in Jamestown closed in 1609.
5. An expert glassblower blew the glass into a bubble.
6. Soft glass bubbles were shaped with tongs and shears.

LESSON 2

Thinking: Comparing and Contrasting (page 194)
Write a paragraph contrasting fossil fuel energy with solar energy. Use the notes below and add your own.

	Solar Power	Fossil Fuels
supply:	unlimited supply	supply limited
waste:	no waste	smoke, ash, smog
cost:	free once installed	expensive to buy

LESSON 3

Writing an Explanatory Paragraph (page 196)
Compare and contrast two kinds of science, for example, botany and zoology. Explore the topic and organize your notes. Be sure to write a topic sentence that states your main idea. Use appropriate transition words to connect your ideas. Write a concluding sentence that summarizes your main idea. Revise and proofread your work carefully.

LESSON 4

Speaking and Listening: Giving Instructions (page 204)
In a paragraph, summarize the guidelines for giving effective oral instructions.

THEME PROJECT TIME CAPSULE

You have read and written explanatory paragraphs about topics that interested you, from music and crafts to history and science. You have shared your explanations with others in different ways.

Now imagine that you have been asked to participate in a project that will explain life in the late twentieth century to people of the future. To do this, you will make a time capsule. What would you want someone in the distant future to know about you and your friends? What items from today's culture would you display? Look at the picture below. Use the picture as the basis for a discussion with your classmates about what makes life today distinct from life in other times. What do you have and do that belongs uniquely to this time and age?

As a class, create a time capsule. Here are some suggestions.

- Collect ten to fifteen items that will fit into a large box, and which you believe represent the present time.
- Try to represent various activities and different viewpoints. What will people of the future want to know?
- Explain why you think each selection belongs in the time capsule.
- Make models or diagrams of any items you cannot actually seal in the capsule.

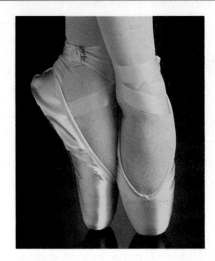

Pronouns

In this unit you will learn about pronouns. Using pronouns is a convenient way to avoid repeating nouns. By not repeating nouns, you can add variety to your writing.

Discuss Read the poem on the opposite page. What "footprints on the sands of time" would you like to leave?

Creative Expression The theme of this unit is *Achievements.* There are many ways to achieve. Write a list of ways in which people can achieve. Write your list in your journal.

Lives of great men all remind us
We can make our lives sublime.
And, departing, leave behind us
Footprints on the sands of time.

—Henry Wadsworth Longfellow,
from "A Psalm of Life"

1 PERSONAL PRONOUNS

A pronoun is a word that can take the place of a noun or a group of words acting as a noun.

You have learned that a noun is a word that names a person, a place, a thing, or an idea. A **pronoun** is a word that can take the place of a noun.

> Andy likes to read. **He** enjoys reading biographies.

A **personal pronoun** is a pronoun that refers to a person or thing. Some personal pronouns are used as the subjects of sentences. These pronouns are called **subject pronouns.**

> Sara reads books about inventors. **She** enjoys them.

Other personal pronouns are used as the objects of verbs or as the objects of prepositions. These pronouns are called **object pronouns.**

> Sara is interested in Edison. She read about **him.**

Subject Pronouns		Object Pronouns	
Singular	**Plural**	**Singular**	**Plural**
I	we	me	us
you	you	you	you
he, she, it	they	him, her, it	them

Guided Practice

Name the correct personal pronoun to use in place of the underlined word or words.

Example: <u>Americans</u> cherish the story of Thomas Edison.
They

1. <u>Thomas Alva Edison</u> was born in 1847.
2. Edison's inventions made <u>Edison</u> famous.
3. One of <u>the inventions</u> was the record player.
4. The carbon microphone was also invented by <u>Edison</u>.
5. <u>Motion pictures</u> were made possible by his work.

 THINK

- How can I decide if a word is a personal pronoun?

REMEMBER

- A **pronoun** is a word that can take the place of a noun or a group of words acting as a noun.
- A **subject pronoun** is used as the subject of a sentence. An **object pronoun** is used as the object of a verb or preposition.

More Practice

A. Write the pronoun that correctly replaces the underlined noun or group of words.

Example: His special gifts made concepts easy for Edison.
        him

6. Thomas Alva Edison was born in Milan, Ohio.
7. The Edisons moved to Michigan when Thomas was seven.
8. Thomas could not adapt to the routine of school.
9. He was educated at home by his mother.
10. As a boy Edison performed physics experiments.
11. Edison set up a laboratory in his cellar, and he tested many laws of physics in the laboratory.
12. At age twelve he got a job to pay for his chemicals.

B. Write each sentence, replacing the underlined noun or group of words with the correct pronoun. Then write whether the pronoun is a **subject pronoun** or **object pronoun.**

Example: Edison's mother influenced his career.
        She influenced his career.
        subject pronoun

13. When Edison was sixteen, Edison learned telegraphy.
14. Electricity fascinated Edison.
15. Edison's first invention was an electric vote recorder.
16. Edison's favorite invention was the phonograph.
17. An electrical system was created by Edison.
18. This system led to America's electric lighting industry.
19. Edison also excelled in many other areas.
20. Edison's companies became a huge corporation.

Extra Practice, page 236

WRITING APPLICATION A Biographical Sketch

Write a brief biographical sketch of an inventor whose achievements interest you. Exchange sketches with a classmate; identify the personal pronouns in each other's work.

2 PRONOUNS AND ANTECEDENTS

You know that a pronoun is a word that can take the place of a noun or a group of words acting as a noun. The word or group of words that a pronoun replaces or refers to is called the **antecedent** of the pronoun.

Antecedent   Pronoun

People can excel even if **they** have disabilities.

Always make sure that the pronoun reference to the antecedent is clear. Rewrite a sentence to avoid any ambiguity.

VAGUE: The instructors taught the students Braille, and they practiced every day.

CLEAR: The instructors taught the students Braille, and the students practiced every day.

A pronoun must agree with its antecedent in **person** (first, second, or third), **number** (singular or plural), and **gender** (masculine, feminine, or neuter).

Beethoven continued to compose music after **he** became deaf. (third-person, singular, masculine pronoun)

Louis Braille invented a **system** of writing for blind people, and **it** is still in use today. (third-person, singular, neuter pronoun)

Guided Practice

Read each sentence. Identify the antecedent of the underlined pronoun.

Example: Disabled people often adjust if <u>they</u> receive encouragement. *people*

1. Helen Keller triumphed over her disabilities, and <u>she</u> became a famous author and lecturer.
2. Her life was extraordinary, and <u>it</u> inspired many people.
3. An illness struck Helen, and it left <u>her</u> blind, deaf, and mute.
4. Her parents sought help, and <u>they</u> hired Anne Sullivan.
5. Anne was a "miracle worker" because <u>she</u> helped Helen so.

 **THINK**

■ How do I choose a pronoun that agrees with its antecedent?

REMEMBER

- The **antecedent** of a pronoun is the word or group of words that a pronoun refers to or replaces. A pronoun must agree with its antecedent in person, number, and gender.

More Practice

A. Write the antecedent of the underlined pronoun.

Example: When Anne began working with Helen, Helen gave <u>her</u> many difficult moments.   *Anne*

6. Anne was hard-working, and <u>she</u> was patient and kind.
7. Helen needed Anne; she greatly depended on <u>her</u>.
8. Anne taught Helen every name had a sound associated with <u>it</u>.
9. After Helen learned sign language by touch, <u>she</u> was able to communicate her thoughts and feelings.
10. Anne taught Helen to read Braille, and taught <u>her</u> to type.
11. These skills encouraged Helen, and <u>they</u> helped her always.
12. In writing about her accomplishments, Helen said that without Anne she could not have achieved <u>them</u>.

B. Write each sentence. Write each pronoun and antecedent.

Example: The struggle for an education was frustrating, but it was also rewarding.   *it struggle*

13. Helen had another good teacher; she was Sarah Fuller.
14. Helen attended a private school, and she read in Braille.
15. Anne accompanied Helen to classes; after school Anne repeated the lectures to her by touch.
16. Helen took exams for Radcliffe College; she passed them.
17. Anne accompanied Helen and assisted her in many ways.
18. Helen won honors, and she won them with Anne's help.
19. After graduation Helen and Anne lived near Boston, where they worked together on Helen's autobiography.
20. Helen undertook many careers, among them author and lecturer.

Extra Practice, page 237

WRITING APPLICATION

Interview someone whom you admire. Then write your interview or write an imaginary interview. Exchange interviews with a classmate and identify the pronouns and their antecedents in each other's work.

COOPERATIVE
LEARNING

3 USING SUBJECT AND OBJECT PRONOUNS

You know that personal pronouns can be in the nominative or objective case. Use the **nominative case** for pronouns that are the subject of a sentence. Use the **objective case** for pronouns that are the objects of verbs or prepositions.

Nominative Case		Objective Case	
Singular	**Plural**	**Singular**	**Plural**
I	we	me	us
you	you	you	you
he, she, it	they	him, her, it	them

1. Use the nominative case for a pronoun in a compound subject. **He** and **I** like cast-iron buildings.
2. Use the objective case for a pronoun in a compound object. Hal went to the museum with **her** and **me.**
3. Use *I* or *me* last in a compound subject or object. Tom and **I** found a photograph of him and **me.**
4. In formal writing, use the nominative case of a pronoun after the linking verb *be.* The recipient was **she.**

Guided Practice

Tell whether the underlined pronoun is in the nominative or objective case.

Example: <u>He</u> and I bought a book about architects.
      nominative

1. David and <u>I</u> read a book about Frank Lloyd Wright.
2. His life and art fascinate David and <u>me</u>.
3. Some think that the greatest American architect was <u>he</u>.
4. When Wright was a young child, <u>he</u> and his mother used blocks and paper to build models of buildings.
5. Several buildings in Chicago were designed by <u>him</u>.

 THINK

- How do I decide whether to use the nominative or objective case of a pronoun?

REMEMBER

- Use the **nominative case** of a pronoun when the pronoun is part of a compound subject.
- Use the **objective case** of a pronoun when the pronoun is part of a compound object of a verb or preposition.

More Practice

A. Write the pronoun that correctly completes the sentence.

Example: Architecture influences (we, us).   *us*

6. Frank Lloyd Wright was a great architect; the modern movement was led by (he, him) and others.
7. Architecture interested both his mother and (he, him).
8. His success was perhaps due to (her, she) and early training.
9. (He, Him) and other young designers worked together.
10. Wright and (them, they) worked on well-known buildings.
11. My favorite architect is (him, he).
12. To both his clients and (him, he), his designs were successful.

B. Write each sentence, replacing the underlined noun or group of words with the correct pronoun form. Then write **nominative** or **objective** to identify its case.

Example: Architects work toward individual styles.
    They work toward individual styles.
    nominative

13. The "Prairie Style" was associated with Wright.
14. The homes were built near Chicago.
15. Low horizontal lines were a part of this style.
16. The architect with the best ideas was perhaps Wright.
17. Wright and his style became famous.
18. The Depression had a severe impact on Wright.
19. Several of his buildings and their designs have been destroyed.
20. His designs for the Johnson Wax Company building and the Guggenheim Museum are among his finest.

Extra Practice, Practice Plus, pages 238–239

WRITING APPLICATION A Descriptive Paragraph

With a partner, select a building or structure that you both like and write a description of it. Ask another classmate to identify the case of each personal pronoun.

4 POSSESSIVE PRONOUNS

Sometimes you use pronouns to show who or what has or owns something. These pronouns are called **possessive pronouns.** A possessive pronoun can take the place of a possessive noun.

> **Margot's** talents are evident in **her** paintings.

Possessive pronouns have two forms. One form is used before a noun. The other form is used alone.

Used Before a Noun		Used Alone	
my	our	mine	ours
your	your	yours	yours
his, her, its	their	his, hers, its	theirs

A possessive pronoun must agree with its antecedent in person (first, second, or third), number (singular or plural), and gender (masculine, feminine, or neuter).

> The **painting** looked better in **its** new frame.

Possessive pronouns are not spelled with apostrophes.

> The colorful pastel painting is **hers.**   (not *her's*)

The contractions *it's, you're,* and *they're* should not be confused with the possessive pronouns *its, your,* and *their.*

Guided Practice

Name the correct possessive pronoun to use in place of the underlined possessive noun.

Example: This is one of Hopper's paintings.   *his*

1. Edward Hopper is William's favorite painter.
2. Hopper's paintings are known for the paintings' realism.
3. Hopper was interested in a painting's mood.
4. Hopper's use of color is simple but strong.
5. Observers' appreciation of a Hopper painting is often great.

 THINK

■ How can I tell the difference between a possessive pronoun and a contraction?

REMEMBER

- A **possessive pronoun** is a personal pronoun that names who or what has or owns something.
- A possessive pronoun is never spelled with an apostrophe.

More Practice

A. Write each sentence. Draw one line under each possessive pronoun and two lines under its antecedent.

Example: We began to appreciate our American stylists.

> <u>We</u> <u>began</u> <u>to</u> <u>appreciate</u> <u>our</u> <u>American stylists.</u>

6. Did you enjoy your visit to the art museum?

7. Mary Cassatt spent most of her life in France.

8. Cassatt's paintings are admired for their style.

9. I like this painting because of its colors.

10. Cassatt admired Peter Paul Rubens's subjects and his style.

11. Studies and travels left their imprint on Cassatt's work.

12. Cassatt's paintings were appreciated for their brushstrokes.

B. Write each sentence, using the correct possessive pronoun in the blank.

Example: Cassatt was born in America, but she developed ____ art in France.

> *Cassatt was born in America, but she developed her art in France.*

13. Cassatt exhibited ____ work in Paris.

14. The artist Edgar Degas saw her work and admired ____ originality.

15. She accepted ____ invitation to show her work.

16. Many artists entered ____ paintings in the exhibit.

17. Few American paintings were as well liked as ____ .

18. Cassatt exhibited again and ____ popularity grew.

19. The critics and public gave Cassatt ____ high regard.

20. Americans were slower to recognize her work for ____ merit.

Extra Practice, page 240

WRITING APPLICATION A Story

Write a brief story that has a famous artist as the main character. Then, exchange compositions with a classmate and identify the possessive pronouns in each other's work.

INDEFINITE PRONOUNS

Indefinite pronouns do not refer to particular people, places, things, or ideas. Most indefinite pronouns are singular. Some are plural.

> **Everyone** *has* a favorite Gershwin song.   (singular)
> **Few** *dislike* his compositions.   (plural)

	Indefinite Pronouns			
Singular	another anybody anyone each either	everybody everyone everything much	neither nobody no one nothing	one somebody someone something
Plural	both	few	many	others	several
Singular or Plural	all	any	most	none	some

Some indefinite pronouns take either a singular or a plural verb, depending on the phrase that follows the pronoun.

> **Most** *of Gershwin's music* **is** popular.   (singular)
> **Most** *of his melodies* **are** memorable.   (plural)

Guided Practice

Identify the indefinite pronoun in each sentence.

Example: Everyone loves Gershwin's music.
>   *Everyone*

1. One of George Gershwin's most popular songs is "Summertime."
2. Another is "I Got Rhythm."
3. Many of the lyrics to his songs were written by his brother.
4. All of Gershwin's songs are American in spirit.
5. Several celebrate his love of life.

THINK

- When using an indefinite pronoun, how do I know whether to use a singular or a plural verb?

REMEMBER

- An **indefinite pronoun** is a pronoun that does not refer to a particular person, place, thing, or idea.
- Use a singular verb with a singular indefinite pronoun. Use a plural verb with a plural indefinite pronoun.

More Practice

A. Write the indefinite pronoun in each sentence.

Example: Almost anyone can hum a Gershwin tune. *anyone*

6. One of America's favorite composers is George Gershwin.
7. As a young boy, nothing but street games interested him.
8. Then something made him realize the beauty of music.
9. After he heard a classmate play the violin, everything in his life took second place to music.
10. All of the boy's free time was spent on music.
11. Most of his early musical instruction was taught by Charles Hambitzer.
12. Several of his songs are now world famous.

B. Write each sentence, using the correct form of the verb.

Example: Some of these influences (was, were) derived from jazz.
Some of these influences were derived from jazz.

13. Many of Gershwin's songs (was, were) written for Broadway.
14. Some of Gershwin's music (was, were) considered classical.
15. One of these compositions (was, were) *Rhapsody in Blue.*
16. Several of his classical compositions (was, were) for piano.
17. Most of his finest music (is, are) included in his folk opera *Porgy and Bess.*
18. Some of those songs (has, have) become American classics.
19. Much of his music (bring, brings) enjoyment.
20. Most of his compositions (is, are) appreciated as important contributions to American culture.

Extra Practice, page 241

WRITING APPLICATION A Comparison

Write a comparison between two kinds of music, books, or foods you enjoy. Then exchange papers with a classmate and identify the indefinite pronouns in each other's work.

6 REFLEXIVE AND INTENSIVE PRONOUNS

A **reflexive pronoun** is a special pronoun that points the action of the verb back to the subject.

Eva congratulated **herself** on the report she wrote.
Mark gave **himself** enough time to do his report.

Singular	myself	yourself	herself, himself	itself
Plural	ourselves	yourselves	themselves	

Never use *hisself* for *himself* and *theirselves* for *themselves*.
Do not use reflexive pronouns where a subject or object pronoun belongs.

> **CORRECT:** Sue and I ate. Tell Sue and me.
> **INCORRECT:** Sue and myself ate. Tell Sue and myself.

Reflexive pronouns may also be used for emphasis, or to intensify a statement. An **intensive pronoun** adds emphasis to a noun or a pronoun already named.

Eva **herself** would like to become a biographer.
Mark bound the paper **himself**.

or

Mark **himself** bound the paper.

Guided Practice

Tell whether each pronoun is used as a reflexive or an intensive pronoun.

Example: Dorothea Dix chose herself a difficult career.
reflexive

1. Dorothea Dix herself led a movement to improve prisons.
2. The prisoners could not easily help themselves.
3. Dix must have pleased herself as changes began.
4. Humane treatment itself was Dix's goal for all institutions.
5. The prisoners themselves expressed appreciation.

?! THINK

- How can I decide whether to use a reflexive pronoun or an object pronoun?

REMEMBER

- A **reflexive pronoun** points the action of the verb back to the subject.
- An **intensive pronoun** is a pronoun that adds emphasis to a noun or a pronoun already named.

More Practice

A. Write each sentence. Underline and label each **reflexive** or **intensive** pronoun.

Example: More women advanced themselves.
          More women advanced <u>themselves</u>.
          reflexive

6. Ida M. Tarbell considered herself a journalist.
7. We ourselves read her work in old newspapers at the library.
8. Tarbell herself had also written a biography of Lincoln.
9. Magazines prided themselves on publishing her articles.
10. She herself investigated corruption in industry.
11. The owner of a magazine himself defended her work.
12. Tarbell brought herself much attention.

B. Write each sentence, filling in the blank with the correct pronoun form. Write whether the pronoun is **reflexive** or **intensive.**

Example: The suffrage movement ____ grew slowly.
          The suffrage movement itself grew slowly.
          intensive

13. Susan B. Anthony ____ led the women's suffrage movement.
14. Elizabeth Cady Stanton supported ____ as a journalist.
15. Women who wanted the vote attached ____ to the movement.
16. The movement ____ began in 1848.
17. Women improved ____ to achieve their goal.
18. We should remind ____ not to take our rights for granted.
19. The original leaders proved ____ .
20. The struggle ____ ended in victory in 1920.

Extra Practice, page 242

WRITING APPLICATION A Speech

Write a brief speech about an issue that is important to you. Then exchange papers with a classmate and identify any reflexive or intensive pronouns in each other's work.

7 INTERROGATIVE AND DEMONSTRATIVE PRONOUNS

An **interrogative pronoun** is a pronoun that introduces an interrogative sentence.

Who is that actor?	**Whose** is this book?
Whom do you prefer?	**Which** is mine?
At **whom** did you laugh?	**What** is your name?

Use *who* as the subject of a sentence. Use *whom* as the object of a verb or as the object of a preposition.

Do not confuse the interrogative pronoun *whose* with *who's*, which is the contraction of *who is*.

Whose is this video?	**Who's** your favorite actress?

Demonstrative pronouns point out things. *This* (singular) and *these* (plural) point out something close. *That* (singular) and *those* (plural) point out something at a distance.

This is a fine film.	**That** is a new movie.
These are my books.	**Those** are worn out.

Demonstrative pronouns replace nouns and stand alone in sentences. If *this, that, these,* or *those* is used directly before a noun rather than in place of a noun, it is functioning as an adjective rather than as a pronoun.

This is a funny movie.   (demonstrative pronoun)
This movie is funny.   (demonstrative adjective)

Guided Practice

Tell whether the pronoun that begins each sentence is an interrogative or a demonstrative pronoun.

Example: This is my favorite scene in the film.
          demonstrative

1. What do you think makes Charlie Chaplin a comic figure?
2. That was Buster Keaton's funniest role.
3. Who was the better actor, Chaplin or Keaton?
4. Whom did Chaplin mimic in *The Great Dictator*?
5. These are old photographs of Chaplin and Keaton.

 THINK

■ How do I decide whether to use *who* or *whom*?

REMEMBER

- An **interrogative pronoun** is a pronoun used to introduce an interrogative sentence.
- A **demonstrative pronoun** is a pronoun that points out something and stands alone in a sentence.

GRAMMAR

More Practice

A. Write and label the **interrogative** or **demonstrative** pronoun in each sentence.

Example: Which is your favorite Chaplin film?
     Which   interrogative

6. Who was considered the greatest rival of Charlie Chaplin?
7. That was Buster Keaton.
8. Of whom do we think when the Little Tramp comes to mind?
9. This was the character that Chaplin made famous.
10. Who was known as "The Great Stone Face"?
11. That was Buster Keaton, and who deserved the name more?
12. Those were exciting years in the history of film.

B. Write each sentence using the correct pronoun.

Example: (Those, This) were the golden years of comedy.
    Those were the golden years of comedy.

13. Chaplin and Keaton both created companies, but (who's, whose) was known as United Artists?
14. (Those, That) is the company that Chaplin formed in 1923.
15. (Who, Whom) had the funnier role?
16. To (who, whom) was a special Academy Award given in 1973?
17. (Whose, Who's) more sympathetic?
18. (This, These) were actors of great comic brilliance.
19. (Who's, Whose) was the greater talent?
20. (Which, Who) of them do you prefer?

Extra Practice, page 243

WRITING APPLICATION A Summary

Write a summary of an episode from one of your favorite movies or books. Then exchange papers with a classmate and identify the interrogative and demonstrative pronouns in each other's work.

8 MECHANICS: Using Abbreviations

Abbreviations are shortened forms of words. Many abbreviations begin with a capital letter and end with a period.

Titles of Persons	**Mr.** Ira Glass **Mrs.** David Ito **Ms.** Jane Kerr **Dr.** Carl Lynn, **Jr.**
Days of the Week	**Sun. Mon. Tues. Wed. Thurs. Fri. Sat.**
Months	**Jan. Aug. Oct.** (but **May June July**)
Streets	**Ave. Dr. Pkwy. Rd. Sq. St.**
Businesses	**Corp. Co. Inc. Ltd. Bros.**
Professional or Academic Degrees	Elsa Richards, **M.D.** Otto King, **Ph.D.**
Times	9:20 **A.M.** 8:10 **P.M.** 33 **B.C. A.D.** 325
Units of Measure	**ft. qt. lb. in. yd. mi. pt. oz. gal.** **m** (meter) **kg** (kilogram) **l** (liter)

Some abbreviations use all capital letters and no periods.

Agencies and Organizations	**VISTA** (Volunteers in Service to America) **NFL** (National Football League)
States	**AL** (Alabama) **IA** (Iowa) **UT** (Utah)

Guided Practice

Name the word that can be abbreviated in each item. Then tell the abbreviation for the word.

Example: Doctor Joseph Dubois   *Doctor Dr.*

1. 400 Courthouse Square
2. 144 feet
3. February 29, 1992
4. Hanna and McKay, Incorporated

THINK

■ How do I decide when I can abbreviate a word?

REMEMBER

- **Abbreviations** are shortened forms of words.
- Many abbreviations begin with a capital letter and end with a period. If necessary, check in a dictionary for help with writing an abbreviation.

More Practice

A. Find the word or words that can be abbreviated in each item. Then write the abbreviation.

Example: Eliot Armstrong, Doctor of Philosophy   *Ph.D.*

5. Tennessee Valley Authority
6. Baton Rouge, Louisiana
7. Antoinette Black and Company
8. Toby Little, Bachelor of Science
9. the year 1940 after Christ's birth
10. American Medical Association
11. the year 55 before Christ's birth

12. one quart
13. 8:35 in the evening
14. 4 yards
15. Thursday: music class
16. Mister Ramon Cabral
17. 15 meters
18. 10:15 in the morning

B. Find the word or words in each sentence that can be abbreviated. Then write the abbreviation.

Example: My father is the president of the Parent-Teacher Association.   *PTA*

19. List the days of the work week across the top of your paper like this: Monday, Tuesday, Wednesday, Thursday, Friday.
20. List these times of the day down the left-hand side of the table: 8:30 in the morning; 10:30 in the morning; 12:30 in the afternoon; 2:30 in the afternoon; 4:30 in the afternoon.
21. Laura James, Doctor of Philosophy, filled out the chart.
22. Use these abbreviations to show how much time you spent reading in each two-hour period: hours, minutes.
23. Date your report as follows: August 1, 1990.
24. Doctor James lives in Chicago.
25. Her address is 6251 Sheridan Road, Chicago, Illinois 60626.

Extra Practice, page 244

WRITING APPLICATION A Chart

Make a chart of the time you spend reading. Use abbreviations when appropriate. Exchange charts with a classmate and check each other's work for correct abbreviations.

9 VOCABULARY BUILDING: Homophones and Homographs

Sometimes words are confused because they sound alike. A **homophone** is a word that has the same pronunciation as that of another word but with a different meaning and usually a different spelling.

Last summer I sat **here** in the stadium.
It was a thrill to **hear** the fans cheer.

I suddenly felt emotional.
A tear formed in my **eye.**

A **homograph** is a word with the same spelling as that of another word but with a different meaning, and sometimes a different pronunciation.

I wiped the **tear** from my eye.
Who made this **tear** in my shirt?

Did you see that ball **fly**?
A **fly** landed on my head.

Guided Practice

Name the homophone that correctly completes the sentence.

Example: An airplane (flue, flew) over the stadium. *flew*

1. There was an (heir, air) of excitement in the ball park.
2. The sky overhead was (blue, blew) and cloudless.
3. The (son, sun) shone brightly.
4. The (great, grate) Jackie Robinson was going to play.
5. Everyone was eager to watch (hymn, him) score.
6. Jack Roosevelt Robinson was (born, borne) in Georgia.
7. Robinson played (for, four) sports: football, track, basketball, and, of (course, coarse), baseball.
8. Robinson was the first black to (be, bee) chosen from (miner, minor) league baseball to play in the major leagues.
9. The Dodgers, then the (team, teem) from Brooklyn, signed him.
10. At first (there, their, they're) was opposition (to, too, two) Robinson because of his color.

?! THINK

■ How can I tell the difference between a homophone and a homograph?

REMEMBER

- **Homophones** are words that sound alike but have different spellings and different meanings.
- **Homographs** are words that are spelled the same but have different meanings and sometimes different pronunciations.

More Practice

A. Write each sentence, using the correct word or words.

Example: Robinson was one of the great (ball, bawl) players.
Robinson was one of the great ballplayers.

11. After the Dodgers (one, won) the pennant in 1947, he was voted rookie of the year.
12. He held the bat with his (rite, write, right) hand.
13. Every chance he had he (wood, would) (steal, steel) a base.
14. His (peak, peek) season was 1949.

B. Read each sentence. Then write the letter of the definition that matches the meaning of the underlined homograph.

Example: The spectators <u>felt</u> the excitement.
      a. sensed
      b. unwoven fabric

15. The Brooklyn Dodger <u>fans</u> cheered Robinson.
  a. enthusiastic spectators   b. cooling devices
16. They were <u>content</u> to watch him slug the ball.
  a. happy   b. material contained; substance
17. When Robinson was the <u>batter</u>, all eyes focused on him.
  a. a baking mixture   b. hitter
18. He was the <u>kind</u> of athlete who excelled in all areas.
  a. gentle   b. type
19. Robinson renewed his <u>contract</u> with the Dodgers.
  a. legal agreement   b. to shrink to smaller size
20. Robinson <u>led</u> the Dodgers to one World Series victory.
  a. soft metal element   b. guided

Extra Practice, page 245

WRITING APPLICATION Sentences

Choose several pairs of homophones from this lesson, or think of some others. For each pair, write a sentence that contains both words. Exchange papers with a classmate and identify and define the homophones in each other's work.

COOPERATIVE
LEARNING

GRAMMAR ——AND WRITING CONNECTION

Combining Sentences

You can sometimes use *who* (for people) and *which* or *that* (for places or things) to combine related sentences.

SEPARATE: The student sang a lovely song. The student is in the chorus.

COMBINED: The student **who is in the chorus** sang a lovely song.

SEPARATE: We went to the awards program. The program took place on Thursday night.

COMBINED: We went to the awards program **that took place on Thursday night.**

SEPARATE: The program lasted an hour. It was delightful.

COMBINED: The program, **which was delightful,** lasted an hour.

Use *that* to introduce information that is essential to the meaning of the sentence. Use *which* to introduce information that is not essential. Information introduced by *which* is set off by commas.

Working Together

COOPERATIVE LEARNING

Think about each pair of sentences. Then tell how you would combine them to make a single sentence.

Example: The crafts award was for weaving. It was given first.
The crafts award, which was given first, was for weaving.

1. We observed the sculpture. The sculpture won the art award.
2. The flutist won an award. The flutist is in my music class.
3. My cousin Paul is a good writer. He won the poetry award.

Revising Sentences

In her journal Carolyn wrote notes about the achievements of her classmates. Help Carolyn revise her notes by combining the pairs of sentences. Use *who*, *which*, or *that*.

4. I admire Francesca's drawings. Her drawings are realistic.
5. Tony dances effortlessly. Tony is also my neighbor.
6. My friend Jason is in my class. Jason says wise things.
7. We laughed at Joe's jokes. The jokes are really witty.
8. Another student tells jokes. The student is in my class, too.
9. My friend Agnes lives in my neighborhood. She is a good singer.
10. Her laugh is musical. Her laugh is unforgettable.
11. Reba runs very fast. She is good at the high jump, too.
12. Carl makes birdhouses. The birdhouses are attractive.
13. My friend Sherri is the class president. The office is an honor.
14. Steven can spell almost any word. It is remarkable.
15. We all work on projects in class. We are proud of them.

WRITER AT WORK

Think about your achievements and the achievements of your classmates. Choose one that you would like to attain in the future. Write a paragraph about it.

When you revise your paragraph, work with a partner to find pairs of sentences to combine. Use *who*, *which*, and *that*.

UNIT CHECKUP

LESSONS

1-2 **Personal Pronouns** (page 212), **Pronouns and Antecedents** (page 214)   Write each sentence. Underline each personal pronoun once and its antecedent twice.

1. Sandra Day O'Connor was born in Texas; she graduated third in her class at law school.
2. Service in Arizona's Senate was important to O'Connor's career; it was headed for distinction.
3. As a judge, O'Connor believed in the rights of individuals under the Constitution, and they always were upheld by her.
4. In 1981, President Ronald Reagan broke tradition when he appointed O'Connor to the Supreme Court.
5. Tom, what do you think of this appointment?

LESSONS

3-4 **Subject and Object Pronouns** (page 216), **Possessive Pronouns** (page 218)   Write each sentence. Draw one line under each **subject** and **object** pronoun and label it. Then draw two lines under each possessive pronoun.

6. Langston Hughes is admired for his beautiful poetry.
7. He was prominent in the Harlem Renaissance, a creative time for urban black life.
8. Collections of his verses were published during Hughes's lifetime; among them is *The Weary Blues*.
9. There are also plays, children's books, and novels by him.
10. Hughes inspired many young black writers, and they and his readers will always remember him.

LESSONS

5-6 **Indefinite Pronouns** (page 220), **Reflexive and Intensive Pronouns** (page 222)   Write each sentence. Draw one line under each indefinite pronoun and two lines under each reflexive or intensive pronoun.

11. Everyone in the world of dance is indebted to Martha Graham.
12. Graham herself is one of the leaders of modern dance.
13. In 1929 she formed her own company, and her dancers performed pieces she had choreographed herself.
14. Some of her dance portraits include poet Emily Dickinson in *Letter to the World* and the bride in *Appalachian Spring*.
15. Another of her well-known dances is *Archaic Hours*.

LESSON 7

Interrogative and Demonstrative Pronouns (page 224)
Write each sentence. Draw one line under each interrogative
pronoun and two lines under each demonstrative pronoun.
Then write how each pronoun is used in the sentence.

16. Who made the first solo flight across the Atlantic Ocean?
17. That was Charles Lindbergh.
18. Whom would you have preferred to meet, Lindbergh or Amelia
Earhart, the first woman to fly solo across the Atlantic?
19. Which of these aviators flew alone from Hawaii to California?
20. This was one of Amelia Earhart's achievements.

LESSON 8

Mechanics: Using Abbreviations (page 226)   Write the abbreviation of each word or group of words. Place periods where
they are needed.

21. Federal Bureau of Investigation
22. Ace Corporation
23. six o'clock in the morning
24. Lewis Ash, Doctor of Philosophy
25. 100 years before Christ's birth

26. Doctor Nash
27. Lee Parkway
28. 2 kilograms
29. 30 ounces
30. Florida

LESSON 9

Vocabulary Building: Homophones and Homographs (page
228)   Write each sentence, using the word or words that
correctly complete the sentence.

31. (For, Four, Fore) many years the polio virus was a threat.
32. (Sum, Some) scientists sought (ways, weighs) to combat this virus.
33. Jonas Salk developed a vaccine (to, two, too) protect people.

Write the letter of the definition that matches the meaning
of the underlined homograph.

34. Albert Sabin developed another kind of vaccine against polio.
a. category   b. sympathetic
35. People no longer feared that they would contract this disease.
a. to become infected with   b. legal agreement

Writing Application: Pronoun Usage (pages 212–224)   The
following paragraph contains five errors in pronoun usage.
Rewrite the paragraph correctly.

36.–40. Whom has made discoveries in immunology? Dr. Jesse W. Lazear
was hisself an experimental subject. A mosquito infected with
yellow fever stung himself. These act proved that mosquitoes
carried yellow fever, but cost Lazear his life. Whom else in
medicine has made such a sacrifice?

Alice, Where Is Wonderland?

Working with a partner, choose a fictional character whom you both would like to "interview." Together, write notes about the character. Then compose a list of questions to "ask" the person. Prepare an imaginary interview to be presented to the class. Determine which roles you and your partner will play. When you practice your interview, strive to create a convincing character as the interviewer or as the person being interviewed. Have your audience identify each type of pronoun you use.

Lives of a Pronoun

Play this game with a partner. Think of a famous American. Have your partner use pronouns—subject, object, personal, possessive, indefinite, reflexive, interrogative, and demonstrative— to ask questions about the identity of the person you have in mind. Exchange roles. See who guesses the answer with the fewest questions.

The word *biography* consists of two word parts. The word part *bio* means "life"; *graphy* means "writing" or "descriptive science." Fill in the blanks in the following sentences with the correct *graphy* words. Use these word parts: photo, geo, tele, calli, xero.

Jigsaw Words

____ is the art of producing beautiful writing.

____ is the science that examines the earth and its life.

____ is a process for copying written or graphic material.

____ is the use of a system for transmitting or receiving communications.

____ is the art or process of producing images on a light-sensitive medium such as film.

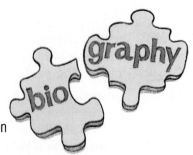

CREATIVE EXPRESSION

In Hardin County

With flint locked guns and polished stocks,
Knee breeches and long homespun socks,
On morning of St. Valentine
Two hunters met in 1809
Across the line from Illinois;
They stopped their mules and voiced their joy.

"Why, Ben, it's been quite a spell
Since I've seen you. The folks all well?
Bring any news from up near town?"
"Why, yes. D'you know John Ezry Brown?
They say that he's a-goin' down
To Washington in all the din
To see Jim Madison sworn in.

"And this young feller Bonaparte
That's fightin' 'cross the sea,
Is slicin' Europe all to bits.
Least that's what they're a-tellin' me."
"Wal, wal, nice day, kinda breezy,
This mule's gettin' quite uneasy.

"Now come and see us some time, do,
And bring the gals and Hepsy, too."
"Yes, some fine day we'll be along,
Got any news to send along?"
"No, nothin' worth a tinker's song.
There's nothin' happens here near me,
Doggondest place you ever see.

"Tom Lincoln lives right over there,
In that log cabin, bleak and bare,
They say they have a little babe,
I understand they've named him 'Abe.'
Yes, Sally said just t'other day,
That nothin' happens down this way."

—Lulu E. Thompson

Try It Out!
A narrative poem tells a story. Write a short narrative poem.

Three levels of practice

Personal Pronouns (page 212)

LEVEL
A. Write each sentence. Underline the personal pronoun, and identify it as a **subject** pronoun or an **object** pronoun.

1. Edison was a famous inventor, and he became a folk hero.
2. Many of Edison's inventions were also manufactured by him.
3. They included lamps and the parts used in a lighting system.
4. The phonograph was unique; it led to the formation of the huge recording industry of today.
5. The electric lighting industry can also be traced to him.
6. Edison invented the kinetoscope, and today's motion picture industry began with it.

LEVEL
B. Write each sentence. Replace the underlined noun or group of words with the correct personal pronoun.

7. Samuel F. B. Morse preceded Edison as an American inventor of importance.
8. Morse was also a gifted portrait painter.
9. As a student he was interested in electricity.
10. His contributions to telegraphy are well known.
11. Morse code, the set of symbols used on the telegraph, is named after Morse.
12. Morse experimented with underwater cables and hoped that one day messages could be sent across the Atlantic Ocean.
13. Morse's invention won great acclaim throughout the world.

LEVEL
C. Write each sentence. Replace the underlined word or group of words with the correct personal pronoun. Then write **subject** pronoun or **object** pronoun after each sentence.

14. Granville T. Woods contributed to the uses of electricity.
15. Woods was nicknamed the "Black Edison."
16. As a young engineer on the railroad, Woods became intrigued by the mysteries of electricity.
17. Books on electricity gave Woods the basis of his knowledge.
18. He invented railway telegraphy, which meant that messages could be sent using telegraph wires running beside the tracks.
19. The automatic air brake was invented by Woods.
20. Woods also devised an electrically heated egg incubator.

EXTRA PRACTICE

Three levels of practice

Pronouns and Antecedents (page 214)

LEVEL

A. Write each sentence. Draw two lines under the antecedent of the underlined pronoun.

1. When Anne Sullivan was a child, she became partially blind.
2. Anne went to the Perkins Institute for the Blind, where the teachers taught her the manual alphabet.
3. Anne had several operations, and they helped her eyesight.
4. Anne was an excellent student, and she graduated at twenty.
5. Because Anne was such a good student at Perkins, the administrator recommended her as Helen Keller's teacher.
6. In 1887 Anne and Helen began their long association, and they soon became friends.

LEVEL

B. Write the personal pronoun for which the underlined word or words are the antecedent.

7. Helen Keller attributed her achievements to Anne.
8. Anne taught Helen essential skills that enabled her to excel.
9. Dedication and love motivated Anne, and they shone through her relationship with Helen.
10. When Helen gave lecture tours, Anne accompanied her.
11. Anne met John Albert Macy, a literary critic, and married him.
12. Before the marriage, Anne explained her relationship with Helen, and Macy accepted her as part of Anne's life.

LEVEL

C. Write each sentence. Fill in the blank with a pronoun that agrees with the underlined antecedent.

13. Anne is remembered as an educator, and ____ is known for her work in promoting the American Foundation for the Blind.
14. Anne also developed new techniques for teaching disabled people, and today's approach is based on ____ .
15. Anne's eyesight became weaker once again, and by 1935 ____ had diminished to near blindness.
16. Anne became ill, and ____ died in New York in 1936.
17. A famous play, entitled *The Miracle Worker*, was written about Anne and Helen, and ____ was later made into a movie.
18. Many young people have been inspired by Anne and Helen, and ____ have chosen careers as teachers of disabled children.

EXTRA PRACTICE

Three levels of practice

Using Subject and Object Pronouns (page 216)

LEVEL

A. Write each sentence. Draw one line under each subject pronoun and two lines under each object pronoun.

1. Charles Bulfinch was a well-known American architect; the Federal style was associated with him.
2. He and Thomas Jefferson, also an architect, met in France.
3. The styles he saw in England also influenced him.
4. Wanting the buildings of Boston to look as elegant as London's, Bulfinch gave them and their city a classical look.
5. They and other buildings designed by him are still admired.
6. He liked classical elements and used them in his buildings.

LEVEL

B. Write each sentence, selecting the correct personal pronoun to complete the sentence. Then write **nominative** or **objective** to identify its case.

7. Frederick Law Olmsted was a gifted landscape architect; when people think of urban parks, they think of (he, him).
8. (Him, He) helped design New York City's Central Park.
9. Olmsted designed public parks; (them, they) are still popular.
10. Olmsted preserved the features of the landscape; he combined (they, them) and his unique designs.
11. New York City has four parks designed by Olmsted; (them, they) and his parks in other cities are national treasures.
12. He is known for the recreational grounds he designed; among (they, them) are the grounds of the U.S. Capitol.

LEVEL

C. Write each sentence, replacing each underlined noun or group of words with the correct pronoun form. Then write **nominative** or **objective** to identify its case.

13. I.M. Pei was born in China; it is Pei whom people recognize as one of the finest architects today.
14. Pei and his partners are known for unusual designs.
15. Among Pei's urban designs are museums and malls.
16. Pei's buildings are sensitive to the natural surroundings.
17. Many of Pei's buildings are unusual; these buildings have brought him wide acclaim.
18. His projects have great range to them.

PRACTICE + PLUS

Three levels of additional practice for a difficult skill

Using Subject and Object Pronouns (page 216)

LEVEL

A. Write each sentence. Draw one line under each subject pronoun and two lines under each object pronoun.

1. Helen and I prepared an oral report on opera.
2. Helen went to the library with me.
3. The librarian was helpful to us.
4. He found three excellent books.
5. He told us about the career of Giuseppe Verdi.
6. We selected Verdi as the subject of the report.
7. Helen asked Donna and me to summarize his life.
8. She would read about the composers who influenced him.

LEVEL

B. Write each sentence, selecting the correct personal pronoun to complete the sentence. Then write **nominative** or **objective** to identify its case.

9. Verdi grew up in a poor family; (he, him) was born in Italy.
10. He took music examinations but failed (they, them).
11. Several teachers tutored (he, him) privately.
12. He wrote his first opera in 1839; (it, they) was unsuccessful.
13. The next few years brought (he, him) much sorrow.
14. (He, Him) lost his wife and two children.
15. (They, Them) died of sudden illness.
16. Verdi thought that the most unhappy man was (he, him).

LEVEL

C. Write each sentence, replacing each underlined noun or group of words with the correct pronoun form. Then write **nominative** or **objective** to identify its case.

17. Soon Verdi's operas made the composer famous in Italy.
18. The composer was also admired as a patriot.
19. Did Nina tell Rita and me about his most popular opera?
20. The opera is named after Aida, an Ethiopian princess.
21. This opera had its first performance in Cairo.
22. Verdi operas are well-known; people still hum his tunes.
23. Verdi loved Shakespeare's plays and used two of the dramas as the basis of tragic operas.
24. The titles of these operas are *Macbeth* and *Otello*.
25. Even in Italian, the works still have broad appeal.

EXTRA PRACTICE

Three levels of practice

Possessive Pronouns (page 218)

LEVEL

A. Write each sentence. Draw one line under each possessive pronoun.

1. Joshua Johnson was a black American painter, and interest in his life and work has grown.
2. Little about Johnson's early life is known; its mysteries are numerous.
3. Historians do not know when or where he was born, but their research shows that he was a free black, not a slave.
4. It is known that Johnson earned his living as a portrait painter.
5. More than eighty portraits are his work.

LEVEL

B. Write each sentence, using the correct form given in parentheses.

6. Georgia O'Keeffe is considered one of America's finest painters; (her, their) paintings are in many museums.
7. O'Keeffe's work drew the attention of photographer Alfred Stieglitz, and (his, its) admiration brought her recognition.
8. O'Keeffe painted rocks, flowers, bones, and clouds; (their, they're) details were magnified in her works.
9. When you see one of O'Keeffe's flower paintings, (your, you're) mind becomes captivated by (it's, its) boldness.
10. O'Keeffe moved to New Mexico, where she began (her, its) series of paintings with a desert motif.

LEVEL

C. Write each sentence. Fill in the blank with a possessive pronoun that agrees with the underlined antecedent.

11. The art of Winslow Homer is popular; ____ seascapes in watercolor are realistic and powerful.
12. Thomas Cole is well known for his paintings of the Hudson Valley; ____ majesty captures the beauty of the scenery.
13. The enormous paintings of the American West by Albert Bierstadt show ____ splendor and diversity.
14. The painting American Gothic is better known than ____ artist, Grant Wood.
15. Marsden Hartley declared himself "the painter of Maine," whose residents and scenery were portrayed in ____ paintings.

EXTRA PRACTICE

Three levels of practice

Indefinite Pronouns (page 220)

LEVEL

A. Write each sentence. Underline the indefinite pronoun, and write whether it is used as a **singular** or a **plural** subject.

1. Few of America's songwriters have composed more songs than Irving Berlin.
2. Most of the music was for Broadway shows and for films.
3. Everyone seems to enjoy hearing "Alexander's Ragtime Band."
4. No one can fail to respond to "God Bless America."
5. One of his musical scores, for *This Is the Army* (1942), won him the Medal for Merit in 1945.
6. Some of his most popular songs are "Always" and "All Alone."

LEVEL

B. Write each sentence. Draw one line under each indefinite pronoun and two lines under the word it refers to.

7. One of the most gifted composers in the United States was Samuel Barber.
8. Some of his honors include winning two Pulitzer Prizes.
9. Many of his compositions reflect his musical brilliance.
10. Both of his operas are among his greatest works.
11. Much of his music was composed for orchestra and chorus.
12. Some of his best music was written for piano.
13. Most of his music received acclaim; one of his concertos won an award.

LEVEL

C. Write each sentence, using the correct form of the verb given in parentheses.

14. One of the great legends of modern American jazz (was, were) Duke Ellington.
15. Most of his music (is, are) admired for its complex melodies.
16. Several of his best-loved compositions (is, are) "Solitude," "Sophisticated Lady," and "Mood Indigo."
17. Another of his well-known compositions (is, are) *Black, Brown, and Beige,* a long concert work.
18. Few of his contemporaries (was, were) as talented as he was, and many of his fans (was, were) thrilled to hear him play.

EXTRA PRACTICE

Three levels of practice

Reflexive and Intensive Pronouns (page 222)

LEVEL
A. Write each sentence. Draw one line under each reflexive pronoun and two lines under each intensive pronoun.

1. The name *muckrakers* itself was given to writers who exposed corruption in industry and government.
2. Elizabeth Cochrane Seaman herself was a muckraker.
3. Writing under the pen name of Nelly Bly, she put herself in situations in which she could expose the truth.
4. She once obtained a factory job herself so that she could write about the awful working conditions there.
5. Another time she interviewed asylum patients themselves about their treatment.
6. The truth itself was Nelly Bly's quest.

LEVEL
B. Write each sentence. Underline and label each **reflexive** or **intensive** pronoun.

7. Lincoln Steffens considered himself a muckraker.
8. Steffens himself worked as a magazine editor.
9. Corruption itself grew as a problem in city governments.
10. Steffens wrote articles about city corruption, and the articles themselves caused action.
11. He prided himself on exposing the need for reforms.
12. Steffens's life itself was interesting.

LEVEL
C. Write each sentence, filling in the blank with the correct reflexive or intensive pronoun form. Identify whether the pronoun is **reflexive** or **intensive.**

13. Novelist Upton Sinclair also called ____ a muckraker.
14. His strong interest in social and industrial reform was ____ reflected in his more than eighty novels.
15. The Chicago stockyards ____ provided the subject for his famous novel *The Jungle.*
16. The novel ____ , with gruesome detail, exposed the horrible conditions in the meat-packing industry.
17. His followers ____ encouraged Sinclair to press for reforms.
18. When his novel *The Dragon's Teeth* won a Pulitzer Prize, Sinclair ____ was proud for this recognition.

EXTRA PRACTICE

Three levels of practice

Interrogative and Demonstrative Pronouns (page 224)

LEVEL

A. Write each sentence. Draw one line under each interrogative pronoun and two lines under each demonstrative pronoun.

1. Who has not laughed at the antics of the Marx Brothers?
2. This was a comedy team that used sight gags, slapstick, wisecracks, and puns.
3. At whom did you laugh most?
4. What could be funnier than Groucho, Harpo, Zeppo, and Chico?
5. Which is their funniest movie, *Horse Feathers, Duck Soup,* or *A Night at the Opera?*
6. These are movies that several generations have enjoyed.
7. If Groucho's wit is compared with Harpo's, whose is sharper?

LEVEL

B. Write each sentence, using the correct pronoun form given in parentheses.

8. (What, Who) is the name of another comedy team?
9. (Who, Whom) do you think of when you hear the word *zany?*
10. (This, These) is the team that depended on slapstick.
11. (Whose, Who's) routine is the funnier, the Three Stooges' or Abbott and Costello's?
12. (Who, Whom) do you like better, Bud Abbott or Lou Costello?
13. The names of two of the Three Stooges were Moe and Curly, but (what, who's) was the name of the third?

LEVEL

C. Write each sentence, filling in the blank with an appropriate interrogative or demonstrative pronoun.

14. ____ does not enjoy the comedy of Laurel and Hardy?
15. ____ are routines that often rely on pantomine.
16. ____ of the two comic actors is the tall, skinny one?
17. ____ do you think is funnier, Stan or Ollie?
18. If you compare Abbott and Costello's brand of humor with Laurel and Hardy's, ____ is more amusing?
19. ____ are the titles of some of Laurel and Hardy's movies?
20. ____ of ____ is their funniest?

EXTRA PRACTICE

Three levels of practice

Mechanics: Using Abbreviations (page 226)

LEVEL
A. Write the abbreviation for each word or group of words.

1. Wednesday
2. Doctor
3. Alabama
4. Road
5. Company
6. October
7. inches
8. after noon
9. 4:00 in the afternoon
10. 76 after Christ's birth
11. United Nations
12. 604 before Christ's birth

LEVEL
B. Find the word or words that can be abbreviated in each sentence. Write the word and the abbreviation.

13. The memo was dated Saturday, January 10.
14. The mineral weighed 15 ounces.
15. The postmark was from Phoenix, Arizona.
16. The street sign indicated Boston Post Road.
17. The recipe called for one pint of tomato juice.
18. A brass plate on the door contained the words Doctor Steele.
19. His card announced that he was William D'Amato, Junior.
20. The schedule indicated that the bus left at 7:00 that morning.
21. The table top was three feet by four feet.
22. Sarah received her Master of Arts degree last spring.
23. I swim at the Young Men's Christian Association pool.
24. The magazine is published by Time, Incorporated.
25. The National Aeronautics and Space Administration is based in Houston, Texas.

LEVEL
C. Each abbreviation below is written incorrectly. Rewrite each abbreviation correctly.

26. Doc.
27. TVA.
28. Sep.
29. 5 am
30. Janu.
31. N.F.L
32. phD
33. fbi
34. ALAB
35. Ace Comp.

EXTRA PRACTICE

Three levels of practice

Vocabulary Building: Homophones and Homographs
(page 228)

LEVEL
A. Write each sentence, using the word or words that correctly complete the sentence.

1. Roberto Clemente was born near San Juan, the (capitol, capital) of Puerto Rico.
2. Clemente was an excellent baseball player, (two, to, too).
3. From 1955 to 1972 he played in the outfield (four, for, fore) the Pittsburgh Pirates.
4. Clemente was the leading league batter (four, for, fore) times.
5. He (lead, led) the Pirates to the world championship.
6. On December 31, 1972, Clemente (died, dyed) when the plane carrying him and four other men plunged into the (see, sea).

LEVEL
B. Write each sentence, using the homophone that correctly completes the sentence. Explain your answer.

7. Arthur Ashe was (born, borne) in Richmond, Virginia, in 1943.
8. In 1968 Ashe became the first black to have (one, won) the U.S. Tennis Open.
9. Ashe won the Australian and Wimbledon titles, (to, too, two).
10. A heart condition forced (him, hymn) to retire.
11. Although he (no, know) longer competes, Arthur Ashe teaches.
12. Ashe helps students to realize (there, their, they're) dreams to (be, bee) world-class tennis players.

LEVEL
C. Read each sentence. Then write the letter of the definition that matches the meaning of the underlined homograph.

13. Billie Jean King has had a fine career in tennis.
    a. a penalty   b. excellent
14. Her tennis matches were always exciting.
    a. contests   b. flammable material for starting fires
15. King worked hard to uphold the status of women's tennis.
    a. unyielding   b. with great effort
16. King has won a long list of championship titles.
    a. a series   b. to tilt to one side
17. Being able to watch Billie Jean King win was wonderful.
    a. to see   b. a timepiece

MAINTENANCE

UNIT 1: SENTENCES

Complete Subjects and Complete Predicates (page 4),
Simple Subjects and Simple Predicates (page 6)   Write each sentence. Underline the complete subject once and the complete predicate twice. Then write both the simple subject and the simple predicate.

1. The brown horse pranced around the paddock.
2. A young boy watched the horse wistfully.
3. His father bought the horse last week.
4. The frisky horse was trained last summer.
5. The proud youngster will show the horse at the fair.

Correcting Fragments and Run-on Sentences (page 12) Write each group of words, correcting the sentence fragments and run-on sentences. Write **correct** next to any word group that is a sentence.

6. Chili is our family's favorite dish, we cooked some yesterday.
7. Everyone's mouth watered for a bowl of it.
8. Murphy added the chili powder, he added too much.
9. The hottest chili in town for lunch.
10. Will throw the chili in the garbage.

UNIT 3: NOUNS

Possessive Nouns (page 70)
Write the following sentences. Underline each singular possessive noun once and each plural possessive noun twice.

11. The schedule for our state's political convention is almost ready.
12. The candidates' statements are exciting.
13. The party's platform was written last week.
14. The women's vote will be important in this election.
15. The election will decide the majority's will.

UNIT 5: VERBS

Action Verbs (page 132),
Direct Objects, Transitive and Intransitive Verbs (page 134),
Linking Verbs (page 138)
Write each sentence. Draw one line under each verb and label each **direct object, predicate noun,** or **predicate adjective.**

16. Beatrix painted pictures of animals.
17. Her paintings are very good.
18. People respect this writer greatly.
19. Beatrix wrote many small books.
20. Beatrix Potter was the author of *The Tale of Peter Rabbit.*

Indirect Objects (page 136) Label each **direct object** and **indirect object**.

21. The store offered customers a special on VCRs.
22. The clerk showed Amos a new model.
23. Amos handed the clerk a check.
24. Amos had bought the class a wonderful gift.
25. The class wrote Amos a thank-you letter.

Making Subjects and Verbs Agree (page 140) Write each sentence, choosing the correct form of the verb.

26. Today tree-ring dates (is, are) more accurate.
27. Tree rings (provide, provides) answers to many scientific questions.
28. Evidence of ancient volcanic eruptions (is, are) visible in tree rings.
29. Sequences of tree rings now (go, goes) back 8,500 years.
30. A tree-ring record (increase, increases) precision in dating archaeological finds.

Present, Past, and Future Tenses (page 142), **Present and Past Progressive** (page 146), **Perfect Tenses** (page 148) Write each sentence. Underline the verb or verb phrase. Then write its tense: **present, past, future, present progressive, past progressive, present perfect,** or **past perfect.**

31. Human-powered vehicles are becoming a reality.
32. The *Gossamer Albatross* had crossed the English Channel in 1979.
33. People in a human-powered submarine, hydrofoil, and helicopter will attempt similar expeditions.
34. Human-powered vehicles test the limits of human strength and endurance.
35. Enthusiasts are hoping for practical applications of the technology, but these have remained elusive.

Irregular Verbs (pages 150, 152) Write each sentence, using either the past or past participle of the verb shown in parentheses.

36. Astronomers have ____ a very distant galaxy. (see)
37. Its light has ____ about 12 billion years to reach the earth. (take)
38. Astronomers ____ the galaxy into view with an infrared telescope. (bring)
39. Several astronomers have ____ about the wonders of the galaxy. (write)
40. The galaxy ____ into existence early in the history of the universe. (come)

Using Commas to Separate Parts of a Sentence (page 154) Rewrite each sentence by adding a comma or commas where needed.

41. Some hawks falcons and golden eagles hunt in pairs.
42. Anna their behavior is not very successful.

43. Only Harris's hawks I hear hunt in groups.

44. Yes they coordinate their hunting tactics.

45. They share their food too.

Word Choice (page 156) Rewrite each sentence, replacing the underlined words with one of the following terms:

**stared   blustered   shrieked
strutted   cheered**

46. The clown talked in a noisy and threatening way.

47. The trapeze artist went proudly over to the ladder.

48. The audience looked at the performers on the high wire.

49. Everyone cried out sharply when the performers nearly fell.

50. The entire audience showed a great deal of approval at the end of the performance.

UNIT 7: PRONOUNS

Personal Pronouns (page 212) Write each sentence. Write the pronoun that correctly replaces the underlined noun or group of words.

51. A book collector browsed in a roadside antiques barn.

52. The collector saw an old book in a pile of pamphlets.

53. He paid the owner of the antiques barn fifteen dollars for the book.

54. He took the book to some antiques dealers.

55. The dealers said the book, *Tamerlane and Other Poems* by Edgar Allan Poe, was one of the rarest books in America.

Pronouns and Antecedents (page 214) Write each sentence. Draw two lines under the antecedent of the underlined pronouns.

56. Wild rice is not really a rice; it is an aquatic grass.

57. Indians who lived near the Great Lakes first grew the plant; they used canoes when they harvested the seeds.

58. The wild seeds are fragile, and they cannot be harvested by machine.

59. My parents and I once watched the harvesting process, and we marveled at the amount of hand labor needed.

60. A cultivated strain has been developed, and it can withstand harvesting by machine.

Using Subject and Object Pronouns (page 216) Write each sentence. Write the pronoun that correctly completes each sentence. Then write **nominative** or **objective** to identify its case.

61. Rolf and (I, me) walked in the woods.

62. I showed (he, him) a jack-in-the-pulpit.

63. The shape of the flower interested (he, him).

64. Jane saw (we, us), and (she, her) wanted the flower.
65. (I and she, She and I) decided woodland flowers should not be picked.

Possessive Pronouns (page 218) Write each sentence. Underline each possessive pronoun and draw an arrow to its antecedent.

66. Addie raked the leaves in her yard.
67. Leon planted some tulip bulbs in his garden.
68. The trees were dropping their colorful leaves.
69. The whole neighborhood likes its autumn outdoor activities.
70. I do not enjoy summer as my friends do.

Indefinite Pronouns (page 220) Write each sentence. Underline each indefinite pronoun. Label each indefinite pronoun as **singular** or **plural**.

71. Each of us has a favorite kind of movie.
72. Some prefer Westerns, while others like horror films.
73. Even today many are fans of musical movies.
74. Because of changing taste, few are made today.
75. Today most are seen on TV or on video tapes.

Reflexive and Intensive Pronouns (page 222) Write each sentence. Underline and iden-
tify each reflexive and each intensive pronoun.

76. I bought myself my first model car kit.
77. The designer himself watched me buy it.
78. My sister once cut herself while making models.
79. I myself knew to be very careful.
80. The models themselves are very handsome.

Interrogative and Demonstrative Pronouns (page 224) Write each sentence. Underline and label each interrogative and demonstrative pronoun.

81. This is near where we camped last year.
82. Which is the site near the waterfall?
83. Oh, yes. That was the best site of all.
84. What did you do with the tent stakes?
85. Where are those?

Homophones and Homographs (page 228) Write the following pairs of words. Identify each pair as **homophones** or **homographs**. Then write brief meanings for each word.

86. days, daze
87. pail, pale
88. rock, rock
89. way, weigh
90. plain, plane
91. wind, wind
92. soar, sore
93. foul, fowl
94. great, grate
95. here, hear
96. hole, whole
97. led, lead
98. raise, raze
99. post, post
100. loan, lone

UNIT
8

Writing Biographical Sketches

Read the quotation and look at the picture on the opposite page. What can a person achieve through reading, thinking, speaking, and writing?

The subject of a biographical sketch is usually someone whom the writer admires. The writer wishes to share his or her admiration of the subject with an audience.

Focus A biographical sketch paints a picture of someone you admire. It usually describes the person's qualities and actions in a way that makes it clear to the reader why the writer admires the person.

Whom do you admire? Who could be the subject of your biographical sketch? On the following pages you will find a biography and some interesting photographs of people who have achieved certain goals. You can use the biography and the photographs to find ideas for your writing.

THEME: *ACHIEVEMENTS*

Let us dare to read, think, speak, and write. . . .

—John Adams

Have you ever wanted to do something that other people were sure that you would not be able to do, and then you did it? How did such an achievement against the odds make you feel?

Edna Gardner Whyte, aerobatic performer and flight instructor, was born at a time when many activities were closed to women. Despite many obstacles, Whyte more than triumphed.

As you read the selection, notice the order in which the writer presents the information.

Rising Above the Obstacles
by Joan Ackermann–Blount

"Isn't this fun?" Edna Gardner Whyte, pioneer woman aviator, has just stalled her plane at 1,500 feet, sending it toppling in a free-fall spin.

Her passenger, someone who doesn't do too well on Ferris wheels, is screaming piteously at the earth that is whirlpooling up toward her, wrapping itself around her head, unfurling like an explosion in a ribbon factory.

"Edna . . . the motor . . . is everything all right?"

"Yes, now relax. I want you to enjoy this."

The engine is back on, the plane has leveled out, and the earth has stopped making monstrous faces at odd angles in the windows.

"Edna . . . please take me down." She has slid so far down in her seat, her head rests on her parachute.[1]

Edna Gardner Whyte, eighty-one, winner of innumerable air races and aerobatic contests, the instructor of more than 4,400 students, a past president of the Ninety-Nines (an international organization for women pilots), a designer and builder of two airports, and the head of three flight schools, has every reason to be calm. Since 1928 she has spent three and a half years of her life, more than 30,000 hours, in the air; she feels as comfortable as an egg in a cake.

Some people have swimming pools in their backyards. Some have trampolines, tennis courts, barbecue pits. Whyte has an airport. To get into the air, all she has to do is walk out her back door into her hangar (attached to her house like a garage), pull out her Cessna-120, climb into it, taxi down a gravel road the length of a city block, and she's on the runway, ready for take-off.

She takes off in her plane as many times in a day as the average person drives off in a car. Since 1928 Whyte has won 128 trophies in closed-course events and in cross-country races, including the Powder Puff Derby, the Women's International Race, and the Sky Lady Derby. She still races three times a year and is often invited to put on aerobatic demonstrations. "I just hope I can race three times a year for the next fifty years," Whyte says.

Still instructing seven days a week, averaging four to six hours of flying time a day, Whyte could use a control tower to

1. The lively introduction uses dialogue to capture the reader's interest.

direct all the traffic zooming in and out of her house at 99 Monocoupe Drive (99 because of the Ninety-Nines; Monocoupe because it's one of her favorite airplanes) in Roanoke, Texas, eighteen miles from Fort Worth.

Whyte sold her home in nearby Richland Hills in March of 1970, after the death of her husband. She cashed in all her stocks and other investments to buy the thirty-four acres of land in Roanoke, where the Friendly Aero Valley Airport now stands.[2]

She needed $5,000 to pour the concrete for her first hangar. "I went to the Small Business Administration, but they told me I was too old and a woman in a man's world." She was only sixty-seven, still in her prime. All her life she'd been told that the sky was a man's world. "Phooey" is what she told the Small Business Administration, and "Phooey" is what she told the designers she hired to draw up plans for the airport, the hangars, and the runway. "I could do better than that," she says, "so I drew up the plans myself."

"The runway didn't have lights for seven years," she says. "When I'd get a call at night that a plane wanted to land, I'd run out in my robe and slippers and put smoke pots on the field."

2. The author has switched from the present time to tell what came before.

Whyte's runway is now 3,500 feet long and 40 feet wide, big enough to accommodate a Learjet, or a bicycle race for eleven medium-size children.

During Whyte's fifty-five-year flying career she has flown fifty-eight models of airplane, and she can rattle off the names as if she were reciting a times table.

It wasn't until last year that Whyte got a chance to fly a military jet, a T-37 Tweety Bird trainer at Reese Air Force base in Lubbock, Texas. "Oh, I wanted to fly a jet so bad," she says. She had been a guest speaker at a banquet for the Pioneer Pilots Association (she is in the Pioneer Pilots Hall of Fame) and had expressed her rage at never having been permitted to fly a jet, because by the time the military had accepted women as jet pilots, she was over the age limit. "They arranged for me to fly one," she says. "When I was up there, I radioed: 'Sleep well, America, you've got an eighty-year-old woman out here flying tonight.' They broadcast that on TV all over the country."

Whyte's greatest dream was to be a pilot for a commercial airline. Three times she applied. The first was in 1933 in Washington, at Central Airlines. "A woman named Helen Richey had just been hired as a pilot," Whyte says. "Well, when she was hired, the men pilots decided they would make a men's union. If you didn't belong to the union, you couldn't fly." Richey was forced to quit, and Whyte wasn't hired.

"The second time, in 1935, I went to Chicago Southern Airlines. They were hiring my own students, students who'd had only 200 or 300 hours while I'd had over 3,000. I put in my application. When they sent me in for my physical, they said I was too short. I was half an inch taller than one of my students who got the job."

The third time she applied, at Braniff in 1938, they gave it to her straight. "The man said to me, 'I'll bet you're Edna Gardner,' and I said, 'Yes, I am.' He asked me some questions, and then he stood up and said, 'Do you really think passengers would get on an airliner if they saw a woman in the front?' I said, 'Sir, I don't know what you mean. Men and women get on my planes all day long.' He said, 'I'm sure it would hurt customer business.' End of interview."

Prejudice against women was a fact of life Whyte always had to deal with in her flying career. When Whyte was learning to fly, women had to be resourceful just to get instructions.

Whyte's passion for speed hit her early in life. Born in Garden City, Minnesota, on November 3, 1902, the descendant of nineteenth-century homesteaders ("I come from hearty stock"), Whyte spent the first years of life on a farm; at age six she was riding horses bareback and seeing how fast she could make them go.

In 1909 her father got a job with the railroad in Seattle, and the family moved West. When Edna was eight, he was killed in a head-on train collision. Soon after, her mother contracted tuberculosis, and Edna and her sister Vera and brother Dean were placed with different relatives in Minnesota, Washington, and Wisconsin. "I think one of the reasons I'm so competitive," Whyte says, "is because I lived with other families when I was young. The daughter of the family would get three petticoats, and I'd get one. It made me defensive. Why else would a woman my age still want to compete so much?"

In 1921 Whyte got her first crack behind the wheel of a borrowed Model T. "I was a bit reckless with it," she says. "I wanted to see how fast it would go, and we ended up rolling over in a ditch."

Five years later she got her first ride in an airplane. She was a nurse at Virginia Mason Hospital in Seattle when one of her patients, recuperated from an automobile accident, offered to take her up in a plane. "We went to Renton Field, and he put me in the cockpit of an OX-5 Jenny," she says. "He showed me how to use the stick—nose up, nose down, nose sideways. We were following the roads, dirt and gravel back then, and I thought it was wonderful."

Whyte was hooked. She found herself an instructor and paid for her flying lessons, $35 an hour, with her $70 a month salary. Whyte applied for her pilot's license in 1928 and got the highest grade on the written exam. "But the man at the Department of Commerce fumbled with my papers and ignored me after the test. I thought I might have done something wrong. I thought, 'I'm in bad graces now.' He made me sit there until the other applicants had gotten their licenses. Then he walked me around the back of a hangar and asked me what I wanted a license for.

'I've never given a woman a license before,' he said, 'and I'm not sure I want to start now.' I told him I studied real hard and that I wanted to make a career in aviation. I cried, and finally he took me up and passed me."

In 1929, Whyte was appointed to the Navy Nurse Corps and stationed at the naval hospital in Newport. In 1932 she applied for a chance to fly across the Atlantic with two male pilots; the trip was organized by the American Nurses Aviation Service for the purpose of studying aviation medicine. Because of her training as a nurse, her connection with the armed services, and her flying experience, Whyte was chosen. It was to be a non-stop flight from New York to Rome, and it was planned that Whyte would parachute over Florence, Italy, as a tribute to Florence Nightingale. The arrangements had been made, but then the government notified Whyte that it would not grant her a leave of absence. In her place, a young woman named Edna Newcomer went with the two men, and the trip ended in disaster; the plane crashed in the Azores. The headline in the October 9, 1932, Boston Sunday *Advertiser* read, UNCLE SAM'S NO SAVES NAVY NURSE FROM DEATH.

"Makes you believe in fate, doesn't it?" says Whyte.

That was the same year that Amelia Earhart soloed across the Atlantic. "Amelia had courage and a strong desire to prove that women could fly," says Whyte, a friend of Earhart's. "She worked so hard to help women. I remember sitting with her at a race once and Amelia saying, 'We have some of the best pilots in the world, but when they go for positions, they don't get hired. The men get the taxpayers' money to learn to fly; they get good positions, retirement money. The women get nothing.'"

During the six and a half years that Whyte was a Navy nurse, she was always flying and spent most of her off-hours giving instruction. By 1935 she realized she was making more money as an instructor than as a nurse, so she resigned from the Navy and went to New Orleans, where she started a flight school, Air College, Inc. "The darned flying bug ruined a perfectly good nurse," she says. When World War II broke out, Whyte sold her hangars, her lease on the land, and her landing strips to the Navy and went to Fort Worth to get her instrument rating.

She also worked on a civilian service contract with the Army Air Corps and trained fighter pilots for combat missions. Her knowledge of aerobatics was crucial to her teaching. "Fighting pilots really have to know aerobatics to kick it around and get the enemy off the trail," she says. In February of 1944, General Hap Arnold decided there were enough military pilots; all pilot training was discontinued, literally overnight. Because she was a registered nurse, Whyte was able to get a commission in the Army Nurse Corps and was sent to Luzon in the Philippines, where she later received recognition for her missions of mercy, flying injured soldiers out in B-52's.

"If I can continue to teach my pilots to be safe," says Whyte, now flying home at night in her Cessna-120, "why, then I'm doing something. It's taken me a lifetime to collect what I have, and I feel like I should use it to do a little good in the world."[3]

3. The author chooses to conclude the sketch with dialogue.

Thinking Like a Reader

1. What obstacles did Edna Whyte overcome to fulfill her ambitions?

2. How have you overcome obstacles to achieve a goal?

Write your responses in your journal.

Thinking Like a Writer

3. How does the writer indicate what kind of person Edna Whyte is?

4. What details does she use?

5. Which details do you find the most effective?

6. If you were to write about someone, whom would you choose? Why?

Write your responses in your journal.

Brainstorm *Vocabulary*

In "Rising Above the Obstacles," the author uses words such as *aerobatic* and *hangar* that are specialized to aviation. However, some ordinary words have specialized meanings. Think of an activity with which you are familiar that might use ordinary words in a special way. For example, *run* is a verb that means "to move quickly on foot." This word has a very different meaning for baseball players and another for bus drivers. In your journal create a personal vocabulary list of words and phrases that have two or more very different meanings. List the general meaning and the meanings special to a particular activity. Use these words in your writing.

Talk It Over *Role Play*

Edna Whyte is a woman who has inspired other people to attempt to achieve their goals. Think of a person who has inspired you, someone with whom you would like to speak. With a partner, imagine that you have the opportunity to telephone the person you admire and discuss the reasons for your admiration. As your partner plays the role of the person you admire, ask at least three questions that relate to the person's accomplishments.

Quick Write *A Book Jacket*

Now that you have been thinking about a person you admire, write a biographical summary about this person like the ones you often see on book jackets. Include those achievements that cause you to admire the person. For example, here is a capsule biography of Edna Whyte.

Born in 1902, Edna Whyte is an aerobatic performer, flight instructor, and airport operator. In the Pioneer Pilots Hall of Fame, this Texas resident has clocked more than 30,000 air hours since 1928. A former nurse, Whyte teaches pilots and wants to do some good in the world.

As you write your "thumbnail" sketch, try to make your audience want to read a complete biography of your subject.

Idea Corner *Think of Ideas*

Think of topics for a biographical sketch. In your journal write whatever ideas come to mind. Make a list of people about whom you would like to write. Try to choose people from a variety of fields; for example, list a singer, a sports figure, an actor, and someone you know personally. After each name write the main reason you find this person interesting. Prepare a list of five questions you would most like to ask each person.

PICTURES ![camera icon] *SEEING LIKE A WRITER*

Finding Ideas for Writing
Look at the pictures. Think about what you see. What ideas
for writing a biographical sketch do the pictures give you?
Write your ideas in your journal.

Carl Lewis, 1988 Olympic champion

Olympic champions Sergei Grinkov and Ekaterina Gordeeva

hiel Chester French's statue of Abraham Lincoln at the Lincoln Memorial

1 GROUP WRITING: A BIOGRAPHICAL SKETCH

COOPERATIVE
LEARNING

A **biographical sketch** is a factual account of someone's life. The **purpose** of a biographical sketch is to inform an **audience** about the person's most important life experiences and achievements. An effective three-paragraph biographical sketch has the following parts.

- Introduction
- Body
- Conclusion

Introduction

An effective introductory paragraph of a biographical sketch might contain a fact or idea that captures the reader's interest. Read the following introduction.

> Did you know that Carolyn Keene, author of the Nancy Drew mysteries; Franklin W. Dixon, author of the Hardy Boys series; and Laura Lee Hope, author of the Bobbsey Twins books, are all the same person? Each was a pseudonym for Harriet Stratemeyer Adams, who wrote nearly two hundred books under these names. Her father had originally created some of these series. After his death Mrs. Adams became the senior partner in the Stratemeyer Syndicate, which produced the books. Although Mrs. Adams did not write all of the books, all had to meet with her approval.

Another way to introduce the subject of this biographical sketch might have been to quote Mrs. Adams or one of her books. In "Rising Above the Obstacles" the writer opens by stating the subject's philosophy of life. Choose an opening that expresses the spirit of your subject.

Guided Practice: Writing an Introduction

As a class, decide on a subject for a biographical sketch. The subject might be an entertainer, a teacher, an inventor, or a subject from history. Find out about the life of the person. Then write a brief introduction for a biographical sketch.

Body

The body of a biographical sketch summarizes the important events, experiences, and achievements in the person's life. These are usually presented in the order in which they occurred in time, that is, **chronological order.**

W R I T I N G

TOGETHER

> Harriet Stratemeyer was born in Newark, New Jersey, in 1892. In 1914 she graduated from Wellesley College. <u>Soon</u> she began to work for her father. <u>Later</u>, she married Russell V. Adams, who worked as an investment banker. <u>Then</u> in 1930 she wrote the first book about her most famous heroine, Nancy Drew. This was *Secret of the Old Clock*, the first book in the popular series of Nancy Drew mysteries.

- How are the events arranged?
- Which words help you understand the order of the events in time?

Notice that the paragraph begins with the birth of the subject and ends with her first major achievement. Chronological order is a logical way to lead the reader through the life of the subject.

Now study the underlined words in the paragraph. These are **transition words** that help the reader to see connections between ideas. Other transition words that show time are *after, before, always, following, immediately, meanwhile, sometimes, until, finally,* and *now.* Other words such as *but, however, like,* and *similarly* are transition words that show comparison.

Guided Practice: Events in Chronological Order

As a class you have written an introduction for a biographical sketch. Now make a list of the important events in the life of your subject and think about which of these you should include in the body of the composition. Choose the information that is most significant. Remember that you are writing a biographical sketch, not a full biography. Because of this, it is necessary to eliminate minor details. Then arrange the events that you have selected in chronological order. Use transition words to help make clear when each of the events happened in time.

Conclusion

The conclusion of a biographical sketch should leave the reader with a significant idea about the subject. Although it is a good practice to tie together ideas you have mentioned before, you should not simply repeat what you have written elsewhere. A conclusion is more than a summary. It often explains an important goal in a person's life or describes his or her personality. Directly quoting the subject is another way to conclude your composition. The conclusion below also continues the chronological order used in the body.

> Mrs. Adams found a way to pursue a satisfying career and at the same time raise a family of four children. In fact, she was with her family and working on a new series of ghost stories on the day she died at the age of eighty-nine.

Guided Practice: Writing a Conclusion

As a class, decide what you should put in the concluding paragraph of the biographical sketch that you have been composing. Discuss different conclusions and make notes for a conclusion that you think would be most effective.

Putting a Biographical Sketch Together

With your classmates you have selected a subject for a biographical sketch and have written an introduction. You have also made a list of the important events and experiences in the person's life and arranged the information in chronological order. For the conclusion, you have made notes on what you want to include.

Guided Practice: Writing a Biographical Sketch

Now write your biographical sketch. Use the introduction you have already prepared. As you write the body, include only the most important facts about the person's life. Be sure to use transition words to help the reader understand when events occurred. Finally, write a conclusion that sums up the person's accomplishments and personality.

Share your biographical sketch with a friend. Ask your friend if he or she thought that the time order of events in the person's life was presented clearly.

Checklist A Biographical Sketch

When you write a biographical sketch, you will want to keep some important points in mind. To help you remember them, make a copy of the checklist for writing a biographical sketch given below. Be sure to add any further points that you want to remember. Keep the checklist in your writing folder. You can refer to it when you write a biographical sketch.

Also be sure to keep the **purpose** of your biographical sketch in mind as you plan your composition. Decide just exactly what it is about your subject that you want to emphasize to inform your **audience.** Begin with an introduction that will capture your audience's attention and also provide a focus for your sketch. Be sure the body of your sketch builds to a strong conclusion.

CHECKLIST

- Remember purpose and audience.
- Begin with an introduction.
- Write the body.
    Include important events.
    Arrange details in chronological order.
    Use transition words.
- Add a conclusion.
- _____

2 THINKING AND WRITING: Understanding Sequence

Think about what you have learned about writing a biographical sketch. You know that the writer can help the reader understand a person's life story by arranging the events in chronological order. By describing the sequence of events in time order, the writer can show a pattern of development in the subject's life.

When writing the body of a biographical sketch, a writer usually begins with the birth and childhood of the subject and ends with the last or most recent events and accomplishments in the person's life.

Look at these notes a student made. The writer plans to write a biographical sketch about John Fitzgerald Kennedy. He has listed many facts about his subject.

—born May 29, 1917, in Brookline, Massachusetts

—graduated from Harvard University, joined U.S. Navy in 1940

—during World War II (1941–1945) commanded PT boat, won honors

—married Jacqueline Bouvier in 1953

—elected as Democrat to House of Representatives for Massachusetts in 1946

—elected to U.S. Senate for Massachusetts in 1952

—wrote Pulitzer Prize-winning biography *Profiles in Courage* in 1957

—elected President of the United States in 1960

—in 1961 launched Peace Corps, sent military advisers to Vietnam

—Cuban Missile Crisis in 1962

—in 1963 signed Atomic Test-Ban Treaty, assassinated on November 22 in Dallas, Texas

---

Thinking Like a Writer

■ How should the notes be arranged to show a logical sequence in time?

Before beginning a biographical sketch, the writer should arrange the events in chronological order. By organizing the details in a logical sequence in time, the writer will be able to show the reader how one event in the person's life leads to another.

THINKING APPLICATION Sequencing

Each of the writers named below is planning to write a biographical sketch. Help each writer arrange information in a time sequence. You may wish to discuss your thinking with your classmates.

1. Dena wants to write a biographical sketch about her math teacher, Jackie Abelino. Read Dena's interview notes. On a separate sheet of paper, write a list of events from Ms. Abelino's life in chronological order.

> Teaching since 1988. Studied at Pennsylvania Ballet 1960–66. Graduated from Southern Oregon State College in 1976. Peace Corps in Guatemala 1978–80. Married Joe 1979. Stopped ballet in 1972 because of injuries. 1977 starts studying modern dance. Moved to New York 1966 to study at School of American Ballet. Born 1950 in Philadelphia. Daughter Jessica born 1982. Worked as an accountant 1976–78.

2. Danny is writing about George Blank, his Little League coach, who Danny thinks should be elected to the local school board. Read Danny's notes. With a classmate, discuss the ordering principles that you think will work best for Danny. Then, on a separate sheet of paper, list the events in the order you think they should appear in Danny's sketch.

> Born 1941. Married Phyllis 1978. Son Phil born 1980. Daughter Kim born 1984. Started own software company 1970. Played minor league baseball 1963–68. University of Wisconsin 1959–63, there majored in Political Science. Developed computer program for teaching softball 1978.

3 INDEPENDENT WRITING: A Biographical Sketch

Prewrite: Step 1

You now have some ideas about biographical sketches. You are ready to choose a subject and gather information in order to write a sketch of your own. Here is how Jaime, a student your age, chose a subject.

Choosing a Topic

Jaime talked with a classmate about possible subjects for a biographical sketch. They discussed the fact that there were members of their own families whose lives interested them very much and whom they wanted to know more about. Jaime decided that his grandmother would make a good subject. He knew that she had led an interesting life. He also knew that she would be happy to tell him about it. Jaime decided that the **purpose** of his sketch would be to inform an **audience** of his classmates.

Exploring Ideas: Making a Time Line

Jaime realized that he would not be able to write everything there was to know about his grandmother. He decided to list the kind of information he most wanted to include. Here is Jaime's list.

1. Family history--born? lived? parents? meaning of name?
2. Childhood experiences--get into trouble? games? movies?
3. Education--school? first job?
4. Marriage--how did you meet Granddad?
5. Family--what was Mom like as a kid?
6. Hobbies? pets?
7. Philosophy of life. Hero?

Jaime decided that the best way of collecting information would be to interview his grandmother. He made a special appointment to meet with her. He took his list of questions with him when he conducted the interview. As his grandmother answered his questions, Jaime made notes of what she said and even wrote down some direct quotations.

After the interview Jaime was having difficulty keeping the events of his grandmother's life in order. He decided to make a time line of her life and chart the major events. This gave Jaime a visual idea of the major events in his grandmother's life. Here is what his time line looked like.

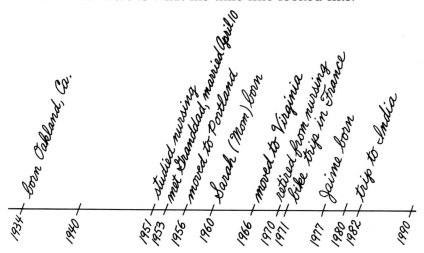

Thinking Like a Writer

■ What details did Jaime include in his sketch?

■ In what order did Jaime organize the details?

■ Is Jaime missing any important information? If so, what information is he missing?

YOUR TURN

Begin planning a biographical sketch by choosing a topic and explaining it. Use **Pictures** or your journal for ideas.

JOURNAL

■ Make a list of ideas.

■ Choose a subject that would be of interest to you and to your audience.

■ Gather information and arrange it in a time line.

■ Add more facts to your time line or cross out unnecessary details at any time.

Write a First Draft: Step 2

Jaime reviewed what he knew about writing a biographical sketch and prepared a planning checklist. He also reviewed the list of questions that he had asked his grandmother and the notes that he had made about her answers.

With this information fresh in his mind, Jaime then wrote his first draft. He did not interrupt the flow of his ideas by correcting his work. He knew he could make changes later. Read the first draft of the introduction of his biographical sketch.

Part of Jaime's First Draft

> She was born during a snowstorm, an unusual event in Oakland, California. They called her Louisa May after her favorite author, Louisa May Alcott. The year was 1934. Louisa had a happy, carefree childhod. She met Granddad at a dance in 1953. She graduated from high School in 1951, during the Korean War. Biology was her favorite subject. Her and a friend wanted to become doctors. They studied medecine. Louisa decided to became a nurse. Her career was changed. She had another path in mind. Three months later they were married. They moved to Portland, Oregon where granddad worked for the forest service

Planning Checklist
- Remember purpose and audience.
- Begin with an introduction.
- Write the body.
- Include important events.
- Arrange details in chronological order.
- Use transition words.
- Add a conclusion.

YOUR TURN

Write the first draft of your biographical sketch. As you write, ask yourself these questions.

- What is my purpose?
- What does my audience need to know for me to achieve my purpose?
- What information should I put in the introduction? the body?
- Are events arranged in chronological order? Have I used transition words to make one event lead to another?

TIME-OUT You might want to take some time out before you revise. That way you will be able to revise your writing with a fresh eye.

Revise: Step 3

After he had finished writing his first draft, Jaime read it over to himself and made some changes that he thought would improve it. Then he asked a classmate, Gloria, to read his draft. He asked her if there were any further changes he should make.

Jaime also looked at his planning checklist to see if he had included the necessary parts in his draft. He realized there was one more point he had missed. Jaime put a check mark next to both points to remind himself to make changes in his draft.

Before he went further, Jaime reread his first draft with **purpose** and **audience** in mind. He asked himself if the information in his sketch truly informed his readers about his grandmother. He also realized that his classmates would be interested in a more personal touch in the body of the sketch. He decided to use the direct quotations there.

As Jaime revised his first draft, he paid special attention to the points on his checklist. Could he improve the introduction or the conclusion? Did he leave out any important information in the body of his composition? Were the events presented in chronological order? Was his use of direct quotations effective? He would wait until later to check for errors in spelling and punctuation.

Look at part of Jaime's revised draft on the next page.

Revising Checklist
- Remember purpose and audience.
- Begin with an introduction.
- Write the body.
- Include important events.
- ✔ Arrange events in chronological order.
- ✔ Use transition words.
- Add a conclusion.

W R I T I N G

PROCESS

Part of Jaime's Revised Draft

in 1934

She was born during a snowstorm, an unusual event

in Oakland, California. They called her Louisa May after

mother's

her favorite author, Louisa May Alcott. ~~The year was 1934.~~

Louisa had a happy, carefree childhod. She met Granddad

at a dance in 1953. She graduated from high School in

Because

1951, ~~during the Korean War,~~ Biology was her favorite

She   *decided*   *First*

subject. ~~Her~~ and a friend wanted to become doctors. They

and then   *Although*

studied medecine, Louisa decided to become a nurse. Her

career was changed. She had another path in mind. Three

months later they were married. They moved to Portland,

Oregon where granddad worked for the forest service

Thinking Like a Writer

WISE
WORD
CHOICE

- What words and phrases did Jaime add? Do you think his additions are effective?
- Which words or phrases did he delete? Do you agree with his choices?
- How did Jaime combine sentences or phrases in order to clarify his meaning and add variety? How does combining them improve the composition?

YOUR TURN

Read over your first draft. Ask yourself the questions below.

- How can I improve the introduction so that it captures my audience's interest?
- What events need to be rearranged to chronological order?
- How can I make my conclusion stronger?
- How could I improve my writing by combining related sentences?

Now revise your biographical sketch. If you wish, share your writing with a friend or classmate and ask him or her for suggestions.

Proofread: Step 4

Jaime knew that he had to proofread his work for errors in spelling, grammar, punctuation, and capitalization. Jaime made a proofreading checklist to help remind him of what he needed to check.

> **PROOFREADING CHECKLIST**
>
> - Did I indent each paragraph?
> - Did I spell each word correctly?
> - What errors in punctuation do I need to correct?
> - What errors in capitalization do I need to correct?
> - What errors in pronoun usage do I need to correct?

Part of Jaime's Proofread Draft

Louisa had a happy, carefree ~~childhod~~ *childhood* She met Granddad at a dance in 1953. She graduated from high school in 1951, during the Korean War. ~~Biology~~ *Because* Biology was her favorite subject. ~~Her~~ *She* and a friend ~~wanted~~ *decided* to become doctors. *First,* They studied ~~medecine~~ *medicine and then* Louisa decided to become a nurse. *although* Her career was changed, She had another path in mind.

YOUR TURN

Proofreading Practice

Below is a paragraph that you can use to practice your proofreading skills. Read the paragraph and find the errors. Write the paragraph correctly on a separate sheet of paper.

> My best freind and me put together a model of the U.S.S. *constitution.* We assembled it all ourself. When we finished, to who did the ship belong. We decided to share it. He would keep it six months and myself would then keep it for six months.

Applying Your Proofreading Skills

Now edit and proofread your own biographical sketch. Before you begin, carefully read your checklist one more time. Then review **The Grammar Connection** and **The Mechanics Connection** below. Use the proofreading marks shown below when you make changes.

THE GRAMMAR CONNECTION

Remember these rules about subject and object pronouns.

- Use a **subject pronoun** when the pronoun is the subject of a sentence.

    He and **I** enjoyed the old photographs.
    They showed another era.

- In formal writing, use a **subject pronoun** after a linking verb.

    The subject of the photograph was Tom and **I.**
    The person with the hat is **he.**

- Use an **object pronoun** when the pronoun is used as a direct object, an indirect object, or the object of a preposition.

    Grandma showed **us** the photographs.
    She keeps **them** here for **me.**

Check your biographical sketch. Have you used subject and object pronouns correctly?

THE MECHANICS CONNECTION

Remember that abbreviations are shortened forms of words.

- Many abbreviations begin with a capital letter and end with a period.

Mr.	Gov.	Tues.
Jan.	St.	Corp.

- Some abbreviations use all capital letters and use no periods.

NATO	TV	YMCA
TX	NBA	CBS

- Some abbreviations use capital letters followed by periods.

A.M.	P.M.	B.C.
A.D.	U.S.A.	P.S.

Check your biographical sketch. Have you used abbreviations correctly?

Proofreading Marks
Indent ⌐I
Add ∧
Add a comma ⋏
Add quotation marks ⌄⌄
Add a period ⊙
Take out ꙅ
Capitalize ≡
Lower-case letter /
Reverse the order ∿

Publish: Step 5

Jaime wanted to share his biographical sketch with his classmates. First, he gave the sketch a title, "A Grand Grandmother," which he thought expressed the main idea of his composition. Then he made a neat final copy of his work. Jaime then made a cover from a portrait of his grand-mother that his sister had drawn. He posted his work on the class bulletin board along with other biographical sketches written by his classmates. The reaction to it was enthusias-tic. Several of his classmates wanted to meet his grandmother and asked if she could come and speak to the class about her experiences as a nurse.

YOUR TURN

Give your biographical sketch a suitable title. Then make a neat, final copy. Think of ways to share your biographical sketch. You might want to use one of the ideas in the **Sharing Suggestions** box below.

SHARING SUGGESTIONS

Read your biographical sketch to a family member or neighborhood friend.	As a class project, collect your biographical sketches to form a *Biography Magazine.*	If the subject of your work is alive, send him or her a copy of your work.

---

4 SPEAKING AND LISTENING: Conducting an Interview

In order to gather information for your biographical sketch, you may have interviewed your subject and perhaps others who know your subject. Interviews can be a useful tool for gathering information in many situations. Knowing how to conduct an interview successfully will help you be more effective when you are the person being interviewed.

When you interview someone, it is important to prepare questions in writing beforehand. Here is an excerpt from Jaime's interview with his grandmother.

Hobbies? Bird watching, bridge, movies, reading, traveling, and "spending time with my grandchildren."
What would you change about your life? nothing.
If you could be anything else, what would you be? tap dancer or vet. At times likes animals more than people.

When you conduct an interview, it will help you to keep some guidelines in mind. These guidelines will help you focus your interview so that you can get both the information you want as well as the details you did not anticipate before the interview.

SPEAKING GUIDELINES: An Interview

1. Be sure the person to be interviewed knows in advance the purpose of your interview.
2. Plan questions that reflect your purpose.
3. Make notes of important information or ask the person if you may tape-record the interview.
4. Be attentive. Ask politely for more details when necessary.
5. Be courteous. Tactfully conclude the interview when the allotted time has been reached. Thank the person.

If you are using the information from your interview in a biographical sketch, review your notes. Select and arrange the information that is most important. Do not change the meaning of what the person said. When you want to tell your audience the exact words of your subject, use quotation marks around the passage.

SPEAKING APPLICATION An Interview

With a partner, think of a situation in which an interview would be appropriate. An interview for a job, for entrance into a school, or by a reporter are possible situations. When you have decided on the situation, write a list of questions and conduct an interview. Your partner will play the role of the subject of the interview. After you interview your partner, he or she will interview you. When you are interviewing, use the following guidelines.

LISTENING GUIDELINES: An Interview

1. Listen for key phrases and ideas mentioned in the interview. Take notes about important points.
2. Listen for unexpected information. Adjust some of your questions, if necessary.
3. Be polite. Allow the person being interviewed to answer your questions without interruption.

THE CURRICULUM CONNECTION

Writing About Health

When you think about health, you might think of doctors, nurses, and hospitals. These people and institutions are an important part of a health-care system, but there is more to maintaining your health than being cured. Many people now believe that preventive medicine is the best path to good health. During the past century, scientists have developed treatments that have all but eradicated diseases that seemed incurable, diseases such as polio, diphtheria, smallpox, and tuberculosis.

You yourself also have the means to maintain your own good health. A healthful diet, cleanliness, adequate exercise, and sufficient rest all contribute to keeping you healthy.

ACTIVITIES

Make a Health Chart

Hygiene is the science of preserving health and preventing disease primarily through cleanliness. Make a list of measures you can take each day that will help you be healthy. Illustrate each item with a drawing or a picture from a magazine. Share your checklist with your classmates and add their ideas to yours.

Make a Menu

Nutrition is important to good health. Do research on the basic food groups that make up a balanced diet. Compile a menu for one day or more—breakfast, lunch, dinner, and snacks. Be sure the foods are nutritionally well balanced and easy to prepare. Look in newspapers, magazines, or cookbooks for menu ideas. You could also interview someone you know who knows about nutrition.

Keep an Exercise Chart

Make a list of the activities in which you participate. Then make a chart of the activities that involve some sort of exercise. The chart can be for a week or a month. Keep a record of how long (or how far) you exercised. Keep it up.

Respond to Literature

The following selection is taken from a biography of Jonas E. Salk, the man who was most responsible for the development of an effective anti-polio vaccine. As you read, notice the qualities that helped Dr. Salk achieve his goal. After reading the selection, write a response. Your response may be a letter to Dr. Salk, a poem about his work, or a biographical sketch of him. Share your response by reading it aloud or by showing your work.

The Reward of a Thing Well Done

Dr. Salk has received no money from the sale of his vaccine, however. Once he was asked who owned the patent on it and replied, "The people . . . could you patent the sun?"

Perhaps one reason why Jonas Salk is so widely known is that he often left the laboratory to explain his vaccine to the public. . . . Jonas Salk did these things out of a strong sense of social obligation, and not because he wanted fame. . . . He knew that the work of other scientists had made the vaccine possible; it was embarrassing to be given so much of the credit. . . . Whether or not his research will bring him another dramatic success in the eyes of the world does not concern Dr. Salk. . . . "I don't want to go from one crest to another," Dr. Salk replied. "And science isn't like novel-writing. To a scientist, fame is neither an end nor even a means to an end. Do you recall what Emerson said?—'The reward of a thing well done is the opportunity to do more.' "

—Sarah K. Bolton, *Famous Men of Science*

UNIT CHECKUP

LESSON **Group Writing: A Biographical Sketch** (page 262)   A good introduction gives the reader a clear idea of what a composition is about. Read the following introduction for a biographical sketch and determine whether it accomplishes its purpose effectively. If it does not, rewrite it.

> Everybody knows who Superman is. He is able to leap tall buildings in a single bound. He also goes faster than a speeding bullet. Superman is really Clark Kent, the mild-mannered reporter for the *Daily Planet*. He changes to Superman only when he decides to fight criminals. I think that Superman is a great hero.

LESSON **Thinking: Understanding Sequence** (page 266)   Here are some notes for a biographical sketch. Arrange them in chronological order and then write a finished paragraph.

James Beard: Chef and cookbook writer. First chef with a demonstration television show, 1945–47. Greatest influence: mother; great cook and owned hotel. 1922 sailed for London, hoped to be an actor. Served World War II as a cryptographic specialist. Born May 5, 1903, in Portland, Oregon. Moved to New York City in 1937. In 1955 opened his first cooking school. Returned to Portland in 1925 and worked for an interior designer.

LESSON **Writing a Biographical Sketch** (page 268)   Write a biographical sketch of one of your classmates for a class yearbook. Conduct an interview in order to get the necessary information. At the same time, your classmate can interview you for his or her biographical sketch. Limit your sketch to one paragraph, but remember to begin with a strong opening statement and close with a concluding sentence that characterizes your subject.

LESSON **4** **Speaking and Listening: An Interview** (page 276)   Imagine that you are going to interview an official in your community for your school newspaper. Your purpose is to find out about the plans for starting a major recycling program. Keep your audience, your schoolmates, in mind. Write three questions that you would ask.

THEME PROJECT *AUTOBIOGRAPHY*

You have learned about writing biographical sketches in order to inform your classmates and friends about the achievements of people you know and admire. You have also read biographical sketches of a number of people who have made contributions in several fields of endeavor.

With your classmates, discuss the tasks and skills you each have acquired and mastered during your lives. Include both physical skills, such as swimming, and mental or emotional skills, such as learning how to budget your time or how to set priorities. You might want to focus on those skills you have acquired during the past year.

Write a brief biographical sketch of yourself, an *auto*biography.

- Begin by making a list of your past achievements.
- Then think about your goals for the future.
- Include information about people and events that have influenced you.
- Ask your family and close friends about what they think your outstanding qualities are.
- Consider writing your autobiography in the form of an interview.

UNIT

9

Adjectives and Adverbs

In this unit you will learn about adjectives and adverbs. Adjectives and adverbs add color and detail to your writing. With adjectives and adverbs, you can paint pictures with words.

Discuss Read the poem on the opposite page. What mood has the poet created?

Creative Expression The unit theme is *Impressions*. To form an impression of something, a writer must first be a keen observer. Choose a subject to observe and write your impression of the subject. Write your thoughts in your journal.

THEME: *IMPRESSIONS*

Nightfall. Large clouds smother the town.
The street lamps stand, drowsy and sorrowful,
and the yellow moon travels between rain and wind.

Anochecido, grades nubes ahogan el pueblo.
Los faroles estan tristes y sonolientos,
y la luna amarilla camina, entre agua y viento.

—Juan Ramon Jimenez

1 ADJECTIVES

An adjective is a word that modifies, or describes, a noun or pronoun.

When you describe people, places, and things, you use words that tell about their size, shape, color, number, or other qualities. Words that describe nouns or pronouns are called **adjectives.**

> **A vast** hall led to **many large** displays of sculpture.
> **Two lovely** statues attracted the **curious** students.

A **predicate adjective** is an adjective that follows a linking verb and describes the subject of the sentence.

> The museum was **huge** and **impressive.**
> Each exhibition seemed **better** than the last.

Present and past participles may be used as adjectives and predicate adjectives.

> The art collection was **interesting** and **inspiring.**
> The **fascinated** students examined the mummy case.

Guided Practice

Identify the adjectives and predicate adjectives. Then name the words they modify.

Example: The new wing contains an ancient temple.
new wing   ancient temple

1. The excited class enjoyed the graceful sculptures.
2. The students, tired and hungry, then ate lunch.
3. The refreshed students continued the tour.
4. They looked at the art from ancient Rome.
5. The majestic columns seemed perfect to them.

 THINK

■ How can I use adjectives effectively in my own writing?

REMEMBER

- An **adjective** is a word that modifies, or describes, a noun or a pronoun.
- A **predicate adjective** is an adjective that follows a linking verb and describes the subject.

More Practice

Write each adjective and the noun or pronoun that the adjective modifies.

Example: Many students studied the colorful tiles from Carthage. *Many students colorful tiles*

6. The interested students paid another visit to the museum.
7. They spent several hours looking at the collection.
8. The strange masks and lean figures were wonderful.
9. The decorative arts from Africa revealed the intricate handiwork of the artists.
10. Arnold liked the beautiful carvings on the musical instruments.
11. Claudia preferred the abstract style of the carvings.
12. Most students enjoy paintings by modern artists.
13. Many students wanted to see the famous paintings from the Renaissance.
14. They were familiar with the historical period and the religious influences on art.
15. Yaeko liked the vivid use of color.
16. Tommy preferred the modern paintings.
17. A few students were tired.
18. David pointed out a bewildering canvas.
19. Robin discussed her favorite painters.
20. The tour was not only educational, but it also was a wonderful outing in the city.

Extra Practice, page 312

WRITING APPLICATION A Descriptive Paragraph

Write a paragraph about a recent group activity in which you participated. Describe what you did and share your impressions of the event. Then exchange paragraphs with a classmate and identify all of the adjectives in each other's work.

2 ARTICLES AND PROPER ADJECTIVES

The words *a, an,* and *the* form a special group of adjectives called **articles.**

The snack consisted of **a** piece of cheese and **an** apple.

The articles *a* and *an* are **indefinite articles** and refer to any one of a group of persons, places, things, or ideas. Use *a* before a word that begins with a consonant sound; use *an* before a word that begins with a vowel sound.

The is called a **definite article** because it identifies specific persons, places, things, or ideas.

A **proper adjective** is formed from a proper noun. A proper adjective always begins with a capital letter. Some proper adjectives have the same form as the corresponding proper nouns.

Wisconsin cheese　　　**September** crop of apples

Most proper adjectives, however, have a different form. They are formed with one of the following endings.

an	ese	ian	ish
Mexico— Mexican	China— Chinese	Canada— Canadian	Spain— Spanish

Guided Practice

Complete each sentence with an indefinite article and identify the proper adjective.

Example: Fried plantain is ___ Caribbean dish.
　　　　　Fried plantain is a Caribbean dish.　Caribbean

1. ___ Southern dish I like is made with okra.
2. ___ Spanish dish called *arroz con pollo* is delicious.
3. Many Italian dishes have ___ tomato-base sauce.
4. ___ bread that my grandmother likes best is Irish soda bread.
5. Margot ate ___ asparagus soufflé in ___ Boston restaurant.

?! THINK

■ How do I know if a word is a proper adjective?

REMEMBER

- **Articles** are special kinds of adjectives. *The* is the **definite article.** *A* and *an* are **indefinite articles.**
- A **proper adjective** is formed from a proper noun and begins with a capital letter.

More Practice

A. Write each sentence. Write the correct indefinite article for each blank and underline each proper adjective.

Example: ____ chef prepared this Portuguese meal.
   A chef prepared this <u>Portuguese</u> meal.

6. Anna's father prepares ____ Indian dish.
7. Ingmar enjoys eating ____ Swedish dish known as *gravlax*.
8. Manhattan clam chowder is ____ appealing soup.
9. Suki cooks ____ delicious Japanese fish soup.
10. Gloria won ____ cooking contest sponsored by ____ South-western restaurant chain.
11. Leonard works as ____ apprentice cook in Chicago.
12. Alfred's specialty is ____ Creole dish made with crawfish.

B. Write each sentence. Fill in the blank with the proper adjective that is formed from the proper noun given in parentheses. Use a dictionary if you need help.

Example: Forms of pasta were created by ____ cooks.   (Italy)
   Forms of pasta were created by Italian cooks.

13. Some ____ dishes are easy to prepare.   (China)
14. Gazpacho is a cold ____ vegetable soup.   (Spain)
15. A ____ dish I like is made with beans and rice.   (Chile)
16. Carol served imported ____ caviar.   (Russia)
17. Dominick often craves ____ food.   (Mexico)
18. ____ scones are traditionally served at tea.   (England)
19. This ____ cheese is good with that bread.   (Denmark)
20. This food is similar to ____ food.   (Brazil)

Extra Practice, page 313

WRITING APPLICATION A Review

Write a review of a real or imaginary international restaurant. Describe several of your favorite kinds of foods. Then exchange papers with a classmate and identify the proper adjectives and articles in each other's work.

3 COMPARATIVE AND SUPERLATIVE ADJECTIVES I

The **positive** form of an adjective does not compare. The **comparative** form of an adjective compares two people or things. The **superlative** form of an adjective compares three or more people or things. Study the following rules.

1. Add *er* to form the comparative and *est* to form the superlative of adjectives with one syllable.

small	small**er**	small**est**
thin	thinn**er**	thinn**est**

2. Add *er* to form the comparative and *est* to form the superlative of many two-syllable adjectives.

lengthy	lengthi**er**	lengthi**est**
tiny	tini**er**	tini**est**

3. If *er* and *est* sound awkward with a two-syllable adjective, use *more* and *most* (or *less* and *least*).

gruesome	**more** gruesome	**most** gruesome
active	**less** active	**least** active

4. Always use *more* and *most* (or *less* and *least*) to form the comparative and superlative forms of adjectives of three or more syllables.

likable	**more** likable	**most** likable
energetic	**less** energetic	**least** energetic

Guided Practice

Tell whether the adjective is comparative or superlative.

Example: The schnauzer is one of the more playful breeds.
　　　　　more playful   comparative

1. The pug is a smaller dog than the beagle.
2. The German shepherd is a larger dog than both.
3. The Irish wolfhound is the tallest breed of all.
4. The cocker spaniel is more popular than the spitz.
5. The golden retriever may be the friendliest of all breeds.

 THINK

- When I am using comparative and superlative adjectives, how do I decide when to use *more* and *most* or *er* and *est*?

REMEMBER

- Add *er* and *est* to form the **comparative** and **superlative** forms of most one-syllable and two-syllable adjectives.
- Use *more* and *most* with some two-syllable adjectives.
- Use *more* and *most* with adjectives of three or more syllables.

More Practice

A. Write each sentence. Underline each adjective and write whether it is **positive, comparative,** or **superlative.**

Example: The bull terrier looked <u>uglier</u> than the <u>other</u> pets.
comparative   positive

6. The biggest dog show is held in the modern sports center.
7. To dog fanciers, it was the most important show of the year.
8. Hank was more excited about going than his sister Kate was.
9. Kate likes dogs but thinks cats make the greatest pets.
10. The dog show was noisier than Hank and Kate had expected.
11. A judge chose one pointer as the most handsome of its breed.
12. Hank saw the greyhounds, the fastest runners of all dogs.

B. Write each sentence. Fill in each blank with the correct form of the adjective(s) given in parentheses.

Example: Are cats ____ than dogs? (wise) *wiser*

13. Are Rottweilers the ____ dogs of all? (fierce)
14. Retrievers seem ____ than pointers. (smart)
15. The ____ dogs were the terriers. (cute)
16. The ____ breed at the show was the poodle. (popular)
17. Setters looked ____ than spaniels. (beautiful)
18. Hank said the Bernese mountain dog was ____ than the St. Bernard. (impressive)
19. It seemed that the ____ breeds at the show had the ____ barks of all. (small; loud)
20. Kate said that cats seemed ____ than dogs. (sly)

Extra Practice, page 314

WRITING APPLICATION A News Article

With a partner write a news article describing a competition, such as a county fair, a crafts show, a sports event, or a horse show. Use comparison or contrast in your description. Then exchange papers with a classmate and identify each adjective and its degree of comparison.

4 COMPARATIVE AND SUPERLATIVE ADJECTIVES II

You have learned that the comparative and superlative forms of most adjectives are formed by adding *er* and *est* or by using *more* and *most* or *less* and *least*. Some adjectives, however, have irregular comparative and superlative forms.

Murray is a **good** chess player.
Suzanne is a **better** chess player than Murray.
Sandy is the **best** chess player of the three.

Study the following chart. Note how different the comparative and superlative forms are from the positive forms.

Positive	Comparative	Superlative
good	better	best
well	better	best
bad	worse	worst
ill	worse	worst
far	farther	farthest
little	less, lesser	least
many/much	more	most

Avoid double comparisons, such as *more better* and *most farthest*. Never use *more* and *most* with adjectives that have irregular comparative and superlative forms.

Guided Practice

Identify the degree of comparison of each underlined adjective.

Example: For me, chess is the <u>most difficult</u> game.
superlative

1. <u>Many</u> people enjoy a game of chess.
2. Learning how to become a <u>better</u> player is a challenge.
3. The <u>worst</u> players do not concentrate on the game.
4. Playing a <u>bad</u> game can be discouraging.
5. Practice, however, will bring <u>more</u> confidence.

 THINK

■ How can I avoid using a double comparison?

REMEMBER

- Some adjectives have irregular comparative and superlative forms.
- Avoid double comparisons by never using *more* and *most* with adjectives that are already compared.

More Practice

A. Write each adjective and its degree of comparison.

Example: A ghost in a snowstorm was the hardest puzzle.
          hardest   superlative

6. This novelty store services the most customers.
7. Jigsaw puzzles are good challenges.
8. Natasha is the best crossword puzzle-solver I know.
9. She can complete a puzzle in less time than anyone else.
10. I'm probably the worst puzzle-solver in the world!
11. Stewart is a better puzzle-solver than most people.
12. Natasha, however, has won more competitions than Stewart.

B. Write each sentence. Fill each blank with the correct degree of comparison for the adjective in parentheses.

Example: Janet likes maze puzzles ____ of all. (good) *best*

13. Crossword puzzles are a ____ test of vocabulary. (good)
14. Carlos is the ____ solver of puzzles in the room. (good)
15. He spends ____ time on a puzzle than anyone else. (little)
16. He thinks that word-search puzzles are the ____ puzzles ever designed. (bad)
17. Diagramless puzzles present the ____ difficulty. (much)
18. Carlos's favorite clues are the ones that contain the ____ information. (little)
19. To become ____ at solving puzzles, Carlos also solves puzzles in Spanish. (good)
20. His goal is to be the ____ crossword puzzle solver in the nation. (good)

Extra Practice, page 315

WRITING APPLICATION An Explanation

Explain and compare two or more games, sports, or hobbies in a brief paragraph. Then exchange papers with a classmate and identify the irregular comparative and superlative forms of adjectives in each other's work.

5 DEMONSTRATIVE ADJECTIVES

When the demonstrative words *this, these, that,* and *those* are used to modify nouns, they are called **demonstrative adjectives.**

> **This** book is interesting.
> **These** books are informative.
> **That** book is beautifully illustrated.
> **Those** books are first editions.

This and *these* are used to point out people, places, and things that are nearby. *That* and *those* are used to point out people, places, and things that are farther away. Avoid using the words *here* and *there* with demonstrative adjectives.

> **CORRECT:** This book is by Charles Dickens.
> **INCORRECT:** This book here is by Charles Dickens.

Remember that the word *them* is an object pronoun. Never use *them* as an adjective to point things out.

> **CORRECT:** I read those books last year.
> **INCORRECT:** I read them books last year.

Guided Practice

Identify each demonstrative adjective and the word it modifies.

Example: This book was signed by the author. *This   book*

1. Bill received that book as a birthday present.
2. Those books were borrowed from the library.
3. This book is a suspenseful thriller.
4. These books were published this year.
5. That biography is about the author of these novels.

?! THINK

- How can I decide whether to use a demonstrative adjective or an object pronoun?

REMEMBER

- *This, that, these,* and *those* may be used as **demonstrative adjectives** that point out people, places, or things.
- Do not use *here* or *there* with a demonstrative adjective.
- Do not use the object pronoun *them* in place of the demonstrative adjective *those.*

More Practice

A. Write each sentence. Draw one line under each demonstrative adjective and two lines under the word it modifies.

Example: All those shelves contain rare books.
  All <u>those</u> <u>shelves</u> contain rare books.

6. That bookstore has wonderful books.
7. I bought this book of poetry there.
8. All of these poems were written by American poets.
9. Robert Frost is my favorite among those poets.
10. The book on that shelf is a biography of Frost.
11. This book of short stories is by the author of that novel.
12. Have you read that new book by those two writers?

B. Write each sentence. Fill in each blank with an appropriate demonstrative adjective.

Example: I borrowed ____ book from her.   *this or that*

13. Would you like to borrow ____ book?
14. If you like, you can borrow ____ mystery.
15. I liked ____ author's first novel.
16. ____ second novel by him is not so good.
17. The authors of ____ books are film critics.
18. They wrote ____ book about the history of American film.
19. I haven't read ____ science-fiction novels.
20. ____ book of word games you gave me and ____ puzzle books provide endless fun.

Extra Practice, page 316

COOPERATIVE
LEARNING

WRITING APPLICATION Directions

With a group of classmates, write directions for finding important parts of your school, such as the library or auditorium. Point out features along the way. Then, as a group, identify the demonstrative adjectives in your work.

---

6 ADVERBS

You know that adjectives describe nouns and pronouns. **Adverbs** are words that describe action verbs, adjectives, or other adverbs.

An adverb may tell *when, where,* or *how* about an action verb.

> Amanda practices tennis **often.**   (*when*)
> She plays at a court **here** in the city.   (*where*)
> She plays the game **well.**   (*how*)

An adverb may also modify an adjective.

> Amanda is **very** athletic.   She is **quite** energetic.

Very and *quite* tell *to what extent* a quality exists and are known as **intensifiers.** Other intensifiers are *almost, completely, extremely, rather, somewhat,* and *too.* Intensifiers precede the words that they modify.

Adverbs may also modify other adverbs.

> Amanda learned tennis **surprisingly** quickly.

Many adverbs are formed by adding *ly* to adjectives.

> graceful—graceful**ly**   magnificent—magnificent**ly**

Not all the words that end in *ly,* however, are adverbs. For example, *friendly, lively, kindly,* and *lonely* are usually adjectives.

Guided Practice

Name each adverb. Then tell what word the adverb modifies and what part of speech it is.

Example: Ellis can make figure-eights perfectly.
>   *perfectly   make   verb*

1. Ellis ice-skates daily.
2. He skates particularly gracefully.
3. He skates outdoors during the winter.
4. He often skates at the indoor rink, however.
5. He is somewhat nervous before a performance.

 THINK

- How can I tell if a word is an adverb or an adjective?

REMEMBER

- An **adverb** is a word that modifies a verb, an adjective, or another adverb.
- Adverbs answer *how, when, where,* or *to what extent.*

More Practice

A. Write each adverb and the word(s) it modifies. Then write the part of speech of the modified word.

Example: Wanda dives quickly into the pool.
       quickly   dives   verb

6. Wanda swims here at school after classes.
7. Like many swimmers, she is very slender.
8. She can swim a mile very fast.
9. Swimming has come naturally to Wanda.
10. Her technique is absolutely magnificent.
11. She can swim forward and backward quite easily.
12. Soon Wanda will represent the United States in the Olympics.

B. Write each sentence. Fill in each blank by using your own adverb or an adverb from the list.

Example: The cheerleaders are ___ enthusiastic. *always*

well	everywhere	loudly	faithfully
very	excitedly	always	yesterday
quite	clearly	rather	readily

13. Hyung was chosen captain of his soccer team ___ .
14. He is ___ the best player on the team.
15. The team's scores have improved ___ dramatically this year.
16. The coach ___ praises the team for its spirit.
17. Many students ___ attend each soccer match.
18. They cheer ___ and ___ .
19. People tell Hyung ___ he goes how ___ proud they are.
20. Hyung acknowledges that his team plays ___ .

Extra Practice, page 317

WRITING APPLICATION A Radio Broadcast

Imagine that you are a broadcaster for a radio sports program. Write a brief description of a sports event. Then exchange papers with a classmate and identify the adverbs and the words they modify in each other's work.

7 COMPARATIVE AND SUPERLATIVE ADVERBS

The comparative form of an adverb compares two actions. The superlative form of an adverb compares more than two actions.

1. Add *er* or *est* to all adverbs with one syllable and to a few adverbs with two syllables. soon, soon**er**, soon**est**

2. For most adverbs with two syllables and all adverbs with more than two syllables, use *more* or *most*. frequently, **more** frequently, **most** frequently

3. Use *less* or *least* to form negative comparisons. quickly, **less** quickly, **least** quickly

4. Do not use *er* with *more* or *est* with *most*, as in "more sooner" and "most hardest."

Some adverbs have irregular comparative and superlative forms. See the chart below.

Adverb	Comparative	Superlative
badly	worse	worst
well	better	best
far (distance)	farther	farthest
far (degree)	further	furthest
little	less	least

Guided Practice

Tell whether the adverb is comparative or superlative.

Example: Ned runs farther than Milton does.   *comparative*

1. Hector exercises more vigorously than Milton.
2. Janet performs aerobics most gracefully of all.
3. Ned runs faster than Hector.
4. Milton runs the most quickly.
5. Laura works out more often than Janet.
6. Jack takes exercise classes more frequently than I do.

THINK

■ How do I decide whether to use *est* or *most* to form a superlative adverb?

REMEMBER

- Use *more* and *most* to form the **comparative** and **superlative** forms of most adverbs. Add *er* and *est* to form the comparative and superlative degrees of one-syllable adverbs and a few adverbs of more than one syllable.
- Do not use *er* with *more* or *est* with *most*.

More Practice

A. Write each adverb and whether it is **comparative** or **superlative.**

Example: Aerobics is given most often at this gym.
　　　　　most often　superlative

  7. Beth exercises more enthusiastically than Mary.
  8. Of all the classes, aerobics is requested most often.
  9. Hakeem uses the equipment the most cautiously.
 10. Luke does push-ups the most enthusiastically.
 11. Brenda finishes the laps around the track sooner than Pat.
 12. Tony trains less rigorously than any other student.

B. Write each sentence. Fill in each blank with the correct comparative or superlative form of the adverb given.

Example: Jim performs ___ when it is cool.   (well)
　　　　　best

 13. Of all the students, Roberto can run ___.   (far)
 14. He performs ___ of all when he is rested.   (well)
 15. Well-rested athletes always perform ___ than usual.   (well)
 16. An athlete who doesn't eat a balanced diet will perform ___ than those who do.   (badly)
 17. Roberto's friend Jim does not run ___ than he does.   (fast)
 18. Jim practices ___ than the other runners do.   (hard)
 19. Joseph exercises the ___ of all the students.   (little)
 20. Larry ran the ___ of all the runners.   (long)

Extra Practice, page 318

WRITING APPLICATION A Story

Write a brief story involving three characters in a foot race. Describe the race. Then exchange papers with a classmate and identify the comparative and superlative adverbs.

8 AVOIDING DOUBLE NEGATIVES

You have already studied several kinds of adverbs. The word *not* is also an adverb. It is a negative word that is often part of a contraction. Remember that a contraction that ends in n't is made up of both a verb and an adverb.

That movie **is not** very entertaining.
That movie **isn't** very entertaining.

Here are some other negative words with their positive forms.

hardly . . . almost	nowhere . . . anywhere
nothing . . . anything	never . . . ever
nobody . . . anybody	none . . . any
no . . . any	no one . . . anyone

Use only one negative word to convey a negative meaning. The use of two negative words with one verb is called a **double negative.** Notice that there are two ways you can correct a sentence that has a double negative.

INCORRECT: The actor hasn't never acted in a good movie.

CORRECT: The actor hasn't ever acted in a good movie.

CORRECT: The actor has never acted in a good movie.

Guided Practice

Read each sentence. Choose the correct word from the parentheses.

Example: Haven't you (never, ever) seen this actor before?
ever

1. The new movie (has, hasn't) hardly been showing a week.
2. The director doesn't have (no, any) talent.
3. Nobody (never, ever) gives his movies good reviews.
4. You won't see such a poor movie (nowhere, anywhere) else.

 THINK

■ How can I avoid using a double negative?

REMEMBER

- A **double negative** is the incorrect use of two negative words to convey a negative meaning.
- Avoid double negatives by using only one negative at a time.

More Practice

A. Write each sentence. Underline each negative adverb.

Example: They couldn't get the stars they wanted for this movie.

5. It is hardly likely that this movie will be a hit.
6. The critics said it wasn't well directed.
7. One critic said that the acting isn't convincing.
8. Another critic thought the movie would never end.
9. Don scarcely saw the movie since he could barely stay awake.
10. I won't go to see it because the reviews were not good.

B. Write each sentence correctly so that it no longer contains a double negative.

Example: It doesn't make no sense to color those old movies.
It doesn't make any sense to color those old movies.

11. There aren't hardly any good movies playing nearby.
12. I don't like nothing but old movies anyway.
13. Old movies aren't screened nowhere in this town.
14. Doesn't nobody want to see a classic movie?
15. Scarcely no one I know goes to old movies.
16. If I didn't have no videocassette recorder, I wouldn't never see old movies.
17. I don't watch no horror movies nor science-fiction movies.
18. I won't watch none of the movies that depict violence.
19. Violent movies don't have no value.
20. They don't never appeal to my friends or me.

Extra Practice, page 319

WRITING APPLICATION A Review

COOPERATIVE
LEARNING

Write a review of a movie or TV show that you did not like. Present your review to a small group. Ask your classmates to check to see if you have avoided using double negatives in your review.

9 USING ADJECTIVES AND ADVERBS

Confusion can arise sometimes between adjectives and adverbs, particularly when they have similar forms.

ADJECTIVES:	good	bad	sure	real
ADVERBS:	well	badly	surely	really

1. Always use *good* as an adjective. Use *well* as an adverb to tell how ably something works or was done.

   Max had always been a **good** cat.   (adjective)
   Even as a kitten he had behaved **well.**   (adverb)

2. Use *well* as an adjective only to describe someone's health or physical appearance.

   As an older cat he had been **well** and active.

3. Always use *bad* as an adjective preceding a noun or as a predicate adjective following a linking verb. Use *badly* as an adverb to describe how an action was performed.

   One day Max looked **bad.**   (adjective)
   The vet said he was in **bad** condition.   (adjective)
   Max's heart was performing **badly.**   (adverb)

4. Use *sure* as an adjective and *surely* as an adverb.

   The vet was **sure** Max would get better.   (adjective)
   Nancy and her family **surely** loved Max.   (adverb)

5. Use *real* as an adjective and *really* as an adverb.

   Max was a **real** friend.   (adjective)
   He was a **really** loyal companion.   (adverb)

Guided Practice

Identify the underlined word as adjective or adverb.

Example: My dog Hansel is my best friend.   *adjective*

1. Dogs and cats are good companions.
2. A dog or a cat becomes a real part of the family.
3. People surely benefit from having a pet.
4. When people feel bad, a pet brings them comfort.
5. People and pets get along well together.

 THINK

- How can I decide whether to use an adjective or an adverb?

REMEMBER

- Use *bad, good,* and *real* to describe nouns or pronouns.
- Use *badly, well,* and *really* to modify verbs, adjectives, or other adverbs.
- Use *well* as an adjective when referring to someone's health.

More Practice

A. Identify the underlined word as **adjective** or **adverb**.

Example: We did not know Toby <u>well</u>.   *adverb*

6. William <u>badly</u> wanted to adopt Toby.
7. William and Toby were already <u>good</u> friends.
8. The neighbors could not care for Toby <u>well</u>.
9. Walking Toby became a <u>real</u> problem for them.
10. The vet, however, was <u>sure</u> that Toby was in good health.
11. William would feel <u>really</u> bad if they gave Toby away.
12. He had always treated Toby <u>well</u>.

B. Write each sentence. Choose the correct word(s).

Example: Pumpkin can land (neat, <u>neatly</u>) on the counter.

13. Pumpkin is an orange cat that behaves (bad, badly) at times.
14. Maria found the cat on a (real, really) dark night.
15. Maria felt (sure, surely) that Pumpkin was a stray that had never had a (real, really) home.
16. She (sure, surely) wanted a pet, and she did not think having a cat would be a (bad, badly) choice.
17. The vet examined Pumpkin (good, well) and said that the cat was (good, well) but too thin.
18. At first, Pumpkin did not adapt (good, well).
19. Pumpkin (bad, badly) scratched a chair and caused (real, really) havoc.
20. Maria began to feel (bad, badly) because she was (real, really) afraid she couldn't keep the cat.

Extra Practice, Practice Plus, pages 320–321

WRITING APPLICATION An Ad

Write an advertisement that describes a pet that you have always wanted to own. Tell about the pet's appearance and behavior. Then exchange papers with a classmate and check for the correct use of adjectives and adverbs in each other's work.

10 MECHANICS: Commas with Addresses, Dates, and Names

Remember the following rules for using commas when you write dates, addresses, the titles of people, and letters.

Use a comma before and after the year when you include both the month and the day. Do not use a comma if you use only the month and year.

> Cindy said that on June 28, 1992, she will move.
> In September 1989 Tim began junior high school.

Use a comma before and after the name of a state or a country when you write it with the name of a city. Do not use a comma between the name of a state and the ZIP code.

> Alfrieda has lived in Philadelphia, Pennsylvania, since last year.
> London, England, is where she was born.
> Pam lives in Williamsburg, VA 23815.

Use commas to set off an abbreviated title or degree following a person's name.

> Susan Schultz, Ph.D., teaches in Los Angeles.
> Jake Jones, Jr., is a good friend of mine.

Use a comma after the salutation of a friendly letter and after the closing of both a friendly and a business letter.

> Dear Gloria,   Your friend,   Sincerely yours,

Guided Practice

Tell where the commas should be placed.

Example: Tucson Arizona is not far from here.
   after Tucson, after Arizona

1. August 31 1991 is the twins' tenth birthday.
2. Axel Pedersen Jr. is an engineer.
3. Anne O'Neill Ph.D. is a teacher.
4. Santa Fe New Mexico is a beautiful city.
5. In March 1989 they moved to Fargo North Dakota.

THINK

- How do I decide where to put commas when I am writing addresses, dates, and names?

REMEMBER

- Use commas to separate the parts of dates and addresses.
- Use commas to set off titles and degrees after peoples' names.
- Use a comma after the closing of a letter and after the salutation of a friendly letter.

More Practice

A. Write each sentence. Add commas where they belong.

Example: Dr. Valdes lives in Chicago Illinois.
Dr. Valdes lives in Chicago, Illinois.

6. Laura Stern D.D.S. lives in Portland Oregon.
7. Mark Valdes M.D. was born on November 4 1959.
8. Evelyn moved to Brunswick Maine in May.
9. Sean visited Washington DC before traveling to Orlando.
10. Phyllis Singh Ph.D. moved to Albany New York.
11. Oscar Sanford Jr. is performing in Chicago Illinois tonight.
12. The Richardsons will be in London England.
13. Thomas Gray Sr. will telephone from Charlotte NC.

B. Write the following letter, using commas correctly.

14.–25.

94 Bank Street
Atrium New Hampshire 03440
January 2 1991

Carol Clark Ph.D.
142 Commerce Street
Detroit Michigan 48207

Dear Dr. Clark:
   On November 29 1990 I bought a GrapicsPlus personal computer in Burlington Vermont. The dealer told me that you designed some special software. Please send me some information about this. I would like to use it for my presentation at Berkeley California on April 17 1991.

Sincerely
Yoshi Keto M.D.

Extra Practice, page 322

WRITING APPLICATION A Letter

Write a letter to a friend who lives in another state. Using names and dates, describe your activities during the past few months. Check for correct comma usage.

11 VOCABULARY BUILDING: Synonyms and Antonyms

Using synonyms can give variety and precision to your writing.

A **synonym** is a word that has nearly the same meaning as another word.

> The water was **calm,** and the beach was **tranquil.**

The words *calm* and *tranquil* are synonyms; they have nearly the same meaning. Writers use synonyms to avoid repetition and to make fine distinctions.

> Luis said the water was **cold,** but Elizabeth said it was **frigid.**

The words *cold* and *frigid* have different shades of meaning. Elizabeth's impression was that the water felt "extremely cold."

An **antonym** is a word that has the opposite meaning of another word.

> Some people say jogging is **beneficial,** while others say it is **harmful** to the body.

Writers use antonyms to make contrasts. The words *beneficial* and *harmful* have opposite meanings, and their use sets up a contrast.

Antonyms can be created by adding the prefixes *un* and *non* to certain words.

> Our skin should be **protected** from ultraviolet rays; if the skin is **unprotected,** it will burn easily.

Guided Practice

Identify each pair of words as synonyms or antonyms.

Example: lazy, industrious   *antonyms*

1. happy, content
2. difficult, easy
3. sincerely, genuinely
4. common, unusual
5. remote, distant
6. enormous, tiny

?! THINK

■ How can I use synonyms and antonyms to improve my writing?

REMEMBER

- A **synonym** is a word that has the same or almost the same meaning as another word.
- An **antonym** is a word that has the opposite meaning of another word.

More Practice

A. Write each pair of words. Next to each pair write whether the words are **synonyms** or **antonyms**.

Example: fast, swift *synonyms*

7. clean, spotless
8. sharp, dull
9. coarse, smooth
10. fair, just
11. typical, characteristic

12. quickly, slowly
13. hard, difficult
14. fully, partially
15. rash, prudent
16. brave, gallant

B. Write each sentence. For each underlined word, substitute a synonym or an antonym.

Example: An owl <u>sat</u> on a tree limb.   (synonym)   *perched*

17. The forest was cool and <u>damp</u>.   (antonym)
18. The pine trees grew tall and <u>straight</u>.   (synonym)
19. <u>Chirping</u> sparrows flew from tree to tree. (synonym)
20. <u>Few</u> squirrels were seen gathering nuts for the winter.   (antonym)
21. A group of beavers were building a <u>simple</u> dam. (antonym)
22. A family of ducks swam <u>gracefully</u> on the lake. (synonym)
23. A <u>large</u> hawk perched <u>arrogantly</u> on a rock ledge. (synonyms)
24. The sunset cast a <u>dim</u> glow on the treetops. (synonym)

Extra Practice, page 323

WRITING APPLICATION A Comparison

Write a paragraph in which you use a variety of adjectives and adverbs to compare and contrast aspects of a rural or urban scene. Then exchange papers with a classmate and identify the synonyms and antonyms in each other's work.

G
R
A
M
M
A
R

GRAMMAR
—AND
WRITING
CONNECTION

Combining Sentences

You can sometimes avoid repeating words in your writing by using words ending in *ing* and *ed* to combine sentences.

> **SEPARATE:** The soloist impressed us. The soloist was singing on the school stage.
>
> **COMBINED:** The soloist **singing on the school stage** impressed us.
>
> **SEPARATE:** A harpist played a lovely song. The harpist was seated in the orchestra.
>
> **COMBINED:** A harpist **seated in the orchestra** played a lovely song.

Sometimes, when you combine sentences, you can place the words ending in *ing* and *ed* before a noun.

> **SEPARATE:** The magician also impressed everyone. The magician was mystifying.
>
> **COMBINED:** The **mystifying** magician also impressed everyone.

Working Together

COOPERATIVE
LEARNING

Think about each pair of sentences. Then tell how you would combine them into a single sentence.

Example: The break dancer amazed the audience.
He was thrilling.
The thrilling break dancer amazed the audience.

1. The teachers liked the students. The students were performing in the talent show.
2. Some parents helped with the program. The program was quite exciting.
3. One parent was located backstage. The parent was stage manager for the show.

Revising Sentences

Below are some more sentences describing a talent show. Combine the pairs of sentences by using words that end in *ing* or *ed*.

4. The audience heard a trio. The trio was playing jazz.
5. People liked the comics best. The comics were stumbling.
6. Some of the actors reviewed their lines. The lines were printed on big posters.
7. Soon the first act had ended. The act was exciting.
8. One actor had a case of stagefright. The stagefright was unexpected.
9. A ballad was sweetly sung. It was very moving.
10. At the curtain call some performers had big smiles. The smiles were spread across their faces.
11. The audience was pleased. They applauded for a long time.
12. The performers were obviously delighted. The performers took several curtain calls.

Write a paragraph that describes the talents of a person you admire. When you revise, work with a partner to find pairs of sentences to combine using words ending in *ing* and *ed*.

UNIT CHECKUP

LESSONS

Adjectives (page 284), **Articles and Proper Adjectives** (page 286)   Write each sentence. Draw one line under each adjective and two lines under each article.

1. Yesterday was Joan's first day back at school after a long bout with the flu.
2. She still felt weak.
3. The recuperating Joan listened to tapes of people speaking the French language.
4. The young student enjoyed this beautiful language.
5. Joan planned a visit with her Canadian cousins in Montreal next summer.

LESSONS

Comparative and Superlative Adjectives I (page 288),
Comparative and Superlative Adjectives II (page 290),
Demonstrative Adjectives (page 292)   Write each sentence. Fill in each blank with the comparative or superlative form of the adjective given in parentheses. Underline each demonstrative adjective.

6. My baby brother was the ____ infant I had ever seen. (tiny)
7. His beautiful face was ____ than this apple.   (round)
8. He looked ____ than that delicate piece of porcelain on the shelf.   (fragile)
9. I promised myself that I would be the ____ big brother in the world.   (good)
10. His arrival brought the ____ excitement of all those family events that I could remember.   (much)

LESSONS

Adverbs (page 294), **Comparative and Superlative Adverbs** (page 296)   Write each adverb and the word(s) it modifies. Label each comparative and superlative adverb.

11. The team members were proud that they had played well and won the tournament fairly.
12. Marty had scored more often than any other player on the school team.
13. Of all the players, Luke defended his position the most vigorously.
14. Sean ran the farthest of all the players on the team.
15. Paul was sad because he thought he had performed badly.

LESSONS **Avoiding Double Negatives** (page 298), **Using Adjectives and Adverbs** (page 300) Write each sentence. Use the correct word given in parentheses.

16. Lois broke her leg (real, really) seriously.

17. She (could, couldn't) hardly get around because of the full cast.

18. The doctor said her leg would mend (good, well).

19. Lois felt (bad, badly) when she couldn't participate in (any, no) school dances.

20. She (sure, surely) looked forward to the day when she wouldn't (ever, never) have to see the cast again.

LESSON **Mechanics: Commas with Addresses, Dates, and Names** (page 302) Write each sentence. Add commas where they belong.

21. Dorothy MacIntyre D.V.M. lives in Norfolk Virginia.

22. Jimmy Scott moved to Dallas Texas on January 26 1989.

23. Malcolm Coakley Jr. lived in Denver Colorado until recently.

24. The orchestra will perform in Chicago Illinois in May 1990.

25. Between November 4 1990 and April 5 1991 my grandparents will be in Tampa Florida.

LESSON **Vocabulary Building: Synonyms and Antonyms** (page 304) Write each sentence. For each underlined word, substitute a synonym or an antonym as indicated in parentheses.

26. It was very breezy before the storm began. (synonym)

27. Tiny chunks of hail began to fall. (antonym)

28. Brilliant flashes of lightning lit the sky. (synonym)

29. Light rain started to fall. (antonym)

30. The swollen river began to overflow. (synonym)

 Writing Application: Using Adjectives and Adverbs (pages 284–300) The paragraph below contains 10 errors in adjective and adverb usage. Rewrite the paragraph correctly.

31.–40. The Russian ballet dancers performed good last night. The better dancer I have ever seen, however, will dance tonight. She dances extremely elegant. We haven't seen no better dancing here. She dances frequentlier in other countries. Her leaps are quickest than her partner's, though his jumps are magnificently than hers. She is more smaller than the others in the company. This dancer felt badly this afternoon and may not feel well enough to dance tonight. If she does, her performance will probably be least energetic than it was last night.

Similes and Metaphors

A **simile** is a figure of speech that states a comparison. Using the word *like* or *as*, a simile states that one thing is like another. A **metaphor** is a comparison in which one thing is spoken of as if it were the other. Work with a partner to think of different words to complete each figure of speech below. Then select the ones that create the most vivid images. Use them in a descriptive paragraph.

The _____ was like a _____.
The _____ was as _____ as silk.
The room was a _____.
The _____ was like a desert.
Her smile was a _____.

INVENTIVE LANGUAGE

Imagine an invention that you think people could use. Be as serious or as whimsical as you like. Then prepare an ad to describe and sell your invention. Use a variety of colorful and precise adjectives to describe your invention and several adverbs to describe how it operates.

FOOD FACTS

Play this game in groups of three students. Take turns saying a sentence that contains an adjective or an adverb that describes food or eating. The other two students should rephrase the sentence using the comparative and the superlative forms of the modifier. Play at least six rounds, and strive to be creative. Assign points for the correct use of adjectives and adverbs.

CREATIVE EXPRESSION

MOUNTAIN WIND

Windrush down the timber chutes
between the mountain's knees—
a hiss of distant breathing,
a shouting in the trees,
a recklessness of branches,
a wilderness a-sway,
when suddenly
a silence
takes your breath away.

—Barbara Kunz Loots

Try It Out!

In this concrete poem, the lines are arranged to picture the subject of the poem. The poet reinforces her picture with sound. First, she uses onomatopoeia, words whose sounds suggest actual sounds, as *hiss* does. She also uses consonance, an effect created by repeating consonant sounds: *chutes, knees, hiss, recklessness,* and *silence.* Try to use onomatopoeia and consonance in a poem of your own.

EXTRA PRACTICE

Three levels of practice

Adjectives (page 284)

LEVEL

A. Write each sentence. Underline each adjective.

1. My parents like classical and popular music.
2. They also like traditional American jazz.
3. Occasionally, I hear them play unfamiliar music.
4. Certain songs must bring back special memories.
5. I know my mother was an avid fan of the Beatles.
6. My thoughtful father keeps a tactful silence.
7. His sentimental expression tells the real story.
8. I suppose my parents were young once, too!

LEVEL

B. Write each sentence. Write each adjective and the word it modifies.

9. Last Saturday was my parents' fifteenth anniversary.
10. My sister and I gave them excellent tickets to the symphony.
11. They celebrated by having dinner at a fancy restaurant and going to the special concert.
12. On Sunday I prepared a delicious breakfast for them.
13. It consisted of freshly squeezed juice.
14. They said that the breakfast was superb.
15. The local newspaper made a perfect gift.
16. A witty article spoke of modern marriage.

LEVEL

C. Write each sentence. Fill in each blank with an appropriate adjective.

17. My father is very ____ around the house.
18. ____ nights a week he cooks dinner, which is ____ by the time my mother gets home.
19. My father has taken a ____ course in ____ cooking.
20. My mother finds gardening to be ____ and ____ .
21. ____ summer she grew ____ kinds of vegetables.
22. ____ spring she will plant a ____ garden along the ____ side of the house.
23. The ____ side of the house receives ____ sunlight.
24. The ____ vegetables grow better where the light is ____ .
25. ____ year my father cooked ____ pounds of string beans.

EXTRA PRACTICE

Three levels of practice

Articles and Proper Adjectives (page 286)

LEVEL

A. Write each sentence. Fill in each blank with the correct definite or indefinite article.

1. Does eating ____ apple ____ day keep ____ doctor away?
2. ____ piece of fruit contains some of ____ vitamins and minerals necessary for good health.
3. Fruit also contains ____ kind of fiber that should be ____ part of every diet.
4. ____ good breakfast is ____ bowl of cereal with fruit.
5. ____ banana is ____ unusual fruit that grows in its own packaging.
6. Bananas are rich in ____ essential mineral potassium and are ____ important vitamin source.

LEVEL

B. Write each proper noun. Next to each noun write the proper adjective that is formed from it. Use a dictionary if you need help.

7. Burma	11. Italy	15. Finland
8. Argentina	12. Kenya	16. Europe
9. Peru	13. Scotland	17. Sri Lanka
10. Poland	14. Morocco	18. Ghana

LEVEL

C. Write each sentence. Fill in the blank(s) with the proper adjective that is formed from the proper noun given in parentheses. Use a dictionary if you need help.

19. Trifle is an ____ dessert made with preserved fruit or jam. (England)
20. Did you ever taste a kiwi, a fuzzy-skinned fruit that is also called the ____ gooseberry? (China)
21. Can you think of anything more ____ than apple pie? (America)
22. A ____ crepe made with raspberries is delicious. (France)
23. I have tasted a ____ dessert made with plantains and a ____ dish made with pineapple. (Chile; Hawaii)
24. Bananas have different names in several ____ countries. (Europe)
25. The ____ word for a pineapple is *ananas*. (Italy)

EXTRA PRACTICE

Three levels of practice

Comparative and Superlative Adjectives I (page 288)

LEVEL

A. Write each adjective. Next to the word write its comparative and superlative forms.

1. big
2. noisy
3. spare
4. thin
5. sensational
6. huge
7. active
8. independent
9. peculiar

LEVEL

B. Write each sentence. Underline each adjective, and write its degree of comparison.

10. I enjoyed going to the antique car show.
11. I think old cars are more interesting than new cars.
12. At the show I saw a rare Bentley that was the most beautiful car I had ever seen.
13. A Rolls-Royce at the show was featured as the most expensive car in the world.
14. A popular car was the Model T Ford.
15. Perhaps the most unusual car at the show was a Packard.
16. The car with two rear axles was strange.
17. The strangest car was the odd-looking Studebaker.

LEVEL

C. Write each sentence. Fill in each blank with the correct degree of comparison for the adjective(s) given in parentheses.

18. A friend and I also went to the flower show held in the ____ convention center. (new)
19. The ____ tulips I had ever seen were on display. (pretty)
20. The many varieties of roses were even ____ to look at than the tulips. (fascinating)
21. My friend was ____ in the tropical flowers than in the regular garden flowers. (interested)
22. Some of the tropical flowers were the ____ of all the varieties exhibited. (strange)
23. The ____ part of the show included many flowers used in making perfume. (sweet)
24. Even the ____ fragrances are further concentrated by several ____ processes. (intense; special)
25. The essences are even ____ than the ____ of the original flowers. (fragrant; strong)

EXTRA PRACTICE

Three levels of practice

Comparative and Superlative Adjectives II (page 290)

LEVEL
A. Write each adjective. Next to each write the comparative and superlative forms.

1. much   3. far   5. well
2. good   4. bad   6. many

LEVEL
B. Write each sentence. Underline each adjective and write its degree of comparison.

7. Maxine is a better math student than Todd.
8. Todd, however, does best in science.
9. The worst grade that he ever got on a science test was 95.
10. One day Maxine did not feel well, and Todd offered her a little help in science lab.
11. Maxine said she would help Todd get better grades in math.
12. Now they are best friends and better students, too.
13. They did more work on their science project than anyone else.
14. Yes, their entry in the recent science fair did well.
15. In fact, it won the most points.

LEVEL
C. Write each sentence. Fill in each blank with the correct form of comparison for the adjective(s) given in parentheses.

16. Although Maria's native language is Spanish, she is one of the ____ English students in the eighth grade.   (good)
17. Maria wants to learn ____ languages than the others.   (many)
18. Maria plans to take ____ courses in foreign languages when she is in high school.   (far)
19. With the ____ effort, she can learn grammar.   (good)
20. Pronunciation of words gives her the ____ difficulty.   (much)
21. So that she can be a ____ speaker, Maria spends ____ time in the language lab.   (good; much)
22. Paolo found that the ____ way to learn French vowel sounds was by listening to records.   (good)
23. He felt that some vowel combinations were ____ from English than others.   (far)
24. To him the French vowels sounded ____ complex.   (much)
25. The placement of sound seemed ____ .   (hard)

EXTRA PRACTICE

Three levels of practice

Demonstrative Adjectives (page 292)

LEVEL

A. Write each sentence. Draw one line under each demonstrative adjective and two lines under the word that it modifies.

1. Did you see this photograph?
2. That young girl in the picture is my grandmother.
3. Those adults in the picture are her parents.
4. These photographs are of my grandfather when he was a boy.
5. In this picture my great-aunt Celia was a baby.
6. In that photograph Aunt Celia was four years old.
7. My favorite photograph is that one.
8. We gave those others to Uncle Ned.

LEVEL

B. Write each sentence. Fill in each blank with the correct demonstrative adjective.

9. Who took ____ photographs?
10. ____ one in particular is very good.
11. ____ nature photographs were taken at the San Diego Zoo.
12. ____ photographer has a lot of talent.
13. Do you like ____ photograph of the lion?
14. ____ print is the best of all ____ prints.
15. ____ photographer has a rare gift.
16. Look at the clarity of light in ____ photographs.

LEVEL

C. Rewrite each sentence so that it is grammatically correct.

17. I saw them photographs in a book.
18. This here photograph is by a famous photographer.
19. That there color photo looks like a painting.
20. This photographs were taken with an instant camera.
21. Them shots capture the beauty of this surroundings.
22. I like these here pictures better than them prints in the den.
23. These one is a bit too dark.
24. Give the first prize to those photographer.
25. That picture frames are too heavy for such delicate images.

EXTRA PRACTICE

Three levels of practice

Adverbs (page 294)

LEVEL

A. Write each sentence. Underline each adverb, and write whether it tells **when, where,** or **how** about the action verb.

1. Victor cleaned his room thoroughly.
2. His cousin Matt will be coming for a visit tomorrow.
3. Matt moved away, and Victor has not seen him recently.
4. Victor arranges his belongings neatly.
5. He stores all of his sports equipment away in the closet.
6. Victor always knows where he puts his things.
7. Matt knows Victor's habits well.
8. Matt borrowed Victor's hockey stick recently.

LEVEL

B. Write each adverb and the word(s) it modifies. Then write the part of speech of the modified word(s).

9. Victor now is anticipating Matt's visit.
10. Victor and Matt have rather similar interests.
11. Both cousins play basketball particularly well, and both are musically talented.
12. They are personally alike, too.
13. Seldom do they talk if they have nothing worthwhile to say.
14. They treat everyone politely, and they are very reliable.
15. They like each other very much.
16. Never has anyone seen them angry.

LEVEL

C. Write each sentence. Fill in each blank with an appropriate adverb.

17. Victor and Matt will attend a football game ____ .
18. ____ they will have dinner with Victor's parents.
19. Victor also got tickets for a concert that is ____ sold out.
20. The rock group is ____ popular with ____ everyone.
21. Victor thinks Matt would be ____ interested in attending.
22. Victor wishes that Matt and he lived ____ to each other because he knows he will feel ____ sad when Matt goes ____ .
23. ____ they are mistaken for twins.
24. They ____ look ____ much alike.
25. Matt and Victor are ____ alike because they are cousins.

EXTRA PRACTICE

Three levels of practice

Comparative and Superlative Adverbs (page 296)

LEVEL

A. Write each adverb. Next to each word write its comparative and superlative forms.

1. early
2. well
3. often
4. badly
5. long
6. little

LEVEL

B. Write each sentence. Underline each adverb and write its degree of comparison.

7. Sarah was eagerly awaiting summer vacation.
8. She would be leaving the city sooner than her friends would.
9. On the last day of class, Sarah arrived earlier than the others.
10. She had slept badly because she was excited about her trip.
11. She was speaking more nervously than usual because she was addressing the whole class.
12. Somehow, she knew that her speech would turn out better than anyone else's speech.
13. Sarah had prepared more carefully than ever.
14. Even the most skillfully written speech can be dull.
15. Jim delivered his speech more confidently than Alex.
16. Sarah thought the best idea was to relax completely.

LEVEL

C. Write each sentence. Fill in each blank with the correct degree of comparison for the adverb(s) given in parentheses.

17. Everyone in the class seemed to listen ＿＿ to Sarah's speech than to anyone else's. (attentively)
18. Sarah spoke ＿＿ than she had before. (well)
19. Of all the topics presented, Sarah's topic was ＿＿ likely to bore the students. (little)
20. Her topic was Italian painting, and she spoke ＿＿ than she had ever spoken in the past. (enthusiastically)
21. Sarah ＿＿ accepted the compliments. (graciously)
22. She ＿＿ told the class that she would be in Italy, traveling ＿＿ away from home than ever before. (excitedly; far)
23. The class reacted ＿＿ than before, and several students ＿＿ asked her what she would visit. (admiringly; eagerly)
24. Sarah said that she ＿＿ wanted to see Florence. (greatly)
25. Rome was ＿＿ important to her than Florence. (little)

EXTRA PRACTICE

Three levels of practice

Avoiding Double Negatives (page 298)

LEVEL

A. Write the contraction for each pair of words below.

1. is not		**5.** do not	
2. would not		**6.** will not	
3. could not		**7.** cannot	
4. has not		**8.** should not	

LEVEL

B. Write each sentence. Draw one line under each contraction. Draw two lines under each negative adverb.

9. I could hardly hear the footsteps close behind me, and when I turned, I saw no one.

10. I told myself that I shouldn't be afraid.

11. It was after midnight, and the moon wasn't visible through the clouds.

12. Nowhere could another pedestrian be seen.

13. Never had I felt so alone and vulnerable.

14. As I hurriedly made my way home, I hoped that something wasn't lurking in an alley.

15. I hadn't ever been so suspicious.

16. Never had I been afraid of my own shadow.

LEVEL

C. Write each sentence correctly so that it no longer contains a double negative.

17. I couldn't hardly believe that I was in danger.

18. In this dull town nothing never happens.

19. I tried to convince myself that it wasn't nothing but my overactive imagination that made me fearful.

20. Then the footsteps got louder and seemed closer, and I knew I hadn't never been so frightened.

21. I couldn't scarcely stop from screaming out loud.

22. When it pounced on me, I wasn't hardly breathing, and then I awoke with the cat staring at me intently!

23. The cat hadn't never jumped on the bed before.

24. At first it didn't look nowhere but at me.

25. I can't never forget hearing the other meow coming from under the bed.

EXTRA PRACTICE

Three levels of practice

Using Adjectives and Adverbs (page 300)

LEVEL

A. Write each sentence. Underline each modifier and write whether it is an **adjective** or an **adverb.**

1. When his grandmother moved, Rick missed her badly.
2. She had always been good to him.
3. He really appreciated her love and good advice.
4. Rick knew that she would not want him to feel bad.
5. She had surely helped him in many ways.
6. Rick was fortunate to have a wonderful grandmother.
7. He was really grateful.
8. To him his grandmother was a real treasure.

LEVEL

B. Write each sentence. Choose the correct modifier to complete each sentence.

9. Cindy felt (bad, badly) when she was not chosen for the team.
10. She had not realized that she did not play (good, well).
11. She (sure, surely) was surprised to see how (good, well) the other students were.
12. She felt (sure, surely) that she could improve.
13. Cindy wanted to become a (real, really) good actor.
14. Perhaps she could forget about playing soccer (bad, badly).
15. Making characters seem (real, really) was (sure, surely) noble.
16. Her (real, really) calling now was (sure, surely).

LEVEL

C. Write each sentence. Fill in each blank with the correct modifier from these pairs: **good/well, bad/badly, sure/surely,** and **real/really.**

17. When Alice moved away, Karen felt ____ .
18. Since first grade they had been ____ friends.
19. Karen would ____ miss sharing confidences with Alice.
20. She was ____ that Alice would make new friends in Texas.
21. Alice was ____ at making friends easily.
22. Karen was ____ looking forward to visiting Alice.
23. Everyone was ____ surprised when Alice moved back.
24. At first Karen's ____ feelings were mixed with ____ feelings.
25. They discovered that their friendship was ____ not simple.

PRACTICE + PLUS

Three levels of additional practice for a difficult skill

Using Adjectives and Adverbs (page 300)

LEVEL

A. Write each sentence. Underline each modifier and write whether it is an **adjective** or an **adverb.**

1. Nancy works hard to be a good journalist.
2. When she interviews people, she is really conscientious.
3. She prepares her questions well.
4. She is sure about her facts.
5. Even if she feels bad, she is polite.
6. She guides the interview surely and courteously.
7. Nancy has a sure instinct for real news.

LEVEL

B. Write each sentence. Choose the correct modifier to complete each sentence.

8. Nancy feels (well, good) about her job.
9. She meets (real, really) interesting people.
10. She handles the pressure of deadlines (good, well).
11. On camera, she looks relaxed and (sure, surely) of herself.
12. She displays (good, well) judgment.
13. Her newscast enjoys (good, well) ratings.
14. Nancy feels that journalism performs a (real, really) service.
15. Many people at the network think she will (sure, surely) be made an anchorperson.
16. No one would feel (bad, badly) if the job were offered to her.

LEVEL

C. Write each sentence. Fill in the blank with the correct modifier from these pairs: **good/well, bad/badly, sure/surely,** and **real/really.**

17. Nancy felt ____ when she was assigned to the White House.
18. She ____ concentrated on her new assignment.
19. None of her questions were received ____ .
20. She handled herself ____ at press conferences.
21. Some advisers to the president complimented her ____ command of the facts on many issues.
22. Some evenings, though, she had to work ____ late.
23. Journalists must cope with ____ pressure sometimes.
24. Many members of a news team help journalists perform ____ .
25. Nancy is enjoying the satisfaction of a ____ career.

EXTRA PRACTICE

Three levels of practice

Mechanics: Commas with Addresses, Dates, and Names

(page 302)

LEVEL
A. Write each item. Use commas correctly.

1. September 26 1984
2. Curtis Jensen Jr.
3. Houston Texas
4. Paula Velez M.D.
5. Brooklyn New York 11201
6. Dublin Ireland
7. June 16 1904
8. Warsaw Poland
9. Oscar Smith D.V.M.

LEVEL
B. Write each sentence. Put commas where they belong.

10. Jeanne Patterson's address is 47 Greystone Lane, Stratford Connecticut 06497.
11. On August 11 1990 we will fly to Rome Italy.
12. Anthony Draper Sr. from Chicago Illinois was the guest speaker.
13. Nadine Brown Ph.D. moved to Lima Ohio this year.
14. The sale begins on December 26 1990 and ends on January 8 1991.
15. Mail your response to me by January 1 1991.
16. The store is at 51 North Main Street, Canton Ohio 14299.

LEVEL
C. Write the following letter, using commas correctly.

17.–25.

211 Sonrisa Way
Boca Raton Florida 32800
October 5 1990

Mr. Alan Palmer Jr.
The Rare Book Shoppe
356 Linden Avenue
Princeton New Jersey 08543

Dear Mr. Palmer:

On December 14 1990 I will be giving a lecture in Eugene Oregon. The topic is the use of herbs in early American folk medicine. Please send me a list of any out-of-print books that you may have on this subject.

Thank you in advance for your assistance.

Sincerely
Ramona Carson Ph.D.

EXTRA PRACTICE

Three levels of practice

Vocabulary Building: Synonyms and Antonyms (page 304)

LEVEL

A. Write each pair of words. Next to each pair write whether the words are **synonyms** or **antonyms.**

1. vague, clear
2. remarkable, nondescript
3. timely, opportune
4. adept, unskilled
5. valiantly, bravely
6. shabby, neat
7. honestly, truthfully
8. vivid, vibrant

LEVEL

B. Write each sentence. For each underlined word, substitute a synonym or an antonym as indicated in parentheses.

9. The party was crowded. (synonym)
10. The music was too soft. (antonym)
11. Everyone seemed to be having an awful time. (antonym)
12. The food tasted wonderful. (synonym)
13. The fruit punch was frosty cold. (synonym)
14. Most guests were reluctant to dance. (antonym)
15. All the guests were dressed formally and seemed friendly. (antonym; synonym)
16. Everyone agreed that it was a boring party. (synonym; antonym)

LEVEL

C. Write one synonym and one antonym for each word.

17. weak
18. random
19. dependable
20. busy
21. stealthy
22. cautious
23. swift
24. prominent
25. meek

UNIT

10

Writing Descriptions

Read the Chinese proverb and look at the picture on the opposite page. How is a book like a garden?

Descriptive writing paints a clear picture with words. When you write a description, you will want your readers to be able to construct a vivid image in their minds of what you have described.

Focus A description creates a vivid picture of a person, place, or thing.

What would you like to describe? On the following pages you will find a story that contains some wonderful descriptions. You will also find some photographs of some very interesting things. You can use the story and the photographs to help you find ideas for writing.

THEME: *IMPRESSIONS*

A book is like a garden carried in the pocket.

—Chinese proverb

LITERATURE
Reading Like a Writer

Have you ever thought about what you would do if you were lost or stranded? How would you survive? What kind of shelter would you make, and how would you get enough food to eat?

Fifteen-year-old Meribah has been stranded inside a cave in an unfamiliar mountain forest for several weeks. It is the middle of winter, and she has only a small fire to keep her warm and protect her from wild animals.

As you read the selection, look for the details the author uses to help you see the mountain forest as Meribah saw it.

from

Beyond the Divide

by Kathryn Lasky

January 1, 1850
*The cave on the gorge between
the Deer and Mill creeks*

The sun filtered through the snow hole at the top of the cave entrance. Meribah had been careful to keep it open during the days of the blizzard to let fresh air in. Bright beams of sunlight played over her face now. She yawned and rubbed her eyes. Her first thought was that she had slept late, but a second thought rushed up and crowded out the first. The snow had stopped! Two blizzards back to back had blocked in the cave and Meribah for a week. There could not be a third one—not so soon, at least. Meribah took her knife and poked open the snow hole a bit wider in order to see out better. In the morning sun the white world sparkled like an immense jewel. To the south and west, bare windswept ridges rose like ranks of ever breaking waves. The mountain forest was sheathed in snow and morning light. Pine trees bristled with a million icy needles. The oak's branching limbs, blazing in the sunshine, appeared like ice lace in the winter stillness. The sharp whiteness of the air pierced Meribah's nostrils and stung her cheeks. She was eager to be out. There was much to do.[1]

But first the mark. Meribah took a flake of obsidian she had found near the cave and scratched a line on the wall. It had been three weeks, not since Goodnough had left—that had been seven—not since her father had died—that had been six—but three weeks since she had left the blood-splattered tent and found this cave. It must be the first of January according to Meribah's calculations. The first of January, she thought. I'm fifteen. How much longer until a real thaw? Until the last of the storms? She rekindled the fire. There was still some doe soup from the hindquarter she had wrested from the birds. In the few days of grace after she had left the tent and before the blizzards, Meribah had found a cache of acorns hidden in a tree hollow in a tightly woven basket. Meribah would never have thought of eating acorns, but the fact that they were in a basket suggested that someone had thought of them as food. Also in the basket were some camass and tiger lily roots—something else she had never thought of eating.

She experimented carefully in eating these new things. She remembered that Mrs. Grant had told her that many things were

1. The writer uses vivid details that create a strong overall impression.

poisonous when eaten raw but not when boiled slowly. So after
a long cooking time, Meribah would take little bites of the new
food. If it tasted all right, she would eat a little more, attentive
to any effects. Acorns became her favorite. In the week of
captivity she had devised different methods for cooking them.
They were very good roasted and eaten whole, which was the
quickest and easiest way. But their flavor was best when she
simmered them slowly, then ground them into a paste and
added some of the sweet birch bark from Mrs. Grant's basket.
The inner bark was especially sweet, and this took the edge off
the slight bitterness of the acorns.

If acorns tasted so good, she reasoned, there might be other nuts and perhaps even seeds that she could enjoy. So she was eager to get out this morning and look. Besides, she felt odd about taking from the basket. It was so clearly somebody else's supply, and the idea of gathering nuts was more appealing than probing the snow for oxen or mule carcasses from wagon trains. It was as if on that bloody night when she had walked out of the tent, taking only what she needed on the sledge, she had left behind a fundamental way of living. The former resources seemed as fragile and unsustaining as the old dreams. It was all fool's gold. Since she had been eating the acorns and boiled roots, she had felt much less hungry than in the days back in the tent when she had been eating squirrel and mouse. Not once since being in the cave had she experienced that peculiar sensation of feeling her skull become paper thin, almost transparent, as if the cavity were bright with too much light. Indeed, Meribah had often felt as though she were outside her body and peering into her own skull. She had not felt that way in days.[2]

In a grove of oaks she dug down under the snow for the acorns. Some were rotten from the dampness, but she found a number of good ones. Nearby she also found hazelnuts and buckeyes. Spotting a small winter bird pecking at a pine cone for its nuts, she decided to try some of these also. Although autumn was the time for gathering nuts and many of Meribah's appeared rotten, she had found ways of peeling away the bad parts, drying them slowly in the heat of warm ashes, and then roasting them, to make them palatable. She headed now on her snowshoes for a grove of birch trees that she remembered.

The snow was becoming softer and more difficult to walk on. She stopped on a bare crest of hill to take off the hood that she had made from the pelt of the squirrel that Goodnough had shot. The snow had never been able to gather on the windswept crest, but an ice lip had formed on its edge. Meribah looked at the glistening rim of ice. Ice burn, she thought as she saw the patches of scorched grass beneath the ice. She had seen this before on the ridges of the gorge, which were often swept bare of snow by the wind. The ice acted as a magnifying glass to scorch whatever grew beneath it. The nurturing warmth of the

2. The author uses details that appeal to the senses.

sun was turned into a fire by the ice. What was supposed to
nourish instead consumed. It was an odd act of nature that
fascinated Meribah.[3]

As she stared down at the icy crest, something caught her
eye. Bright and red as jewels, they sparkled under the ice on a
cushion of scorched grass. "Raspberries!" she cried, and
dropped to her knees. She took out her knife and chipped
through the ice. Raspberries for her birthday. The berries were
plump and ripe. In another hour they would have been burned.
There were perhaps three handfuls, which she ate right there.
They were not meant to be saved. They were meant to be eaten
there, straddling that thin silver rim of ice at the top of a new
world. With the sweet juice of a miracle in her mouth, Meribah
looked out toward the march of snowy peaks.

That night by her fire she thought about the raspberries. She
could still taste their sweetness. No summer berry would ever
taste as sweet. She would always have the taste of these, cling-
ing and more real than a memory. She began to think about
things that cling. Her father, he was gone, but yet she lived with
him, seeing his face, hearing his voice. It was as if he were still
there with her, a presence streaming through the minutes of her

3. The ordering of details is clear and vivid.

life like a current in a river. Miracles, Meribah decided, were not meant to be pondered too hard or studied too deeply. They just happened, and one felt blessed by them.

The next morning the sun poured into the cave, and Meribah, feeling warm and still blessed, looked over at her substantial cache of nuts. She decided that perhaps she should replenish the woven basket in the tree hollow. She set out immediately after her breakfast of acorn mush sprinkled with pine nuts, a new flavor that she liked as much as the acorns.

The snow nearly reached the lower edge of the tree hollow, but the basket was still there. Meribah had not realized before how lovely the basket was. Not only was it tightly woven but beautifully shaped into an almost perfect oval with elaborate designs. When she reached into it to put in her acorns, she gasped. The basket had been refilled, and this time there were more camass roots and dried apples! This was meant to be pondered.

There had been evidence of Indians everywhere between Mill Creek and Deer Creek. Especially since she had left the tent to come to the cave, Meribah had seen many signs—obsidian chips from toolmaking, heavy flat stones used for grinding. She had even taken one such stone back to the cave to grind her own acorns. She was surprised not that there were Indians but that a sign had been made to her. As little as Meribah had seen earlier of the California Indians, just after they had crossed Fandango Pass, she realized that these Indians were different from the ones of the plains. She and Goodnough had talked about these differences. The Pitt River Indians, which included the Mill Creeks of this region and those to the north and east where the Pitt River originated, were neither painted nor be-feathered. They seemed to blend in with the forests and rugged terrain in which they lived. Unlike the Plains Indians, they sought no contact with the emigrants for either trade or con-frontation. Withdrawal seemed to be their pattern. Very rarely was a Mill Creek ever seen by a white person, and yet they seemed to have the run of the gorges, the hills, and the forests between the Mill and Deer creeks. Meribah was stunned now as she stood holding the dried apples and camass roots in her hands. A clear sign had been given, a contact of sorts had been made. What did it mean?

Each day the basket was replenished in a small way—a root, a piece of dried deer meat or salmon, some nuts. Meribah continued to look for her own food sources. She did not feel it right to take everything from the basket or to become reliant solely on her secret benefactor. The notion of total reliance on anyone except herself was becoming an alien one to Meribah. But she did continue to visit the tree hollow almost daily— never, however, catching a glimpse of the basket's replenisher. Between the basket and Meribah's own successes in finding nuts, food was not the problem that it had been several weeks before.

Thinking Like a Reader

1. How did Meribah survive in the forest?
2. What would you have done if you were Meribah?

Write your responses in your journal.

Thinking Like a Writer

3. What does the author describe to convey what Meribah experienced? Which details does she provide?
4. Which descriptions did you like best? Which ones created the most vivid pictures in your mind?
5. If you were writing a description about a place that is or was important to you, how would you describe it?

Write your responses in your journal.

Brainstorm *Vocabulary*

In *Beyond the Divide* the author creates a picture of the winter setting around Meribah with descriptions such as "the white world sparkled like an immense jewel" and "the oak's branching limbs . . . appeared like ice lace in the winter stillness." Think of an interesting place that you know. It might be your own neighborhood or a distant place that you have visited. You might also want to try to describe it at a particular time of year. In your journal create a personal vocabulary list of words and phrases that capture the images that come to mind. You can use these words in your writing.

Talk It Over
Describe a Place You Know

In *Beyond the Divide* Kathryn Lasky often describes things by making comparisons. For example, she compares the mountain ridges with breaking waves. The author also uses vivid words in her descriptions. She tells about the "sharp whiteness" of the snow-covered forest. Imagine that you have just come back from vacation and want to tell a friend about some place you thought was interesting. Choose a partner and describe what you saw. Try to create clear images for your listener. Use comparisons and vivid language.

Quick Write *A Travel Brochure*

Now that you have been thinking about a place you would like to describe, try writing the description as if you were writing a travel brochure. A brochure is a pamphlet or booklet that describes something in a vivid way. For example, if you had just come back from a camping trip, you might write about campsites.

The well-kept campsites are located along a narrow ridge overlooking a sparkling, clear lake. Each site is equipped with running water and a modern outdoor grill. Thick groves of pine trees and leafy shrubs provide a sense of privacy as well as welcome shade during the day. The convenient sites are large enough to accommodate spacious tents or small recreational vehicles. The pure, pine-scented air and refreshing breezes from the lake will delight you and your entire family.

Idea Corner *Places of Interest*

Think about topics for writing a description. In your journal, write whatever ideas come to mind. You might start by writing some general topics, such as "Vacation Spots," "Interesting Places in My Hometown," or "Interesting Sights I Have Seen." Under each general topic, list the subjects that you might like to describe. Jot down any descriptive words or phrases that come to mind.

PICTURES  *SEEING LIKE A WRITER*

Finding Ideas for Writing
Look at the pictures. Think about what you see. What ideas
for writing a description do the pictures give you? Write
your ideas in your journal.

Moore's *Family Group*

1 GROUP WRITING: A DESCRIPTION

COOPERATIVE
LEARNING

The **purpose** of descriptive writing is to create a clear and vivid picture of a person, a place, or a thing. A good description makes the subject clear and vivid to your audience by using the following elements.

- Overall Impression
- Sensory Details
- Ordering Details

Overall Impression

Read the following paragraph. Notice that the topic sentence is underlined. Does it attract your attention so that you want to read further?

> The giant sequoia trees of the Mariposa Grove create a dream-like world in which nature has been created on a giant scale. On the average, the trees stand over 250 feet tall and weigh as much as 2 million pounds. At the base of the older trees, the trunks are 30 to 40 feet across. The trunks are covered with rough strips of bark as large as a person's arm. Pale green moss grows on the bark, giving these huge pillars an almost ghost-like appearance as they taper towards the sky. High above, as much as 150 feet from the ground, loom huge branches that carry the canopy of green, scale-like needles. As the wind blows through the grove, the giant trees creak in the immense silence, as if the emphasize their age. When it rains, the clean scent of pine needles fills the air, creating a fresh fragrance everywhere. Visitors to the Mariposa Grove cannot help feeling humbled by the majesty of the giant sequoias.

The topic sentence states a general idea or feeling, or **overall impression,** of what the Mariposa Grove is like. In addition, the topic sentence immediately captures the interest of the reader. All of the details in the paragraph support the overall impression stated in the topic sentence and help recreate the writer's experience in the mind of the reader.

Guided Practice: Creating an Overall Impression

As a class, decide on a familiar or special place that you would like to describe. If you wish, use one of the topics listed below. Discuss ideas with each other. Then write a topic sentence that states your overall impression of the place.

an old barn   the school cafeteria at lunch time
a busy beach   your community's main shopping area

Sensory Details

Sensory details are details that appeal to one of the five senses. They are often used in descriptive writing to describe how things look, sound, taste, feel, or smell. Sensory details are used to help create an overall impression in a description.

In the description of the giant sequoia trees in the Mariposa Grove, sensory details contribute to the overall impression of the forest environment.

■ Which sensory details are used to describe the grove?
■ To which senses do these details appeal?

Guided Practice: Using Sensory Details

Recall the place that you, as a class, have chosen to describe. Reread your topic sentence. Then think of some sensory words and phrases that you might use in your description. As a class, make a chart similar to the one below. List sensory words and phrases that add to the overall impression of the place you are describing.

Sight	Sound	Smell	Touch	Taste
pale green	creak	clean smell	rough	refreshing

Ordering Details

You are already familiar with some ways in which to order details in a paragraph. **Chronological order** is the time order in which things happen. The writer of the paragraph about sequoia trees used **spatial order.** Spatial order is used to describe the location or size things have in relationship to one another. For example, you learn that when a person stands next to a giant tree, he or she feels very small. When a person looks at the trees from a distance, they seem to be bigger, not smaller. Some words and phrases that can indicate spatial order include *next to, in the distance, in front of, in back of, top, bottom, above,* and *below.*

If a description is to be clear and easy to understand, be sure to organize the details carefully. You might decide to use a spatial order that moves from near to far, or bottom to top, or inside to outside.

Guided Practice: Ordering Details

As a class, examine the details you have selected for the topic that you have chosen to describe. Think about a clear and logical way to order the details. Discuss several possible methods before making a final decision.

Putting a Description Together

With your classmates you have written a topic sentence that gives an overall impression of a place you wish to describe. You have also listed some sensory words that you might use in your description. You have also decided how you want to order the details.

Another element of descriptive writing is **figurative language.** Figurative language is a way of making comparisons in order to give color and vividness to what you write. Three kinds of figurative language are **simile, metaphor,** and **personification.**

- A **simile** directly compares two things, using the words *like* or *as.*

    The trees were like silent guards.
    The owl was still as a stone.

- A **metaphor** is an indirect comparison of two things. It describes one thing as if it were something else.

    The sky was an ocean of deep blue.
    The lit window was a beacon in the night.

- **Personification** gives human characteristics to objects, ideas, or animals.

    The branches whispered in the wind. They spoke a secret language to all who would listen.

Guided Practice: Writing a Description

As a class, add more sensory details to each category of the chart that you have already made. Eliminate any details that do not contribute to the overall impression. Then write supporting sentences that use the details from your chart. Use a method of ordering that works best for the subject that you have chosen. Discuss with your classmates the most effective organization. Be sure to use figurative language.

Checklist Descriptive Writing

When you write a description, you will need to keep some points in mind. Below is a checklist for writing a description. Copy it and add any other points to it that you want to remember when you are writing a description. Keep the checklist in your writing folder and use it when you write.

> **CHECKLIST**
>
> - Remember purpose and audience.
> - Include an overall impression.
> - Use sensory details.
>   - Sight
>   - Sound
>   - Smell
>   - Touch
>   - Taste
> - Order details logically.
> - _____

2 THINKING AND WRITING: Classifying

You have learned some important points about writing a description. A topic sentence should state the overall impression. Sensory details will help to expand and enrich your description. Ordering the details in your paragraph will help make it clearer. Using figurative language will help to give special meaning to what you write.

You have listed some sensory words that you may wish to use in a descriptive paragraph about a place. Your writing will be more interesting if you include words or phrases that appeal to several of the senses. Sensory details bring a description to life.

One way to review the sensory words and phrases is to **classify** them, or group them in a chart according to categories. That way you can see how many of the senses you have referred to and how often. A chart will also help you to determine whether the words you have chosen will add to the overall impression of your description. Look at this chart of sensory words from a writer's journal. The writer had decided to describe an old sailing ship she had visited. Notice that she has included some words for four of the five senses. Because her visit did not involve the sense of taste, she did not include it on her chart.

Sight	Sound	Smell	Touch
iron cannons	creak	moldy	rough
tall masts	splash	fishy	damp
old timbers	echo	damp	slippery
large sails	lapping		
sea gulls			

Thinking Like a Writer

- What overall impression might the use of these sensory details support?
- How can classifying sensory details help you to write an effective description?

THINKING APPLICATION Classifying Sensory Details

You know that classifying sensory details can help you make your descriptions more effective.

A. Read the following sentences that describe a meadow on an early summer morning. Classify each detail according to one or more of the fives senses—sight, sound, smell, touch, or taste.

1. The sunlight caressed each contour of the grassy expanse.

2. The fresh, cool dampness of the air tempted the lungs to fill with its sweetness.

3. Thin clouds stretched across the startling blue of the sky.

4. Each step was cushioned by gently crackling grass.

5. A cool breeze stirred the grasses and made them nod.

B. Each of the writers below is planning to write a description. Make a list of sensory details that each might include. Then make a chart to classify the details. How many of the senses have you included? You may want to discuss your thinking and share your charts with other students. Be prepared to explain your choices.

COOPERATIVE
LEARNING

1. Leon is writing a description of a new park in his town. He wants to create the overall impression of happy activity. What are some sensory words and phrases that he might use?

2. Rosa is writing a description of a new restaurant that she visited. She wants to create the overall impression that the food and service were enjoyable and that the restaurant was a pleasant place.

3. Candice is writing a description of an amusement park that she visited. She wants to create an overall impression that the visit was exciting.

4. Mike is writing a description of a baseball game that he attended. His main concern is to create an overall impression of an exciting game and the noisy, good cheer of the spectators.

5. Tanya is writing a description of an art museum that she visited. She wants to create the overall impression of the beauty and variety of the works of art that she saw. What kinds of sensory details might she use?

3 INDEPENDENT WRITING: A Description

Prewrite: Step 1

You have learned the main elements of a good description. Now you are ready to choose a topic for a description of your own. This is how Edward, a student your age, chose a topic.

Choosing a Topic

First Edward made a list of general topics about some places that he thought might be interesting to describe.

my neighborhood	amusement parks
✓ vacation in California	trips to the country
museums	sporting events

Edward thought about each of the general topics on his list and decided that his visit to Yosemite National Park in California would be the most interesting. Then he began to narrow his topic so he could cover it in one paragraph.

Edward decided he would write about his visit to Bridalveil Falls. He liked that topic best and thought that it would be the most interesting.

Exploring Ideas: Clustering Strategy

Edward explored his topic by making a cluster. Here is what his cluster looked like.

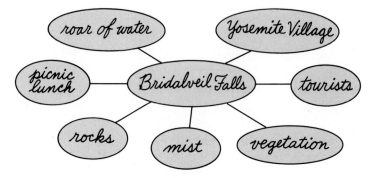

Edward thought he had some good ideas for his description. He decided that his **audience** would be his classmates. His **purpose** for writing would be to describe his visit to Bridalveil Falls so that his classmates could experience it the way he did.

Before beginning to write, Edward closed his eyes and tried to picture how the falls looked. As he thought, he added more details to his cluster and crossed some out.

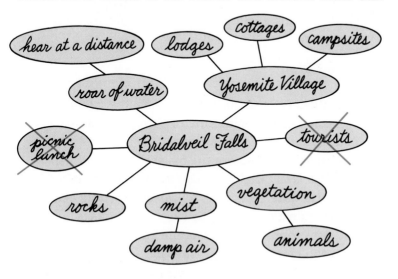

Thinking Like a Writer

■ What details did Edward add to his cluster?

■ What details did he decide to cross out?

■ Why do you think he crossed out those details?

YOUR TURN

Think of a place you would like to describe. Use **Pictures** or your journal for ideas.

JOURNAL

■ Make a list of topics.

■ Choose the topic you like best.

■ Narrow your topic if it is too broad.

■ Think of the overall impression you want to make and state it in a topic sentence.

■ Think about your purpose and audience.

Now make a cluster to explore your topic. Remember, you can add to or take away from the cluster at any time.

Write a First Draft: Step 2

To help him remember the important parts of an effective description, Edward had made a planning checklist. He took out his checklist and used it as he began the first draft of his description.

Then Edward wrote his first draft. He did not stop to make corrections in his work. At this point he was more concerned with putting his ideas down on paper while they were fresh in his mind. He knew he could make any necessary changes and corrections later.

Edward's First Draft

> Bridalveil Falls is the place to visit. The falls lie deep in the california mountains in Yosemite National park. Lodges, cottages, and campsites are available in Yosemite Village. High above the canyon floor a shaft of water falls from the rocky wall. A white viel spreads as the water falls with a roar to the rocks below. The falls are named good. At the base of the falls, a fine mist rises to make the air damp. The vegetation here thrives on the moisture. It is lusher here than in other areas. Signs of abundant wildlife are evident everywhere.

YOUR TURN

Write the first draft of your description. As you prepare to write, ask yourself the following questions.

■ What does my audience need to know to form a clear picture of my subject?

■ What overall impression do I want to give? How can I best express it?

■ What sensory words and phrases can I use?

■ How can I use figurative language to make my writing more interesting?

TIME-OUT You might want to take some time out before you revise. That way you will be able to revise your writing with a fresh eye.

Revise: Step 3

After he finished his first draft, Edward read it over to himself to see if he needed to make any improvements. Because he also wanted someone else's opinion, Edward showed his writing to a classmate.

Your paragraph has many good details, but I think you need to give a stronger overall impression.

You're right. My topic sentence is weak.

Edward wanted to be sure to use his friend's comment when he revised his description. To help him remember, he took out his planning checklist and put a check mark next to the point about including an overall impression. Edward now has a checklist to use as he revises.

As Edward revised his first draft, he referred to his checklist. Should he add sensory details? Were the details arranged logically? Should he eliminate information? He knew that he could wait until later to check for errors in spelling, capitalization, and grammar.

Edward also thought about **purpose** and **audience.** He reminded himself that his purpose in writing was to describe Bridalveil Falls so that someone reading his paragraph could imagine its beauty and fascination. He reasoned that his classmates, who were his audience, would be interested in many of the same aspects of the falls that he had found interesting. He hoped that some of his classmates would want to visit there after reading or hearing his description.

Read Edward's revised draft on the next page.

Revising Checklist
- Remember purpose and audience.
- ✔ Include an overall impression.
- Use sensory words and details.
  - Sight
  - Sound
  - Smell
  - Touch
  - Taste
- Order details logically.

Edward's Revised Draft

Bridalveil Falls is ~~the place to visit.~~ *filled with natures wonders.* The falls lie deep in the california mountains in Yosemite National park. ~~Lodges, cottages, and campsites are available in Yosemite Village.~~ High above the canyon floor a shaft of water ~~falls~~ *leaps* from the rocky wall. ~~A white viel~~ *Farther down* spreads as the water ~~falls~~ *tumbles* with a roar to the rocks below. The falls are named good. At the base of the falls, a fine mist rises to make the air damp. The *lush* vegetation here thrives on the moisture. *and* ~~It is lusher here than in other areas.~~ Signs of abundant wildlife are evident everywhere.

powerful

Thinking Like a Writer

- How did Edward change his topic sentence? Why did he make that change?
- Which sensory words did Edward add? How do they improve his paragraph?
- Which sentence did he cross out? Why do you think he crossed it out?

YOUR TURN

As you read your revised draft, ask yourself these questions.

- How can I make my overall impression clearer?
- How can I capture the interest of my readers?
- How can I arrange the details in my description more logically?
- Can I add any sensory words to make my writing more vivid?
- How can I use figurative language to give added meaning to what I have written?
- How can I improve my writing by combining sentences?

If you wish, ask a friend to read your description and make suggestions. Then revise your paragraph.

Proofread: Step 4

After revising his work, Edward knew he hadn't finished correcting his description until he proofread it carefully.

PROOFREADING CHECKLIST

- Did I indent my paragraph?
- Did I spell all words correctly?
- What punctuation errors do I need to correct?
- What capitalization errors do I need to correct?
- Did I use adjectives and adverbs correctly?

Part of Edward's Proofread Draft

Bridalveil Falls is ~~the place to visit.~~ *filled with nature's wonders.* The falls lie deep in the california mountains in Yosemite National park. ~~Lodges, cottages, and campsites are available in~~ ~~Yosemite Village.~~ High above the canyon floor a shaft of water *powerful* falls *leaps* from the rocky wall. A white viel *Farther down* spreads as the water falls *tumbles* with a roar to the rocks below. The falls are ~~named good.~~ *well named.*

YOUR TURN

Proofreading Practice

Find the errors. Write the corrected paragraph on a separate sheet of paper.

Independence Hall in philadelphia Pennsylvania is the cradel of american liberty. On July 4 1776 the Declaration of Independence was signed there the whole process of separation from England began. Even today the hole building glows with the spirit of freedom

Applying Your Proofreading Skills

Now proofread your description. Refer to the proofreading checklist. Review **The Grammar Connection** and **The Mechanics Connection,** too. Use the proofreading symbols shown on this page.

THE GRAMMAR CONNECTION

Remember these rules about comparing adjectives.

- Add *er* to one-syllable adjectives when comparing two things or people.

  The Sears Tower is **taller** than the Empire State Building.

- Add *est* to one-syllable adjectives when comparing three or more things or people.

  The Sears Tower is the **tallest** building in the world.

- Use *more* or *most* (or *less* or *least*) when comparing some two-syllable adjectives and adjectives of three or more syllables.

  The Taj Mahal is **more graceful** than the White House.
  Many people think it is the **most beautiful** building of all.

Check your description. Have you used adjectives correctly?

THE MECHANICS CONNECTION

Remember this rule about proper adjectives.

- Capitalize adjectives formed from proper nouns.

  Arabian oil   **Chinese** porcelain   **French** restaurant

Review your paragraph. Have you capitalized proper adjectives?

Proofreading Marks
Indent ⁋
Add ∧
Add a comma ⩘
Add quotation marks ⩔ ⩔
Add a period ⊙
Take out ⤴
Capitalize ≡
Lower-case letter /
Reverse the order ∿

Publish: Step 5

Edward looked forward to reading his description to his classmates. After he made a neat final copy of his description, he asked his teacher for some time to give an oral presentation of his writing. Later, several of his classmates asked him questions about Bridalveil Falls. Many wanted to know more about the vegetation and animals that he had seen there. Edward was glad to answer their questions. Talking about the falls helped him to remember what it was like to be there. He promised the class that he would bring in photographs from the trip so that they could see some of the wonders for themselves.

YOUR TURN

Make a neat, final copy of your description. Think of ways to share your work. You might want to use one of the ideas in the **Sharing Suggestions** box below.

SHARING SUGGESTIONS

Create a book of places. Illustrate each description that you include.	Include your description in a letter to a friend.	Use your description as part of an article for the school newspaper.

4 SPEAKING AND LISTENING: Telling About a Place

You have just written a description of a place that you know. Your description included a topic sentence that gave an overall impression of the place. It also included sensory details and figurative language that expanded and enriched your overall impression. You also arranged the details in a logical order. Now you can use what you know about writing a description to prepare and present a short talk.

First, you will want to prepare a note card to use as a reference. You do not have to write out everything on your note card. A talk should not sound as if you are reading. Jot down only the main points and a few important details.

Below is an example of a note card for a talk.

> Notes   Impressions of Mystic Seaport
>
> 1. like stepping back in time
> 2. located on picturesque harbor
> 3. taste of salt in sea air
> 4. streets and shops from turn of the century
> 5. smell of sawdust, straw, and old wood
> 6. tours of reconstructed sailing ships

Notice that the first point states an overall impression. What other points are listed? What sensory details are included?

When you present your talk, use the following guidelines.

SPEAKING GUIDELINES: A Description

1. Remember your **purpose** and **audience.**
2. Give your overall impression of the place. Include sensory details and figurative language to support this impression.
3. List the main points and details on a note card and practice using it.
4. Arrange your main points and details in a logical order. Consider using chronological order or spatial order.
5. Look at your audience when you speak. Use a normal, relaxed tone of voice.
6. Say your words clearly so they can be heard and understood. Do not speak too quickly.

- Why is it important to give an overall impression of the place?
- Why is it important to use sensory details and figurative language?
- Why is it important to present the details in an order that makes sense?

SPEAKING APPLICATION A Description

Prepare a note card to use when delivering a short talk about a place that is special to you. It might be some place in your home town, a favorite vacation spot, or a special place you like to visit. Use the speaking guidelines to help you prepare your notes. Your classmates will be using the following guidelines as they listen to your description.

LISTENING GUIDELINES: A Description

1. Listen for a strong topic sentence.
2. Listen for the overall impression.
3. Listen for sensory details and figurative language.
4. Listen for an order of details that makes sense.

THE CURRICULUM CONNECTION

Writing About Art

From the New Stone Age some 10,000 years ago to the present, people have been expressing themselves through the graphic arts. For those who lived during the New Stone Age, art was what they drew on the walls of caves. Today, graphic and plastic arts take many forms: drawings, paintings, collages, sculptures, photographs, or an assemblage of found objects.

You can view art in many places. Museums display large collections of art for the public. Sculpture can often be seen in public and private buildings. You can also learn about art by reading reference books, or books about a particular art form or artist. One of the best ways to learn about art, however, is to experience it yourself and think about the impression it makes on you.

ACTIVITIES

Create a Collage
A collage is a picture made by gluing objects to a flat surface. A collage can be colorful, symbolic, pictorial, amusing, or any combination of these. Choose such materials as photographs from magazines, cloth, pressed flowers, newspaper, and even three-dimensional objects, such as buttons. Arrange your objects on a flat surface until you find a pleasing pattern, and then glue them onto the support. Collages can be created by an individual or by a group. When you finish, display your work.

Describe a Painting
Look at a painting or reproduction of one in a book. Think of how you would describe the painting. First, write notes about your impressions. Then, write a description for someone who has never seen the painting. Describe both the subject represented in the painting as well as the mood or idea that you think the artist is trying to express. Remember to include sensory words and figurative language in your description.

Respond to Literature

The following comments about modern art were made in the 1950s by the American painter Jackson Pollock. First, read the comments and think carefully about what Pollock is saying. It may help you to look at the painting by Pollock shown on this page to understand what he means when he says modern painters "work from within." Then, respond to Pollock's ideas in the form of an essay, an editorial, or a letter that either agrees or disagrees with what Pollock is saying. In your writing, support your response by describing a specific modern painting.

Thoughts on Modern Painting

All cultures have had means and techniques of expressing their immediate aims—the Chinese, the Renaissance, all cultures. The thing that interests me is that today painters do not have to go to a subject matter outside of themselves. Most modern painters work from a different source. They work from within. . . . And the modern artists have found new ways and new means of making their statements. It seems to me that the modern painter cannot express this age—the airplane, the atom bomb, the radio—in the old forms of the Renaissance or of any other past culture. Each age finds its own technique . . . the strangeness will wear off, and I think we will discover the deeper meanings in modern art.

—B.H. Friedman, *Jackson Pollock: Energy Made Visible*

UNIT CHECKUP

LESSON 1

Group Writing: A Description (page 336)   Read the paragraph below. On a separate sheet of paper, write the sentence that states the overall impression. Identify figurative language and list sensory words the writer uses.

The sights and sounds of the carnival created a world far removed from everyday life. The sweet smell of cotton candy hung in the air, and the acrid taste of dust lingered in the mouth. No one seemed to notice the gritty feeling that surrounded them. Above the clatter of the crowd could be heard the sounds of children laughing, and sometimes crying. Gaily colored tents created a bizarre backdrop for even stranger sights within. Machines with outstretched arms whirled like awesome monsters dancing to some unknown melody.

LESSON 2

Thinking and Writing: Classifying (page 340)   Review the list of sensory words that you just wrote. Make a chart and classify the words according to the sense that each appeals to. Then add ten other words to your chart that you think would be effective in a description of a carnival.

Sight	Sound	Smell	Touch	Taste

LESSON 3

Writing a Description (page 342)   Imagine that you are a famous explorer. You have just returned from exploring a tropical forest that no one had ever seen before. Write a description of the forest. Use sensory words and figurative language in your writing.

LESSON 4

Speaking and Listening: Telling About a Place (page 350) On a piece of paper, make a note card for a brief talk about "The First Place I Remember." You will be giving the speech to your classmates, and your purpose will be to inform them about one of your earliest memories. You may want to do some freewriting or even write a short rough draft before you make your note card. Remember to speak clearly and look at your audience.

In this unit you have learned about the elements that make up a descriptive paragraph. You and your classmates have written descriptions of places and shared your impressions of those places with each other. You have also learned that art is another area in which impressions play an important part.

Look at the photograph of the modern sculpture below. What does this shape suggest to you? What do you think the artist had in mind? This kind of art is meant to create an impression rather than to portray something realistically. Discuss with your class-mates the impression made on you by this work of art.

Alexander Calder's *Flamingo*

As a class, create a classroom art gallery. Beside each work of art, display your impressions and descriptions of each work.

- Assemble original student paintings, drawings, sculptures, collages, and photographs.
- Mount or display each work in a space set up as an art gallery.
- Include descriptions and captions for each art work.
- If you wish, hold a contest with prizes awarded for the best works of art—and for the best descriptions!

UNIT

11

Prepositions, Conjunctions, and Interjections

In this unit you will learn about prepositions, conjunctions, and interjections. These little words help you include more information in sentences.

Discuss Read the poem on the opposite page. From what perspective does the tortoise view the world?

Creative Expression The unit theme is *Perspectives*. Because each of us is different, each of us has a different perspective, or view of things. Think about something that you view from a certain perspective. It might be a political issue or the way you view the seasons. Write about this topic from your perspective. Write your thoughts in your journal.

THEME: *PERSPECTIVES*

**NIGHT THOUGHT
OF A
TORTOISE
SUFFERING FROM
INSOMNIA
ON A LAWN**

*The world is very flat—
There is no doubt of that.*

—E. V. Rieu

1 PREPOSITIONS AND PREPOSITIONAL PHRASES

A preposition is a word that shows the relationship between a noun or a pronoun and another word in a sentence.

Prepositions are often used to describe the location of things.

> The politician **from** Dallas flew **to** New York.

Here is a list of common prepositions. Notice that some prepositions consist of more than one word.

about	before	except	on	until
above	behind	for	out	up
across	below	from	over	with
after	beneath	inside	past	within
against	beside	into	since	without
among	between	like	through	because of
around	down	of	to	except for
as	during	off	under	on account of

A **prepositional phrase** is a group of words that begins with a preposition and ends with a noun or a pronoun. The noun or the pronoun that follows the preposition is called the **object of the preposition.**

> Her speech was **about a new proposal.**

Guided Practice

Name the preposition and the object of the preposition in each sentence.

Example: The politician spoke to the voters.   *to voters*

1. She proposed a plan for a new park.
2. A large tract of land will be needed.
3. Money from local taxes will purchase the land.
4. The park will be built beside a lake.
5. People in the audience began to mutter.

 THINK

■ How do I recognize a group of words as a prepositional phrase?

REMEMBER

- A **preposition** is a word that relates a noun or a pronoun to another word in a sentence.
- A **prepositional phrase** is a group of words that begins with a preposition and ends with a noun or a pronoun that is the **object of the preposition.**

More Practice

A. Write the prepositional phrase in each sentence. Draw one line under the preposition and two lines under its object.

Example: Politicians stood on the platform. <u>on</u> <u><u>the platform</u></u>

6. One politician solicited opinions from the crowd.
7. People in the community were divided.
8. Some citizens disliked the idea of a new park.
9. They complained about high taxes.
10. Other citizens offered support for it.
11. They spoke with equal conviction and concern.
12. After the meeting people continued the discussion.

B. Write each sentence. Fill in the blank with an appropriate prepositional phrase.

Example: The opposition spoke ____ .
          against the project.

13. Many park supporters wrote ____ .
14. Their letters appeared ____ .
15. One ____ listed the park's benefits.
16. Benches will be placed ____ .
17. An enclosed zoo ____ would be built.
18. Recreation facilities would be located ____ .
19. Having picnic grounds ____ was suggested.
20. Some ____ formed committees ____ .

Extra Practice, page 382

WRITING APPLICATION A Letter to the Editor

Imagine a new park is planned for your town. Write a letter to the editor of a local paper telling why you approve or disapprove of the park. Then exchange letters with a classmate and identify the prepositional phrases in each other's letters.

2 USING PRONOUNS IN PREPOSITIONAL PHRASES

You often use a pronoun as the object of a preposition. When the object of a preposition is a pronoun, use an object pronoun.

> The surveyor spoke to **them** about cable TV.

Sometimes a preposition has a *compound object,* or an object consisting of two or more words joined together by a conjunction.

> The surveyor had spoken to **him** and **her.**

When you use the word *me* in a compound object, make sure that it comes last. This practice is not a grammatical rule as much as it is a politeness.

> The surveyor spoke to my parents and **me.**

Avoid using a reflexive pronoun as the object of a preposition when an object pronoun is needed.

> **CORRECT:** Survey questions were divided among us.
> **INCORRECT:** Survey questions were divided among ourselves.

Guided Practice

Choose the word or words that correctly complete each sentence.

Example: He distributed brochures among (they, them).
> *them*

1. The surveyor spoke with our neighbors and (us, ourselves).
2. He also spoke to (myself, me) for some time about cable television.
3. Then he asked many questions of (my sister and I, my sister and me).
4. Were there enough TV stations for our parents and (her, she)?
5. Which shows were popular with (me and my friends, my friends and me)?

 THINK

- How do I determine which pronoun to use as the object of a preposition?

REMEMBER

- When the **object of a preposition** is a pronoun, use an object pronoun.
- When *me* is part of a compound object of a preposition, place it last.
- Do not use a reflexive pronoun when an object pronoun is needed.

More Practice

A. Write the word or words that correctly complete each sentence.

Example: Dad gave a color TV to my brother and (I, me).   *me*

6. Cable TV became available to (ourselves, us) some time ago.
7. Our neighbors watch programs of interest to (them, they).
8. My parents subscribe mainly for (me and my brother, my brother and me).
9. To my sister and (they, them), TV is of little importance.
10. My father watches sports programs with (we, us), however.
11. For my mother and (he, him), network TV is satisfactory.
12. Except for (my brother and me, my brother and I), nobody watches much TV.

B. Write each sentence correctly.

Example: The survey applied to my brother and I.
The survey applied to my brother and me.

13. The surveyor learned these facts from me and my brother.
14. My mother and father also spoke with himself.
15. He asked many questions of them and we.
16. The cable company paid he and another surveyor.
17. The whole town was surveyed by they.
18. For both he and she, the survey was a difficult task.
19. My mother and father discussed costs between themselves.
20. There were few disagreements among my siblings and I.

Extra Practice, Practice Plus, pages 383–384

WRITING APPLICATION An Essay

What are your opinions about cable TV or about TV in general? Express your opinions in an essay. Then exchange essays with a classmate. Make sure your classmate has used pronouns correctly in prepositional phrases.

3 PREPOSITIONAL PHRASES AS ADJECTIVES AND ADVERBS

You know that adjectives describe nouns and pronouns. When a prepositional phrase is used to describe a noun or a pronoun, it functions as an adjective.

> Stars **of baseball** earn huge salaries.
> Many **of the other players** do not.

A prepositional phrase that is used as an adjective is called an **adjective phrase.**

Always place an adjective phrase as close as possible to the noun or pronoun that it modifies. Otherwise, you may convey a meaning that you do not intend.

> MISPLACED: Players earn high salaries *with good agents.*
> CORRECT: Players *with good agents* earn high salaries.

You have also learned that adverbs often modify verbs. A prepositional phrase that modifies a verb is called an **adverb phrase.** An adverb phrase can tell *where, when, why,* or *how* an action takes place.

> Highly paid stars draw crowds **to the stadium.** (Where?)
> They never play **during bad rainstorms.** (When?)
> Many athletes play **for the glamour.** (Why?)
> Most stars play **with consistent skill.** (How?)

Guided Practice

Identify the prepositional phrase in each sentence. Then tell whether it is an adjective phrase or an adverb phrase.

Example: Retirement for most players comes early.
> *for most players   adjective phrase*

1. Most baseball careers begin in the minor leagues.
2. A young player of talent may be noticed quickly.
3. Scouts for the teams carefully study new prospects.
4. Nevertheless, some of the better players are overlooked.
5. A minor-league player often remains overlooked for years.
6. Starting salaries of major leaguers are high.

THINK

■ How do I decide whether a prepositional phrase is an adjective phrase or an adverb phrase?

REMEMBER

- An **adjective phrase** is a prepositional phrase that modifies a noun or a pronoun.
- An **adverb phrase** is a prepositional phrase that modifies, or tells more about, a verb, an adjective, or an adverb.

More Practice

A. Write the prepositional phrase in each sentence. Then write whether it is an **adjective phrase** or an **adverb phrase.**

Example: A good player can go to another team.
to another team   adverb phrase

7. After three years their careers often skyrocket.
8. Players can demand a hearing by an arbitrator.
9. Both sides name a salary of a precise amount.
10. The arbitrator decides between the two amounts.
11. There is no room for compromise.
12. The arbitrator bases salaries on past performance.

B. Write each sentence. Underline each prepositional phrase. Draw two lines under the word it modifies. Write whether the phrase is an **adjective phrase** or an **adverb phrase.**

Example: Changes occur after the season.
Changes occur *after the season.*
adverb phrase

13. A baseball player plays under contract.
14. He often negotiates the contract before each season.
15. Many of the players hire agents.
16. The agent handles negotiations for new contracts.
17. By age forty most players retire.
18. Injuries to players sometimes shorten their careers.
19. Players must earn money during their playing years.
20. In the major leagues, baseball is big business.

Extra Practice, page 385

WRITING APPLICATION A Letter

In a letter to a magazine, express your opinion about high salaries in professional sports. Exchange your work with a classmate. Identify every prepositional phrase in each other's work as an adjective or an adverb phrase.

4 CONJUNCTIONS

Conjunctions connect parts of sentences. A **coordinating conjunction** may connect two subjects, two predicates, two objects of a preposition, or two simple sentences. *And, but, or,* and *nor* are used as coordinating conjunctions.

COMPOUND SUBJECT:
Luis **and** Anna are careful shoppers.

COMPOUND PREDICATE:
Good shoppers compare prices **and** clip coupons.

COMPOUND OBJECT OF A PREPOSITION:
Information in ads **or** circulars can be incorrect.

COMPOUND SENTENCE:
Most ads are honest, **but** many tell half truths.

You can also use pairs of words called **correlative conjunctions** to connect parts of sentences.

> **Common Correlative Conjunctions**
>
> | both . . . and | neither . . . nor | either . . . or |
> |---|---|---|
> | not only . . . but also | whether . . . or | just as . . . so |

Some ads **not only** mislead **but also** confuse.

Guided Practice

Identify the conjunction in each sentence. Then tell whether it joins a compound subject, compound predicate, compound object of a preposition, or the parts of a compound sentence.

Example: Sales are advertised in newspapers or circulars.
    or   compound object of a preposition

1. Many brands and products are sold by supermarkets.
2. Both store brands and national brands are also marketed.
3. National brands are advertised on TV and radio.
4. Managers place them on shelves or give them displays.
5. Store brands not only cost less, but they also give satisfaction.

 THINK

■ How can I effectively use conjunctions in my writing?

REMEMBER

- A **coordinating conjunction** is a single word used to connect parts of a sentence or to connect two sentences.
- **Correlative conjunctions** are pairs of words used to connect parts of a sentence or to connect two sentences.

More Practice

A. Write the coordinating conjunction or correlative conjunctions in each sentence. Then write whether the conjunction joins a **compound subject, compound predicate, compound object of a preposition,** or **compound sentence.**

Example: Some ads either mislead or confuse.

either . . . or   compound predicate

  6. Many ads omit some facts and exaggerate others.
  7. Facts from unnamed surveys or studies are sometimes cited.
  8. Favorable studies are used, but others are ignored.
  9. Ads appeal not only to reason but also emotion.
 10. People speak with sympathy and persuasion.
 11. Famous actors or athletes often give endorsements.
 12. We may admire them, but should we buy things they endorse?

B. Write each sentence; give the appropriate conjunctions.

Example: ___ quality ___ price are considerations.

Both quality and price are considerations.

 13. Some shoppers ___ buy impulsively, ___ they ___ buy indiscriminately.
 14. Good shoppers make a list ___ stick to it.
 15. They make a list of needs, ___ they consider specials.
 16. ___ ads ___ prominent shelf positions fool them.
 17. ___ at home ___ at the store they compare prices.
 18. They calculate prices by the ounce, gram, ___ pound.
 19. How can you ___ your friends be good shoppers?
 20. Shop wisely ___ compare prices.

Extra Practice, page 386

WRITING APPLICATION An Editorial

Write an editorial about an issue that is important to consumers. Then exchange editorials with a classmate. Identify the conjunctions and the types of compounds they join in each other's work.

5 MAKING VERBS AGREE WITH COMPOUND SUBJECTS

As you know, the verb must always agree with the subject of the sentence. In a **compound subject** that contains two or more simple subjects joined by a conjunction, the conjunction determines whether the verb that follows it should be singular or plural.

When two or more subjects are joined by *and* or by *both . . . and*, the verb is plural.

> The automobile **and** the factory *create* smog.
> **Both** Los Angeles **and** London *have* smog.

When two or more subjects are joined by *or, nor, either . . . or*, or *neither . . . nor*, the verb agrees with the simple subject that is closest to it.

> The city **or** the state *fights* pollution.
> **Neither** car owners **nor** the manufacturer *wants* smog.
> **Either** smoke **or** gases *cause* smog.

Guided Practice

Choose the correct form of the verb in parentheses for each sentence.

Example: Carbon monoxide and other pollutants (cause, causes) poor air quality.
cause

1. Factory fumes or car exhaust (create, creates) air pollution.
2. Air inversion and lack of wind (make, makes) it worse.
3. Wind or rainstorms sometimes (clear, clears) the air.
4. Either the city or the state (test, tests) air quality.
5. Neither businesses nor the state (want, wants) pollution.

 THINK

- How can I tell whether a compound subject requires a singular or a plural verb?

REMEMBER

- When two or more subjects are joined by *and* or *both . . . and,* the verb is plural.
- When two or more subjects are joined by *or, nor, either . . . or,* or *neither . . . nor,* the verb agrees with the subject that is closest to it.

More Practice

A. Write the correct form of the verb in parentheses for each sentence.

Example: Automobile and factory exhaust (foul, fouls) the air. *foul*

6. Ground pollution and water pollution (is, are) problems.
7. Solid waste or detergents (pollute, pollutes) many rivers.
8. Neither factory chemicals nor dumped garbage (help, helps).
9. Both landfills and town dumps (is, are) overflowing.
10. Biodegradable waste or conservation (is, are) the answer.
11. Either businesses or the state (clean, cleans) our rivers.
12. Neither politicians nor we (want, wants) pollution.

B. Write each sentence, using the correct form of the verb in parentheses. Underline each conjunction.

Example: Acid rain and foul air (harm, harms) our forests.
    Acid rain <u>and</u> foul air harm our forests.

13. Both air pollution and water pollution (is, are) deadly.
14. Neither animals nor humanity (remain, remains) unaffected.
15. Asthma and emphysema (occur, occurs) in humans.
16. The ear or the eye (is, are) sometimes affected.
17. Fish or land animals (drink, drinks) polluted waters.
18. Either tar or oil (damage, damages) birds' wings.
19. Neither birds nor fish (survive, survives) extensive pollution.
20. Both cities and the countryside (suffer, suffers) greatly.

Extra Practice, page 387

WRITING APPLICATION A Report

COOPERATIVE LEARNING

With a partner, discuss the problems people are creating by polluting the environment. Then write a report about an environmental problem. Exchange papers with another pair of classmates and correct any errors in subject-verb agreement that you find.

6 CONJUNCTIVE ADVERBS

Coordinating and correlative conjunctions can join simple sentences to form compound sentences. Conjunctive adverbs can do the same.

A **conjunctive adverb** is an adverb or an adverb phrase that joins simple sentences to form a compound sentence.

> Many travel by car. Others prefer trains.
> Many travel by car; **however,** others prefer trains.

Note that a semicolon is placed before a conjunctive adverb and a comma is put after it.

Study this chart of common conjunctive adverbs.

Conjunctive Adverbs	Use
also, besides, furthermore, moreover, in addition	show addition
however, nevertheless, still, yet	show contrast
otherwise, on the other hand	show an alternative
consequently, therefore, thus, as a result, so	state a result
likewise, similarly	state similarity
in fact, for example, for instance	clarify or illustrate

Guided Practice

Name the conjunctive adverb in each sentence.

Example: Trains were once luxurious; thus, they were popular.   *thus*

1. Car travel has advantages; however, I prefer trains.
2. Trains travel on tracks; therefore, traffic jams are rare.
3. Train travel is peaceful; in fact, many people take naps.
4. Passengers can read; in addition, they can walk around.
5. Train stations are usually downtown; likewise, bus stations are also convenient.

 THINK

■ How can I use conjunctive adverbs to combine sentences?

REMEMBER

- A **conjunctive adverb** is an adverb or an adverb phrase that joins simple sentences to form a compound sentence.
- When you join sentences with a conjunctive adverb, put a semicolon before it and a comma after it.

More Practice

A. Write *two* conjunctive adverbs that you could use to combine each pair of sentences.

Example: Trains are slow. They are more comfortable.
        nevertheless   however

  6. I can take the train. I can go by bus.
  7. The train ride is more scenic. The bus is cheaper.
  8. The tracks are being repaired. Many trains are late.
  9. The bus is usually on time. The bus station is more conveniently located.
10. The train is comfortable. There is plenty of leg room.

B. Write each pair of sentences as a compound sentence joined by an appropriate conjunctive adverb.

Example: Air travel is faster. It is more expensive.
     Air travel is faster; however, it is more expensive.

11. Airplanes are very fast. Transportation to the airport can be slow.
12. New York's airports are miles from Manhattan. Other airports are far from the center of town.
13. Highways near airports are busy. Arriving passengers may be delayed for hours.
14. Flights are often overbooked. Bad weather and congested air space cause many delays.
15. Airlines offer many discounts. The fare to Florida is surprisingly inexpensive.

Extra Practice, page 388

WRITING APPLICATION An Essay

Write an essay about your favorite mode of travel. Include at least five compound sentences joined by conjunctive adverbs. Then exchange papers with a classmate and check each other's use of conjunctive adverbs.

7 INTERJECTIONS

You know that exclamatory sentences express strong feelings. Occasionally you can use a single word or phrase to express a strong emotion.

An **interjection** is a word or a group of words that expresses a strong feeling. It has no grammatical connection to any other words. An interjection may be part of a sentence or it may stand alone.

Common Interjections				
Ah	Gee	Gosh	Oh, my	Wow
Aha	Good heavens	Phew	Oh, no	Yippee
Hooray	My goodness	Hey	Oops	Rats

Use a comma after an interjection that occurs at the beginning of a sentence.

Wow, movies have become very expensive!

Always use an exclamation mark after an interjection that stands alone. It usually suggests a stronger feeling than an interjection that is used as part of a sentence.

The price went up another dollar! **Oh, my!**
My goodness! Who can afford such high prices?

Interjections are not used often in formal writing. They usually are used in informal dialogue.

Guided Practice

Identify the interjection in each sentence.

Example: Wow! That was a great thriller.   *Wow!*

1. Hey, have you seen any good movies lately?
2. Well, the new movie at Cineplex is pretty good.
3. My goodness! That movie was awful!
4. All those slimy monsters! Ugh!
5. Oh, boy, do you have strange taste!

 THINK

■ When should I use an exclamation mark after an interjection?

REMEMBER

- An **interjection** is a word or group of words that expresses strong feeling.
- Use a comma after an interjection at the beginning of a sentence. Use an exclamation mark after an interjection that stands alone.

More Practice

A. Write the interjection in each sentence.

Example: Phooey, I have seen this before.
Phooey

6. We finally bought a videocassette recorder. Yippee!
7. Big deal! We've had one for years!
8. Wow, aren't VCRs great?
9. Why, we hardly use ours any more.
10. No kidding! Don't you like renting movies?
11. Hey, who wants to sit at home and watch movies?
12. Well, VCRs are great for us couch potatoes!

B. Write each sentence. Fill in each blank with an appropriate interjection. Add the correct punctuation after each interjection.

Example: ____ You spent the weekend with a movie?
Really! You spent the weekend with a movie?

13. Quincey finally made a good movie. ____
14. ____ his last twenty-six films were all terrible!
15. The last one was four hours long. ____
16. ____ did those desert scenes make me thirsty!
17. ____ this movie is a little different.
18. ____ there are no camel chases?
19. ____ What's a Quincey film without a camel?
20. ____ he rides an elephant? That *is* different!

Extra Practice, page 389

WRITING APPLICATION A Dialogue

COOPERATIVE
LEARNING

With a partner, write a dialogue in which two people express their opinions about a particular movie or movie star. Include at least five interjections. Then exchange your paper with another pair of classmates and check each other's use of interjections and punctuation.

MECHANICS: Using Semicolons and Colons

Use a **semicolon** to join parts of a compound sentence when a coordinating conjunction such as *and, or,* or *but* is not used.

> Spring floods destroy farmland; insects ruin crops.

Use a semicolon to join parts of a compound sentence when the parts are long and are subdivided by commas, even if a coordinating conjunction is used.

> Farmers must face floods, droughts, and insects; but they also live close to nature's beauty.

Use a **colon** to introduce a list of items that ends a sentence. Use a phrase such as *the following* before the list.

> Farmers in our area grow **the following** hothouse flowers: orchids, lilies, and anemones.

Use a colon to separate the hour and the minute when you write the time of day and after the salutation of a business letter.

> Many farmers begin work at 5:15 in the morning.
> Dear Sir or Madam:

Guided Practice

Add the correct punctuation to each sentence.

Example: Country life is calm people rarely hurry.
> *Country life is calm; people rarely hurry.*

1. Some like the country others find it boring.
2. In the country I am usually in bed by 9 1 5.
3. City dwellers attend concerts, plays, and films and they enjoy visiting museums and fine department stores.
4. Country dwellers often enjoy the following activities hiking, fishing, swimming, and skiing.
5. Country dwellers live close to nature they experience nature's wonders first-hand.

 THINK

- How can I decide whether to use a semicolon or a comma and a conjunction to separate the parts of a compound sentence?

REMEMBER

- Use a **semicolon** to join parts of a compound sentence when a coordinating conjunction is not used, or when the sentence parts are long and contain commas.
- Use a **colon** before a list, in the time of day, and after the salutation in a business letter.

More Practice

A. Write each sentence. Add semicolons and colons where they are needed.

Example: Cities are crowded I stay away.
Cities are crowded; I stay away.

  6. The city has the following advantages more jobs, higher pay, and better government services.
  7. City dwellers often pay high rents, prices, and taxes and they endure overcrowding and noise pollution.
  8. Many farmers begin work before 6 0 0 every morning.
  9. Some farmers are successful others go bankrupt.
 10. Rural Americans avoid big-city crowds, traffic, and noise but rural life is not without problems.

B. 11.–20. Write this section of a business letter. Add semicolons and colons where they are needed.

Dear Senator Bligh
   The life of a farmer is not easy and recent changes in trade laws, loan programs, and other government policies have not made it easier. Most farmers rise at 5 1 5 they often work until 9 1 5 at night. Farmers fight soil erosion and insect infestations and they experience natural disasters such as floods, droughts, and windstorms. They are often in debt many must spend in the spring for a profit in the fall. Farmers require the following a lower dollar, higher market prices, and more government aid. Please think of the farmer please support the farmer. Much of the future depends on your actions we depend on you.

Extra Practice, page 390

WRITING APPLICATION A Letter

Write a letter to an elected official. Express your opinions about a problem and suggest ways to correct it. Be sure that you have used semicolons and colons correctly.

GRAMMAR

9 VOCABULARY BUILDING: Prefixes

A **prefix** is a word part added to the beginning of a word or to another word part in order to change its meaning.

Prefix	Meaning	Example
de	from	**de**fect
dis	opposite or lack of	**dis**like
in*	without, not	**in**direct
mis	wrongly, badly	**mis**matched
non	not	**non**violent
un	not, opposite of	**un**friendly
uni	one	**uni**form
bi	two	**bi**weekly
tri	three	**tri**angle
anti	against	**anti**slavery
con, com, co	with, together	**con**text, **com**pare
ex	out of	**ex**hale
fore	before	**fore**warn
inter	between	**inter**national
post	after	**post**war
pre	before	**pre**pay
pro	forward	**pro**mote
re	again	**re**read
sub	under	**sub**marine

* *In* changes to *il* before *l*: *illogical*. *In* changes to *im* before *b*, *m*, or *p*: *imbalance*. *In* changes to *ir* before *r*: *irreplaceable*.

Guided Practice

Change the underlined words into a word that uses a prefix.

Example: The student body was <u>led wrongly</u>.   *misled*

1. Many students were <u>not happy</u> with the student council.
2. Members <u>behaved badly</u> during council meetings.
3. The president's performance was <u>below standard</u>.
4. The principal <u>opened</u> elections <u>again</u>.

 THINK

- How can learning prefixes help me build my vocabulary?

REMEMBER

■ A **prefix** is a word part added to the beginning of a base word. A prefix changes the meaning of the base word to which it is added.

More Practice

Change the underlined words to a single word that uses a prefix. Write that word.

Example: Some school elections are <u>badly managed</u>.
mismanaged

5. After our recent election, most of the old council was <u>removed from the throne</u>.
6. Some schools hold <u>twice-yearly</u> elections.
7. In other schools a second election is <u>not regular</u>.
8. The students <u>claim out</u> loud about any proposed changes.
9. It is <u>not legal</u> to vote more than once.
10. The president and secretary run as <u>candidates together</u>.
11. Students in their first year are <u>not eligible</u>.
12. Former presidents cannot be <u>elected again</u>.
13. Some school elections fail because students are <u>not interested</u>.
14. Much time is spent in <u>before-election</u> campaigning.
15. One faction is <u>against football</u>.
16. Another <u>posed forward</u> changes in favor of students.
17. Some candidates promises are often <u>not credible</u>.
18. Other candidates address problems that are <u>not existent</u>.
19. This year's candidates show little <u>sight beforehand</u>.
20. I am <u>not satisfied</u> with the candidates.

Extra Practice, page 391

WRITING APPLICATION An Editorial

Write an editorial about a school or local election. Include at least ten words with prefixes. Exchange papers with a classmate and identify the prefixes in each other's work. Explain the meanings of the words in which the prefixes appear.

GRAMMAR
—AND
WRITING
CONNECTION

Subject-Verb Agreement

You know that a verb must agree with its subject. In some sentences a prepositional phrase modifying the subject comes between the subject and the verb. When a prepositional phrase intervenes, be sure that the verb agrees with the subject and not with the object of the preposition.

When the subject of the sentence is singular, use the singular form of the verb.

The **history** of rockets **begins** in ancient China.

When the subject of the sentence is plural, use the plural form of the verb.

Rockets at this time **were** mainly fireworks.

Working Together

COOPERATIVE
LEARNING

Identify the subject and the correct form of the verb for each sentence.

Example: The movement of rockets (is, are) powerful.
movement is

1. The use of rockets (predate, predates) the use of gunpowder.
2. Rockets of all sorts (has, have) been used in many ways.
3. Signals at night (is, are) made by flares on rockets.
4. Illumination of wide areas (is, are) possible with flares.
5. The idea of jet engines (come, comes) from rocketry.
6. A rocket for fireworks (is, are) only two feet long.
7. Rockets for space travel (is, are) more than 360 feet high.
8. The great size of rockets (is, are) due to their fuel tanks.
9. Thousands of gallons of fuel (is, are) needed for flight.
10. Rockets for exploration and research (travel, travels) far.

Revising Sentences

Terry misunderstood the lesson about making the subject of the sentence agree with the verb. He wrote the following sentences in which some verbs agree incorrectly with the object of the intervening prepositional phrase. Rewrite Terry's sentences, correcting those that are 'wrong.

11. Many of these rockets carry satellites.
12. Hundreds of satellites are in orbit around the earth.
13. Pictures of earth's weather is relayed from satellites.
14. Information for scientific studies are sent back to earth.
15. Human space flights to the moon is made by rocket.
16. A journey to Mars is a dream for the future.
17. Trips to Mars has been made by satellites.
18. Conditions on that planet is hostile to life.
19. The cap of ice on Mars offers hope of life.
20. The dream of scientists involve plants from our planet.

Explore your ideas and feelings about space exploration. Write a paragraph that explains what you think about this issue. Include the opinions of people who might disagree with you. Explain why you think their ideas are weak. When you revise your paragraph, work with a partner to be sure that the subjects of your sentences agree with the verbs.

UNIT CHECKUP

LESSON 1 Prepositions and Prepositional Phrases (page 358) Write the prepositional phrase in each sentence. Then label the preposition **P** and its object **OP.**

1. In 1960 a presidential debate was first televised.
2. The debate was between Kennedy and Nixon.
3. There are now debates on many TV stations.
4. From them we learn the candidates' views.

LESSON 2 Using Pronouns in Prepositional Phrases (page 360) Choose the correct pronoun for each sentence.

5. For Joe and (I, me) last night's debate was fascinating.
6. Some issues were of special concern to Mom and (he, him).
7. The issues stirred emotions in him and (she, her).
8. There were many arguments between (them, themselves).

LESSON 3 Prepositional Phrases as Adjectives and Adverbs (page 362) Write the prepositional phrase in each sentence. Then write whether it is an **adjective phrase** or an **adverb phrase.**

9. An election for president draws worldwide attention.
10. The TV networks cover it in great detail.
11. Before the election they take many polls.
12. Some of our politicians have criticized these polls.

LESSON 4 Conjunctions (page 364) Write the conjunction or pair of conjunctions in each sentence and the type of compound it helps to form: **subject, predicate, object of a preposition,** or **compound sentence.**

13. Both the Republican and the Democrat seek votes.
14. Voters may register in parties or remain independent.
15. They vote in both primaries and general elections.
16. I voted on Tuesday, and I cast my vote carefully.

LESSON 5 Making Verbs Agree with Compound Subjects (page 366) Write the correct form of the verb for each sentence.

17. Both television and radio (carry, carries) political debates.
18. A reporter or a civic leader (moderate, moderates) most debates.
19. The budget or sales tax (is, are) often the chief topic.
20. Neither foreign affairs nor trade (is, are) neglected.

LESSON **Conjunctive Adverbs** (page 368)   Write each pair of sentences as a compound sentence joined by an appropriate conjunctive adverb.

21. The media provide valuable election coverage. Some people have criticized certain practices.

22. Pre-election polls are taken. Exit polls are taken on Election Day.

23. Newscasters seek scoops. They make predictions of winners.

24. Predictions can affect voters. Some may not vote.

 LESSON **Interjections** (page 370)   Write the interjection and the punctuation that should follow it.

25. Hey did you hear the election results?

26. Oh have they finally tabulated the results?

27. It took over two weeks? Wow

28. My goodness That election was close!

 LESSON **Mechanics: Using Semicolons and Colons** (page 372)
Write each sentence. Add semicolons or colons.

29. The following issues have dominated this year's election taxes, the budget deficit, and trade.

30. One candidate is a senator the other is a governor.

31. One knows more about budgets, taxes, and other economic issues but the other is a foreign-policy expert.

32. The polls close at 7 1 5 tonight.

 LESSON **Vocabulary Building: Prefixes** (page 374)   Rewrite each sentence, changing the underlined words to a single word that uses a prefix. Change word order if necessary.

33. Our state senator is against reform.

34. He sponsored a major law on commerce between states.

35. He also thinks this law was handled badly in Congress.

36. Analyses after the election will be in the newspaper.

 Writing Application: Using Prepositions, Conjunctions, and Interjections (pages 358–370)   The following letter contains thirteen errors. Rewrite the letter correctly.

37.–49.   Wow what do you think about the World Series? The local team appeals to Dad and I however our favorite of the pitchers work for the other team. Neither Dad or I prefers one whole team. This letter to yourself asks for your opinion. Gosh Dad and Mom wishes you lived closer. You and Anne stimulates opinions. As for myself, well I miss you, too. You do make visits thus life is bearable.

Stringing Phrases

Prepositional phrases can often be strung together, with each new phrase usually modifying the object of the preposition in the phrase before it. For example: I found the can on the top shelf in aisle A of the supermarket on the corner of Main Street. Taking turns with a partner, create a similar "prepositional phrase string." Make the string of phrases as long as you can and as funny as you like.

ADVERB OR PREPOSITION?

Play this game in groups of three. The first person calls out a word from the list below. The second person then correctly uses that word as an adverb in a sentence. For example: The doctor is not *in* yet. Next, the third person correctly uses the same word as a preposition in a sentence. For example: They both work *in* the same office. Then rotate the players. Keep a score.

in	across	about	past	under
out	above	near	over	around

MOVIE TITLES

Play this game in groups of three. The first player is to make up as many original movie titles as possible with the word *and* in them. The second player's titles must have the word *but* in them; the third player must use *or*. Scores can be kept.

Under the Weather

Prepositional phrases are often used as idioms. An *idiom* is a common expression in which words take on new meanings. For example, when we say that a person is "in hot water," we mean that he or she is in trouble. When we say that an idea is "off the wall," we mean that it is not sensible. Try to list and define ten more prepositional phrases used as idioms. If you have trouble, check a dictionary. Most dictionaries list and define idioms near the ends of entries for key words in those idioms. For example, "in hot water" would appear near the end of the entry for *hot* or *water*.

Can You Haiku?

A haiku is a very short poem of Japanese origin. Classically, it has seventeen syllables, arranged in three lines of five, seven, and five syllables, in that order. Its theme is often about nature. A haiku seeks only to present a few sharp images; the details and meaning are left to the imagination of the reader. Try writing some haiku of your own, choosing some aspects of nature as your topic.

Dewdrops, limpid, small—
   and such a lack of judgment shown
    in where they fall!

         —Soin (c. 1660)

EXTRA PRACTICE

Three levels of practice

Prepositions and Prepositional Phrases (page 358)

LEVEL

A. For each sentence, write the noun or pronoun that is the object of the underlined preposition.

1. Some wild plants are harmful on contact.
2. Among the plants of this type is poison ivy.
3. Its toxic sap causes severe irritation of the skin.
4. Poison ivy is common in the East.
5. Over half of America's population is susceptible.
6. Many plants in American gardens are poisonous.
7. The lovely foxglove contains two kinds of poison.

LEVEL

B. Write each prepositional phrase.

8. Berries from the nightshade plant are deadly.
9. The seeds on tall lupines are their most toxic part.
10. The seed pods hang from the stems like pea pods.
11. Poison ivy affects people in different ways.
12. Some people are immune to it from birth.
13. Others develop an immunity after frequent contact.
14. Children with immunities may not retain them.
15. They may become sensitive as teenagers or adults.

LEVEL

C. Write each sentence. Underline each prepositional phrase. Label each preposition and its object.

16. Poison ivy can be destroyed by certain chemicals.
17. However, its poison will linger after its death.
18. People sometimes burn infected wood as firewood.
19. The smoke of the wood can still transmit the poison.
20. You can pick up poison ivy directly from the plant.
21. You can also get it from infected pets and clothes.
22. Its poison has lingered on clothing for months.
23. Poison ivy grows as a vine or a shrub.
24. It often twists itself around other plants.
25. Its leaves, found in threes, turn red in autumn.

EXTRA PRACTICE

Three levels of practice

Using Pronouns in Prepositional Phrases (page 360)

LEVEL

A. Choose the pronoun that correctly completes each sentence.

1. Gardening is good exercise for David and (I, me).
2. Roses are grown by my neighbors and (me, myself).
3. For Alice and (he, him), roses are a passion.
4. An argument arose between the garden club and (they, them).
5. The club members apologized to (we, us).
6. Organic gardening is popular with my neighbors and (I, me).
7. It poses no danger to our pets or (us, ourselves).

LEVEL

B. Write whether the underlined pronoun is **correct** or **incorrect.** If it is incorrect, write the correct pronoun.

8. For both farmers and <u>we</u>, insects are nuisances.
9. Ladybugs kill our garden pests for <u>us</u>.
10. With mantises and <u>them</u>, we control pests naturally.
11. Chemical insecticides are used by Alice and <u>himself</u>.
12. These are unhealthy for <u>themselves</u> and their pets.
13. A debate began between Alice and <u>myself</u>.
14. We settled the dispute between <u>us</u>.
15. There would be no more quarrels between <u>ourselves</u>.

LEVEL

C. Write each sentence correctly.

16. Mrs. Lisi spoke to David and I.
17. She spoke with ourselves about her nursery.
18. For gardeners like me and you, pest control is a luxury.
19. For farmers and she, it is a necessity.
20. Organic pest controls are good enough for myself and you.
21. They may be too inefficient for farmers and herself.
22. Mrs. Lisi explained this to David and myself.
23. She spoke with ourselves for some time.
24. David's family brought the problem to ourselves.
25. Differences of opinion arose between they and us.

PRACTICE + PLUS

Three levels of additional practice for a difficult skill

Using Pronouns in Prepositional Phrases (page 360)

LEVEL
A. Choose the word or words that correctly complete each sentence.

1. Photography is a favorite hobby for Tom and (I, me).
2. New cameras were given to each of (we, us) on our birthdays.
3. For Tom and (I, me), taking pictures is fun and exciting.
4. Between (us, ourselves), we have all the materials for developing our own pictures.
5. This process gives pleasure to Tom and (I, me).
6. We seldom have arguments between (us, ourselves).
7. The photographs have won much praise for (we, us).
8. Everyone enjoys looking at (they, them).
9. For Tom and (I, me), the pleasure is in the process.

LEVEL
B. Write whether the underlined pronoun is **correct** or **incorrect**. If it is incorrect, write the correct pronoun.

10. Rich and Leah sold the bike to Olive and <u>me</u>.
11. We asked several questions of him and <u>she</u>.
12. We thought the price might be too high for <u>ourselves</u>.
13. A debate began between Olive and <u>myself</u>.
14. We wanted a good bike for our brothers and <u>ourselves</u>.
15. Craig examined the bike with Olive and <u>me</u>.
16. The price was considered by both <u>he</u> and us.
17. There are no differences of opinion among <u>ourselves</u>.

LEVEL
C. Write each sentence correctly.

18. The salesperson came over to me and Mei.
19. He explained to ourselves the different cameras.
20. For photographers like ourselves, a good camera is a necessity.
21. Mr. Simpson showed ourselves an automatic focus camera.
22. The price seemed too high to Mei and myself.
23. There was no difference of opinion between we.
24. We discussed a cheaper camera for ourselves.
25. Mr. Simpson explained it to she and me.

EXTRA PRACTICE

Three levels of practice

Prepositional Phrases as Adjectives or Adverbs (page 362)

LEVEL

A. For each sentence, write the adjective phrase or adverb phrase that modifies the underlined word.

1. Like aphids, <u>slugs</u> are destructive garden pests.
2. They quickly strip the <u>growth</u> of young plants.
3. They leave a telltale <u>trail</u> of slime behind.
4. Shallow <u>dishes</u> of grape juice drown slugs.
5. You can also deter them with <u>ashes</u> from the fireplace.
6. Most slugs <u>feed</u> in early morning.
7. As a last resort, <u>use</u> poisonous pellets overnight.

LEVEL

B. Write whether the underlined phrase in each sentence is an adjective phrase or an adverb phrase.

8. Place pellets <u>of metaldehyde</u> around flower beds.
9. The pellets work <u>like bait or traps</u>.
10. <u>After contact with them</u>, the slugs disintegrate.
11. Woodchucks are cute creatures <u>of the forest</u>.
12. However, <u>in the garden</u> they cause havoc.
13. Pets <u>like cats and dogs</u> will discourage woodchucks.
14. Place mothballs <u>around nonedible plants</u>.
15. Finally, protect your vegetables <u>with a sturdy fence</u>.

LEVEL

C. Write each sentence. Draw one line under each prepositional phrase and two lines under the noun, pronoun, or verb that it modifies. Identify each phrase as an **adjective phrase** or an **adverb phrase.**

16. Insects attack plants of many kinds.
17. Crops on farms are especially vulnerable.
18. On farms many growers use insecticides.
19. Chemicals like DDT destroy insect populations.
20. Some of them also harm the environment.
21. In small gardens, avoid such drastic measures.
22. Soapy water deters a number of insect pests.
23. A spray of harmless oil sometimes works.
24. Apply these solutions after each rainfall.
25. Also remove large troublesome insects by hand.

EXTRA PRACTICE

Three levels of practice

Conjunctions (page 364)

LEVEL

A. Write the conjunction in each sentence.

1. Animals or people can be harmed by toxic chemicals.
2. Not only pesticides but also some fertilizers contain them.
3. Both farmers and gardeners can fertilize organically.
4. Either compost or bone meal fertilizes organically.
5. Organic fertilizer is not dangerous, nor is it costly.
6. Phosphorus and other nutrients are needed by most plants.
7. Soils with nutrients are fertile and produce higher yields.

LEVEL

B. Write the coordinating or correlative conjunctions in each sentence. Then write whether the conjunction joins a **compound subject, compound predicate, compound object of a preposition, compound adjective,** or **compound sentence.**

8. The top layer of thin or sandy soil often lacks nutrients.
9. Other soils lose them through constant use and erosion.
10. Fertilizers replace lost nutrients, and they add new ones.
11. Liquid fertilizers work fast, but powders cost less.
12. Powders release nutrients in a slow but steady way.
13. Either fish meal or ground bone provides nitrogen.
14. Phosphorus is found in both bone meal and manure.
15. In cottonseed meal and wood ash, potassium is found.

LEVEL

C. Write each sentence. Underline each conjunction or pair of conjunctions. Then identify the type of compound that the conjunction or pair of conjunctions helps to form.

16. The measure of acidity or alkalinity is called pH.
17. Evergreens, like yews and azaleas, need acid soil.
18. Both primroses and lilies like slightly acid soil.
19. Most other plants prefer to grow in neutral or alkaline soil.
20. Either lime or eggshells will increase alkalinity.
21. Not only does peat moss add acid, but it also adds other nutrients.
22. It loosens soil and promotes good drainage.
23. Neither lime nor peat moss is very expensive.
24. Both are sold at nurseries and variety stores.
25. Special liquids also add acid, but they cost more.

EXTRA PRACTICE

Three levels of practice

Making Verbs Agree with Compound Subjects (page 366)

LEVEL

A. Write the correct form of the verb for each sentence.

1. The daffodil and the onion (is, are) close relatives.
2. Either March or April (brings, bring) daffodils.
3. Both a daffodil and a tulip (grows, grow) from bulbs.
4. Bone meal or bulb foods (helps, help) them grow.
5. Neither bulb foods nor bone meal (is, are) costly.
6. Neither the tulip nor the daffodil (is, are) hard to grow.
7. Both they and the crocus (require, requires) planting.

LEVEL

B. Write whether the underlined verb in each sentence is **correct** or **incorrect.** If it is incorrect, write the correct form of the verb.

8. Catalog houses or your local nursery <u>sell</u> the bulbs.
9. Either Dad or Mom <u>plants</u> bulbs each year.
10. The dahlia and the anemone also <u>grows</u> from bulbs.
11. Neither the dahlia nor the anemone <u>is</u> hardy.
12. Cold winters or an early frost <u>kill</u> them.
13. Mulches or a cold frame <u>protect</u> flowers from frost.
14. Neither a cold frame nor mulches <u>preserve</u> dahlias.
15. A hothouse or indoor winter storage <u>are</u> necessary.

LEVEL

C. Write each sentence, correcting any incorrect verb forms. If there are no errors, write **correct.**

16. Both my parents and my sister enjoy gardening.
17. One flower or another are always in bloom.
18. Their daffodils and their peony is twenty years old.
19. Either my parents or my sister weed the garden.
20. A mulch or a ground cover curb weed growth.
21. Neither my parents nor my sister like hybrid roses.
22. Insects or a fungus attack them too readily.
23. Either frost or bad drainage destroy their roots.
24. Both my parents and my sister prefers other flowers.
25. Their pride and joy is the twenty-year-old peony.

EXTRA PRACTICE

Three levels of practice

Conjunctive Adverbs (page 368)

LEVEL

A. Write the conjunctive adverb in each sentence.

1. Many plants like sun; however, others prefer shade.
2. Photosynthesis requires light; thus, most plants need sunshine.
3. Shady areas are not totally dark; consequently, some sunshine does reach plants in them.
4. Primroses are fragile; thus, hot sun can kill them.
5. Hostas like shade; moreover, sun spoils their colors.
6. Hot sun kills violas; similarly, it may ruin pansies.
7. Day lilies do well in sunshine; on the other hand, they also flourish in shady spots.

LEVEL

B. Write each sentence. Underline the conjunctive adverb and add the correct punctuation.

8. Azaleas like high shade in fact they do best under trees.
9. Deciduous trees lose their leaves each year as a result they cast little shade in springtime.
10. Many spring-blooming plants thrive under deciduous trees for example daffodils do well under them.
11. Some gardeners like annuals however others like perennials.
12. Annuals die each year therefore they must be resown.
13. Many are easily grown from seeds as a result most annuals cost less than perennials.
14. Perennials are dormant in winter consequently they survive.

LEVEL

C. Write each pair of sentences as a compound sentence joined by an appropriate conjunctive adverb.

15. Trees are actually perennials. Spring-blooming bulbs are a special kind of perennial.
16. Some plants are perennial in the South. In the North they cannot survive the cold winters.
17. Many perennials are native plants. Phlox is American.
18. Annuals bloom for many weeks. Perennials have shorter flowering periods.
19. Perennials grow slowly. Some take two years to bloom.
20. Grow annuals for a quick display. Grow perennials for enduring satisfaction.

EXTRA PRACTICE

Three levels of practice

Interjections (page 370)

LEVEL

A. Write each sentence and underline every interjection.

1. Boy! Gardening is hard work!
2. Well, it's also enjoyable and rewarding.
3. Those tomatoes are huge. Wow!
4. Oh, they're from special seeds.
5. You grew them from seeds? My goodness!
6. Hey, it wasn't that difficult. I started them indoors.
7. No kidding! I thought they took years to grow.
8. My word, how could they? They're annuals.
9. Gee, it still seems like a lot of trouble.
10. Well, there's nothing like home-grown tomatoes. Yummy!

LEVEL

B. Write each sentence. Fill in each blank with an appropriate interjection. Add the correct punctuation after each interjection.

11. I hate spiders. ____
12. ____ many of them benefit the gardener.
13. ____ What do they do?
14. ____ they feed on insects that eat plants.
15. I didn't know that! ____
16. ____ a few of them are poisonous, but most are harmless.
17. ____ there's a big spider right there! ____
18. ____ he is a big one! Actually, that's not a spider; it's a daddy longlegs.
19. ____ that isn't the same as a spider?

LEVEL

C. Write a sentence for each interjection. Punctuate your sentence correctly.

20. Gee
21. My goodness
22. Wow
23. Hey
24. Boy
25. Yippee

EXTRA PRACTICE

Three levels of practice

Mechanics: Using Semicolons and Colons (page 372)

LEVEL

A. Write each sentence, adding a semicolon or a colon.

1. The ecology club meets on Mondays at 3____15 P.M.
2. Members are researching endangered species ____ one member, for example, is investigating the California condor.
3. Many wild animals are near extinction ____ a number of wildflowers are also in danger.
4. The following birds are already extinct ____ the passenger pigeon, the dodo, and the great auk.
5. The moa was a huge bird ____ it became extinct centuries ago.
6. A report will be given ____ it concerns the rescue of the egret.

LEVEL

B. Write each sentence. Add semicolons or colons.

7. The gray whale, the tiger, and the panda are all in peril but the bald eagle is making a comeback.
8. Laws protect the following endangered species the brown pelican, the red wolf, and the whooping crane.
9. Trilliums are endangered picking them is prohibited.
10. The buffalo was in danger however, laws protected it.
11. Other endangered species are as follows mountain gorillas, the Florida panther, and the yak.
12. Our work is very important we care about our world.

LEVEL

C. 13.–20. Write the following business letter. Add semicolons and colons where they are needed.

Dear Congressman Fletcher

   You are hereby invited to our school symposium about the environment. The symposium will take place at 1 1 5 P.M. on April 12. Your interest in environmental issues is well known consequently, you can contribute enormously. We plan to cover the following topics acid rain, toxic waste, and endangered wildlife. We will also discuss garbage disposal and we will relate this to water, air, and ground pollution. Your work with the problems of depleted fisheries, acid rain, and water pollution has made you an expert and your contributions to our symposium will be appreciated. The meeting should be over by 5 1 5 P.M. Please telephone we look forward to hearing from you.

EXTRA PRACTICE

Three levels of practice

Vocabulary Building: Prefixes (page 374)

LEVEL

A. Answer each question by writing the best answer of the three choices given. Use your knowledge of prefixes.

1. Is a triad a group of (a) one, (b) two, or (c) three?
2. A sublevel is the (a) basement, (b) main floor, or (c) top floor.
3. An ingrate is (a) grateful, (b) not grateful, or (c) trapped.
4. When an author foreshadows, does the story (a) surprise us at the end, (b) give clues beforehand, or (c) explain later?
5. If you wrote a postdated check on March 3, might it be dated (a) March 2, (b) March 3, or (c) March 4?

LEVEL

B. Write each word in column I. Next to it, write its definition from column II. Use your knowledge of prefixes.

I	II
6. antitoxin	a. stop (something) from working
7. bifocals	b. spread out
8. compatriot	c. unable to read or write
9. deactivate	d. unskillful; amateurish
10. disregard	e. lacking reverence; sinful
11. expand	f. eyeglasses with double lenses
12. forefather	g. countryman
13. illiterate	h. ancestor
14. impious	i. substance that counteracts a poison
15. inexpert	j. ignore

LEVEL

C. Rewrite each sentence, changing the underlined words into a single word that uses a prefix.

16. Most seed companies put out twice-yearly catalogs.
17. We usually order again from the same company.
18. Their seeds are not expensive and grow well.
19. They also sell both toxic and not toxic pesticides.
20. Orders paid beforehand save on delivery costs.
21. An anxious gardener will work the soil again.
22. A good gardener will not cover any lumps in the soil.
23. Too much cultivation is not necessary.
24. Seeds should not be planted at not regular intervals.
25. Seedlings must eventually be planted beyond.

UNIT
12

Writing Editorials

Read the quotation by James Michener on the opposite page. From what perspective does Michener view writing?

An editorial is written to present the writer's views and ideas in a way that persuades an intended audience to take a certain action or to feel the way the writer feels. The purpose of an editorial is to persuade.

Focus Persuasive writing urges the audience to accept an opinion or to take an action.

What subject would you choose to write about in a persuasive essay? On the following pages you will find an essay that includes persuasion. You will also see some interesting photographs that show things about which people hold certain views. You can use the essay or the photographs to find ideas for writing.

*I love writing. I love the swirl and swing
of words as they tangle with human emotions.*

—James A. Michener

Have you ever wanted to give up on a big job, but then decided you could handle it? What thoughts and reasons made you change your mind?

A college student is having a difficult time writing a term paper. He mentions this while interviewing the author of the subject of the term paper, James Michener. "Tackle the Big Jobs" is Michener's response to the student's problem.

As you read the selection, note the opinions that the writer expresses and his reasons for his beliefs.

TACKLE THE BIG JOBS by JAMES MICHENER

During the summer vacation a fine-looking young man, who was majoring in literature at a top university, asked for an interview, and before we had talked for five minutes, he launched into his complaint.

"Can you imagine?" he lamented. "During vacation I have to write a three-thousand-word term paper about your books." He felt very sorry for himself.

His whimpering irritated me, and on the spur of the moment I shoved at him a card which had become famous in World War II. It was once used on me. It read:

> Young man, your sad story
> is truly heartbreaking.
> Excuse me while I fetch a
> crying towel.

My complaining visitor reacted as I had done twenty years earlier. He burst into laughter and asked, "Did I sound that bad?"

"Worse!" I snapped. Then I pointed to a novel of mine which he was using as the basis for his term paper. "You're belly-aching about a three-thousand-word paper which at most will occupy you for a month. When I started work on *Hawaii*, I faced the prospect of a three-million-word term paper. And five years of work. Frankly, you sound silly."[1]

This strong language encouraged an excellent discussion of the preparation it takes to write a major novel. Five years of research, months of character development, extensive work on plot and setting, endless speculation on psychology, and concentrated work on historical backgrounds.

"When I was finally ready to write," I replied under questioning, "I holed up in a bare-wall, no-telephone Waikiki room and stuck at my typewriter every morning for eighteen months. Seven days a week I wrestled with the words that would not come, with ideas that refused to jell. When I broke a tooth, I told the dentist I'd have to see him at night. When DeWitt Wallace, the editor of the *Reader's Digest* and a man to whom I am much indebted, came to Hawaii on vacation, I wanted to hike with him but had to say, 'In the late afternoon. In the morning I work.' "

1. Mr. Michener has strong opinions and gives reasons to back them up.

I explained to my caller that I write all my books slowly, with two fingers on an old typewriter, and the actual task of getting the words on paper is difficult. Nothing I write is good enough to be used in first draft, not even important personal letters, so I am required to rewrite everything at least twice. Important work, like a novel, must be written over and over again, up to six or seven times. For example, *Hawaii* went very slowly and needed constant revision. Since the final version contained about 500,000 words, and since I wrote it all many times, I had to type in my painstaking fashion about 3,000,000 words.

At this news, my visitor whistled and asked, "How many research books did you have to consult?"

"Several thousand. When I started the actual writing, there were about five hundred that I kept in my office."

"How many personal interviews?"

"About two hundred. Each two or three hours long."

"Did you write much that you weren't able to use?"

"I had to throw away about half a million words."

The young scholar looked again at the card and returned it reverently to my desk. "Would you have the energy to undertake such a task again?" he asked.

"I would always like to be engaged in such tasks," I replied, and he turned to other questions.

Young people, especially those in college who should know better, frequently fail to realize that men and women who wish to accomplish anything must apply themselves to tasks of tremendous magnitude. A new vaccine may take years to perfect. A Broadway play is never written, cast, and produced in a week. A foreign policy is never evolved in a brief time by diplomats relaxing in Washington, London, or Geneva.

The good work of the world is accomplished principally by people who dedicate themselves unstintingly to the big job at hand. Weeks, months, years pass, but the good workman knows that he is gambling on an ultimate achievement which cannot be measured in time spent. Responsible men and women leap to the challenge of jobs that require enormous dedication and years to fulfill, and are happiest when they are so involved.

This means that men and women who hope to make a real contribution to American life must prepare themselves to tackle big jobs, and the interesting fact is that no college or university

in the world can give anyone the specific education he will ultimately need. Adults who are unwilling to reeducate themselves periodically are doomed to mediocrity.[2]

For in American life, the average man—let's leave out doctors and highly specialized scientists—can expect to work in three radically different fields before he retires. The trained lawyer is dragged into a business reorganization and winds up as a college president. The engineer uses his slide rule for a short time, finds himself a sales expert, and ends his career in labor relations. The schoolteacher becomes a principal and later on heads the town's Buick agency.

Obviously no college education could prepare a young man for all that he will have to do in his years of employment. The best a college can do is to inspire him with the urge to reeducate himself constantly.

I first discovered this fact on Guadalcanal in 1945, when the war had passed us by and we could see certain victory ahead. Relieved of pressure, our top admirals and generals could have been excused if they loafed, but the ones I knew well in those days took free time and gave themselves orderly courses in new fields. One carrier admiral studied everything he could get on tank warfare. The head of our outfit, William Lowndes Calhoun, spent six hours a day learning French.

I asked him about this. "Admiral, what's this big deal with French?"

"How do I know where I'll be sent when the war's over?" he countered.

2. The order of the reasoning here is strong and sound.

But what impressed me most was the next tier of officers, the young Army colonels and the Navy commanders. They divided sharply into two groups: those who spent their spare time learning something and those who didn't. In the years that followed, I noticed in the newspapers that whenever President Truman or President Eisenhower chose men for military positions of great power, they always picked from the officers who had reeducated themselves.

More significant to me personally was my stay with the brilliant doctors of an Army hospital in the jungles of Espiritu Santo. The entire staff of a general hospital in Denver, Colorado, had been picked up and flown out to care for our wounded, and they experienced days of overwork followed by weeks of tedium. In the latter periods the doctors organized voluntary study groups by which to further their professional competence.

By good luck, I was allowed to participate in a group that was analyzing alcoholism, and one night the leader asked me, as we were breaking up, "What are you studying, Michener?" The question stunned me, for I had been studying exactly nothing.

I drove back through the jungle and that very night started working on something that I had been toying with for some months. In a lantern-lit, mosquito-filled tin shack, I started writing *Tales of the South Pacific.*

I have been the typical American in that I have had widely scattered jobs: teacher, businessman, soldier, traveler, writer. And my college education gave me no specific preparation for any of these jobs.

But it gave me something much better. I attended Swarthmore College, outside Philadelphia, and by fantastic luck, I got there just as the college was launching an experiment which was to transform the institution and those of us who participated. At the end of my sophomore year, the faculty assembled a group of us and said, "Life does not consist of taking courses in small segments. A productive life consists of finding huge tasks and

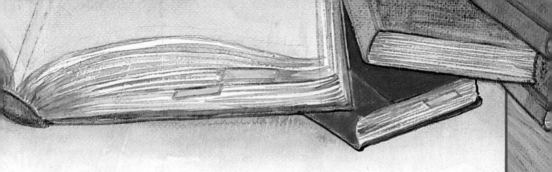

mastering them with whatever tools of intelligence and energy we have. We are going to turn you loose on some huge tasks. Let's see what you can do with them."

Accordingly, we were excused from all future class attendance and were told, "Pick out three fields that interest you." I chose logic, English history, and the novel. The faculty said, "For the next two years go to the library and learn what you can about your fields. At the end of two years, we'll bring in some outside experts from Harvard and Yale, whom you've never seen, and they will determine whether or not you have educated yourselves."

What followed was an experience in intellectual grandeur. The Swarthmore professors, realizing that when I was tested they would be tested, too, helped me to gain as thorough an education as a young man could absorb. For it was in their interest to see that I understood the fine points of the fields I had chosen.

When the two years ended, the visiting experts arrived, and for a week they probed and tested and heckled. At the end of this exciting time, one of the examiners told me, "You have the beginning of a real education."

He was right. Nothing that I studied in college has been of use to me in my various jobs. But what I did learn was how to learn, how to organize, how to write term papers. If my education had ended the week I stood before those strange examiners, I would have proved a fairly useless citizen.

While I was reflecting on these matters, my young scholar asked, "If you were a young man today and wanted to be a writer, what kind of education would you seek?"

I replied, "I'd choose some very difficult field and try to master it. I'd seek out professors who really poured it on. Long term papers and many of them, tough laboratory work."

"Why?" he pressed.

"Because we learn only those things at which we have to

work very hard. It's ridiculous to give a bright fellow like you a three-thousand-word term paper. It ought to be fifteen thousand words—or thirty. Tackle a real job. Then, when you're through, you're on the way to facing big jobs in adult life.''

My visitor made a few marks in his notebook, then asked, ''When you were in college, the scientific revolution hadn't occurred yet. Today, would you stick with liberal arts—things like logic and history—or would you switch to science, where the good jobs are?''

I didn't hesitate a minute on this one. ''Unless I had extraordinary aptitude in the sciences, I'd stick with liberal arts every time. The pay isn't as good. The jobs aren't waiting when you graduate. And when you want to get married, it's tough to tell your girl's father, 'I'm studying philosophy.' But forty years from now the scientists in your class will be scientists. And the liberal arts men will be governing the world.''

The idea was so startling that my young visitor wished to discuss it further. ''You mean there's a chance for fellows like me?''

''Every year your prospects grow brighter,'' I insisted. ''The more complex the world becomes, the more desperately it needs men trained in liberal arts. For the government of the world must always rely upon the man with broad human knowledge. And the government of a business or a university or a newspaper requires the same kind of man.''

''Why?'' he asked, forgetting his notebook.

''Because governing anything requires knowledge of men, a balanced judgment, a gift for conciliation, and, above all, a constant weighing of good versus bad. Only men with broad educations can perform such tasks.''

''Can't scientists do this?'' he asked.

''They surely can. If, after they graduate, they give themselves courses in the humanities.''

I finished our interview by telling a story. ''In 1942 the United States Navy was hungry for talent, and four of us were taken into a small room where we sat around shivering in our shorts. A grim-faced selection committee asked the first would-be officer, 'What can you do?' and the man replied, 'I'm a buyer for Macy's, and I can judge very quickly between markets and prices and trends.' The selection board replied, 'But you can't

do anything practical?' The man said no, and he was shunted
off to one side.

"The next man was a lawyer, and when the board asked him
if he could do anything practical, he had to confess, 'I can
weigh evidence and organize information,' and he was rejected.

"I was the third in line, and when I answered, "I know
language and a good deal of history,' the board groaned, and I
was sent shivering away.

"But when the fourth man said boldly, 'I'm from Georgia
Tech and I can overhaul diesel engines,' the committee jumped
up, practically embraced him, and made him an officer on the
spot."

"That's what I mean," my young scholar pointed out.

"At the end of the war," I continued, "the buyer from Macy's
was assistant to the Secretary of the Navy, in charge of many
complex responsibilities requiring instant good judgment. He
gave himself courses in naval management and government
procedures until he became one of the nation's real experts.

"The lawyer wound up as assistant to Admiral Halsey, and in
a crucial battle, deduced where the Japanese fleet had to be. He
came out covered with medals.

"I was given the job of naval secretary to several Congressional committees who were determining the future of America in the South Pacific. And what was the engineer doing at the end of the war? He was still overhauling diesel engines."

"You're sure there's hope for the liberal-arts man?" the young scholar repeated.

"If he learns to tackle the big jobs—the big ones historically or morally or culturally or politically."

We parted on that note, but when he had gone, I realized that I had not made my statement nearly strong enough. I should have said, "The world is positively hungry for young men who have dedicated themselves to big jobs. If your present professors aren't training you for such work, quit them and find others who will drive you. If your present college isn't making you work to the limit of your ability, drop out and go to another that will. Because if you don't discipline your brain now, you'll never be prepared for the years when it's a question of work or perish."[3]

Parents or professors who do not encourage their young to tackle big jobs commit a moral crime against those young people. For we know that when the young are properly challenged, they will rise to the occasion, and they will prepare themselves for the great work that remains to be done.

3. Michener's persuasive language is straightforward, direct.

Thinking Like a Reader

1. What opinion about "tackling the big jobs" does Michener express?
2. Do you agree or disagree with Michener? Why?

Write your responses in your journal.

Thinking Like a Writer

3. What reasons does the writer give to support his opinions?
4. Which factual details inspire the college student to change his mind about the need to work hard to get ahead?
5. If you met a famous author, what questions would you ask?
6. How would you try to persuade someone to agree with you on an important issue?

Write your responses in your journal.

LITERATURE

Brainstorm *Vocabulary*

In the opening paragraphs of "Tackle the Big Jobs," James Michener uses such vivid verbs as *launched, shoved, burst,* and *snapped.* These verbs give his writing vigor and color. Reread "Tackle the Big Jobs" and pay special attention to the other verbs that Michener uses. Decide if you think he always chose the best verb. Also decide if you think the wording in the dialogue is different from the wording in the text itself. Using Michener as a guide, make a personal vocabulary list of verbs that appeal to you and write them in your journal. Add to this list as you encounter interesting verbs in both speech and in writing. You can use these verbs in your writing.

Talk It Over *Face the Facts*

Work with a small group. Decide on one issue that you feel is worthwhile exploring, such as one of the many problems concerning environmental pollution, a school clean-up campaign, or forming a needed school club. Then take a stand on the issue. Discuss what information you would need to write an editorial supporting your opinion. You might wish to meet with another group of classmates to compare opinions on different topics.

Quick Write *T-Shirt Slogan*

Think of a problem in society that concerns you. Decide on one reason that might persuade people to do something about the problem. Write the reason as it might be displayed on a T-shirt. For example: FOR HEALTHY BODIES— MORE MONEY FOR SCHOOL SPORTS! If possible, illustrate your work. Write slogans for several different issues. Try to make your slogans witty and memorable. Then share them with your classmates. Compare slogans for similar topics. Let your class vote for the best slogans, the wittiest slogan, the best illustrations, and so forth. Make little paper T-shirts with the winning slogans and illustrations for display in the classroom.

Idea Corner *Think of Topics*

Think about some school or community problems or issues about which people have different opinions. Then decide what you think about two or three of these topics. You probably have some ideas right now. In your journal write down whatever ideas come to mind. You might list timely topics such as "Pros and Cons of Co-ed Sports," "The Importance of Good Diet and Exercise," or "Support Luis for Class Officer." Then list facts, reasons, or examples that support your opinions.

PICTURES  *SEEING LIKE A WRITER*

Finding Ideas for Writing

Look at the pictures. Think about what you see. What ideas for persuasive writing do the pictures give you? Write your ideas in your journal.

STUDENT HOT LINE

3 CHEERS FOR THE ATHLETES ON TO THE OLYMPICS

U.S. PEACE COUNCIL

BC's Carole Simpson

Below: McNamara confronting the umpire

1 GROUP WRITING: AN EDITORIAL

COOPERATIVE LEARNING

Editors write editorials on topics that are important. The **purpose** of an editorial is to persuade an **audience** to believe or act in a certain way. To be convincing, editorials must contain facts or reasons to support the opinion. Several points will help you write an effective editorial.

- Facts and Opinions
- Order of Reasons
- Persuasive Language

Facts and Opinions

Read the following editorial.

> The time has come, we believe, for our school district to adopt the California model of three semesters of instruction with a month of vacation between each semester. Many students think that they benefit from one long rest away from school. However, recent studies show that students are more likely to retain information when the breaks between semesters are shorter. Still, there are those who contend that they would be robbed of vacation time. Remember, the amount of vacation time would be the same; it would only be distributed differently. Yet, others claim that the summer vacation comes at the best time of the year. Nevertheless, a student poll shows that a variety of seasonal vacation activities would be greatly welcome. Students and parents, if you agree that a change would be beneficial, let officials know what you think.

The underlined sentence gives an **opinion**, a statement that expresses personal feelings about a topic. You cannot prove that an opinion is true. An opinion often contains **judgment words**, such as *believe*, *best*, *least*, *most*, *probably*, *should*, and *worst*.

The supporting details in the editorial give reasons and facts. A **fact** is a statement that can be proved to be true or false. You can check a fact by personal observation or research. Facts are used to support opinions.

Guided Practice: Facts and Opinions

As a class, agree upon a topic for an editorial. Explore some ideas with your classmates. First write a sentence that states an opinion about a problem or situation. Then make a list of facts that support the opinion expressed. For example:

Opinion: There should be three referees, instead of two, officiating at basketball games.

Fact: The game is so fast that two referees miss violations; for example, they miss calling many line violations.

Order of Reasons

Your ideas should be organized so that they make sense to the readers you are trying to convince. The reasons supporting the opinion expressed should be arranged in an **order of importance**. This means that your most important reason should be presented first. Often some of the reasons anticipate opposing arguments. A concluding sentence restates the opinion that has been proved and either calls for action or permits readers to draw their own conclusions.

Look back at the paragraph on page 406 again.

- Which details present reasons and facts?
- Which sentences anticipate an opposing argument?
- Which sentence calls for an action to be taken?

Guided Practice: Ordering Details

Recall the topic that you have chosen for an editorial. Think of reasons to support your opinion and organize your facts. As a class, make a chart like this one.

Order of Reasons—Fact File

Three referees should officiate basketball games.

Reason 1: Referees could call fouls more closely.
    Fact: Two referees miss many fouls under basket.

Reason 2: Three referees would prevent quarrels more easily.
    Fact: Two referees can't fully anticipate quarrels.

Reason 3: Three referees could check line more closely.
    Fact: Two referees can't consistently check 3-point line because too much is going on.

Persuasive Language

Look at the paragraph on page 406 again. Notice that the paragraph provides solid reasons about the problem instead of emotional appeals. Specific facts instead of broad generalizations are used. Extreme, emotional words have been avoided. Notice, too, there is anticipation of arguments opposed to the point of view expressed. This shows that the writer has carefully considered both sides of the question. In the concluding sentence's call to action, readers are allowed to make up their own minds. The language is persuasive and reasonable.

Transition words can help your readers follow your reasoning smoothly. Here are some examples.

To state an opinion: in my experience; in my opinion
To present facts: according to; another; first; the facts show
To deal with opposing viewpoints: although; despite; still

Guided Practice: Persuasive Language

Rewrite the following paragraph using reasons and persuasive language. Include transition words where appropriate.

I love child-proof bottle caps. These great caps save many children's lives. People who complain about them should be punished. All bottles with dangerous contents must have child-proof caps.

Putting an Editorial Together

With your classmates, you have written a topic sentence stating an opinion for an editorial. You have also listed some reasons and facts that support your opinion. Here is how one student chose facts supporting his opinion.

FACT FILE—NOTES		
Reason #1	Reason #2	Reason #3
call fouls better	prevents quarrels more easily	check 3-point line more consistently
—under basket	—fights can get out of hand	—foot over line?
—bad language		—hand over line?
—who fouls first?	—nudging by players	—how fast ball shot?
	—coach coming in	—foot before line?

Guided Practice: Writing an Editorial

Now finish writing your editorial. Write three detail sentences to support the opinion expressed in your topic sentence. In your detail sentences, include reasons and facts from your Fact File. Be sure to arrange the reasons in their order of importance. Use clear, logical, persuasive language. When appropriate, use transition words that show relationships between ideas. Be sure to consider opposing opinions.

Share your editorial with some friends. Ask them if they think your editorial is logical and convincing.

Checklist An Editorial

When you write an editorial, a checklist will help you remember key points. Copy the sample checklist below and place it in your writing folder. You can refer to the checklist later when you write your own editorial.

> **CHECKLIST**
>
> - Remember purpose and audience.
> - State an opinion in the topic sentence.
> - Present strong supporting facts and reasons.
> - Use order of importance.
> - Use transition words.
> - Write a strong concluding sentence.
> - _____

WRITING TOGETHER

2 THINKING AND WRITING: Faulty Methods of Persuasion

As a writer and reader of editorials you should be aware of **faulty methods of persuasion**. These methods attempt to persuade the reader without using sound reasons and facts. Here are some of the most common types:

Bandwagon is a method that encourages the reader to think in a certain way because that is supposedly the way everyone else thinks. One problem with this thinking is that not everyone believes in just one viewpoint. Another is that numbers alone do not make something right. For example, just because almost everyone at one time thought the sun revolved around the earth, that did not make the belief correct.

Charged words call up strong or extreme emotions. An editorial might call a preferred candidate "confident" while referring to the opposition as "arrogant" (overly confident in a know-it-all way). The use of charged words is unacceptable in an editorial.

Either-or thinking oversimplifies an issue by suggesting that there are only two choices about a subject when there may be more. For example, the statement "Vote for Jane, or our school will go down the drain!" fails to acknowledge that other candidates also could make a contribution to the school. The slogan implies that there are only two choices— either you vote for Jane or the school is in deep trouble.

Slanted facts present only one side of an issue while withholding important facts. The statement that "Jon speaks English poorly" is faulty if it neglects to include the fact that Jon has been in this country for only six months. In this case the facts are slanted *against* Jon. The fact that Jon is a recent immigrant could also be slanted in his favor: "Jon offers a fresh point of view."

Thinking Like a Writer

- Why do you think it is important for the writer of an editorial to recognize faulty methods of persuasion?
- What examples of these faulty methods can you find in advertisements?

If you were County Supervisor of Health, which of the following editorials would be more convincing? With your classmates, discuss the reasons for your choice.

A. Input Industries, Inc., claims it wants to prevent drowning accidents by filling in the abandoned quarry on Route 4. We know, however, that the money grubbers are really after the big bucks they will be paid for every ton of garbage they dump. The company's stupid delivery trucks will run over our kids, and toxic chemical wastes will contaminate our air. Everybody is of one mind— either we stop the dumpers now, or the people in the community should move out of the area!

B. Although it has expressed a desire to prevent swimming accidents, Input Industries, Inc., will perform a disservice to our community if it is permitted to fill the abandoned quarry with 10,000 cubic yards of debris. The risk of accidents caused by incoming trucks carrying landfill far outweighs the possibilities of future swimming accidents in the quarry. We can always find guards to watch the swimming area. However, preliminary scientific tests show that the harmful effects of chemical toxic wastes will linger long after Input Industries has done its work.

After you have selected the editorial that is more effective, find examples of the following faulty methods of persuasion in the editorial you did not choose.

1. Bandwagon
2. Charged words
3. Either-or thinking
4. Slanted facts

   After you and your classmates have identified the faulty methods of persuasion in the editorial that is less effective, as a class or in small groups, rewrite that editorial. In your rewriting, eliminate the bandwagon thinking, change the charged words to neutral words, take out the either-or thinking, and make the slanted facts objective. When you have finished, compare your rewritten editorial with the editorial that you originally decided was the more effective. Now which of these two editorials is more convincing? Discuss the reasons for your decision.

3 INDEPENDENT WRITING: An Editorial

Prewrite: Step 1

Up to this point you have learned the important elements to include in an editorial. You are now ready to choose a topic of your own for writing an editorial. Joyce, a middle school student, chose a topic in this way.

Choosing a Topic

First, Joyce wrote a list of topics and issues she might want to explore. Next, she considered her opinions on each topic. Finally, she chose the topic that seemed best.

> *homeless people*
> *crime problem in the state*
> *need for new auditorium*
> ✓ *bicycle safety* — *ok, write about need for following rules*

Joyce liked her last topic best. She thought she would narrow the topic to what to do about cyclists who break rules. She had a feeling they should be suspended from riding. She needed to think more about the reasons.

Joyce explored her topic further by making a **cluster** of facts and reasons showing how violations affected people.

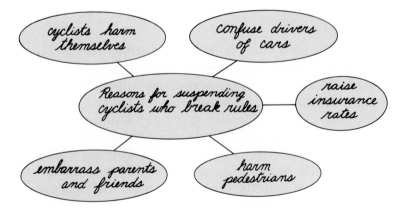

Exploring Ideas: Clustering Strategy

Joyce thought she had some good ideas. She knew her **purpose** would be to convince an **audience** of students that cyclists who repeatedly violated safety regulations should be suspended from further cycling.

After Joyce decided on the purpose and audience for her editorial, she added more details to her cluster.

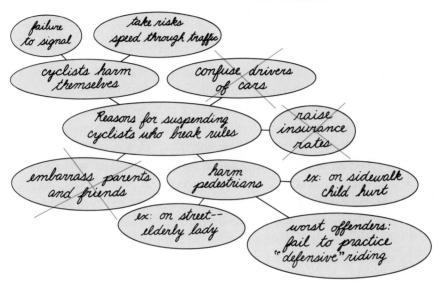

Thinking Like a Writer

- What did Joyce delete?
- What did she add?
- Why do you think she deleted and added these items?

YOUR TURN

Think of a topic for an editorial. Use **Pictures** or your journal for ideas. Follow these steps.

JOURNAL

- Make a list of topics.
- Choose the one that most interests you.
- Narrow the topic if it is too broad.
- Decide on your opinion.
- Think about your purpose and audience.

Now make a cluster for exploring your topic. Write down facts and reasons that support your opinion.

Write a First Draft: Step 2

To help with her first draft, Joyce made a checklist of points to remember. She used her planning checklist as she wrote.

Joyce has decided to include a title for her editorial, as many newspaper editorials do. She is now ready to write her first draft.

Joyce's First Draft

Calling All Cyclist's

Bicycle-riders of all ages who over and over violate traffic rules should be suspended from riding. Our neighborhood has been recently hit by a number of bicycle accidents, for example, two weeks ago a little boy was hit by a crazed cyclist speeding on the sideweek. Last week a cyclist jumped a red light and was hit by a car. Cyclists who do not obey rules are not only dangerous to pedestrians. they are dangerous to theirselves. Some cyclists are tempted by the supposed thrill of speeding through traffic mazes they are apparently willing to risk injuries to theirselves. The worst offenders, we know, are the so-called "innocent" cyclists who do not practice "predictable, defensive" riding. Yesterday a young rider failed to use a hand signal. He was brushed by a car and swerved into an elderly lady.

Planning Checklist
- Remember purpose and audience.
- State an opinion in the topic sentence.
- Include strong supporting facts and reasons.
- Use order of importance.
- Use transition words.
- Write a strong concluding sentence.

While Joyce was writing her first draft, she was interested in putting her thoughts on paper. She did not stop to correct errors because she knew that she could fix them later.

YOUR TURN

Write your first draft. As you prepare to write, ask yourself these questions.

- What do I want to persuade my audience to think or do?
- Which facts and reasons will support my arguments?
- How can I best organize the details?

TIME-OUT You might want to take some time out before you revise. That way you will be able to revise your writing with a fresh eye.

Revise: Step 3

After she finished her first draft, Joyce read it to herself. She had considered submitting her editorial to the school newspaper, so she wanted it to be especially good. Because she wanted some suggestions for improvement, Joyce shared her draft with a partner.

I like most of the ideas in your editorial, Joyce, but there are a couple of points that were not convincing.

Really? Would you tell me which ones?

Joyce then looked back at her planning checklist. She noticed that she had forgotten to include a strong concluding sentence. She checked this on her list so that she would remember to add this important element. Joyce realized that her planning checklist would also work well as a revising checklist, so she made a fresh copy to use as she revised.

Using her checklist as a guide, Joyce began revising her editorial. Were her supporting facts strong enough? Did she present her ideas in the order of importance? Did any information need to be added or eliminated?

Joyce recalled that her purpose was to persuade her readers to share her opinions. She also reminded herself that her audience was her schoolmates. She then reread her first draft with these points in mind. Joyce decided that her ideas and language were appropriate for her purpose and her audience and that with a few changes in spelling and punctuation, her essay would work well.

Look at Joyce's revised draft on the next page.

Revising Checklist
■ Remember purpose and audience.
■ State an opinion in the topic sentence.
✔ Include strong supporting facts and reasons.
■ Use order of importance.
■ Use transition words.
✔ Write a strong concluding sentence.

WRITING PROCESS

Calling All Cyclist's

Bicycle-riders of all ages who ^*repeatedly* over and over violate traffic

rules should be suspended from riding. Our neighborhood

has been recently hit by a number of bicycle accidents, for

example, two weeks ago a little boy was hit by a crazed

cyclist speeding on the sideweek. Last week a cyclist

jumped a red light and was hit by a car. Cyclists who do

not obey rules are not only dangerous to pedestrians. *but also* they

are dangerous to theirselves. Some cyclists are tempted by

the supposed thrill of speeding through traffic mazes they

are apparently willing to risk injuries to theirselves. The

worst offenders, we ^*believe* know, are the so-called "innocent"

cyclists who do not practice "predictable, defensive" riding.

For example,
^Yesterday a young rider failed to use a hand signal. He

was brushed by a car and swerved into an elderly lady.

A responsible community should ban irresponsible cyclists.

Thinking Like a Writer

WISE
WORD
CHOICE

- Which faulty methods of persuasion did Joyce change?
- Which sentence did she add? Why did she add it?
- How does combining sentences improve the paragraph?
- How does adding a transition word improve the paragraph?

YOUR TURN

Read your first draft. Ask yourself these questions.
- How can I make my supporting facts and reasons stronger?
- What transition words could I add to clarify my ideas?
- How could my concluding sentence be more effective?
- How would combining sentences improve my writing?

Now revise your editorial.

Proofread: Step 4

After she revised her draft, Joyce knew that her work was not complete until she proofread her editorial. She made a proofreading checklist to use while she checked her work.

PROOFREADING CHECKLIST

- Did I indent my paragraph?
- Did I spell all words correctly?
- What punctuation errors do I need to correct?
- What capitalization errors do I need to correct?

Part of Joyce's Proofread Draft

Calling All Cyclist's

¶ Bicycle-riders of all ages who ~~over and over~~ *repeatedly* violate traffic

rules should be suspended from riding. Our neighborhood

has been recently hit by a number of bicycle accidents, for

example, two weeks ago a little boy was hit by a ~~crazed~~

cyclist speeding on the ~~sideweek~~ *sidewalk.* Last week a cyclist

jumped a red light and was hit by a car. Cyclists who do

not obey rules are not only dangerous to pedestrians, ~~they~~ *but also*

~~are dangerous~~ to ~~theirselves.~~ *themselves.*

YOUR TURN

Proofreading Practice

Use the paragraph below to practice your proofreading skills. Rewrite it correctly on a separate piece of paper.

Proper diet and exercise are important to ourselves however, they are often-neglected. Balenced meals with a variety of food is highly desirable. The nutritional value in meals are often difficult to know. Seek advice, its up to you.

WRITING

Applying Your Proofreading Skills

Reread your proofreading checklist and read **The Grammar Connection** and **The Mechanics Connection** below. Then proofread your editorial. Use the proofreading marks to indicate changes.

THE GRAMMAR CONNECTION

Remember these rules about using pronouns in prepositional phrases.

- Always use an object pronoun as the object of a preposition.

  Doug was eating lunch with **us.** Diana told the joke to **him.**

- When the object of a preposition is compound and one of the objects is the pronoun *me*, *me* should always be last.

  Doug repeated the joke to Beth and **me** immediately.

- Be careful not to use a reflexive pronoun when an object pronoun is needed.

  The joke took on special meaning for **us.** (not *for ourselves*)

Check your editorial to be sure that you have used pronouns in prepositional phrases correctly.

THE MECHANICS CONNECTION

Remember these rules about using semicolons.

- Use a semicolon to join the two parts of a compound sentence when a coordinating conjunction such as *and, or,* or *but* is not used.

  The joke was extremely funny; we would always laugh at the first line.

- Use a semicolon to join the two parts of a compound sentence when they are long and contain commas, even if a coordinating conjunction is used.

  The punch line, which came at the end, was never reached; but we would laugh like hyenas anyway.

- When the two parts of a compound sentence are joined by conjunctive adverbs such as *however, yet, nevertheless,* and *thus,* use a semicolon before the conjunctive adverb and a comma after it.

  We grew tired of the joke; however, it refused to disappear.

Check your editorial to be sure that you have used semicolons correctly.

Proofreading Marks
Indent ¶
Add ∧
Add a comma ∧
Add quotation
marks ⌄ ⌄
Add a period ⊙
Take out ⌇
Capitalize ≡
Lower-case
letter /
Reverse the
order ∩

Publish: Step 5

Before submitting her editorial to the school newspaper, Joyce decided to share her views about bicycle safety with her family. She made a neat, final copy of her paragraph and took it home in a folder. She read it to her family after dinner. Her family agreed that her writing was good and her reasoning was sound. They encouraged her to submit the editorial to the school paper. Joyce did, and her work appeared in print two weeks later. Many of Joyce's intended audience, her classmates, read the editorial and commented on its contents. Several of her schoolmates responded to Joyce's ideas by means of letters to the editor.

YOUR TURN

Make a neat, final copy of your editorial. The ideas for sharing your work in the **Sharing Suggestions** box below may be helpful.

SHARING SUGGESTIONS

Create a collection of "Editorial Perspectives." Illustrate your work.	Send a copy of your editorial to a city official or to a member of congress for your area.	Make a tape recording of your editorial. Ask a local radio station to donate time for student editorials.

4 SPEAKING AND LISTENING: Conducting a Debate

You have just written an editorial about a topic that interests you. Your editorial included reasons and facts to back up your opinion. Now you can use what you know about persuasion in a debate. In a debate you will be speaking either for or against a proposition.

A **proposition** is a topic sentence rephrased as a question. For example:

> Should our school district adopt the California model for dividing the school year?

In a **traditional debate,** a moderator appoints the time-keeper and judge(s), calls the group to order, and acts as chairman for the debate. After speaking briefly to stimulate audience interest in the topic, the moderator makes sure the debate runs smoothly during the presentation of arguments (**constructive speeches**) and the refutation of arguments (**rebuttals**). The moderator calls upon the debaters in the following order.

Constructive Speeches	Minutes*	Rebuttal Speeches	Minutes*
First affirmative	6	First negative	4
First negative	6	First affirmative	4
Second affirmative	3	Second negative	3
Second negative	3	Second affirmative	3

* Suggested time; make adjustments as necessary.

The affirmative debaters speak in favor of a proposition. The first affirmative speaker introduces the question, defines terms, and presents the affirmative side's view of the issues.

The negative speakers speak against the proposition. The first negative speaker presents the opposition case and opposes the claims of the first affirmative speaker.

The second affirmative speaker opposes arguments made by the negative speaker and continues the case for the affirmative side. The second negative speaker delivers the final speech for that side.

During an intermission, each team meets to decide which debater will oppose the specific arguments of the other team during rebuttal. Notice that the reverse order of speakers during rebuttal offsets the affirmative's advantage in starting the debate. The rebuttal involves direct clashes of evidence and tests the debaters' ability to speak spontaneously.

Usually judges determine the winning team, but sometimes the audience votes for the team they think the better.

When you debate, observe these speaking guidelines.

SPEAKING GUIDELINES: Debating

1. Your purpose is to support or oppose a proposition.
2. Be prepared by knowing the other side of the proposition.
3. Your arguments should be presented logically, clearly, and politely. Do not use faulty methods of persuasion.
4. Prepare a brief outline listing reasons, facts, and examples.
5. During a debate, use note cards for quick reference only.
6. Debate against arguments; never make personal attacks.

- Why is it important to use good reasons and examples?
- Why is it important to know the other side of the proposition in question?

When you listen to a debate, you listen in order to decide which side has presented the more convincing argument.

SPEAKING APPLICATION Debating

Think of a topic of concern to you that would also be a good topic for debating with a group of classmates. The topic should be one about which opinions may differ—for and against. Gather factual information to support your opinion on the topic. Make a note card and use the speaking guidelines to help you prepare. Your classmates will be using the following guidelines as they listen to the debate.

LISTENING GUIDELINES: Debating

1. Listen for the opinions of each speaker.
2. Listen for supporting facts and arguments.
3. Listen for effective responses to the arguments.
4. Listen for faulty or unfair methods of persuasion.

THE CURRICULUM CONNECTION

Writing About the Media

An important aspect of communication through the **media** is persuading people to accept ideas or to take action. In addition to magazines and newspapers, people express their opinions through television and radio. In all of these media, images and words combine to put messages across.

Many people who work in the media are journalists. They specialize in collecting news and information and reporting it to the public. Television, radio, newspapers, and magazines all use news articles and editorials that are either printed or read aloud. Besides words, still photography and moving pictures are also important in both print and television journalism.

ACTIVITIES

Be an Announcer

Work with a partner. Create and present an editorial as a radio announcer would. Be sure to consider opposing opinions. Then tape your editorial. Play it for your classmates. Perhaps you can broadcast it over your school's public address system.

Create a Program

Do research about how a television studio presents the news. Then, with your classmates, set up a "television studio" in your school. Write brief editorials on issues that concern you. Take turns acting as various TV studio personnel, including announcers who read the editorials aloud to the rest of class.

Collect Editorials

Ask members of your class to seek out printed editorials from local and national newspapers, news magazines, and other more general magazines. Collect editorials over a period of time. Appoint a "review board" to select the most interesting editorials. Have a committee mount the editorials in a folder that can be available for anyone in the class to read.

Respond to Literature

Many advertisements are directed at the public by the media. Read the following selection about advertising and its effect. Write a response to the ideas in the form of a story, essay, or report.

The Point of Advertising

Advertisements are all like tacks placed in the road, and the mind of the American consumer is somewhat like an automobile tire. The outer layers of the tire, made of black, smoke-cured apathy, are resilient and hard to pierce. But a good sharp tack can do it, and a superior tack can go on and puncture the inner tube. When that happens, the consumer comes to a shuddering halt, and the man who put the tack in the road, or hired somebody else to do it for him, steps out of the bushes and sells the consumer an icebox. There is nothing wrong with this—most of the time the consumer needs the icebox anyway, and in buying it he performs a function vital to the operation of the economy.

Advertisers are very good at making tacks. They can make big sharp ones—the concept of mildness, for example, has lacerated countless tires in its time. They can make medium-sized tacks—the celebrity testimonial is an example of that sort, standard and solid, likely to cause some punctures but not guaranteed to work every time. Or the advertisers can make little tacks like the singing commercials, one of which may not make much of a dent, but which can be effective in large numbers when strewn across the consumer's road.

—Robert Graham, "Adman's Nightmare"

UNIT CHECKUP

Group Writing: An Editorial (page 406) Copy these sentences on a separate sheet of paper. Then write if the sentence is a **fact** or an **opinion** and underline the judgment word(s) in each opinion.

1. The United Nations does the best job in the world of keeping peace.
2. The U.N. has two main branches, the General Assembly and the Security Council.
3. The U.N. is the most important building in the world.
4. The General Assembly probably does a better job than the Security Council.
5. The Security Council consists of five nations that can use veto power.
6. The U.N. is located in New York City on First Avenue.

LESSON 2

Thinking and Writing: Faulty Methods of Persuasion (page 410) Write each sentence. Underline the word or words that create a faulty method of persuasion. Then label each faulty method as **bandwagon, charged words, either-or thinking,** or **slanted facts.**

1. The drama club's production of *The Fantasticks* was their worst production because no one really enjoyed it.
2. Some people wondered about the quality of those loathsome costumes.
3. The production was so bad that the club should disband.
4. Terry Benson, a substitute, was not very interesting in the role of the Mute.
5. *The Fantasticks* is the last production the drama club will attempt this year.

LESSON 3

An Editorial (page 412) Imagine that you are the editor of *Teenage Life*. Write an editorial for the magazine. The editorial should state your opinion about an important aspect of the lives of young people today. Be sure to include several facts and reasons to support your opinion.

LESSON 4

Speaking and Listening: Conducting a Debate (page 420) In a paragraph, summarize the guidelines for speaking and listening effectively in a debate.

THEME PROJECT

CARTOONS

Using logic and reasoning when you write an editorial helps you learn how to put your feelings in perspective. Newspapers, magazines, and other media use logic to persuade people to accept an editorial point of view. Sometimes logic can be made visual, which presents itself in the form of the editorial cartoon.

Thomas Nast, the great American cartoonist, drew the cartoon below. It is an excellent example of how a cartoon can produce a smile and make a point at the same time. Discuss with your classmates what the cartoon means to you and the point it makes.

WHO STOLE THE PEOPLE'S MONEY? — DO TELL . N.Y.TIMES.   'TWAS HIM.

As a class, create a collection of editorial cartoons about important issues in your school, in your community, in the nation, or in the world.

- Find examples of editorial cartoons in newspapers and magazines. Discuss them with your classmates.
- Draw original editorial cartoons for issues that you care about.
- Include brief captions for the cartoons you create.
- Write editorials to go with the cartoons.
- Share your collection with other classes.

13

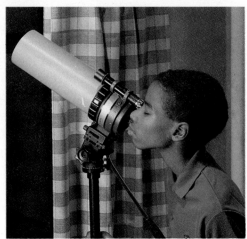

Complex Sentences and Verbals

In this unit you will learn about more kinds of sentences. You can add variety to your writing by using many different kinds of sentences.

Discuss Read the haiku on the opposite page. What image do you see?

Creative Expression The theme of this unit is *Galaxies*. Galaxies are distant, awesome, somewhat unknown. Think of something that is awesome and unknown to you. Write three questions you would like answered about the topic you have chosen. Write your questions in your journal.

THEME: *GALAXIES*

*A full moon comes up,
and stars, stars uncountable,
drown in a green sky.*

—Shiki

1 SENTENCES AND CLAUSES

An independent clause has one complete subject and one complete predicate and can stand alone as a sentence.

You have learned that a simple sentence is a group of words that expresses a complete thought and contains one subject and one predicate. You also know that a compound sentence is made up of two or more simple sentences. Each simple sentence within a compound sentence is called an **independent clause.**

In the compound sentences below, each independent clause is underlined.

> <u>Do you want to read</u>, or <u>do you want to gaze at stars?</u>
> <u>The telescope arrived</u>; <u>he set it up immediately.</u>
> <u>The telescope wasn't large</u>; however, <u>it was powerful.</u>

Notice that a comma precedes the conjunction that joins the independent clauses in a compound sentence. A semicolon joins the independent clauses if they are not joined by a conjunction. A semicolon precedes a conjunctive adverb, such as *however,* and a comma follows it.

Guided Practice

Tell whether each sentence is simple or compound.

Example: The distance from the earth to the sun is 93,000,000 miles.   *simple sentence*

1. The sun is vital to all life.
2. The sun is in the center, and the earth revolves around it.
3. The diameter of the sun is 860,000 miles.
4. Never look directly at the sun; however, you can observe it indirectly.
5. Sunspots occur often; in 1960 there were more than 200.

THINK

- How can I recognize an independent clause?

REMEMBER

- A **simple sentence** has one complete subject and one complete predicate; a **compound sentence** has two or more simple sentences called independent clauses.

- An **independent clause** has a subject and a predicate and can stand alone as a sentence.

More Practice

A. Write whether each sentence is **simple** or **compound.**

Example: Nuclear reactions within the sun produce its energy.   *simple*

  6. The sun is very hot inside, but its surface is hotter.
  7. Almost all of our light comes from the sun.
  8. The surface, or photosphere, is frequently studied.
  9. The light affects us, and the solar wind affects us, too.
 10. Space exploration has renewed our interest in the sun.
 11. We rely on the sun for life, but it is an ordinary star.
 12. The sun is not a particularly large star.
 13. Many stars are much larger; they make the sun seem tiny.

B. Write each sentence and whether it is **simple** or **compound.** If it is a compound sentence, underline each independent clause. Add needed commas and semicolons.

Example: The sun produces heat its energy maintains life.
   The sun produces heat; its energy maintains life.
   compound

 14. People have speculated about the sun for centuries.
 15. Eclipses were recorded and sunspots were noticed later.
 16. The sun was once revered however now it is studied.
 17. The northern lights are called the aurora borealis.
 18. The sun is our nearest star thus it seems brightest.
 19. Heat from the sun makes life on the earth possible.
 20. Sunlight is beneficial it can also be harmful.

Extra Practice, page 456

WRITING APPLICATION An Essay

Imagine that you have just learned that the earth is not the center of our solar system. Write an essay about the importance of this discovery. Then exchange papers with a classmate and identify the independent clauses.

2 COMPLEX SENTENCES

You have learned that an independent clause has a subject and a predicate and that it can stand alone as a sentence. A **subordinate clause** also has a subject and a predicate, but it cannot stand alone as a sentence.

> **Whenever people studied the nighttime sky,** they have noticed a difference between stars and planets.

Subordinate clauses are introduced by **subordinating conjunctions**.

Subordinating Conjunctions			
after	before	though	whenever
although	if	unless	where
as	since	until	whereas
because	than	when	wherever

A sentence made up of an independent clause and one or more subordinate clauses is called a **complex sentence.** In a complex sentence, a comma is used after a subordinate clause that comes at the beginning of a sentence. A comma is usually not used before a subordinate clause that comes at the end of a sentence.

Guided Practice

Identify the subordinate clause in each sentence.

Example: The distinction between stars and planets is clear because the planets move at a faster rate.
because the planets move at a faster rate

1. Although stars seem stationary, planets are moving.
2. Stars twinkle because Earth's atmosphere moves.
3. Though stars move, we can barely detect their motion.
4. Stars emit light whereas planets reflect the sun.
5. Because Earth rotates, the stars appear to rise and set.

 THINK

- How can I tell which clause in a complex sentence is the subordinate clause?

REMEMBER

- A **subordinate clause** has a subject and a predicate, but it cannot stand alone as a sentence.
- A **complex sentence** contains an independent clause and one or more subordinate clauses.

More Practice

A. Write the subordinate clause in each sentence.

Example: Mountains exist on Mars as they exist on Earth.   *as they exist on Earth*

6. Though both are planets, they are very different.
7. Uranus has thirteen more moons than Neptune has.
8. Unless we learn otherwise, little water exists on Mars.
9. If you want to observe a planet, you might watch Venus.
10. An object weighs more on Jupiter than it weighs on Earth.
11. Though Ptolemy thought the sun orbited Earth, he erred.
12. Copernicus discovered the truth after he made careful studies.

B. Write each sentence. Draw one line under the subordinate clause, two lines under the subordinating conjunction.

Example: Although Uranus has rings, Saturn's are more spectacular.
Although Uranus has rings, Saturn's are more spectacular.

13. Pluto was unknown before it was seen in 1930.
14. As you know, *Voyager I* relayed the best pictures.
15. The planets numbered nine after Pluto was found.
16. Wherever gravity exists, atmosphere exists.
17. I think of gases whenever I hear of Jupiter.
18. Although Jupiter is a planet, it is huge.
19. Its atmosphere is deadly since it is ammonia.
20. Though Mars's atmosphere is thin, it is less toxic.

Extra Practice, page 457

WRITING APPLICATION A Journal Entry

Imagine that you are an amateur astronomer. Write a journal entry describing the observations that you might make on a clear night. Try to include complex sentences in your journal entry.

3 ADJECTIVE CLAUSES

You know that a complex sentence contains an independent clause and a subordinate clause. Sometimes the subordinate clause acts as an adjective. An **adjective clause** modifies a noun or a pronoun in the independent clause of a complex sentence.

An adjective clause often begins with a relative pronoun, such as *who, whom, whose, which,* and *that.* The relative pronoun relates the clause to the word or words that the clause modifies.

> Jan Oort, **who studied comets,** was an astronomer.
> Carl Witt, **whom you studied,** discovered an asteroid.
> The Crab nebula, **whose light we can still see today,** exploded in 1054.
> Ceres, **which is an asteroid,** is 600 miles across.
> The comet **that we saw** had a nucleus, coma, and tail.

Adjective clauses also begin with *where* and *when.*

> Are there areas **where you can find meteor craters?**
> Joe likes summer, **when meteor showers are likely.**

Guided Practice

Identify the adjective clause in each sentence.

Example: The word *nova,* which is Latin, means "new."
         which is Latin

1. A supernova that explodes can expand for years.
2. The light, which is powerful, can be seen through a telescope.
3. Supernovas contain areas where radiation is very strong.
4. Kepler is the astronomer who saw a supernova in 1604.
5. Brahe, whom many do not know about, saw one in 1572.
6. Nan, whose report is about astronomy, can define *nova.*
7. A nova is a star that brightens suddenly.
8. Some people who were at the conference had seen a nova.
9. One member, about whom little was known, wrote about it.
10. The star, which had been invisible, became a bright light.

 THINK

■ How do I recognize an adjective clause?

REMEMBER

- An **adjective clause** is a subordinate clause that modifies, or describes, a noun or pronoun in the independent clause of a complex sentence.
- An adjective clause usually begins with a **relative pronoun,** such as *who, whom, whose, which,* or *that.*

More Practice

A. Write each sentence. Underline the adjective clause. Draw a second line under the relative pronoun.

Example: Astronomy, which is always enjoyable, offers many ideas for compositions.
Astronomy, <u>which is always enjoyable,</u> offers many ideas for compositions.

11. A nova is often a double-star system that contains stars called a red giant and a white dwarf.

12. A nova is not a phenomenon that happens frequently.

13. A supernova, which is rarer, is even brighter.

14. A supernova, whose explosion is great, is beautiful.

15. Did any humans observe the Veil Nebula explosion, which occurred thousands of years ago?

B. Write each sentence. Draw one line under the adjective clause and two lines under the word it modifies.

Example: A nova is a star whose intensity increases.
A nova is a <u>star</u> <u>whose intensity increases.</u>

16. Supernovas are phenomena that occur only every few hundred years.

17. They have been seen in our galaxy, where they rarely occur.

18. Carl Sagan, who has written many books, is an astronomer.

19. People who watched *Cosmos* learned about supernovas.

20. The times when supernovas occur cannot be predicted.

Extra Practice, page 458

WRITING APPLICATION An Eyewitness Account

Imagine that you are watching the night sky when a supernova explodes. In your journal write an eyewitness account of what you saw. Exchange papers with a classmate and identify the adjective clauses in each other's work.

4 ESSENTIAL AND NONESSENTIAL CLAUSES

You have learned that an adjective clause describes a noun or pronoun in the independent clause of a complex sentence. Also an adjective clause generally begins with a relative pronoun—*who, whom, whose, which,* or *that.*

The man **who first explained night** was Aristarchus.

The adjective clause in the sentence above is not set off by commas because the clause is *essential.* It tells *which* man.

An **essential clause** is an adjective clause that is necessary to the meaning of the word that it modifies. Do not use commas to set off an essential clause from the sentence.

An adjective clause can give extra information that is nonessential. If the clause is taken out, the meaning of the word that it modifies remains unaffected.

The observatory, **which is a lovely building,** is huge.

A **nonessential clause** is an adjective clause that is not necessary to the meaning of the word that it modifies. Use commas to set off a nonessential clause.

Guided Practice

Identify the adjective clause in each sentence. Tell whether it is an essential or a nonessential clause.

Example: Scientists whom I most admire are astronomers.
whom I most admire   essential clause

1. Hipparchus drew maps that show the position of many stars.
2. People believed in the geocentric theory, which placed the earth at the center of the universe.
3. The man who developed this theory was called Ptolemy.
4. Galileo, whose work is famous, continued the scientific quest.
5. Scientific method, which is based on observation, was used.
6. He is the man whom we credit as its modern innovator.
7. Brahe studied a supernova that is now called "Tycho's star."
8. He used a quadrant, whose value is still known by navigators.

THINK

- How do I know whether an adjective clause is essential or nonessential?

REMEMBER

- An **essential clause** is necessary to the meaning of the word it modifies and is not set off by commas.

- A **nonessential clause** gives extra information about the word it modifies and is set off by commas.

More Practice

A. Write the adjective clause in each sentence. Then write whether the clause is **essential** or **nonessential.**

Example: Astronomy, which is difficult, has rewards.
which is difficult   nonessential

9. Copernicus, who lacked a telescope, made major discoveries.
10. He challenged the idea that Earth was the center of all.
11. This astronomer, who died in 1543, changed our view.
12. An important astronomer who followed was Johannes Kepler.
13. The discoveries that Kepler made also added knowledge.
14. His scheme, which explained planetary motion, is famous.

B. Write each sentence. Underline the adjective clause and label it as **essential** or **nonessential.** Add needed commas.

Example: Kepler who assisted Brahe observed the planets.
    Kepler, *who assisted Brahe*, observed the planets.
    nonessential

15. Kepler made laws whose ideas influenced Newton.
16. Galileo used a lens that increased the image.
17. Herschel built a telescope whose mirror was four feet across.
18. This telescope which was then the largest was built in 1789.
19. A mirror that could capture more light was needed.
20. This light which was concentrated made dim objects visible.

Extra Practice, page 459

WRITING APPLICATION A Letter

Imagine that you are an amateur scientist. Write a letter to a friend about a new instrument that you have just used. Exchange letters with a classmate and identify the essential and nonessential clauses in each other's work.

---

5 ADVERB CLAUSES

Subordinate clauses can also act as adverbs. An **adverb clause** is a subordinate clause that modifies, or tells more about, the verb in the independent clause of a complex sentence. Like an adverb, an adverb clause tells *how, when, where, why,* or *under what conditions* the action occurs.

> HOW: **As if the heavens had opened,** meteors streaked across the sky.
>
> WHEN: **After the meteor shower was over,** the viewers cheered.
>
> WHERE: **Wherever Sid looked,** he saw meteors.
>
> WHY: Meteors seldom strike the earth **because they incinerate.**
>
> CONDITIONS: **Unless you have seen a meteor fall,** you cannot imagine it in all of its glory.

An adverb clause usually begins with a **subordinating conjunction,** such as *because, when, since, though, until, if,* or *although.*

If an adverb clause comes at the beginning of the sentence, it is set off by a comma.

> After he cleaned the lens, Mike looked at the moon.

Guided Practice

Identify the adverb clause in each sentence.

Example: Earth seems tiny when you think of galaxies.
when you think of galaxies

1. Whenever the galaxy is mentioned, we refer to our galaxy.
2. You can see other galaxies if you use a strong telescope.
3. Some are invisible unless you use a radio telescope.
4. The number of galaxies is unknown because space is vast.
5. Although many galaxies are spiral, some have other shapes.
6. Unless you are looking toward the Milky Way, galaxies appear as patches of light.
7. Though we can see 150 galaxies, millions more exist.

 **THINK**

- How can I identify an adverb clause?

REMEMBER

- An **adverb clause** is a subordinate clause that modifies the verb in the independent clause of a complex sentence.

More Practice

A. Write the adverb clause in each sentence.

> When the ancient Greeks saw the Milky Way,
> they thought it was a road to the gods.
> *When the ancient Greeks saw the Milky Way*

8. You cannot see galaxies there because dust clouds cover them.

9. Since our own galaxy is so close, we study it with ease.

10. Because our galaxy rotates, you can think of it as a carousel.

11. Since one trip around the galaxy takes the sun 250 million years, it has made only twenty trips.

12. This estimate is true if the universe is four billion years old.

13. When we have more knowledge, we can be more accurate.

B. Write each sentence. Draw one line under the adverb clause and two lines under the verb it modifies. Add commas where needed.

Example: Our galaxy changed shape as forces acted on it.
> Our galaxy <u>changed</u> shape <u>as forces acted on it</u>.

14. We saw the galactic cluster as we scanned the heavens.

15. If you could see our galaxy from afar you would see its arms.

16. Whereas many once thought the solar system was at the center of our galaxy we now know that it is in the Orion Arm.

17. Before you consider other galaxies think about the "Locals."

18. When you are south of the equator look for our two closest galaxies, the Large and the Small Magellanic Clouds.

19. If you see them you will understand their name.

20. Since they are southern they are named for that explorer.

Extra Practice, Practice Plus, pages 460–461

WRITING APPLICATION A Group Report

COOPERATIVE
LEARNING

Imagine that you are part of a team that discovers a new galaxy. Form a group and write a report that describes the discovery and the new galaxy. Check each other's work to be sure that you have used adverb clauses correctly. Present your report to the class.

6 NOUN CLAUSES

You have learned that subordinate clauses can function as adjectives or adverbs. Other subordinate clauses act as nouns.

> **Whoever observes the night skies** can understand the appeal of astronomy.

The subordinate clause in the sentence above is the subject of the sentence. Since this kind of clause acts as a noun, it is called a **noun clause.**

You can use noun clauses in the same ways that nouns are used—as a subject, a direct object, an object of a preposition, or a predicate noun.

SUBJECT: **How astronomers excel** is my essay topic.

DIRECT OBJECT: Amateurs can pursue **whatever interests them.**

OBJECT OF A PREPOSITION: They focus on **what they prefer.**

PREDICATE NOUN: The observatory is **where Mel spent evenings.**

Because noun clauses are subordinate clauses, the sentences in which they appear are complex sentences. Some of the words that can introduce noun clauses are *how, that, why, what, whatever, when, where, which, whichever, who, whom, whoever, whomever,* and *whose.*

Guided Practice

Identify the noun clause in each sentence.

Example: Whatever Luis sees in the sky interests him.
Whatever Luis sees in the sky

1. The constellations are what Luis is studying.
2. He reads whatever he can find about astronomy.
3. Success of the program depends on whoever volunteers time.
4. That astronomy is so popular is not surprising.
5. Do you know which star is the brightest?

 THINK

- How can I recognize noun clauses?

REMEMBER

- A **noun clause** is a subordinate clause that functions as a noun.
- A noun clause can be a subject, a direct object, an object of a preposition, or a predicate noun.

More Practice

A. Write the noun clause in each sentence.

Example: Why astronomers use telescopes is obvious.
Why astronomers use telescopes

  6. Whoever studies the night sky observes many wonders.
  7. Binoculars can also increase what the viewer sees.
  8. Paul will lend his binoculars to whoever wants them.
  9. The chart gave us an idea about which stars could be seen.
10. Her topic is how Galileo found Jupiter's satellites.
11. Now she wonders which satellites she can see.
12. What she really needs is a more powerful telescope.

B. Write each sentence and underline each noun clause. Then write whether the clause is used as a **subject,** a **direct object,** an **object of a preposition,** or a **predicate noun.**

Example: At whichever setting Bob used, Mars was out of focus.
At whichever setting Bob used, Mars was out of focus. object of a preposition

13. A crater on the moon was what he wanted to see.
14. Why there are rings around Saturn is Laura's question.
15. Her research topic depended on what books she found.
16. When the meteor shower began was important.
17. Jonathan is who found the giant crater.
18. A prize will be given to whoever finds a larger one.
19. Which telescope we use depends on the weather.
20. The image you see will be whatever conditions permit.

Extra Practice, page 462

WRITING APPLICATION An Announcement

COOPERATIVE LEARNING

Imagine that you are forming an astronomy club with some of your classmates. With a partner, write an announcement that will explain current and future projects of the club. Exchange papers with another pair of classmates and identify the noun clauses in one another's work.

7 PARTICIPLES AND PARTICIPIAL PHRASES

The present participle of a verb is formed by adding *ing* to the verb. The past participle is usually formed by adding *ed*. A participle can be the main verb in a verb phrase.

Earth's shadow had **darkened** the moon.

Participles can also function as adjectives.

The **eclipsed** moon was a wonderful sight.

Sometimes a participle used as an adjective is part of a participial phrase. A **participial phrase** is a group of words that includes a participle and other words that complete its meaning.

Shining on that May night, the moon was bright.

The disk **suspended in the sky** then became dark.

A participal phrase that is placed at the beginning of a sentence is set off by a comma.

A participial phrase can appear before or after the word it describes. Always place the phrase as close as possible to the word it modifies, or the meaning of the sentence may become unclear. A misplaced participial phrase may be not only misleading, but also humorous.

CORRECT: We saw the moon reappear **glowing eerily.**
MISPLACED: **Glowing eerily,** we saw the moon reappear.

Guided Practice

Identify the participle in each sentence. Tell whether it is the main verb in a verb phrase or is used as an adjective.

Example: Sue is reading about the phases of the moon.
reading   main verb

1. The moon can be an exciting sight.
2. The moon is orbiting the earth.
3. The orbiting moon goes through different phases.
4. Is the moon waxing toward a full moon?
5. No, it is waning toward a new moon.

?! THINK
- How can I recognize a participial phrase?

REMEMBER

- A **participle** is a verb form that can be used as an adjective to modify a noun or a pronoun.
- A **participial phrase** is a group of words that includes a participle used as an adjective and words that complete its meaning.

More Practice

A. Write the participle in each sentence. Then write whether the participle is used as the **main verb** or as an **adjective.**

Example: The moon is divided into highlands and plains.
divided   main verb

6. Craters dot the scarred surface of the moon.
7. These craters were caused by crashing meteorites.
8. The same side of the moon is always facing the earth.
9. The orbiting moon affects the earth's tides.
10. The spinning earth orbits the sun.
11. In 1687 Isaac Newton had explained how this affected tides.
12. This also involved the changing position of the sun.

B. Write each sentence. Draw one line under each participial phrase and two lines under the word it modifies.

Example: Varying in degree, the three types of eclipses are total, partial, and annular.
<u>Varying in degree</u>, the three <u><u>types</u></u> of eclipses are total, partial, and annular.

13. The total eclipse, blocking the whole sun, is the most dramatic.
14. Dancing around the moon, the sun's corona is spectacular.
15. Seeing a solar eclipse, people were frightened.
16. A type of eclipse recurring every eighteen years is predictable.
17. Astronomers, knowing the prediction, awaited the eclipse.
18. Using dark lenses for protection, they watched the sun disappear from view.

Extra Practice, page 463

WRITING APPLICATION A Descriptive Paragraph

Imagine that you are seeing an eclipse of the sun for the first time. Write a brief description of your feelings. Then exchange papers with a classmate and identify the participles and participial phrases in each other's work.

8 GERUNDS

You know that a participle is a verb form that can be used as an adjective. Another verb form, called a **gerund,** can be used as a noun. Gerunds are formed in the same way as present participles—by adding *ing* to the base form of the verb.

> **Photographing** is the purpose of modern telescopes.

A gerund can serve as the subject, as the direct object, as the object of a preposition, or as a predicate noun.

> SUBJECT: **Theorizing** is something astronomers do.
>
> DIRECT
> OBJECT: Astronomy requires **understanding.**
>
> OBJECT OF A
> PREPOSITION: Astronomers advance by **studying.**
>
> PREDICATE
> NOUN: Seeing is not always **believing.**

A **gerund phrase** is a group of words that includes a gerund and the other words that complete its meaning.

> **Theorizing about planets** is something astronomers do.

To determine whether a verb form ending in *ing* is used as a main verb in a verb phrase, as a present participle used as an adjective, or as a gerund, examine the sentence. If the verb form is being used as a noun, it is a gerund.

Guided Practice

Identify the underlined word as a main verb, as a participle used as an adjective, or as a gerund.

Example: Borrowing names for astronomical bodies from myths is a long tradition.   gerund

1. Two moons called Phobos and Deimos are orbiting Mars.
2. The names, meaning "fear" and "terror," are from mythology.
3. They are the horses pulling the chariot of Mars.
4. Astronomer Asaph Hall is credited with naming the moons.
5. Predicting their orbits is Hall's major contribution.

 THINK

■ How can I recognize that a verb form is a gerund?

REMEMBER

- A **gerund** is a verb form ending in *ing* that is used as a noun.
- A **gerund phrase** is a group of words that includes a gerund and the words that complete its meaning.

More Practice

A. Write whether the underlined word is the **main verb** in a verb phrase, a **participle** used as an adjective, or a **gerund.**

Example: Astronomers were <u>observing</u> Mars for signs of life.
               main verb

  6. In 1877 Schiaparelli reported <u>seeing</u> canals.

  7. <u>Hoping</u> to find these canals, Lowell built an observatory.

  8. <u>Landing</u> on Mars was the mission of *Viking* in 1976.

  9. Tests <u>requiring</u> soil samples were made by *Viking.*

10. <u>Waiting</u> for <u>exciting</u> news can be <u>annoying.</u>

11. The first results were <u>disappointing.</u>

12. <u>Looking</u> for signs of life was <u>exciting.</u>

B. Identify each gerund phrase. Then write whether it is a **subject,** a **direct object,** an **object of a preposition,** or a **predicate noun.**

Example: Seeing the topography of Mars is exciting.
         Seeing the topography of Mars   subject

13. Probing Mars directly was the purpose of *Viking.*

14. By showing Mars close up, the photos were most revealing.

15. Realizing the height of Olympus Mons thrilled us all.

16. Other volcanoes can be seen by examining the photographs.

17. *Viking* continued exploring by digging for soil samples.

18. After testing these samples, many stopped hoping for signs of life on Mars.

19. Designing the tests was a difficult task.

20. Finding no signs of life disappointed many.

Extra Practice, page 464

WRITING APPLICATION A Proposal

Imagine that you are an artist who is commissioned to paint a huge landscape of Mars. Write a proposal about what you would show in your painting. Exchange papers with a classmate and identify the gerunds and gerund phrases in each other's work.

9 INFINITIVES

You have studied gerunds, which are verb forms used as nouns. An **infinitive** is another verb form that can be used as a noun. An infinitive is formed by using the word *to* with the base form of the verb.

An infinitive used as a noun can be the subject, the predicate noun, or the direct object in a sentence.

SUBJECT: **To measure** is an essential part of astronomy.

PREDICATE
NOUN: Another important skill is **to observe.**

DIRECT
OBJECT: Astronomers also need **to think.**

An **infinitive phrase** is a group of words that includes an infinitive and other words that complete its meaning.

> **To study radio waves** is hard work.
> Remember **to adjust the instruments carefully.**

Do not confuse an infinitive with a prepositional phrase that begins with *to*. *To* followed by a verb is always an infinitive.

PREPOSITIONAL
PHRASE: Radio astronomy adds **to our knowledge.**

INFINITIVE
PHRASE: **To measure distances** is its function.

Guided Practice

Tell whether the underlined words are an infinitive, an infinitive phrase, or a prepositional phrase.

Example: <u>To listen</u> requires an astronomer's patience.
infinitive

1. Karl Jansky wanted <u>to hear radio waves from space.</u>
2. Radio astronomy contributes <u>to our understanding of space.</u>
3. <u>To collect radio waves</u> gives us contact with the universe.
4. <u>To listen</u> is <u>to learn.</u>
5. <u>To work at the edge of the universe</u> requires large radio dishes.

 THINK

- How can I tell infinitives and prepositional phrases apart?

REMEMBER

- An **infinitive,** formed with the word *to* and the basic form of the verb, can be used as a noun.
- An **infinitive phrase** is an infinitive and the other words that complete its meaning.

More Practice

A. Write whether the underlined words are an **infinitive,** an **infinitive phrase,** or a **prepositional phrase.**

Example: Sue wanted <u>to include radio waves in her report</u>.
       infinitive phrase

  6. She turned <u>to the back</u> of the book.
  7. Her first step was <u>to check the index</u>.
  8. She found entries that ranged from *airglow* <u>to *radio waves*</u>.
  9. Turning <u>to the page</u>, she saw an entry for *thermal emissions*.
 10. <u>To read further</u> seemed pointless <u>to her</u>.
 11. She decided <u>to pose a question</u> <u>to an astronomer</u>.
 12. <u>To continue</u> was <u>to risk disappointment</u>.

B. Write each sentence. Underline and label each **infinitive, infinitive phrase,** and **prepositional phrase.** Write whether each infinitive or infinitive phrase is used as a **subject,** as a **predicate noun,** or as a **direct object.**

Example: To study the stars is rewarding.
       <u>To study the stars</u> is rewarding.
       infinitive phrase   *subject*

 13. The image cannot be increased to a larger size.
 14. To launch telescopes into space is one solution.
 15. Their purpose is to determine distances.
 16. Quasars send radio waves directly to the earth.
 17. To be informed about quasars is to study continually.
 18. Some scientists want to devote their efforts to that goal.

Extra Practice, page 465

WRITING APPLICATION A Description

   Imagine you are Galileo, the first person to observe the features of the moon through a telescope. Using infinitives and infinitive phrases, describe what you see as you gaze at the moon. Exchange descriptions with a classmate and check each other's work for correct use of infinitives.

10 MECHANICS: Using Commas With Clauses

You have learned that a clause is a sentence part that contains a subject and a predicate. Remember the following rules for using commas when you write sentences that contain clauses.

1. Use a comma before the conjunctions *and, or,* and *but* when you join two independent clauses to form a compound sentence.

    Will Clark investigate the sun, or will he study Mars?

2. Use commas to set off an adjective clause that gives information that is not essential to the meaning of the word it modifies.

    He went to the library, **which was nearby,** for data.
    The material **that he found** was excellent.

3. Use a comma after an adverb clause that begins a sentence.

    After Clark finished his research, he wrote a topic outline.

Guided Practice

For each sentence tell where a comma or commas are needed.

Example: When the sky is clear 6,000 stars are visible to the naked eye.   *comma after clear*

1. A small telescope which is inexpensive is a valuable aid.
2. Telescopes that are very powerful reveal distant galaxies.
3. Each galaxy that is visible contains billions of stars.
4. The Milky Way which is our galaxy is rather small.
5. The vastness of the universe became even more apparent when the telescope was used.
6. Galileo gazed upward and he saw hundreds of "new" stars.
7. Hubble whose studies were advanced explained the size of the galaxy.

 THINK

■ How do I know when to use commas to set off clauses?

REMEMBER

- Use a comma before the conjunction *and*, *or*, or *but* in a compound sentence.
- Use commas to set off a nonessential adjective clause.
- Use a comma after an adverb clause that begins a sentence.

More Practice

A. Write each sentence, adding commas where needed.

Example: Using ancient charts Galileo explored the skies.
Using ancient charts, Galileo explored the skies.

8. After he studied his charts Herschel found unknown stars.
9. Other scientists suspected that spiral galaxies were common.
10. Radio astronomy which was a new tool aided investigation.
11. The nearest star to our solar system is Alpha Centauri which is four light-years away.
12. Gerald Hawkins who is an astrophysicist offers new theories.

B. Write each sentence, adding commas where needed. Then write whether the sentence is **compound** or contains an **adjective clause** or an **adverb clause.**

Example: *Apollo 11* was launched and the world awaited the lunar landing.
Apollo 11 was launched, and the world awaited the lunar landing.   compound

13. People were amazed as the rockets fired.
14. After viewers saw the takeoff they still gazed up.
15. Men who would go to the moon boarded the module.
16. As he piloted the module Collins spoke to the others.
17. Armstrong whom we watched on TV stepped out.
18. He was moved and as he spoke his voice cracked.
19. Aldrin was the second man on the moon and he left footprints in the lunar soil.
20. They planted an American flag before they reentered the module.

Extra Practice, page 466

An Article

Write an article about an exciting event, such as a new scientific discovery or something that happened to you for the first time. Then ask a classmate to identify the different clauses and check the commas in your article.

11 VOCABULARY BUILDING: Suffixes

A **suffix** is a letter or a group of letters that is added to the end of a base word. The addition of a suffix changes the part of speech of a word and sometimes the meaning.

Noun-Forming Suffixes

Suffix	Meaning	Example
an	one who is of	Europe**an**
er, or	one who or that which	mark**er**, act**or**
ian	one skilled in	magic**ian**
ion	act, state, or result of	act**ion**
ism	act, practice, or process of	patriot**ism**
ist	one who works at, practices, or adheres to	chem**ist**
ment	act, condition, or result of	agree**ment**
ness	quality, state, or condition	kind**ness**
tion	act, state, or result of	informa**tion**

Adjective-Forming Suffixes

Suffix	Meaning	Example
able, ible	able to, capable of being	manage**able**, divis**ible**
an	of or belonging to	Mexic**an**
ful	full of, marked by	help**ful**
ic	like	hero**ic**
ish	like, suggesting	boy**ish**
less	lacking, without	fear**less**
y	showing, suggesting	smok**y**

Guided Practice

Name the suffix in each word.

Example: employment   *ment*

1. gleeful
2. action
3. artist
4. impish
5. readable
6. operator

THINK

- How does the addition of a suffix change a word?

REMEMBER

- A **suffix** is a word part added to the end of a base word. A suffix changes the part of speech and sometimes the meaning of the base word to which it is added.

More Practice

A. Write each word and underline the suffix. Then define the word, using a dictionary if necessary.

Example: hugeness—*state of being huge*

  7. mathematician   **9.** starry   **11.** amazement

  8. meteoric   **10.** visible   **12.** physicist

B. Write each sentence. Complete the word by writing the appropriate suffix. Use a dictionary to help you.

Example: The photographs of Mars were remark ____.
    The photographs of Mars were remarkable.

13. It was hard to see Mars in the blurr____ photograph.
14. Often align____ of stars is a problem.
15. A geolog____ studied the surface of Mars.
16. An astronomer is truly a spectat____.
17. When a star explodes, it increases in bright____.
18. Stars shine because of a nuclear react____.

19. Mars is covered with redd____ rocks.
20. Astronauts are often cited for hero____.
21. The loca____ of quasars was an exciting discovery.
22. Scientific theor____ offer possible answers.
23. An astronom____ observes the skies.
24. The clearly vis____ channels on Mars indicate the one-time act____ of water.
25. Telescop____ observa____ can be beauti____.

Extra Practice, page 467

WRITING APPLICATION A Journal Entry

Observe the night sky on a clear evening. Note everything you see. Write about your observations in your journal. Circle every suffix you used.

GRAMMAR ——AND—— WRITING CONNECTION

Parallel Structure

To make your writing clearer, more logical, and more enjoyable, it is important that you understand how to develop parallel structure in your sentences. **Parallel structure** is a style of writing in which parts of a sentence that are similar in meaning are expressed with similar grammatical forms. For example, when Neil Armstrong stepped onto the surface of the moon, he said, "That's one small step for man, one giant leap for mankind." Compare this in terms of clarity, logic, and style to "Even though I am only taking one little step, it still represents something larger."

NOT PARALLEL: Ancient people named groups of stars after gods, goddesses, and also gave some the names of animals.

PARALLEL: Ancient people named groups of stars after gods, goddesses, and animals.

NOT PARALLEL: How could these people see figures in the sky so clearly and with ease?

PARALLEL: How could these people see figures in the sky so clearly and easily?

Working Together

COOPERATIVE LEARNING

With a classmate, talk about each sentence and tell how its structure can be made parallel.

Example: The constellation that I know best and I like it the most is Ursa Major.
The constellation that I know best and like most is Ursa Major.

1. Observing the constellations is awesome and gives a thrill.
2. We are reminded of myths, legends, and also remember heroes.
3. The values of ancient people become apparent and are appreciated.

Revising Sentences

Rewrite each sentence so that it has parallel structure.

4. The study of the constellations is not important to studying astronomy.
5. Learning the names of groups of stars has more to do with mythology than with astronomical studies.
6. Many astronomers are aware of technical terms, complicated formulas, and problems in science.
7. Astronomers know about mathematics and physics, but they may not know about things mythological.
8. Mr. Green enjoys knowing the constellations, to point them out, and telling their stories.
9. He is unusual because he is a scientist, an astronomer, and writes.
10. In college he studied literature, physics, and liked astronomy.
11. This may account for his many interests, wide ranging knowledge, and he held different jobs.
12. The first things he points out to a newcomer are the Big Dipper, Polaris, and shows them the Little Dipper.
13. He finds enjoyment in being with people, pointing out constellations, and to tell the myths of the constellations.

WRITER AT WORK

Below is the beginning of a paragraph. Rewrite these sentences for parallel structure. Then do some research and add more sentences. Also make sure that these have parallel structure.

The constellation of Ursa Major is best known as the Big Dipper, and Ursa Minor is called the Little Dipper. In Latin, *ursa* means "bear," and *major* has the meaning of "big," and "little" is the meaning of *minor*.

Man's First Step on the Moon. Original oil painting by Norman Rockwell (detail).

UNIT CHECKUP

LESSON

1

Sentences and Clauses (page 428)   Write the independent clause(s) in each sentence.

1. Jan wondered about his research paper.
2. Is it like other kinds of writing, or is it different?
3. He thought about topics; he wanted an interesting one.
4. He listed ideas, and suddenly he thought of a good topic.

LESSON
2

Complex Sentences (page 430)   Write the subordinate clause in each sentence.

5. Ever since Jan could remember, he had liked Greek myths.
6. Although there were many gods, Jan liked Hermes the most.
7. Whenever Zeus needed a messenger, he sent for Hermes.
8. When Hermes appears in Roman myths, his name is Mercury.

LESSON

3

Adjective Clauses (page 432)   Write each sentence. Draw one line under the adjective clause and two lines under the word it modifies.

9. Jan visited the library, which was across town.
10. The librarian, who was always pleasant, helped him.
11. Jan saw a book whose authors he recognized.
12. One author, whom he looked up, had written many books.

LESSON
4

Essential and Nonessential Clauses (page 434)   Write each sentence. Underline each essential clause once and each nonessential clause twice.

13. Jan, who had never done a research paper, took notes.
14. He narrowed his topic, which made it easier to handle.
15. Jan, who had found many books, made a bibliography.
16. The bibliography that he compiled would help later.

LESSON

5

Adverb Clauses (page 436)   Write each sentence. Draw one line under the adverb clause and two lines under the word it modifies.

17. After Jan found his topic, he checked the card catalog.
18. The card catalog would help because it lists books by subject.
19. Where he saw references to Hermes, he noted the call number.
20. Jan continued his search until he had enough material.

Noun Clauses (page 438)   Write each noun clause.

21. What the card catalog lists is three ways of finding books.
22. Subject cards tell which books contain material on the subject.
23. Author cards show whatever titles an author has written.
24. Checking a title card is how you find specific books.

Participles and Participial Phrases (page 440)   Write each sentence and underline each participle or participial phrase.

25. Jan had gathered a stack of three-by-five cards.
26. Finding something interesting, he noted it on a card.
27. Sometimes he included a summarized passage.
28. Reading something important, he quoted it exactly.

Gerunds, Infinitives (pages 442, 444)   Identify each **gerund, gerund phrase, infinitive,** and **infinitive phrase.**

29. Taking notes is a vital part of writing reports.
30. Quoting word by word is a waste of time.
31. To save time is necessary; to summarize is wisest.
32. Directly quoting only important passages is best.
33. To quote is to use the writer's exact words.
34. Showing quotations requires using quotation marks.

Mechanics: Using Commas with Clauses (page 446)   Add needed commas.

35. Sorting the note cards Jan placed them in stacks.
36. Rereading the cards he found some in the wrong pile.
37. One pile was very large and it produced three new categories.
38. Jan who had finished sorting had begun to write an outline.

Vocabulary Building: Suffixes (page 448)   Write the appropriate suffix.

39. It is help____ to ask what questions the paper answers.
40. Jan felt like a writ____ as he developed his thesis.
41. His convic____ about the quality of his research increased.
42. When he finished, Jan had a feeling of accomplish____.

Writing Application: Clauses and Phrases (pages 428–446)
This paragraph contains seven errors in the use of clauses and phrases. Rewrite the paragraph correctly.

43.–49.   Pompeii was a busy Roman port and it was a resort for wealthy Romans. When Vesuvius that is a volcano erupted in A.D. 79 the city was buried under tons of ash. Rediscovered in 1748 Pompeii that is remarkably well preserved has been excavated.

Dangling Sentences

Sentences with misplaced participial phrases can create some very amusing images. For example: Scrubbing the dog, the phone rang. Form groups of three students and on strips of paper write funny sentences with misplaced participial phrases. Then join your class-mates and make mobiles with the sentence strips. Corrected sentences should be written on the reverse side of each strip in a different color. For example: As I was scrubbing the dog, the phone rang.

Laughing with Limericks

Limericks are a popular form of poetry. A limerick is a humorous five-line poem in which the first, second, and fifth lines rhyme with one another and have three stressed syllables, while the third and fourth lines rhyme with each other and have only two stressed syllables. A good limerick must be funny. Read these.

There was a young lady from Niger,
Who smiled as she rode on a tiger.
   They came back from the ride
   With the lady inside,
And the smile on the face of the tiger.

A canner, exceedingly canny,
One morning remarked to his granny,
   "A canner can can
   Anything that he can,
But a canner can't can a can, can he?"

Write your own limerick. Match the meter and rhyme scheme of the two examples. Remember to make your limerick humorous. The humor might be based on a pun, as in "A canner, exceedingly canny."

WHO ARE YOU?

Work with a partner. Divide a sheet of paper length-wise. Label the two columns *Dependent Clauses* and *Independent Clauses*. In each column, take turns writing sentences about people you know. Each sentence should contain a dependent clause and an independent clause beginning with the word *who*. Take turns reading the sentences aloud. Give points for correct punctuation.

Suffix Symbols

Imagine that you have discovered this strange symbol in a far-off galaxy.

Suffixes

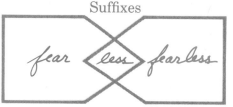

Having this symbol will bring you luck, but only if you *carefully* follow these instructions.

1. Recopy the symbol neatly so that it fits on a sheet of paper.
2. Label the space where the figures overlap *Suffixes* and print such suffixes as *able, er,* and *ic.*
3. In the figure on the left write words or word parts that you can match with the suffixes.
4. In the figure on the right write the words formed. One example has been provided. May good luck be with you!

Everyone Is a Star

Fold a piece of paper in half and then in half again. You now have four equal squares. Label the squares *Noun Clause, Adjective Clause, Adverb Clause,* and *Artwork*. In each of the first three spaces, write a sentence for a friend. The sentences should include the kind of clause indicated. In the last space draw a picture or make a collage that illustrates the content of your sentences. Exchange papers with your friend.

EXTRA PRACTICE

Three levels of practice

Sentences and Clauses (page 428)

LEVEL
A. Write whether each sentence is a **simple** or a **compound** sentence.

1. An essay develops ideas about a topic.
2. A research paper is different from an essay.
3. You develop a thesis, but you use facts to support it.
4. Research often must be done at a library.
5. A research paper includes a bibliography.
6. Jill took notes from many sources.
7. Is a bibliography in alphabetical order?
8. Sources are important; they are marked by footnotes.
9. Greg knew his topic; however, he needed information.
10. He chose golf, his best sport; but he limited the topic.

LEVEL
B. Write each sentence. Write whether it is **simple** or **compound.** If it is compound, underline the independent clauses.

11. The scope of a topic is important.
12. This subject may be too broad; you must focus on one part.
13. You may select several topics at first.
14. One topic was magic; another was ice cream.
15. Bill selected a topic, and he limited it.
16. He likes cars; therefore, he chose the Model T.
17. Mac is thinking about choosing water-skiing.
18. Would you want to learn about roller-skating?

LEVEL
C. Write each sentence. Then write whether the sentence is **simple** or **compound.** If the sentence is compound, underline the independent clauses. Add commas and semicolons where needed.

19. Judy likes many things but she likes horses best.
20. Her topic is too broad she decides on thoroughbreds.
21. The racehorse she chooses is Secretariat.
22. He won many races he also set course records.
23. Is it better to win or is it better to set records?
24. Secretariat won the Triple Crown.
25. Secretariat showed his greatness by achieving this feat.

EXTRA PRACTICE

Three levels of practice

Complex Sentences (page 430)

LEVEL
A. Write the subordinate clause in each sentence.

1. While she sorted the note cards, Judy reread them.
2. An order of ideas came to her as she sorted the notes.
3. Before she began the outline, she studied her note cards.
4. Although she discarded some cards, most were relevant.
5. Since the cards were in order, she made an outline.
6. She wrote sentences because they would be easier to read.
7. Bill worked on his outline until he found the gaps.
8. Before he could continue, he needed to do more research.
9. He used the town library because it has more resources.
10. Although it was late, he arrived before the library closed.

LEVEL
B. Write each sentence. Then draw one line under the subordinate clause and two lines under the subordinate conjunction.

11. When you write, it is important to acknowledge your sources.
12. Use quotation marks when you use the exact words of the original writer.
13. If you use ideas from a source, you must still give credit.
14. Whenever you use a book, list it in the bibliography.
15. Add each book to your list as you go along.
16. Sources of ideas can be confused unless you keep notes.
17. As you write, you often combine ideas from various sources.
18. State your topic and thesis as you begin your paper.
19. This will help as you start.

LEVEL
C. Write each sentence. Draw one line under each subordinate clause. Draw two lines under the subordinate conjunction and add commas where needed.

20. Although Bill liked all cars he focused on one in particular.
21. He considered several cars until he remembered the Model T.
22. Whereas others were older this one was more popular.
23. Though black was the only color used the car was handsome.
24. In 1908 the Model T was seen wherever you saw cars.
25. Henry Ford succeeded because he used mass production.

GRAMMAR

Three levels of practice

Adjective Clauses (page 432)

LEVEL

A. Write the adjective clause in each sentence.

1. Greg, who had completed his research, sorted his note cards.
2. He found a card that lacked a reference.
3. He finally found the book that he had used.
4. He returned the book to the shelf where he had found it.
5. He had done work that was unnecessary.
6. Greg, whose outline was complete, reviewed his work.
7. He rewrote a sentence whose structure was awkward.

LEVEL

B. Write each sentence. Draw one line under the adjective clause and two lines under the word it modifies.

8. Now he needed someone who could check the outline.
9. Another person would have a perspective that was fresh.
10. Greg gave the outline to his father, who was very helpful.
11. Are you a person who puts off writing research papers?
12. The time when you must begin to write always arrives.
13. A good topic, which is important, is the first step.
14. Avoid a topic whose scope is too broad.
15. A person who does research must limit the topic.
16. Think of the overall point that you must make.
17. Use sources whose information relates to the topic.
18. An outline, which is really a guide, is always helpful.

LEVEL

C. Write each sentence. Draw one line under the adjective clause and two lines under the word it modifies. Add commas where needed.

19. You will write notes that include quotations.
20. Many ideas will come from people who are authorities.
21. Write a first draft whose order follows your outline.
22. You will write a paper that has three distinct parts.
23. The first part whose content sets forth the main idea is the introduction.
24. The second part that you write is the body of the paper.
25. The conclusion which should tie together the ideas in your paper is the final part.

EXTRA PRACTICE

Three levels of practice

Essential and Nonessential Clauses (page 434)

LEVEL

A. Write the adjective clause in each sentence. Label the clause as **essential** or **nonessential.**

1. Mary, whose topic is dolphins, made notes on cards.
2. The notes that she made were helpful.
3. Dolphins was not the first topic that she tried.
4. Her first idea, which she gave up, was hot air balloons.
5. A friend who read widely first interested Mary in dolphins.
6. The friend, whose name is Juanita, told a tale.
7. The story, which is true, tells of a dolphin trait.
8. Dolphins, which have some sort of language, communicate with each other.
9. The animals that she admires are bottlenosed dolphins.
10. Those that I like are whales.

LEVEL

B. Write each sentence, and underline the adjective clause. Label the clause as **essential** or **nonessential.**

11. Dolphins save other dolphins that are in trouble.
12. This trait, which many do not know, is remarkable.
13. One swims underneath, pushing the other up to breathe the air that it must have.
14. The dolphin that receives the aid may survive.
15. Dolphins have also saved people who are drowning.
16. Some accounts that document these incidents are ancient.
17. Have you heard of a movie whose subject is dolphins?

LEVEL

C. Write each sentence, and underline the adjective clause. Label the clause as **essential** or **nonessential.** Add commas where needed.

18. Drawings whose dates are unknown show dolphins rescuing drowning sailors.
19. Another drawing that is very old is even clearer.
20. Mary read about a number of dolphins that saved humans.
21. This behavior which was new to her became her topic.
22. She made notes of every incident that she could find.
23. Her note cards which she put in order suggested an outline.
24. She changed some sentences that were in the outline.
25. She wrote an introduction that stated the thesis.

EXTRA PRACTICE

Three levels of practice

Adverb Clauses (page 436)

LEVEL

A. Write the adverb clause in each sentence.

1. Before Sam started his research paper, he thought carefully.
2. He made plans whenever a project was due.
3. If he used the time well now, he might save time later.
4. Although Sam had many interests, he wrote down only six.
5. Unless he found something better, he would use one of these.
6. After he thought about topics, Sam selected one.
7. Since the topic was too broad, he limited it.
8. He reworked the idea until it was something he could cover fully in his paper.

LEVEL

B. Write each sentence. Draw one line under the adverb clause. Draw two lines under the verb that it modifies.

9. Fran wrote a brief outline because it gave her work form.
10. Whenever new ideas occurred to her, she added them.
11. Because Fran had written research papers before, she was sure of her skills.
12. After she thought her topic over, she went to the library.
13. Before she started, the librarian gave her some ideas.
14. The *Readers' Guide* helped as Fran began.
15. Though the *Guide*'s title is longer, she shortened it for notes.
16. She added *to Periodical Literature* when she wrote formally.
17. When she used the *Readers' Guide*, she turned to D.
18. She smiled because many articles were listed.

LEVEL

C. Write each sentence. Draw one line under the adverb clause and two lines under the verb it modifies. Add commas where needed.

19. Unless the articles were about dolphins Fran ignored them.
20. After she read some articles she switched to books.
21. She went to the card catalog because she sought books.
22. Fran looked at author cards until she thought of a better way.
23. She turned to subject cards because they were more useful.
24. When she found a book she read the table of contents.
25. She also turned to the back because the index was useful.

PRACTICE + PLUS

Three levels of additional practice for a difficult skill

Adverb Clauses (page 436)

LEVEL

A. Write the adverb clause in each sentence.

1. After the students had turned in their research reports, they discussed their topics.
2. Tony had chosen Alexander Cartwright because Tony was interested in the rules for playing baseball.
3. Although Bob did not have a green thumb, he chose tulips.
4. Julie had researched the Globe Theatre since she was interested in Shakespeare.
5. Because John had once visited the Statue of Liberty, he had written about its construction.

LEVEL

B. Write each sentence. Draw one line under the adverb clause and two lines under the verb that it modifies.

6. Craig had thought long before he picked a final topic.
7. Whenever Craig reads a book, he reads adventure stories.
8. When Craig needed a topic, he researched the career of Dumas.
9. Wherever Ken went, he saw mailboxes.
10. Since Ken had always been curious about the postal service, his topic was the Zip code system.

LEVEL

C. Write each sentence. Draw one line under the adverb clause and two lines under the verb it modifies. Add commas where needed.

11. Since Wendell is an avid model railroad fan he submitted a paper about the first railroad in the United States.
12. When Cynthia chose her research topic she chose Yellowstone.
13. Although many ideas appealed to her Marge selected the development of the Braille system.
14. George's topic had been killer bees until he changed it.
15. Because he couldn't find sound information about this topic George chose the migration of Canada geese.

EXTRA PRACTICE

Three levels of practice

Noun Clauses (page 438)

LEVEL

A. Write the noun clause in each sentence.

1. Art is what interests Hank.
2. He goes to whatever art shows are in town.
3. He hopes that he will become an artist someday.
4. He discusses art with whoever is in the gallery.
5. What particularly interests Hank is painting.
6. Watercolors are what interested him earlier.
7. Where he spends much time is in the art room.
8. Whoever is looking for him will often find him there.

LEVEL

B. Write each sentence, and underline the noun clause.

9. Hank wonders how he can use his interests in a report.
10. Can he use his interests for what is needed?
11. Why Hank chose Claude Monet is clear.
12. Scholars say that Monet was the first Impressionist.
13. Hank remembers when he visited Paris last summer.
14. Why he went was to see the art museums.
15. He visited whatever museum was in his guidebook.
16. One day he followed whichever was the most interesting street.
17. What he found was a museum of paintings by Claude Monet.
18. How he ever found that museum is still a mystery.

LEVEL

C. Write each sentence and underline the noun clause. Then write whether the clause is used as a **subject,** a **direct object,** an **object of a preposition,** or a **predicate noun.**

19. Whatever he had once thought of Monet changed.
20. There were many prints for sale for whoever wanted them.
21. Why there were so many prints was soon apparent.
22. The truth is that there were hundreds of paintings.
23. Monet is responsible for what Hank knows about color.
24. His reward was that he found many topics.
25. Hank focused on whatever Monet wrote for new artists.

EXTRA PRACTICE

Three levels of practice

Participles and Participial Phrases (page 440)

LEVEL

A. Write the participle in each sentence. Then write wnether the participle is the **main verb** of a verb phrase or is used as an **adjective.**

1. Jim was thinking about pyramids for his paper.
2. He found several illustrated books on the subject.
3. Some pyramids were built before 3000 B.C.
4. They were amazing structures made of stone.
5. Huge blocks of limestone were dragged from afar.

LEVEL

B. Write each sentence. Draw one line under each participial phrase and two lines under the word that it modifies.

6. Recognized as the best example is the Great Pyramid at Giza.
7. It is huge, covering thirteen acres and standing fifty feet taller than St. Peter's in Rome.
8. Commanding that much territory, it is a perfect square except for one small error.
9. Constructed of limestone, it is 480 feet tall.
10. The Great Pyramid, leading the list of the ancient world's great wonders, was unsurpassed for 4,500 years.

LEVEL

C. Write each sentence. Draw one line under each participial phrase. Then draw two lines under the word that it modifies. Add commas where needed.

11. Citing the Great Pyramid as an example one book said that there were 100,000 slave workers present at all times.
12. Dragging the stones from quarries they rolled them on logs to the construction site.
13. Each stone was immense weighing two and a half tons.
14. Reaching the pyramid men and cattle pulled each stone up ramps to its proper place.
15. The work continued for twenty years interrupted only by floods.

EXTRA PRACTICE

Three levels of practice

Gerunds (page 442)

LEVEL

A. Write whether the underlined word is a participle used as the **main verb** in a verb phrase, a participle used as an **adjective,** or a **gerund.**

1. Mary was <u>thinking</u> about her research paper.
2. She knew that an <u>interesting</u> paper would take much research.
3. Mainly she thought about the process of <u>researching</u>.
4. She remembered <u>recalling</u> her friend's story.
5. <u>Finding</u> articles in the *Readers' Guide* was important.
6. The card catalog assisted her in <u>locating</u> books.
7. Then she was <u>browsing</u> through the table of contents.
8. <u>Skimming</u> pages also helped her see what it was about.
9. <u>Checking</u> the index had been even more helpful.

LEVEL

B. Identify each gerund or gerund phrase. Then write whether it is used as a **subject,** a **direct object,** a **predicate noun,** or an **object of a preposition.**

10. Mary would enjoy writing about dolphins.
11. She had prepared herself by researching carefully.
12. Putting it off any longer would be foolish.
13. There was no time like the present for starting.
14. Outlining the major points would also be helpful.
15. Mary sat down and started preparing an outline.
16. Outlining helped give her paper logical structure.

LEVEL

C. Write each sentence, and underline each gerund or gerund phrase. Then write whether it is used as a **subject,** a **direct object,** a **predicate noun,** or an **object of a preposition.**

17. By following an outline, she kept to the point.
18. Besides, she could always refer to her note taking.
19. Note taking is good preparation for writing.
20. Writing makes her ideas flow.
21. Showing connections is another benefit.
22. Developing ideas is part of the process of writing.
23. Putting something down on a blank page was difficult.
24. Writing a paper is more complex than revision.
25. Revising her work was easier because she knew the subject.

EXTRA PRACTICE

Three levels of practice

Infinitives (page 444)

LEVEL
A. Write whether each underlined group of words is an **infinitive,** an **infinitive phrase,** or a **prepositional phrase.**

1. To throw a boomerang takes skill.
2. People think the boomerang always returns to the thrower.
3. The purpose of a boomerang is to sail.
4. However, some go in a straight line to the target.
5. To travel over 100 yards is common for a good boomerang.
6. To think of boomerangs as only Australian is incorrect.
7. In Egypt to throw a boomerang was a sport for the nobility.
8. People in India began to hunt with boomerangs.
9. To throw boomerangs was a Hopi Indian skill.

LEVEL
B. Write each sentence. Underline each infinitive or infinitive phrase.

10. A characteristic of boomerangs was to sail far with great force.
11. A boomerang begins to spin as it sails.
12. The spin helps to lift the boomerang.
13. To comprehend this is difficult.
14. To understand the gyroscope is to understand this principle.
15. Try to remember that boomerangs can be traced to prehistory.
16. The characteristic of a boomerang is to make a return.
17. To turn to the left is a strong tendency in most boomerangs.
18. Its function is to make a complete circle before grounding.

LEVEL
C. Write each sentence. Underline each infinitive, infinitive phrase, or prepositional phrase beginning with *to.* Then write whether each infinitive or infinitive phrase is used as the **subject,** the **predicate noun,** or the **direct object.**

19. The thrower must learn to place the fingers at the end.
20. To throw it overhand is also necessary.
21. To add a sharp flick of the wrist is also essential.
22. Another trick is to throw it into the wind.
23. The skill is to coordinate all these movements.
24. The verb *boomerang* means "to backfire."
25. Almost everyone would like to throw a boomerang; however, to catch one appeals only to a few.

EXTRA PRACTICE

Three levels of practice

Mechanics: Using Commas with Clauses (page 446)

LEVEL
A. Write each sentence, adding a comma or commas where needed. If no commas are needed, write **correct.**

1. The first fountain pens which were developed in England more than 150 years ago replaced quill pens.
2. An American who started producing fountain pens in 1880 was L. E. Waterman.
3. Waterman's pens seized the public's imagination and they became popular immediately.
4. The fountain pens that you can find today are filled with ink in different ways.
5. When you fill a pen the ink is drawn into the reservoir.

LEVEL
B. Write each sentence, adding commas where needed. If no commas are needed, write **correct.**

6. Another pen that is common uses cartridges of ink.
7. You insert a cartridge that opens when you tighten the pen.
8. What is the writing instrument that most people use today?
9. The ballpoint pen which you probably use regularly has replaced the fountain pen.
10. A ballpoint pen which has a ball bearing at its tip has a simple design.

LEVEL
C. Write each sentence, adding commas where they are needed. Then write whether you added a comma or commas to punctuate a **compound sentence,** an **adjective clause,** or an **adverb clause.**

11. This ballpoint which was known as a "biro" was widely used in Britain.
12. The first ink that was used in ballpoints was printer's ink.
13. Because it leaked it posed a problem that was serious.
14. The spring that retracts the point catches and this allows the point to be exposed.
15. A much simpler method which you find on disposable ballpoints uses a thin plastic rod.

EXTRA PRACTICE

Three levels of practice

Vocabulary Building: Suffixes (page 448)

LEVEL

A. Write each word and underline the suffix. Then define the word, using a dictionary if necessary.

1. artist
2. employment
3. dampness
4. erasable
5. optimism

6. mythic
7. joker
8. greenish
9. misty
10. reaction

LEVEL

B. Write each sentence. Complete the word by writing the appropriate suffix. Use the dictionary to help you.

11. The observa____ of the lodestone was first made in China.
12. The discovery is trace____ to the first century B.C.
13. The develop____ of the compass began in A.D. 1100.
14. Sail____ were the primary users of the compass.
15. By 1250 the Scandinav____ were using the compass.
16. Europe____ benefited greatly from this invention.
17. The compass has been invalu____.
18. How would you know direc____ if the sun was not visible?
19. A compass is important when the weather is cloud____.

LEVEL

C. Write each sentence. Complete the word by writing the appropriate suffix. Then define the word, using a dictionary if necessary.

20. Later a difference was discovered between true north and magnetic north known as a magnetic varia____.
21. An iron needle will become magnet____ by rubbing it against a lodestone.
22. In early compasses the needles would lose their magnet____.
23. Scient____ have often used compasses.
24. In the nineteenth century compasses encountered more interference because ships were more metal____.
25. The solution was to make a careful adjust____ of each compass in each ship.

MAINTENANCE

UNIT 1: SENTENCES

Complete Subjects and Complete Predicates (page 4), **Simple Subjects and Simple Predicates** (page 6) Write each sentence. Underline the complete subject once and the complete predicate twice. Then write both the simple subject and the simple predicate.

1. Three spiders spin webs in the barn.
2. A red-and-black ladybug crawls over a leaf.
3. A praying mantis with spindly legs strikes a saintly pose.
4. My young brother studies bugs.

Correcting Fragments and Run-on Sentences (page 12) Write each group of words, correcting the sentence fragments and run-on sentences. Write **correct** next to any group of words that is a sentence.

5. The poet saw a field of daffodils, he wrote a poem about them.
6. Memorized the poem last week.
7. Our daffodils bloomed earlier this month.
8. The white and yellow blossoms with orange centers.

UNIT 3: NOUNS

Possessive Nouns (page 70) Write the sentences. Underline each singular possessive noun once and each plural possessive noun twice.

9. The opera company will present Verdi's *Aida*.
10. The singers' music is on the top shelf.
11. The soprano's aria will be rehearsed next.
12. The chorus's entrance was late.

UNIT 5: VERBS

Action Verbs (page 132), **Direct Objects, Transitive and Intransitive Verbs** (page 134), **Linking Verbs** (page 138) Write each sentence. Draw one line under each verb and two lines under each direct object, predicate noun, or predicate adjective. Over each verb write **tr.** for *transitive*, **int.** for *intransitive*, or **l.** for *linking*.

13. John makes jewelry of silver and gold.
14. He works at his shop all day.
15. He is a highly competent craftsman.
16. He sets a gemstone into a pendant.

Making Subjects and Verbs Agree (page 140)   Write each sentence, choosing the correct form of the verb in parentheses.

17. A bright, luminous comet (swing, swings) in a long orbit around the sun.
18. Each comet (have, has) a nucleus, a coma, and a tail.
19. Amateur and professional astronomers (track, tracks) the path of the comet.
20. The tail of a comet (streak, streaks) toward the sun.

Indirect Objects (page 136) Write each sentence. Write **d.o.** above each direct object and **i.o.** above each indirect object.

21. Mr. Darrow lent Homer a clarinet.
22. The bandmaster assigned him a solo part.
23. Homer asked the teacher a question.
24. The teacher sent the class an invitation.

Present, Past, and Future Tenses (page 142), **Present and Past Progressive** (page 146), **Perfect Tenses** (page 148)   Write each sentence. Underline the verb or verb phrase. Then write its tense: **present, past, future, present progressive, past progressive, present perfect,** or **past perfect.**

25. Recognition is coming to women inventors at last.

26. People have ignored women inventors for many years.
27. Eleanor Raymond and Maria Telkes had developed solar heating for homes without fair credit.
28. Jocelyn Bell had discovered the pulsar, but her professor received a Nobel Prize for it.

Irregular Verbs I (page 150), **Irregular Verbs II** (page 152) Write each sentence, using either the past or past participle of the verb shown in parentheses.

29. I had ____ a very large bubble.   (blow)
30. The cat ____ after it.   (run)
31. The cat has ____ forward toward it.   (spring)
32. The cat ____ its paw at the bubble.   (swing)

Using Commas to Separate Parts of a Sentence (page 154)   Rewrite each sentence by adding a comma or commas where needed.

33. Lew what kinds of dance do you study?
34. I take lessons in ballet tap dancing and folk dancing.
35. Ballet I understand takes the most skill.
36. Yes the steps are very precise.

UNIT 7: PRONOUNS

Using Subject and Object Pronouns (page 216)   Rewrite the sentences, choosing the pronoun that correctly completes each one. Then write **nominative** or **objective** to identify the case of the pronoun.

37. Sharon, Fred, and (I, me) swam in the waters of the Great Salt Lake.
38. I dared (he, him) to dive to the bottom.
39. (She, Her) and I watched through our goggles.
40. The salt water kept (he, him) afloat.

Possessive Pronouns (page 218)   Write each sentence. Underline each possessive pronoun and draw an arrow to its antecedent.

41. The Katzes took their vacation in the Rockies.
42. Charlotte left her suitcase at the motel.
43. David took wonderful pictures with his new camera.
44. The motel owners supplied extra towels for us at their pool.

UNIT 9: ADJECTIVES AND ADVERBS

Adjectives (page 284), **Articles and Proper Adjectives** (page 286)   Write each sentence. Draw one line under each adjective and two lines under each proper adjective. After each sentence, write each article and possessive pronoun.

45. A magnificent French tapestry hangs on the gray walls.
46. Priceless Oriental rugs cover the floors.
47. Their rich treasures are in the great mansion.
48. The Italian library contains his fine books.

Comparative and Superlative Adjectives I (page 288), **Comparative and Superlative Adjectives II** (page 290)   Write each sentence. Fill in each blank with the correct degree of comparison for the adjective in parentheses.

49. Serena's collection of tiles is ____ than a museum's. (large)
50. It is the ____ private collection in this town.   (important)
51. Serena paints ____ tiles than Rosa.   (good)
52. Rosa destroyed the ____ of her tiles.   (bad)

Adverbs (page 294)   Write each sentence. Underline each adverb and draw an arrow to the word it modifies. Then write what part of speech the modified word is.

53. Felix often plays croquet outdoors.
54. He wields his mallet rather wildly.
55. He often sends his ball straight through the wicket.
56. Every day Felix diligently practices his shots.

Comparative and Superlative Adverbs (page 296)
Write each sentence. Underline each adverb and write its degree of comparison as **positive, comparative,** or **superlative.**

57. Patrick bags groceries after school quite often.
58. He works harder at his job than Ivan.
59. Ivan bags more slowly but less haphazardly than Bill.
60. Annie rings up the sales faster than Doris.

Avoiding Double Negatives
(page 298) Rewrite each sentence, correcting the double negatives.

61. Daniel hadn't never ridden in a helicopter before.
62. Helicopters aren't flown nowhere near his home town.
63. Hardly no one he knows has flown in a helicopter.
64. Doesn't no one want to see Daniel's takeoff?

Using Adjectives and Adverbs
(page 300) Write each sentence. Choose the correct modifier to complete each sentence.

65. Roger makes (real, really) (good, well) pottery.
66. He feels (good, well) about his work.
67. He was (sure, surely) that he had not fired this batch (bad, badly).
68. He (sure, surely) will be able to get these pots.

Using Commas with Addresses, Dates, and Names
(page 302) Write each sentence. Add commas where needed.

69. Morris Barrie Jr. will travel to Chicago Illinois.
70. His appointment is with Myra Spencer Ph.D a chemist.
71. She works at Clancy Chemical Company 131 Michigan Avenue Chicago Illinois 60611.
72. Morris signed a contract with the company on July 18 1988 for research on a new plant food.

Synonyms and Antonyms
(page 304) Write each pair of words. Next to each write whether the words are **synonyms** or **antonyms.**

73. nimble, spry
74. heavy, light
75. clear, murky
76. strange, odd
77. flimsy, strong
78. afraid, scared
79. sane, lucid
80. idle, busy

UNIT 11: PREPOSITIONS, CONJUNCTIONS, AND INTERJECTIONS

Prepositions and Prepositional Phrases (page 358)
Write each sentence. Draw a

line under each prepositional phrase. Then draw a second line under the preposition and under its object.

81. Many cities have buildings with cast-iron facades.
82. Using cast iron in construction work began in the last part of the eighteenth century.
83. Cast iron was first used for bridges in England.
84. The dome of the United States Capitol is made of cast iron.

Using Pronouns in Prepositional Phrases (page 360) Rewrite these sentences, correcting the pronoun errors. If there are no errors, write **correct.**

85. Geoff will travel with my parents and I.
86. For both he and I the trip will be fun.
87. Geoff and myself divided the packing chores.
88. You can write to him and me at this address.

Conjunctions (page 364) Write each sentence. Underline the coordinating or correlative conjunctions and write the type of compound that they helped to form.

89. Nick and Ana study the menu carefully and thoroughly.
90. They will avoid elegant but expensive dishes.

91. Neither the chef's salad nor the fruit plate appeals to Ana.
92. Nick wants crab gumbo, but he doesn't see it on the menu or on the list of specials.

Making Verbs Agree with Compound Subjects (page 366) Rewrite each sentence, using the correct present-tense form of the verb in parentheses.

93. Neither team members nor the coach (arrive) on time.
94. The bats and a glove (be) near the bench.
95. Either the pitcher or the catcher (lead) the warm-up.
96. Both the infielders and the outfielders (be) alert.

Prefixes (page 374) Rewrite each sentence, turning the underlined words into a single word that uses a prefix. Place the word where it reads best.

97. Will you remove the frost from the refrigerator?
98. This can of beets is labeled wrongly.
99. Eric prefers grapes with no seeds in them.
100. Eva, you must heat the oven in advance.

UNIT 13: COMPLEX SENTENCES AND VERBALS

Sentences and Clauses (page 428), **Complex Sentences** (page 430) Write each sentence. Underline each independent clause once and each subordinate clause twice. Then write whether the sentence is **compound** or **complex.**

101. When archaeologists dug in Central America, they found many Mayan clay whistles.

102. At first the objects were dismissed as toys; however, they really were musical instruments.

103. Some whistles were simple, but others were complex.

104. Although Mayan culture flourished between A.D. 200 and 900, many of the instruments are much older.

Adjective Clauses (page 432) **Adverb Clauses** (page 436), **Essential and Nonessential Clauses** (page 434) Write each sentence. Draw one line under the subordinate clause. Then write whether it is an **adjective clause** or an **adverb clause** and mark the noun or verb it modifies. Set off nonessential adjective clauses with commas.

105. Because the technology is now available, Rose has become a "desktop publisher."

106. When Rose bought a personal computer, she began her publishing career.

107. Rose used a printer which became expensive before she got her computer.

108. The printing shop used a huge typesetting machine that formed pieces of metal type into columns.

Participles and Participial Phrases (page 440) Write each sentence. Underline each participle or participial phrase used as an adjective. Then write the word the participle or participial phrase describes.

109. The elephants trumpeting through the brush are fast.

110. Leading the herd, an old female is entering the water.

111. The elephants bathing in the river have cooled themselves.

112. Trained elephants have helped people work.

Infinitives (page 444) Write each sentence. Underline each infinitive or infinitive phrase. Identify each as **subject** or **direct object** of the verb.

113. To grow day lilies is easy.

114. One species manages to grow almost anywhere.

115. Even with neglect, the plants continue to multiply.

116. However, to develop new varieties is difficult.

Suffixes (page 448) Write each sentence. Complete each one by finding the proper suffix from the list below.

**ance   ize   ful   ical
or   tion   er   ic   ism**

117. An edit____ will review the manuscript.

118. She will give critic____ to the writ____.

119. She will be very care____ with the geograph____ references.

120. Even a wonder____ novel must have exact inspec____.

UNIT
14

Writing Research Reports

Read the quotation and look at the picture on the opposite page. What kinds of questions do you ask yourself when you read?

When you write a research report, you combine and summarize information that you have gathered from your reading. You look in many different sources for your information.

Focus A research report provides information about a limited topic based on facts gathered from different sources.

What topic would you like to research? On the following pages you will find a science article and some photographs that may give you some ideas for writing.

THEME: *GALAXIES*

*The answers you get from literature depend
on the questions you pose.*

—Margaret Atwood

Have you ever observed the evening sky and wondered about the mysteries of the universe? How far away are those bright objects? Could they be occupied by intelligent life—or any life at all?

Records from the earliest civilizations show that people who studied the skies developed many different explanations for what they saw there.

As you read the selection below, look for facts that ancient peoples used to explain their observations.

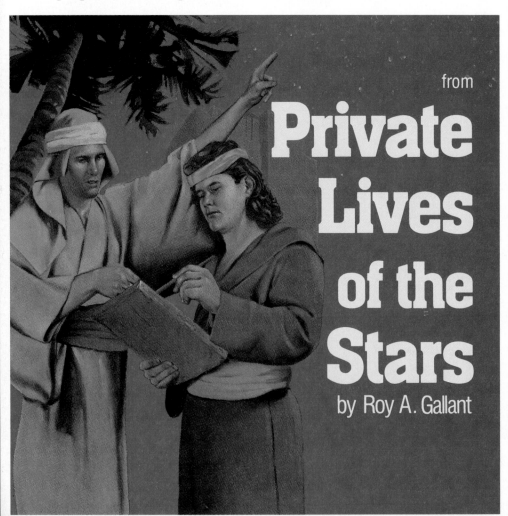

from

Private Lives of the Stars

by Roy A. Gallant

For as long as there have been people, they have studied the sky as a source of wonder and mystery. More than 5,000 years ago ancient stargazers, writing on blocks of clay, recorded the changing positions of the planets Mercury and Venus as they saw those planets move among the stars. They also kept records of the changing shape of the Moon as it went through phases, and of the Sun during eclipses. For those early stargazers, any object seen in the heavens was called a star. The planets were called wandering stars because they seemed to move among the stars. Comets were called hairy stars because of their long tails. And what we know today to be meteors were called shooting stars because they were thought to be stars falling to earth. The stars themselves were seen to flow endlessly across the heavens as a group. Because they were not seen to move about every which way like snowflakes in a blizzard, they were called fixed stars.

As we ask many questions about the universe today, so did the stargazers of old. Those questions surely included: What are the stars? Where do they come from? Are they alive? How big are they? Does Earth shine like a star? What is the place of Earth, and of the Sun, in the universe?[1]

The answers to those questions were not to come for a very long time. And when they did, they came slowly. At the time we are talking about—a few thousands of years ago—science did not exist. There were no chemists to explain what the stars are made of, and no physicists to explain how the stars move or how far away they are. And there were no telescopes through which to study the stars. Without science, people those many centuries ago made up stories, called myths, to explain what they saw in the sky. They made the sky a home for gods, demons, and spirits who ruled the world and were thought to control the lives of all people.

Among those who looked on the Sun as a god were New Mexico's Zuni Indians. According to Zuni creation myth, originally there were no people on Earth's surface. They were all crowded into a large, dark dungeon four levels underground. The Sun-god felt sorry for the imprisoned people, so he called his two sons to his side and said, "Let the people into the light."

1. The writer states his topic in the form of questions.

The two sons went down to Earth and entered the four lower worlds. Each world became darker and darker. When the sons finally reached the people, they said, "We have come for you."

"Bring us to the Sun," the people cried.

As the people followed the two boys, their eyes hurt during the long climb to the lighter third world and the even lighter second world. "Is this the bright world where we are to live?" asked the people. "Not yet," answered the two boys.

When the people stepped out into the fresh air and bright light, they were at first blinded. The Sun's rays pained them so that tears streamed from their eyes. And as their tears mixed with the soil, buttercups and sunflowers began to grow.

"This is the world," the people said.

Try for a moment to put yourself in the place of the old stargazers thousands of years ago. Imagine yourself studying the night sky for the first time and being asked to explain what you saw.

One thing you would most likely believe is that Earth is the center of the universe. Probably you would also say that Earth does not move in any way. Also, that the stars, Sun, and all other sky objects circle about Earth. That is what your senses would tell you.

After all, you cannot *feel* Earth move as it rotates, or spins, on its axis. The astronomer Tycho Brahe, about 300 years ago, said that Earth could not be spinning around like a top. If it did, he argued, birds would have their perches whipped out from under them. Neither can you feel Earth move as it revolves, or circles, about the Sun. And doesn't the Sun appear to rise over the same horizon each morning and set below the opposite horizon in the evening? And what about the Moon? It, too, appears to glide across the great sky dome in much the same way. Earth feels comfortably fixed and motionless in space, while all other objects seem to move around it. This is what people's senses tell them. And, after all, "seeing is believing." Or is it?

What about the height of the great sky dome? It was unknown to the stargazers of old. No one knew how to measure the height of the sky. Surely it was higher than the mountains, but how much higher no one could say. More than 2,500 years ago, people called the Babylonians built huge towering temples called ziggurats. Their tops, which reached into the sky, were supposed to be the meeting place of gods and men.

The Sumerians were an even older people who lived in what is now Iraq about 5,000 years ago. They worshiped several gods and associated the Moon, Sun, and other sky objects with those gods. Like people, the gods were thought to have personal feelings and so they had to be comforted when they became upset.

During an eclipse of the Sun, the Sun-god was thought to be in great pain because he was being attacked by demons. The pain was worse during the first half of the eclipse as the Sun-god shone fainter and fainter. The instant an eclipse began, the priests lit a torch on the temple altar and began to say special prayers to save the fields, rivers, and other parts of the land. Meanwhile, all the people were told to cover their heads with their clothing and to shout loudly. That always seemed to end the eclipse and bring things back to normal.

Who could say that such action did not work? After all, the eclipse ended and the land and rivers were not harmed. So great was the people's fear of unusual events in the sky that few were likely to have enough courage to do nothing at all to find out if the eclipse would end on its own, instead of having to be "frightened" away.

Around 500 B.C., Greek scholars turned away from the old superstitions about the Sun, Moon, and planets being gods who ruled over all events and life on Earth. The Greeks had named the planets after their gods, as had other cultures before and after them.

Babylonian gods	Greek gods	Roman gods	Role or association
Samash	Helios	Sol	Life, energy
Sin	Selene	Luna	Lunacy
Nabu	Hermes	Mercury	Messenger of gods
Ishtar	Aphrodite	Venus	Love and fertility
Nergal	Ares	Mars	War
Marduk	Zeus	Jupiter	King of gods
Ninib	Kronos	Saturn	Time

This new breed of scholars felt that associating the planets, stars, and other sky objects with gods was an obstacle to finding out what those objects were made of and what made them shine. They felt that they must look for natural causes, not supernatural ones.

One such scholar thought of Earth as a flat "table" hanging in space. All the stars and planets, he said, were made from moisture rising from the ground. As the moisture rose, it became thin and changed to fire. And so the stars were born. Another Greek scholar thought of the stars as clouds that each night were set on fire and rose into the heavens. Still another also said that the stars were made of fire, and that each one rested in a bowl. At night when the stars are visible, he said, the mouths of the bowls are turned toward us and we see their fire. But during the day the bowls turn upward and hide the stars from view.[2]

2. The author has gathered information from many sources to develop his topic.

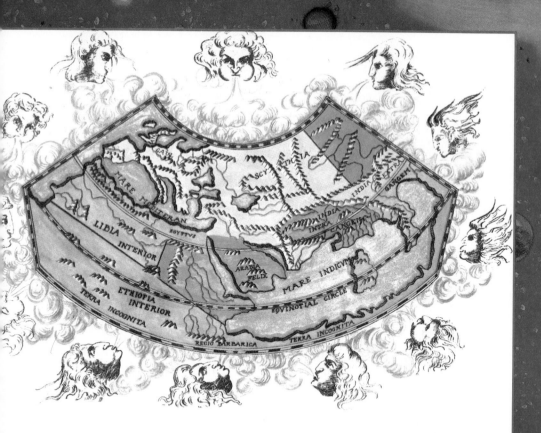

How did the Greek scholars of long ago explain, by natural causes, the nightly parade of stars across the sky? They pictured the sky dome as the upper half of a great hollow glass ball that turned slowly. Earth was at the very center and did not move. The surface of this glass ball marked the outer edge of the universe. All the stars were stuck onto its surface. Some were brighter and others dimmer, but all were the same distance from central Earth. Once a day the glass ball made one complete turn. As it did, it carried the stars around with it.

Many of the ideas of the scholars of ancient Greece seem odd to us today. But as time passed, the Greeks got better at explaining many of the things they saw in the sky. They were the first to reason that Earth is not motionless in space. They said that Earth must be spinning around like a top, and that that spinning motion makes the stars and Sun only *appear* to parade across the sky. They became the first to show that Earth was shaped like a ball instead of being flat, and they measured its size accurately. They also worked out the Moon's size and distance from Earth. The Greeks of old were the first to think

that the Sun was at the center of the Solar System and that
Earth and all the other planets circled the Sun. Unfortunately,
however, an astronomer who lived later (Ptolemy, around A.D.
150) taught that Earth was the center of the Solar System, and
that the Sun and planets all revolved about us. It took 1,500
years to correct that false view.

Thinking Like a Reader

1. How did various cultures differ in explaining the heavenly bodies?
   How were their explanations similar?
2. What mysterious aspects of nature have you wanted explanations
   for or have you investigated?

Write your responses in your journal.

Thinking Like a Writer

3. How do you think the writer gathered information for this piece of
   writing?
4. Which details best help you understand how these ancient peoples explained what they saw in the night sky?
5. Which details were the most interesting to you?

If you were going to research a topic, what might it be? In your
journal, write a list of questions you would be interested in answering.

Brainstorm *Vocabulary*

In *Private Lives of the Stars* the author mentions *meteors*, *comets*, and *ziggurats*. Chances are that you recognize the first two words, but ziggurats are probably objects that you know nothing about unless you happen to be familiar with ancient Babylonian architecture. Think of a subject or hobby that you have studied and its distinctive vocabulary. For example, one special word you may have learned as a collector of model cars is *scale*. In your journal write down your subjects of interest and words and phrases learned while studying these. Use these words in your writing.

Talk It Over *Opinion Poll*

When you conduct research, you are carefully gathering information about a subject in order to prove or discover facts. One way of learning information is to ask a group of people for their opinions about a subject. Politicians, for example, have pollsters ask voters their opinions about important issues. As a class, decide on a poll that you would like to conduct. For instance, you might want to learn which magazine is the most widely read in your class. Then, supported by facts and figures from your poll, you can request a subscription for the school library. Decide on the size of the group to be interviewed, then prepare a list of questions to ask them. The answers, when compiled, will reflect the group's opinion.

Quick Write *Write a Summary*

In order to compile research efficiently, the researcher must be able to summarize source materials. You would not want to copy an entire book or article related to your topic. Rather, you would take notes that reflect the main ideas presented in the source material. Skim *Private Lives of the Stars* on pages 476–482 and write a summary of seventy-five words or less covering its main ideas.

Idea Corner *Think of Topics*

Think of topics on which you might write a research report. In your journal write whatever ideas come to mind. Then write down questions that you would like to have answered about each topic. Use the 5 *W*'s and *H*—*who? what? when? where? why?* and *how?*—when you frame your questions. Here is an example.

Topic: Caring for cats

Questions: *What* type of food does my cat need?

Where should my cat sleep?

When should I take my cat to the vet?

Who are the vets in my community?

Why does my cat bite?

How can I keep my cat healthy?

PICTURES *SEEING LIKE A WRITER*

Finding Ideas for Writing

Look at the pictures on these pages. Think about what you
see. What ideas for writing a research report do the pictures
give you? Write your ideas in your journal.

Above: Explaining the motion of objects

Below: The Great Nebula of O

ent monument of Stonehenge on England's Salisbury Plain

er, as photographed by *Voyager 1*

1 GROUP WRITING: A RESEARCH REPORT

COOPERATIVE
LEARNING

The **purpose** of a research report is to provide an **audience** with factual information about a topic. In order to write a research report, the writer must investigate the topic. The report itself is the presentation of the findings. Writing a research report involves several important steps.

- Finding Information and Taking Notes
- Making an Outline
- Writing Paragraphs from an Outline

Finding Information and Taking Notes

Sources of information for your research report include encyclopedias, magazines, and books. It is best to use the encyclopedia only as a starting point, as a tool that will help you to focus your search for other information. In addition to general encyclopedias, a library's reference section holds a variety of dictionaries, almanacs, and subject encyclopedias. *The Readers' Guide to Periodical Literature* is another valuable reference. This publication is a monthly index listing magazine and newspaper articles.

The card catalog lists every book in the library by author, title, and subject. Once you have found a book that you think will be useful, look in its index and table of contents to check the amount and kind of information it contains.

The list of sources you use in preparing your research report is called your **bibliography**. For each source, it is a good idea to make a bibliography card, a 3 x 5-inch card containing information about the source.

Encyclopedia

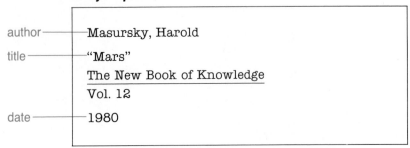

author——— Masursky, Harold
title ——— "Mars"
The New Book of Knowledge
Vol. 12
date ——— 1980

Book

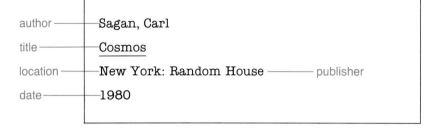

author —— Sagan, Carl

title —— Cosmos

location —— New York: Random House —— publisher

date —— 1980

Magazine

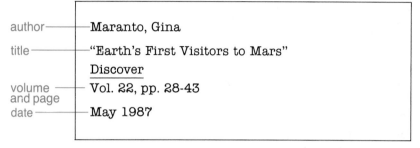

author —— Maranto, Gina

title —— "Earth's First Visitors to Mars"
Discover

volume and page —— Vol. 22, pp. 28-43

date —— May 1987

Keep a record of the information you may want to use by summarizing it in your own words on a 3 x 5-inch note card.

Read the following paragraph.

The very small amounts of oxygen, nitrogen, and water vapor in the atmosphere of Mars make it unlikely that the planet could support the kind of living things that we know on Earth. However, some kinds of life could exist that are not based on these substances.

Here is a note card based on the paragraph.

title —— The New Book of Knowledge

author —— Harold Masursky

subject —— Mars—possibility of life

summary —— —small amts. of oxygen, nitrogen, and water vapor can't support life as we know it on Earth
—author thinks possibility that "some kinds of life exist that are not based" on above elements

page —— p. 111

Keep in mind these guidelines about taking notes.

1. Do not write every word. Begin with a key idea and write down the explanatory details below. Do not copy an entire article or even a paragraph; make notes from only the information that pertains to your topic.
2. Use abbreviations. In order to write more quickly, some writers use a standard shorthand. Others make up their own personal shorthand.
3. When you find an idea expressed so well that you want to quote the author, put quotation marks around words taken directly from the source. Whenever you write down someone else's exact words, you must place those words in quotation marks.

Guided Practice: Finding Information and Taking Notes

As a class, choose a topic from the list below or think of a topic on which you all agree. Then, individually, find one source on your topic and make a bibliography card and a note card using that source. You might want to compare your cards with those of your classmates.

New Year's customs	scuba diving	plant life
Olympic games	pop songs	aerobics

Making an Outline

Once you have taken adequate notes, it is helpful to make an outline. Since you do not want your report to be a shapeless mass of information, you must find a way to tie together the information so that it is meaningful for you and for your readers. Recall how the information in your sources was organized. Your note cards will also give you ideas for making an outline.

Review your note cards. How can you summarize the main points your report will make? Focus for now on one controlling idea that you can develop with details in your research report. Such a controlling idea is called a **thesis statement**.

Example: Though recent space probes show no evidence, some scientists continue to believe in the possibilities of life on Mars.

Look at this example of a **sentence outline**, which organizes information logically into main topics (with Roman numerals) and subtopics (with capital letters).

I. People are interested in Mars for several reasons.
   A. Mars has several earthlike characteristics.
   B. Mars seems to be more visible than other planets.
II. Mars was the object of renewed interest during the late nineteenth century.
   A. Professor Lowell developed the theory of an older, wiser race in 1834.
   B. Giovanni Schiaparelli observed the canals in 1877.
III. Modern science looks at Mars.
   A. In 1970s *Mariner 9* pictures disprove canals.
   B. Some scientists continue to consider life on Mars.

In an outline, place roman numerals before main topics. Place capital letters before subtopics. Subtopics are indented. Your outline must always have at least two main topics and two subtopics. That is, if you have a I, you must have a II; if you have an A, you must have a B. Remember that you cannot divide a topic into one part. Each number or letter is followed by a period. Each entry begins with a capital letter.

Guided Practice: Making an Outline

Recall the subject for which you have gathered information and made notes. Organize your note cards into categories. With your classmates, discuss what you want to say about your subject. Finally, referring to your note cards, write a thesis statement and a sentence outline for your report. Your outline should have at least three main topics and at least two subtopics for each main topic.

Writing Paragraphs from an Outline

Your outline is a guide from which to write your report. Each paragraph of the report corresponds to a main topic in your outline. The main topics become topic sentences for paragraphs; the subtopics become supporting sentences.

Your report should have at least three paragraphs. In the first paragraph include an introduction that tells readers what the report is about. The last paragraph will state your conclusion. The middle of the report will contain the facts and information you have learned from your research.

The Mysteries of Mars

People have long been curious about the possibilities of life on the planet Mars. Although recent space probes have shown no evidence of life on Mars, the myth of Martian life persists. There are many reasons why the idea of life on Mars continues to tickle the imagination. Mars, although inhospitable to human life, seems to be the most earthlike of the eight other planets in our solar system. It has polar icecaps, a seasonal pattern of change, a twenty-four-hour day, and the same tilt on its axis as Earth. In addition, it is the nearest planet with a visible surface. It was probably because the surface of Mars was so easy to see that nineteenth-century observers focused their attention on the "red planet" and wrote stories about intelligent life on Mars.

In 1834 American astronomer Percival Lowell established an observatory in Flagstaff, Arizona. It was Lowell who developed the major theories about Martian life. He deduced that the planet had been inhabited by an older and wiser race who built canals to conserve water on this arid planet. In 1877 Giovanni Schiaparelli, an Italian astronomer, made the first map of Mars. The map showed what he called canals on the surface of Mars. Because canals are man-made, the discovery encouraged others to think in terms of intelligent life on Mars.

By the 1970s space probes had provided more accurate photographs of Mars. These photographs revealed no evidence of canals or any other proof of intelligent life. Yet, scientists continue to ponder the possibility of life on Mars. Microbiologists, for example, have developed tools that could measure the presence of microorganisms on Mars. Astronomer Carl Sagan points out that it is still too early to reach conclusions about life on Mars.

At the end of your report include your bibliography—the list of sources that you used in preparing the report—on a separate sheet of paper. Organize your bibliography alphabetically by the authors' last names. Note the indentation and punctuation.

Bibliography

Maranto, Gina. "Earth's First Visitors to Mars." Discover,
    Vol. 22, May 1987, pp. 28–43.

Masursky, Harold. "Mars." The New Book of Knowledge,
    Vol. 12, 1980 edition.

Sagan, Carl. Cosmos. New York: Random House, 1980.

Putting a Research Report Together

With your classmates you have gathered information and written a thesis statement for a research report. You have also developed an outline to organize your information.

Guided Practice: Writing a Research Report

Using your thesis statement and outline, write a three-paragraph research report. Use the main topics from your outline as topic sentences. Write detail sentences for the subtopics. Use details from the notes you have compiled.

Share your report with a friend. Ask your friend if he or she learned anything new about the subject.

Checklist A Research Report

One way to remember the important elements of a research report is to make a checklist. The checklist will remind you of points concerning your research report.

Make a copy of this checklist and add other points you want to remember. Use it when you write your report.

CHECKLIST

- Remember purpose and audience.
- Find information and take notes.
- Organize note cards into groups.
- Write a thesis statement.
- Make an outline.
- Write paragraphs based on the outline.
- Include a good introduction and conclusion.
- _____

2 THINKING AND WRITING: Cause-and-Effect Relationships

If you lean too far back in a straight-back chair, chances are that you will fall. In addition to illustrating the law of gravity, this situation is also a simple example of a cause-and-effect relationship. Gravity is the **cause**, and falling on the floor is the **effect**. Look around and you will notice many other instances of cause-and-effect relationships.

CAUSE	EFFECT
use too many electrical appliances	fuse blows
open can of cat food	cat comes running
wind blows around apple tree	apples drop
plant seeds in fertile, moist soil	seeds grow
put yeast dough in warm place	dough rises

Expressing ideas in terms of cause-and-effect relationships can be an effective way of organizing your writing, especially in a research report. When you write, think about leading your reader logically from one fact to the next. You might begin with the cause and lead to the effect.

Because Mars appears to have more in common with Earth than any other planet in our solar system, both the United States and the Soviet Union have committed more resources to the study of Mars than to the study of any of the other planets.

If you want to emphasize the effect, you might place it first by rewriting the sentence.

Both the United States and the Soviet Union have committed more resources to the study of Mars than to the study of any other planet in our solar system because Mars has the most similarities to Earth.

Often an effect can have several potential causes. For example, if a plant dies it could be because it did not have sufficient water or sunlight or because it had too much water or sunlight. Causes also can sometimes have several effects. Gravity may cause the chair to fall, but it also might cause the chair to break.

Thinking Like a Writer

- What examples of cause and effect can you add to the examples above?
- When have you used cause-and-effect explanations in your writing?

THINKING APPLICATION Cause and Effect

COOPERATIVE
LEARNING

Cause and effect is something we all encounter every day, in school and out, in living as well as in writing. Work out these cause-and-effect problems.

1. With a classmate, observe the physical qualities of your classroom. Write a list that describes a few of these qualities or effects. Then for each quality, write the cause or causes. Here is an example.
    Effect: Very warm in the afternoon and cool in the morning
    Cause: Room faces west.
2. The research report about Mars on page 490 states, "Mars seems to be the most earthlike of the eight other planets in our solar system." With a classmate, write a list of the details (causes) that lead to such a conclusion.
3. With a classmate, make a list of cause-and-effect relationships that apply to what you have studied in other classes. Consider classes such as physical education and health as well as social studies, science, and mathematics.
4. Carefully study the cartoon by the American artist Reuben ("Rube") Goldberg, who is most famous for his clever cause-and-effect drawings. Work with classmates to create your own cartoon in the Goldberg style.

---

3 INDEPENDENT WRITING: A Research Report

Prewrite: Step 1

Now that you have learned the elements of writing a research report, you are ready to write one of your own. This is how Thea, a student your age, chose a topic for her research report.

Choosing a Topic

Thea was fascinated by the idea that several ancient cultures had used the stars to create calendars that would help them in their farming. Using this idea and other information she had learned in her classes, Thea brainstormed a list of possible topics in the form of questions. Here is Thea's list.

1. How could astronomy help farmers?
2. How did the calendar develop?
3. What were some of the early tools of astronomy?

Thea continued her search for a topic by looking up the key words *astronomy* and *calendar* in an encyclopedia and finding a long list of entries for each. Thea then went to the card catalog and looked under *astronomy*. She found a book titled *Early Man and the Cosmos*. From the table of contents Thea learned that the book opened with a chronological table comparing developments in different cultures. Thea knew that she had found a major reference source and made a bibliography card for it. She also found *Cosmos* by Carl Sagan. By skimming these two books, Thea found out that several places still had remains of monuments that might have been tools for astronomical observation or measurement. Thea knew that she was on the right track.

At this point Thea decided that she would write her report about one of these ancient monuments. After returning to the encyclopedia index and the card catalog, she decided to write her report about Stonehenge in England. Thea made this choice because she had always been interested in Stonehenge and because there was an abundance of information about it. Now that she had selected her topic, Thea decided her **purpose** would be to inform an **audience** of her classmates about Stonehenge.

At this point, Thea felt she needed to focus her research even further, so she made a list of questions that would guide her reading. Here are some of her questions.

—What does Stonehenge look like?
—Who built Stonehenge, and how did they build it?
—What was its purpose?
—Is it still used today?

Exploring Ideas: Taking Notes and Making an Outline

By this time, Thea had quite an extensive bibliography. To keep track of her sources, she made a bibliography card for each source she used. Look at this bibliography card that Thea made.

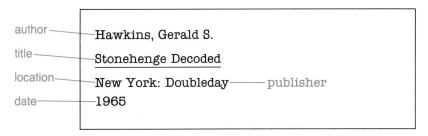

author	Hawkins, Gerald S.
title	Stonehenge Decoded
location	New York: Doubleday ——— publisher
date	1965

Next, Thea read her sources for information and summarized the information on note cards, like the one below.

title	Early Man and the Cosmos
author	Evan Hadingham
subject	Excavations—diggings
summary	1) half of monuments not excavated
	2) Many monuments dug up by archaeologist Wm. Hawley. He did a sloppy job and caused problems for later excavations.
pages	pp. 43-44

Notice that sometimes Thea used her own abbreviations, which were clear in meaning to her. If you do use abbreviations, make sure you remember their meaning for later reference.

When Thea had completed a number of note cards, she felt she had enough information to make an outline. She read over her note cards and wrote a thesis statement—the main idea for her report. She then used her notes to make a sentence outline. Notice that she used Arabic numerals to add details under her subtopics.

Thesis statement: Stonehenge is believed to be the oldest existing astronomical monument, but no one is sure of its purpose.

I. Stonehenge is the best-preserved monument from the New Stone Age.
   A. It is impossible to prove how it was used.
   B. Stonehenge is located in southern England.
   C. Stonehenge is composed of many sizes of stones.
      1. Stones are topped by lintels.
      2. Ditches surround the structures.
   D. The monument faces the rising sun.
II. Many theories about the purpose of Stonehenge have been made.
   A. Some called Stonehenge a Druid temple.
   B. One theory credits Merlin, the magician.
   C. Archaeologists dispute the Druid theory.
      1. Druids worshiped the moon, not the sun.
      2. Stonehenge was built 1000 years before the Druids.
   D. Hawkins developed new theories about Stonehenge by computer.
III. Scientists have difficulty in reaching definite conclusions about the purpose of Stonehenge.
   A. Half of Stonehenge remains unexcavated.
   B. Early excavations were not complete.
   C. Stonehenge was rebuilt several times.
   D. Stonehenge can be compared to other ancient monuments.

Thea reminded herself that her purpose for writing was to give her classmates information about Stonehenge and perhaps inspire them to want to learn more. Before beginning to write, Thea imagined that she was an archaeologist explaining Stonehenge to a group of students. At this point, she made some changes in part of her outline.

III. Scientists have difficulty in reaching definite conclusions about how Stonehenge was used.

    A. Half of Stonehenge remains unexcavated.

    B. Early excavations were not complete.

    C. Stonehenge was rebuilt several times.

    D. Stonehenge can be compared to other monuments.

Thea was now satisfied with her outline. She knew that her outline was logical and had a beginning, a middle, and an ending. This meant that when she followed her outline as she wrote out her first draft, the report would also be logical and have good form.

Thinking Like a Writer

- What did Thea add?
- What did she delete?
- Why do you think she made these changes?

YOUR TURN

Think of a topic on which you would like to write a report. Use **Pictures** or your journal to help you think of ideas. Follow these steps.

- Make a list of topics and questions.
- Choose the topic you like best.
- Narrow your topic if it is too broad.
- Think of questions about your topic that you would like answered.
- Think about your purpose and audience.

Gather sources, take notes, and make an outline.

Write a First Draft: Step 2

Thea knew what a research report should include, and she had made a planning checklist. Thea was now ready to write her first draft, giving a paragraph to each of her outline's major points.

Part of Thea's First Draft

Stonehenge is the oldest existing astronomical monument. It is impossible to prove for sure how it was used. Stonehenge is in Southern England, eights miles north of Salisbury Plain. It is the best perserved monument from the New Stone age. Egypt's Abu Simbel and the ziggurats of Babylonia were built much later.

Today we can see only the ruins of Stonehenge. Like there are these ditches surrounding the main stones, and lots of tall stones with lintels on top. These lintels show that the people who built it were from the mediterranean originally. The people were prehistoric, that is, of the period before recorded history.

As Thea was writing her first draft, she focused on putting her ideas down on paper. She was not concerned about grammatical errors at this time because she knew that she could correct them later.

Planning Checklist
- Remember purpose and audience.
- Find information and take notes.
- Organize the note cards into groups.
- Write a thesis statement.
- Make an outline.
- Write paragraphs from the outline.
- Include a good introduction and conclusion.

YOUR TURN

After reviewing your planning checklist, write the first draft of your research report. As you prepare to write, ask yourself these questions.

- What is the main idea that I want to state?
- How can I best use my outline when writing paragraphs?
- What facts and details will explain my main point?
- What important ideas should I state in my introduction and conclusion?

TIME-OUT You might want to take some time out before you revise. That way you will be able to revise your writing with a fresh eye.

Revise: Step 3

After she finished writing the first draft of her research report, Thea read it over to herself. She knew that there were problems with her work. Then she shared her writing with a classmate because she wanted some suggestions for improvements. In their conference, Thea's friend reminded her that when writing about architecture and archaeology, a special vocabulary is often used. Thea knew that some of her classmates would be confused by these terms. She had the choice of either explaining these terms or using simpler, less precise terms. Thea decided that she must explain the terms.

Your report is really interesting, but some of the details weren't clear. For example, what is a lintel?

I can clear that up. Thanks, Jon.

Thea then reread her first draft. As she finished, she realized that she had not written a strong concluding sentence for her introduction. Realizing that she might have overlooked other important points, Thea decided that she should refer to her checklist as she revised her report.

Using her checklist as a guide, Thea revised her report. Were her introduction and conclusion strong? Did she write paragraphs that covered the topics in her outline? Did she need to add or eliminate any information? She did not correct errors such as those in spelling or punctuation. She would fix those mistakes later.

Look at some of Thea's revisions on the next page.

Revising Checklist
- Remember purpose and audience.
- Find information and take notes.
- Organize the note cards into groups.
- Write a thesis statement.
- Make an outline.
- Write paragraphs from the outline.
- ✔ Include a good introduction and conclusion.
- ✔ Define unusual terms.

Part of Thea's Revised Draft

Stonehenge is the oldest existing astronomical monument,~~,~~ *but* it is

impossible to prove ~~for sure~~ how it was used.~~,~~ *Standing* Stonehenge is in
Stonehenge

Southern England, eights miles north of Salisbury Plain.~~.~~ It is the

best perserved monument~~,~~ *of* ~~from~~ the New Stone age. Egypt's Abu
of Egypt

Simbel~~,~~ and the ziggurats of Babylonia were built much later.

Today we can ⟨see⟩ ⟨only⟩ the ruins of Stonehenge. ~~Like there are~~
many *rectangular*
~~these~~ ditches surrounding~~,~~ the main stones, and lots of tall~~,~~ stones
horizontal top pieces called *prehistoric*
~~∧~~ with lintels ~~on top~~. These lintels show that the~~,~~ people who built ~~it~~
Stonehenge
~~∧~~ were~~,~~ from the mediterranean originally. ~~The people were~~
— originally

~~prehistoric, that is, of the period before recorded history.~~ *We are*
not sure why, but the monument faces the
rising sun.

Thinking Like a Writer

- What sentence did Thea add? Why do you think that she added it?
- What sentence did she delete? Why do you think that she deleted it?
- Which sentences did she combine? How does combining them improve her writing?

YOUR TURN

Read your first draft. Ask yourself these questions.

- Have I included enough information so that my topic is clear to my audience?
- How can I make my thesis statement clearer?
- How can my introduction and conclusion be stronger?
- Do I use any terms that may need to be explained?

If you wish, ask a friend to read your work and make suggestions. Then revise your research report.

Proofread: Step 4

Thea was pleased with the changes that she made in her draft. However, she knew that she had to proofread her research report.

Part of Thea's Proofread Draft

Stonehenge is the oldest existing astronomical monument. ~~It is~~ *but*

impossible to prove ~~for sure~~ how it was used. ~~Stonehenge is~~ in *Standing*

~~Southern England, eights~~ miles north of Salisbury Plain, ~~It~~ is the *Stonehenge*

best (perserved) monument ~~from~~ the New Stone age. ~~Egypt's~~ Abu *preserved* *of* *of Egypt*

Simbel and the ziggurats of Babylonia were built much later.

Today we can (see only) the ruins of Stonehenge. ~~Like there are~~ *many* *rectangular*

~~these~~ ditches surrounding the main stones, ~~and lots of~~ tall stones *horizontal top pieces called* *prehistoric*

with ~~lintels on top.~~ These lintels show that the people who built ~~it~~ *Stonehenge*

were from the mediterranean ~~originally.~~ ~~The people were~~ *originally*

~~prehistoric, that is, of the period before recorded history.~~ *We are not sure why, but the monument faces the rising sun.*

YOUR TURN

Proofreading Practice

Practice your proofreading skills by finding the errors in the paragraph below. Then write it correctly.

Even though science is based on facts. It cant always tell the truth about the passed. Gerald hawkins who is a great theoretical scientist used a computer to make a theory about how ancient people used Stonehenge. Although guessing this was a great step in the study of ancient astronomy. Being highly educated this guess comes from a remarkable man.

Proofreading Checklist
- Did I indent each paragraph?
- Did I spell all words correctly?
- What punctuation errors do I need to correct?
- What capitalization errors do I need to correct?
- Are there sentences that I should combine?

Applying Your Proofreading Skills

Now proofread your research report. Use the proofreading marks to make changes. Before you begin, refer to your checklist again and review **The Grammar Connection** and **The Mechanics Connection** below.

THE GRAMMAR CONNECTION

Remember these rules about the placement of participial phrases.

■ When a participial phrase is placed at the beginning of a sentence, it is always set off with a comma.

Enjoying good food, I spend much time in the kitchen.

■ Always try to place a participial phrase as close as possible to the noun or pronoun that it describes. A misplaced participial phrase is not only misleading but also is often laughable.

My family, appreciating my skills, enjoys the meals.

or

Appreciating my skills, my family enjoys the meals.

but not

Appreciating my skills, the meals are enjoyed by my family.

Check your research report for the correct use of participial phrases.

THE MECHANICS CONNECTION

Remember these rules about using commas with clauses.

■ Place a comma after an adverb clause that introduces a sentence, but not before one that comes at the end of a sentence.

Because the kitchen is tiny, only two cooks can work there.

or

Only two cooks can work there because the kitchen is tiny.

■ Set off nonessential adjective clauses with commas. Essential adjective clauses do not call for punctuation.

Dad, who enjoys eating, is not skilled in the kitchen.
The person who helps the most is my mom.
Cooking, which is fun, builds the appetite.
I enjoy a meal that is well prepared.

Check your research report for the correct punctuation of adverb and adjective clauses.

Proofreading Marks
Indent ¶
Add ∧
Add a comma ⌄
Add quotation marks ⌄ ⌄
Add a period ⊙
Take out ✄
Capitalize ≡
Lower-case letter /
Reverse the order ∩

Publish: Step 5

After Thea finished proofreading her report, she gave it a title, "Stonehenge: The Unsolved Riddle." She thought this title expressed her thesis statement clearly. She made a neat final copy of her report and bound it in a folder. The report was placed in the classroom where her classmates could read it. Several of her classmates asked her questions about Stonehenge. The class decided that they were interested in learning more about astronomical monuments.

YOUR TURN

Make a neat final copy of your research report. Remember to include your bibliography. Use your best handwriting or type your report. Do not forget to give your report a title that will interest readers. Think of a way to share your report with your class. You might find some ideas in the **Sharing Suggestions** box below.

SHARING SUGGESTIONS

Give an oral presentation of the report to your class. Use visual aids where appropriate.	Illustrate your report with diagrams, photographs, and drawings. Create a class encyclopedia, using your report.	Share your research report with members of your science or social studies class or with your teacher in one of those subjects.

4 SPEAKING AND LISTENING: Giving an Effective Oral Report

You have just written a research report about a topic that interests you. Your work on the report probably taught you facts and ideas about an unfamiliar subject. Now you can use this information as the topic for an oral report.

Giving an oral report can be thought of as an opportunity to teach a class. As you prepare to give an oral report, think of some techniques that your teachers and other speakers use to hold your attention, such as establishing good eye contact. You might use some of these techniques when you give your report. Remember that there is more to giving an oral report than simply reading aloud your written report. Preparation is an important part of the process.

The best way to prepare for an oral report is to make note cards that you can refer to when you give your report. On your note cards write only the main points and some important details that support them. Since it is easy to confuse names and dates, it is a good idea to include those on your note cards if they are important to your presentation. Referring to your original outline might remind you of the main points of your report.

The note card below was prepared by Thea for an oral report about Stonehenge.

> Notes   Stonehenge
>
> 1. Oldest astronomical monument; unknown exactly how used.
> 2. Located on Salisbury Plain, southern England.
> 3. Rebuilt several times. Earliest 3000 B.C.
> 4. Probable use: chart movement of sun.
> 5. 1740 William Stukely: Druid temple. Later disproved.
> 6. Gerald Hawkins 1963 computer analysis; key finding.
> 7. 1979, provides new Heel Stone theory.

Notice that the thesis statement is listed on the note card. What other points are listed?

When you give an oral report, it will help you to keep some guidelines in mind. These speaking guidelines will help you to focus your talk.

SPEAKING GUIDELINES: Giving an Oral Report

1. Keep your **purpose** in mind when you plan. Consider questions that your **audience** might ask.
2. Prepare note cards from which to speak. Include your thesis statement, the main points of your report, and any important details.
3. Practice your delivery with a friend or with a tape recorder.
4. Follow your outline or notes. Begin each part of your report with a clear topic sentence.
5. Look at your listeners frequently. Speak to them directly. Avoid reading your report word for word.
6. Speak clearly and distinctly. Vary the speed, volume, and tone of your voice. Use gestures where appropriate.

- Why is a thesis statement important when I am giving an oral report?
- Why is practicing an oral report important?

SPEAKING APPLICATION Giving an Oral Report

Prepare an oral report that is based on your research report. Compose a note card to use when you are giving your talk. Use the speaking guidelines to help you prepare. Your classmates will be taking notes as well as using the following guidelines as they listen to your report.

LISTENING GUIDELINES: Hearing an Oral Report

1. Listen to understand the thesis statement and the main ideas of the report.
2. When you take notes, write the thesis statement and main ideas in your own words.
3. Listen for important details, such as names and dates, and write them down.
4. Listen for points about which you would like to know more. Ask the speaker questions.

THE CURRICULUM CONNECTION

Writing About Mathematics

In this unit you have analyzed both the elements of a research report and the research process itself. You then followed this process and wrote a research report. While you researched your topic, you may have made use of some mathematical concepts.

The word *mathematics* is from a Greek word that means "inclined to learn," and, indeed, the study of numbers has proved valuable in almost every field of knowledge. Most early scientists were also mathematicians. Modern researchers in such nonscientific fields as history and sociology have also found themselves using mathematical tools like **statistics** and **percentages** to measure the past and make predictions about the future. It is the rare field that has not felt the impact of the computer, which is a practical application of complicated mathematical theories. Although there may be times when mathematics seems very removed from everyday life, you most likely make use of mathematical concepts every day.

ACTIVITIES

Practical Math

Write a list of various subjects studied in school. Then, next to each subject, note how mathematics might be used as a tool in this field. Next, list your activities on a typical day. Circle the ones that could involve some mathematical concepts. Share your findings with your classmates.

Gather Statistics

With your class, select an area that you can research directly. For example, perhaps you want to determine the local or national political figure most popular among the students in your school. Conduct a public opinion poll and chart your findings in a way that will allow you to make comparisons between different groups. For example, do younger people differ from older people in their opinions?

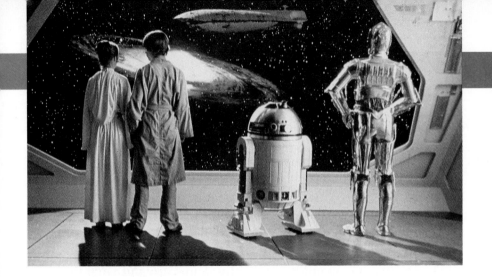

Respond to Literature

Computers and robots operate by means of mathematical principles. In the selection below, robot inventor Hans Moravec speculates about the future of robots. After reading the passage, write a response to it in the form of an essay, a story, or a research report.

Future Robots

"If we had intelligent bicycles, kids would never need training wheels to learn how to ride. Tiny computers and sensors could easily balance the bicycle. They would also be able to take sonar and infrared sensor readings and avoid collisions. The bike would keep its rider out of trouble. It would be like the rider's guardian angel.

"Robots already have something very special that we humans lack," says Moravec. "That something is telepathy. Robots can read each other's minds using microwaves. Then they can use microwaves to send information around the globe and even across outer space.

"Humans living in a world of telepathic robots won't have a clue," says Moravec. "Millions of robots will be trading information. A person who tried to make sense of all this would be like a tourist who stands in an alley and tries to make sense of a whole city."

This strange world of robots doesn't scare Hans Moravec. He believes technology can be used to help people. He's always believed the possibilities are almost limitless.

from "Hans on Robots" by Fred D'Ignazio

UNIT CHECKUP

Group Writing: A Research Report (page 486)   Edith is planning a research report on the uses of solar power. She was absent from school when the teacher told the class how to write a bibliography and take notes. Help Edith to use the correct form for her bibliography by writing the following information correctly on a separate sheet of paper. If there is any information missing, write what kind of information is needed.

1. Mothers of invention by Ethlie Ann Vare and Greg Ptacek. 1988. William Morrow and Company, Inc./New York
2. Fill 'er up—with sunlight, *Smithsonian Magazine*, volume 18, Number 11, February 1988
3. Funk and Wagnalls *New Encyclopedia* 1973

Thinking: Cause-and-Effect Relationships (page 492) Scientists, detectives, and students all must understand cause-and-effect relationships in order to do their work. Listed below are four situations that need a detective. For each situation, construct a logical chain of events that could have resulted in the situation described.

1. George comes home from school and enters the kitchen for a snack. On the kitchen table are a glass of spilt milk, a half-empty jar of peanut butter, and an empty bread bag.
2. The houseplant on the window sill has died.
3. The school play was a great success.
4. Terry hit a home run.

Writing a Research Report (page 494)   Imagine that you are a researcher who will write a report on energy. Narrow your topic. Then identify sources and gather information for a three-paragraph report. Organize your notes into an outline and write a thesis statement. Be sure to include an effective introduction and conclusion in your research report. Also include a bibliography at the end of your report.

Speaking and Listening: Giving an Effective Oral Report (page 504)   Write a paragraph summarizing the important points that you should remember in preparing and presenting an effective oral report.

THEME PROJECT SPACE STATION

You have read and discussed several aspects of space exploration and discovery. The excitement of exploration and discovery has inspired many scientists to write about their research. There is another kind of writing closely related to science. Look at the picture below.

Ever since Jules Verne wrote *From the Earth to the Moon* and H.G. Wells took his readers to Mars in *War of the Worlds*, science-fiction writers, on imaginative journeys, have taken us into future worlds. Talk with your classmates about science-fiction novels and movies that you have enjoyed. Discuss the aspects that seem to be pure fiction and the aspects that are based on scientific fact. What aspects of outer space and the galaxy interest you most?

With your classmates, create a space station or shuttle.

- Do research to find out about space stations and space shuttles.
- Create props, sets, space maps, and charts.
- Write dialogue for the crew of the space station.
- Write fact files, explanations, and informative articles that would be helpful to the crew of a space station.

Writer's Reference

C O N T E N T S

LANGUAGE STUDY
H A N D B O O K

GRAMMAR

Sentences

A **sentence** is a group of words that expresses a complete thought.

There are four sentence types.
A **declarative** sentence makes a statement.

> I have a pen pal in England. (ends with a period)

An **interrogative** sentence asks a question.

> Do you write often? (ends with a question mark)

An **imperative** sentence gives a command or makes a request.

> Give me her address. (ends with a period)

An **exclamatory** sentence expresses strong feeling.

> Look at the length of this letter! (ends with an exclamation mark)

The **complete subject** of a sentence includes all the words that tell what or whom the sentence is about.

> The first paragraph describes the weather.

The **complete predicate** of a sentence includes all the words that tell what the subject does or is.

> A huge storm blew down trees and power lines.

A **compound subject** is two or more simple subjects with the same predicate.

> Wind and rain did a great deal of damage.

A **compound predicate** is two or more simple predicates with the same subject.

> The telephone service came and went.

A **run-on sentence** is two or more sentences that are incorrectly written as one.

> The river near her house overflowed the town was flooded.

Divide a run-on sentence into several sentences or join the independent clauses correctly.

> The river near her house overflowed. The town was flooded.
> The river near her house overflowed, and the town was flooded.

A **sentence fragment** is a group of words that is only part of a sentence. It does not have both a subject and a predicate, and it does not express a complete thought.

> The shops on the main street. (fragment: no predicate)
> Were knee-deep in water. (fragment: no subject)

Add a subject or a predicate to a fragment to complete a sentence.

> The shops on the main street were knee-deep in water.

A **compound sentence** contains two or more simple sentences joined by *and, but,* or *or*.

> The neighbors came, **and** they helped save the wares.

An **independent clause** has one complete subject and one complete predicate. It expresses a complete thought, and it can stand alone as a sentence.

> **Firemen diverted the water**, and **much harm was prevented.**

A **subordinate clause** is a group of words that has a subject and a predicate, but it cannot stand alone as a complete sentence.

> Because the water was so deep.

A **complex sentence** contains an independent clause and one or more subordinate clauses.

> Many things were ruined because the water was so deep.

An **adjective clause** is a subordinate clause that is used as an adjective.

> People **who lived nearby** suffered much damage.

An **adverb clause** is a subordinate clause used as an adverb.

> Some people fled their houses **when the water rose.**

Nouns

A **noun** is a word that names a person, place, thing, or idea.

> merchant   storeroom   tree   courage

A **concrete noun** names something that you can see or touch.

> bench   finger   barn   airplane

An **abstract noun** names something that you cannot see or touch, such as an emotion or an idea.

> pleasure   anger   bravery   democracy

A **proper noun** is a noun that names a particular person, place, or thing.

> Paul Revere   Scotland   Great Pyramid

A **collective noun** is a noun that names a group of people or things.

> choir   flock   team   Congress

A **compound noun** is formed from two or more words that work together as a single noun.

> bedroom   Robin Hood   mother-in-law

A **plural noun** is a noun that names more than one person, place, thing, or idea.

> waiters   towns   teacups   liberties   mice

An **appositive** is a word or group of words that follows and defines or identifies a noun.

> Mr. Benson, **the principal,** gave a short speech.

Verbs

An **action verb** is a word that expresses action.

> laugh   fly   think   distract

A **linking verb** is a verb that links the subject of a sentence to a noun or an adjective in the predicate.

> Florence Nightingale **was** a brave woman.

A **direct object** is a noun or pronoun that receives the action of a verb.

> She nursed **soldiers** during the Crimean War.

A verb with a direct object is a **transitive verb.** A verb that does not have a direct object is an **intransitive verb.**

An **indirect object** is a noun or pronoun that answers the question *to whom? for whom? to what?* or *for what?* after an action verb.

> Florence Nightingale gave **nurses** lessons in caring for patients.

A verb is in the **active voice** when the subject of a sentence performs the action. Verbs in the active voice may or may not have a direct object.

> We **enjoyed** the party.

A verb is in the **passive voice** when the subject receives the action of the verb. Verbs in the passive voice do not have a direct object.

> The party **was enjoyed** by us.

The time expressed by a verb is called its **tense**. The three simple tenses are **present** (the action is happening now), **past** (the action has already happened), and **future** (the action will happen in the future).

> We **study** the problems of hospital care.   (present)
> We **studied** about sanitation yesterday.   (past)
> We **will study** about modern medicine tomorrow.   (future)

A **verb phrase** consists of a main verb and all of its helping verbs.

> Much progress **has been made** during the last century.

The **present progressive** form of a verb expresses an action or condition that is continuing in the present. It consists of the helping verb *am, is,* or *are* and the present participle of the main verb.

> We **are enjoying** the study unit. (present progressive)

The **past progressive** form of a verb expresses an action or a condition that continued for some time in the past. It consists of the helping verb *was* or *were* and the present participle of the main verb.

> I **was reading** about inoculation. (past progressive)

The **perfect tenses** of a verb express actions that happened at an indefinite time in the past.

> We **have voted.**   (present perfect)
> Before we voted, I **had registered.**   (past perfect)
> By noon we **will have decided.**   (future perfect)

Most verbs add *d* or *ed* to form the past tense. (wait—*waited*; close—*closed*) An **irregular verb** does not use this pattern. You must memorize the irregular verb forms. Here are some examples of irregular verbs.

Present	Past	Past with Helping Verb
be	was	(*have, has,* or *had*) been
begin	began	(*have, has,* or *had*) begun
blow	blew	(*have, has,* or *had*) blown
come	came	(*have, has,* or *had*) come
do	did	(*have, has,* or *had*) done
drive	drove	(*have, has,* or *had*) driven
go	went	(*have, has,* or *had*) gone
have	had	(*have, has,* or *had*) had
hide	hid	(*have, has,* or *had*) hidden
see	saw	(*have, has,* or *had*) seen
set	set	(*have, has,* or *had*) set
take	took	(*have, has,* or *had*) taken

Pronouns

A **pronoun** takes the place of one or more nouns and the words that go with the nouns.

> The big ship sailed. **It** sailed.

An **antecedent** is a word or group of words to which a pronoun refers.

> **The owner of the ship** was pleased, and *he* smiled.

A **subject pronoun** is a pronoun that is used as the subject of a sentence.

> I, you, he, she, it, we, they

An **object pronoun** is a pronoun that is used as a direct object, an indirect object, or as the object of a preposition.

> me, you, him, her, it, us, them

A **possessive pronoun** shows who or what owns something.

> Used before a noun: my, your, his, her, its, our, their
> Used alone: mine, yours, his, hers, its, ours, theirs

An **indefinite pronoun** is a pronoun that does not refer to a particular person, place, or thing.

> all, any, anyone, each, every, everybody, few, nobody

A **reflexive pronoun** points the action of the verb back to the subject. Reflexive pronouns end in *self* or *selves*.

> He hurt **himself**.

An **intensive pronoun** is a pronoun that adds emphasis to a noun or pronoun already named. Intensive pronouns end in *self* or *selves*.

> The ship **itself** was safe at sea.

An **interrogative pronoun** is a pronoun used to form questions.

> **What** is that? **Which** is the one you brought?

A **demonstrative pronoun** is a pronoun that points out specific persons, places, things, or ideas and stands alone in a sentence.

> this   that   these   those

Adjectives

An **adjective** is a word that modifies a noun or pronoun.

> **heavy** weights   **happy** family

The words *a, an,* and *the* are special adjectives called **articles**. *A* and *an* are **indefinite articles** because they do not refer to a particular person, place, thing, or idea. *The* is called a **definite article** because it identifies a specific person, place, thing, or idea.

A **proper adjective** is formed from a proper noun and begins with a capital letter.

> **French** toast   **Eisenhower** jacket

A **comparative adjective** compares two nouns. To form a comparative adjective, add *er* or use the word *more* with the adjective.

> the **larger** mast   the **more important** issue

A **superlative adjective** compares more than two nouns. To form a superlative adjective, add *est* or use the word *most* with the adjective.

> the **heaviest** weight   the **most beautiful** scene

A **demonstrative adjective** points out something and describes nouns by answering the question *which one?* or *which ones? This* (singular) and *these* (plural) are used to refer to things nearby. *That* (singular) and *those* (plural) are used to refer to things at a distance.

> **this** cat   **these** stamps   **that** house   **those** maps

Adverbs

An **adverb** is a word that modifies a verb, an adjective, or another adverb.

> The ship sailed **slowly.**   The masts were **very** tall.
> The people waved **rather slowly.**

A **comparative adverb** compares two actions. Comparative adverbs are usually formed with the word *more*.

> She danced **more gracefully** than her partner.

A **superlative adverb** compares more than two actions. Superlative adverbs are usually formed with the word *most*.

> His answer was the **most cleverly** phrased of all.

Prepositions

A **preposition** is a word that relates a noun or pronoun to another word in a sentence.

> We went **with** my uncle.

A **prepositional phrase** is a group of words that begins with a preposition and ends with a noun or pronoun.

> He drove **to the theater.**

The noun or pronoun that completes a prepositional phrase is called the **object of the preposition**.

> We bought tickets at the **entrance.**

If a prepositional phrase tells *how, where,* or *when,* it is an **adverb phrase**.

> We sat **in the third row.**

If a prepositional phrase tells *how many, what kind,* or *which one,* it is an **adjective phrase**.

> We heard every word **of the play.**

Conjunctions

A **conjunction** is a word that joins words or groups of words. A **coordinating conjunction** is a single word that joins words or groups of words.

> Sue **and** Bill   the tree in the yard **or** the one next to it

Correlative conjunctions are pairs of words that are used to join words or groups of words.

> **both** big **and** heavy   **neither** Bert **nor** Elsa

Interjections

An **interjection** is a word or group of words that expresses strong feeling.

> Wow!   Gee whiz!   Ha!   Oh no!

VERBALS

Participles

A **present participle** is formed by adding *ing* to a verb. A present participle may be used as a part of a verb phrase or as an adjective.

> The **shining** brass was **shimmering** in the sunlight.

A **past participle** is usually formed by adding *ed* to a verb. A past participle may be used as a part of a verb phrase or as an adjective.

> The **heated** pipe had **burned** a hole in the rug.

A **participial phrase** is a group of words that includes a participle and other words that complete its meaning.

> **Pushing the door open,** the horses roamed into the yard.

A **misplaced participial phrase** is a participial phrase that is not placed near the word it modifies, thus misleading the reader.

> I saw a steeple **walking down the street.**

Gerunds

A **gerund** is a verb form that ends in *ing* and is used as a noun.

> **Running** is good for your lungs.

A **gerund phrase** is a group of words that includes a gerund and other words that complete its meaning.

> **Playing team sports** is also excellent exercise.

Infinitives

An **infinitive** is formed with the word *to* together with the base form of a verb. An infinitive is often used as a noun in a sentence.

> **To win** is not as important as **to play.**

An **infinitive phrase** is a group of words that includes an infinitive and other words that complete its meaning.

> Everyone wants **to contribute his or her best effort.**

MECHANICS

PUNCTUATION
Periods

Use a period at the end of a declarative sentence.

> The day was bright and sunny.

Use a period at the end of an imperative sentence.

> Put that needle back in the pincushion.

Use a period or periods with many abbreviations.

> Dr.   St.   A.M.   gal.   Jan.

Use a period after initials.

> P.T. Barnum   John F. Kennedy

Commas

Use a comma before the conjunction in a compound sentence.

> I read the newspaper, and then we ate dinner.

Use a comma or commas to set off the name of a state or country after the name of a city.

> Alex was born in Racine, Wisconsin, on Labor Day.
> He lived for many years in London, England.

Use a comma or commas to set off the year in a complete date.

> The Bastille was stormed on July 14, 1789, in Paris.
> (but: The Bastille was stormed in July 1789 in Paris.)

Use commas to separate three or more items in a series.

> Red, white, and green are on the Italian flag.
> We looked on the bed, in the drawer, and in the closet.

Use a comma after the greeting and closing of a friendly letter.

> Dear Aunt Rose,   Sincerely yours,

Use a comma to show a pause after an introductory word or phrase.

> Well, do you know the answer?
> Yes, there may be no answer.

Use a comma or commas to set off a word or phrase that interrupts the flow of thought.

> It is, you might say, a question of taste.

Use a comma or commas to set off a noun of direct address.

Please, Richard, what was the question?   May I go, sir?

Use a comma or commas to set off the word *too* when it is used to mean "also."

May I go, too?   You, too, may find the answer.

Apostrophes

Use apostrophes (') in contractions to show where a letter or letters are missing.

couldn't   o'clock   I'm

Use apostrophes with nouns to show possession. Add *'s* to singular nouns or plural nouns that do not end in *s*.

John**'s** model   women**'s** shoes

Add an apostrophe to form the possessive of plural nouns that end in *s*.

cousins' house   dogs' leashes

Colons

Use a colon before a list of similar items, especially after the expressions "as follows" or "the following."

The box contained the following: letters, bills, receipts, notes, and memos.

Use a colon after the greeting in a business letter.

Dear Sir or Madam: Dear Doctor McCormack:

Use a colon to separate the hour and the minute when you use numerals to indicate the exact time of day.

4:14 P.M.   12:36 A.M.   (but: *five o'clock in the morning*)

Semicolons

Use a semicolon (;) to join parts of a compound sentence when a coordinating conjunction such as *and, but,* or *or* is not used.

Baltimore became a major port; New York declined.

Use a semicolon to join parts of a compound sentence when the parts are long and are subdivided by commas, even if a coordinating conjunction is used.

Airplanes have radically changed how we move cargo; and shipping by rail, water, and truck has changed greatly.

Hyphens

Use a hyphen to show the division of a word at the end of a line. Always divide the word between its syllables. If you are uncertain of how a word is divided into syllables, look it up in a dictionary.

> Forests and their products are of the greatest importance to people.

Use a hyphen in compound numbers.

> forty-seven   thirty-three letters

Use a hyphen or hyphens in certain compound nouns.

> great-grandmother   attorney-at-law

Dashes

Use a dash to show that a thought or a speech was unfinished or interrupted. If the sentence continues, use a second dash to mark the end of the interruption.

> Christopher Columbus discovered—oh, you know that.
> Mr. Williams—he is friend of mine—is the director.

Titles

To indicate italics, underline the titles of full-length books, movies, plays, and television programs. Put quotation marks around the titles of poems, short stories, one-act plays, magazine articles, song titles, and other short works.

> <u>Mutiny on the Bounty</u>   <u>Collier's Encyclopedia</u>
> "The Night the Bed Fell"   "Trees"   "Forever Young"

Capitalize the first word and all important words in the titles of books, plays, short stories, poems, movies, and TV programs.

> *The Once and Future King*   *The Taming of the Shrew*
> "Why I Live at the P.O."   "America the Beautiful"

Writing Quotations

Capitalize the first word of a quotation, no matter where it appears in a sentence.

> James Lawrence said, "Don't give up the ship."

Do **not** capitalize the beginning of explanatory words unless they are the first words of the sentence.

> "Follow the yellow brick road," said the Munchkins.
> The lion cried, "If I only had a heart."

Do **not** capitalize the second part of an interrupted quotation unless it begins a new sentence.

"I'll get you," the witch snarled, "**a**nd your little dog, too."

Use a comma to separate the explanatory words at the beginning of a sentence from the quotation that follows.

John Paul Jones said, "I have not yet begun to fight."

Use a comma instead of a period at the end of a statement or command in a quotation at the beginning of a sentence.

"Take out a clean piece of paper," the teacher announced.

Punctuate quoted questions or exclamations in the usual way. The end punctuation goes *before* the second quotation mark. Do not capitalize the first letter of the explanatory words.

"What can I do to help?" **t**he poised gentleman asked.

Abbreviations

Abbreviations are shortened forms of words. Many abbreviations begin with a capital letter and end with a period.

Titles of persons can be abbreviated.

Dr. William McCabe   Edwin R. Lane, Sr.

Days of the week and months of the year are often abbreviated.

Oct. (October)   Tues. (Tuesday)

There are many common abbreviations used in addresses.

St. (street)   Blvd. (boulevard)   Ave. (avenue)

You will often see these abbreviations in company names.

Co. (company)   Corp. (corporation)   Inc. (incorporated)

Professional or academic degrees are often abbreviated.

Janice Williams, Ph.D.   Robert Stein, M.D.

Abbreviations are used with time of day and with years.

8:01 P.M.   2000 B.C.   A.D. 970

Units of measure are often abbreviated in scientific or informal writing.

2 qt. (two quarts)   80 m (eighty meters)

Some abbreviations use all capital letters and no periods. These include agencies and organizations.

VISTA   PTA   OAS   USMC

Postal Abbreviations

Use the United States Postal Service abbreviations for state names. Notice that each abbreviation consists of *two* capital letters. No period follows these abbreviations.

AL (Alabama)	LA (Louisiana)	OH (Ohio)
AK (Alaska)	ME (Maine)	OK (Oklahoma)
AZ (Arizona)	MD (Maryland)	OR (Oregon)
AR (Arkansas)	MA (Massachusetts)	PA (Pennsylvania)
CA (California)	MI (Michigan)	RI (Rhode Island)
CO (Colorado)	MN (Minnesota)	SC (South Carolina)
CT (Connecticut)	MS (Mississippi)	SD (South Dakota)
DE (Delaware)	MO (Missouri)	TN (Tennessee)
FL (Florida)	MT (Montana)	TX (Texas)
GA (Georgia)	NE (Nebraska)	UT (Utah)
HI (Hawaii)	NV (Nevada)	VT (Vermont)
ID (Idaho)	NH (New Hampshire)	VA (Virginia)
IL (Illinois)	NJ (New Jersey)	WA (Washington)
IN (Indiana)	NM (New Mexico)	WV (West Virginia)
IA (Iowa)	NY (New York)	WI (Wisconsin)
KS (Kansas)	NC (North Carolina)	WY (Wyoming)
KY (Kentucky)	ND (North Dakota)	(DC—District of Columbia)

CAPITALIZATION

Capitalize the name and initials of specific persons, places, or things.

John Wayne   Boca Raton   Holy Grail

Capitalize titles of respect when they are part of a specific name.

Admiral Farragut   President Harry Truman

Always capitalize the first-person pronoun *I*.

Capitalize words that show family relationships only when they are used as substitutes for a person's name.

I told Mother that the washing machine broke.
(*but*: My mother already knew it was broken.)

Capitalize the names of religious books.

The Bible is divided into many books.

Capitalize the names for the days of the week and the months of the year.

Thursday   Saturday   December   June

Capitalize the names of holidays and religious days.

May Day   Christmas   Thanksgiving   Yom Kippur

Capitalize the names of cities, states, countries, and other specific geographic locations.

Missouri   **Kansas City**   Ethiopia   Rio Grande

Capitalize the titles of specific clubs and organizations.

American **B**allet Theatre   Marine **B**ank   Kiwanis

Capitalize the names of political and ethnic groups.

Republicans   **R**ussians   Seminole Indians

Capitalize proper adjectives.

Persian rugs   Christian ethics   Carolina hills

Capitalize all the words in the greeting of a letter.

Dear Sir: My Dear Friend,

Capitalize only the first word in a letter's closing.

Sincerely yours,

Capitalize the names of important historical events and documents.

Battle of **B**unker Hill   World War I   Bill of Rights

Capitalize the names of foreign languages.

Latin   Swedish

USAGE

Subject-Verb Agreement

Subjects and verbs must agree in number. If a subject is singular, the verb must be singular in form as well. If a subject is plural, the verb must be plural in form.

> The happy **student works** hard.
> The happy **students work** hard.

If a compound subject is connected by *and*, use a plural verb. If a compound subject is connected by *or*, use the verb that agrees with the second part of the subject.

> Terry **and** Alice **were** at the gym. (plural)
> Terry **or** Alice **is** almost always there. (singular)

The subject and verb must agree even when the subject appears after the verb.

> There **are** several basketball **nets** in the locker.

The subject and verb must agree even when a phrase comes between them.

> The **man** with the name tags **is** the coach.

In sentences beginning with *here* or *there*, look for the subject after the verb. *Here* or *there* is never the subject.

> Here **is** the **key** to the locker.

In some interrogative sentences a helping verb may come before the subject. Look for the subject between the helping verb and the main verb.

> **Does** the **coach** need the nets now?

Pronouns

When a pronoun is used as a subject, use a subject pronoun.

> The coach and **he** practiced free throws.

When a pronoun is used as a direct object, an indirect object, or the object of a preposition, use an object pronoun.

> We saw **them** in the locker room.
> They gave **us** permission to practice.
> The coach threw the ball to **him.**

Pronoun Antecedents

Be sure pronoun antecedents are clear. Some sentences have to be reworded so that the antecedent is clear.

> Jason threw the ball to Scott; he missed. (unclear)
> Jason threw the ball to Scott; Scott missed. (clear)

Pronouns and Contractions

Because several pronouns and contractions are homophones, they are often confused.

Pronoun	Contraction
its (possessive form of *it*)	it's (contraction of *it is* or *it has*)
their (possessive form of *they*, used before a noun)	they're (contraction of *they are*)
theirs (possessive form of *they*, stands alone)	there's (contraction of *there is* or *there has*)
whose (possessive form of *who*)	who's (contraction of *who is* or *who has*)
your (possessive form of *you*)	you're (contraction of *you are*)

Adjectives

Do not use *more* or *most* with adjectives that already show comparison.

> Jason is larger than Scott.   (correct)
> Jason is more larger than Scott.   (incorrect)

Some adjectives are irregular. That is, they do not form their comparative forms in the usual way.

Adjective	Compares Two Nouns	Compares More Than Two Nouns
good	better	best
bad	worse	worst
much	more	most
little	less	least

To make an adjective into an adverb, add **ly** to the end of many adjectives.

> wide—widely   beautiful—beautifully

Adverbs

No, *never*, *not*, *hardly*, and *scarcely* are negative adverbs. A **double negative** is the incorrect use of two negatives in one sentence. Use only one negative in a sentence.

> I have **not** seen any.   (correct: single negative)
> I have **not** seen **none.**   (incorrect: double negative)

Good—Well, Bad—Badly

Good and *bad* are adjectives. They tell about nouns.

> It is a **good** book.   It has a **bad** cover.

Well and *badly* are adverbs. They describe verbs.

> The story began **well.**   The cover closed **badly.**

Use *well* and *bad* when talking about health.

> I am not feeling **well** today. I felt **bad** yesterday, too.

Misplaced Modifiers

Place phrases as close as possible to the words they modify. Otherwise, the sentence may be confusing.

> I saw a man on the bus **with a crutch.** (unclear)
> I saw a man **with a crutch** on the bus. (clear)

THESAURUS FOR WRITING

What Is a Thesaurus?

A thesaurus is a reference that can be very useful when you are writing. It provides synonyms for many common words. Synonyms are words that mean almost the same thing.

The thesaurus can help you find more interesting words and more exact words to use in your writing. For example, you may write this sentence.

> Her hair was *wet* from the sudden rainfall.

Wet is not a very interesting word, and it says very little about her hair. If you look up the word *wet* in the thesaurus, you will find these words: damp, moist, soggy, sopping, drenched, dank. Using one of these words would make your sentence more interesting and more exact.

Using the Thesaurus

The words in a thesaurus are listed in alphabetical order. If you want to find a word, look it up as you would in a dictionary. If the word is listed in the thesaurus, you will find an entry such as this one for the word *cold*.

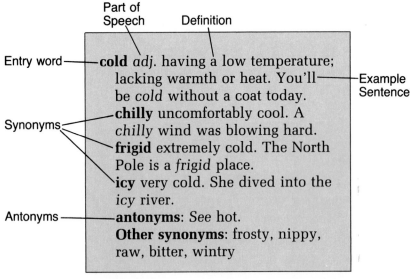

The word *cold* is called an entry word. The information that follows is called the entry. The entry for *cold* gives the part of speech, a definition of the word, and an example sentence. Below that are synonyms; each synonym is indicated by dark type. Each synonym is defined, especially in how it differs from *cold*, and is used in an example sentence. In some entries you will find words listed as "other synonyms." These are similar in meaning to the entry word, but they are not defined in the thesaurus. A dictionary can provide additional information about these words.

In some entries you will also find antonyms. Antonyms are words with opposite meanings, such as *tall* and *short*. The antonyms help you understand the meaning of the entry word.

Cross-references

In some cases you will find cross-references. For example, if you look up the word *allow*, you will find this cross-reference: "*See* let." This means that you should look up the word *let*; the word *allow* will be listed under *let*. You may also find a cross-reference in an entry. For example, if you look up the word *strange*, you will find a list of synonyms and a cross-reference that says "*See also* unusual." This means that you will find more information about *strange* under the entry word *unusual*.

The thesaurus can help make you a better writer by helping you find just the right word for what you want to say.

A

agree *v.* to say "yes"; to have the same opinion; to be in harmony. We *agreed* about our responsibilities.
assent to express acceptance (of an idea, proposal, etc.). The mayor *assented* to the plan.
concur to have the same opinion. I *concur* with your argument.
consent to give permission or approval. Dad *consented* to our going on the trip.

allow *See* let.

angry *adj.* feeling or showing anger. She was *angry* with me.
choleric easily irritated or angered. Ed is such a *choleric* person that we have to be careful what we say to him.
enraged filled with rage; angry beyond control. The *enraged* bull charged at the red cape.
furious extremely angry. Ann was *furious* when she read the letter.
incensed filled with anger. Why is she so *incensed* about this?
resentful feeling bitter or indignant. Peter has always been *resentful* of my success.
Other synonyms: outraged, irate, infuriated, irascible, cross, irritated, displeased

answer *v.* to give a spoken or written response. She never *answered* my question.
reply to say in response. When he asked, what did you *reply*?
respond to give an answer. We should *respond* to her request.

retort to reply, usually sharply, to criticism or a remark. "He's not so great," Nick *retorted*.
antonyms: ask, inquire

ask *v.* to put a question to. *Ask* the policeman for directions.
inquire to seek information by asking questions. Perry called to *inquire* about renting the house.
query to seek a formal answer to a question. She *queried* the office manager for information.
question to try to get information (from someone). Judge Warner *questioned* the witness about the crime.
antonyms: *See* answer.

awful *adj.* causing fear, dread, or awe. We heard an *awful* shriek.
dreadful causing great fear. Polio was once a *dreadful* disease.
frightful causing fright. A *frightful* roar came from the cave.
horrible arousing feelings of horror. What a *horrible* accident!
terrible causing terror or awe. The *terrible* battle ended today.
Other synonyms: dire, shocking, ominous, horrifying, ghastly

B

beautiful *adj.* full of beauty; having pleasing qualities. This leather work is *beautiful*.
attractive appealing or pleasing, but not in an exceptional way. That's an *attractive* blouse.
gorgeous extremely beautiful or richly colored. The autumn leaves were a *gorgeous* sight.

lovely beautiful in a comforting way. She has a *lovely* voice.
pretty pleasing or attractive, often said of something small or dainty. That's a *pretty* ring.
antonyms: ugly, unattractive
Other synonyms: stunning, striking, appealing, handsome

big *adj.* of great size. We jumped into a *big* pile of leaves.
enormous much greater than the usual size. Jason had an *enormous* bowl of salad.
gigantic like a giant in size. Two *gigantic* horses pulled the heavy sled.
huge extremely big. I had a *huge* sandwich for lunch.
large of great size; big. It's a *large* house with ten rooms.
antonyms: *See* little.
Other synonyms: monstrous, massive, humongous, titanic

brave *adj.* willing to face danger; without fear. The *brave* diver leapt from the cliff.
bold showing courage; fearless. They made a *bold* rescue.
courageous having courage. The *courageous* climber reached the peak of the mountain.
daring willing to take risks. The *daring* acrobat flew into the air.
antonyms: afraid, fearful
Other synonyms: intrepid, fearless, dauntless

break *v.* to come apart; to separate into pieces. Who *broke* the egg?
crack to break without fully separating. Our new oak table *cracked* right down the middle.
fracture to break or split. She *fractured* her ankle.
shatter to break suddenly into many pieces. The vase *shattered* when it hit the floor.
Other synonyms: split, splinter, smash, burst

bright *adj.* filled with light; shining. Their *bright* headlights blinded me for a moment.
brilliant shining or sparkling with light. She was wearing a *brilliant* diamond necklace.
glistening shining with reflected light. He dived into the *glistening* pool.
luminous giving off light. The *luminous* coals glowed in the dark.
shiny shining; bright. She gave her brother a *shiny* dime.
antonyms: dark, dull

C

cheap *adj.* low in price; inferior in quality or value. He plans to buy a *cheap* boat and fix it up.
cut-rate sold or selling at a reduced or cheap price. She buys her shoes at a *cut-rate* store.
economical operating cheaply; inexpensive. A wood stove is an *economical* source of heat.
gaudy tastelessly bright or ornate. Louise got a *gaudy* purple hat for her birthday.
inexpensive low in price. The Palms is an *inexpensive* hotel.
antonym: expensive

clean *adj.* without dirt or stain. Do you have a *clean* towel?
immaculate perfectly clean. His room is always *immaculate*.
pure free from contamination.

We bought *pure* spring water.
spick-and-span fresh, neat, and clean. The kitchen floor was *spick-and-span*.
spotless extremely clean. These glasses are *spotless*.
antonyms: dirty, filthy, messy

cold *adj.* having a low temperature; lacking warmth or heat. You'll be *cold* without a coat.
chilly uncomfortably cool. A *chilly* wind was blowing hard.
frigid extremely cold. The North Pole is a *frigid* place.
icy very cold. She dived into the *icy* river.
antonyms: See hot.

collect *v.* to gather or bring (things) together. Theo will *collect* cans for the fund drive.
assemble to gather or bring together, especially people. The members *assembled* for lunch.
compile to collect and put together (information), as in a list or report. Please help me *compile* a list of addresses.
gather to bring together in one place or group. Lyn *gathered* many plants for her plant book.

cook *v.* to prepare food for eating, using heat. Let's *cook* some eggs.
bake to cook in an oven. This casserole *baked* for an hour.
broil to cook by exposing to a flame or other source of intense heat. We can *broil* hamburgers on the charcoal grill.
fry to cook in a pan over direct heat, using hot oil or fat. Let's *fry* some peppers and onions.
roast to cook with very little moisture, in an oven or over an open fire. You should *roast* the turkey for about four hours.
Other synonyms: sauté, boil

cry *v.* to shed tears. Debi started to *cry* when the movie ended.
bawl to cry loudly. That baby *bawled* all morning long.
sob to cry with short gasps. Ned *sobbed* at his friend's funeral.
weep to show grief, joy, or other strong emotions by crying. Mom began to *weep* at my graduation.
whimper to cry with weak, broken sounds. The puppy *whimpered* because of the thorn in his paw.
whine to make a high-pitched, mournful cry of pain or distress. Jimmy *whined* all the way to the summer camp.
antonyms: See laugh.

D

do *v.* to carry out. Please *do* your chores before breakfast.
achieve to bring about an intended result. Mr. Lane worked hard to *achieve* his goal.
contrive to bring about, especially with difficulty. The convict *contrived* his escape.
execute to complete, often when told to do so; to put into effect. The guard *executed* his orders.
perform to carry out to completion. Sherry *performed* the bone dance at the ceremony.

dry *adj.* not wet; free of moisture. He put *dry* sand on the floor.
arid dry as a result of having little rainfall. This was an *arid*

region before the dam was built.

desiccated completely dried up. We found a *desiccated* fish on the beach.

parched dried out by heat. Her throat was *parched* with thirst.

sere withered; dry. The meadow was brown and *sere*.

antonyms: See wet.

E

easy *adj.* requiring little mental or physical effort; not difficult. That was an *easy* test.

effortless seeming to require little effort. She made the dance look so *effortless*.

facile not hard to do or achieve; done easily and quickly. That is a *facile* plan for a difficult problem.

simple not complicated. He used a *simple* recipe for pancakes.

antonyms: difficult, hard

F

far *adj.* a long way off; not near. It is too *far* to walk in one day.

distant extremely far. We heard the howl of a *distant* wolf.

remote faraway, in an out-of-the-way place. They moved the capital to a *remote* area.

antonyms: near, close

fast *adj.* moving or done with speed. That was a *fast* game.

quick done in a very short time. Can you give me a *quick* haircut?

rapid with great speed, often in a continuing way. The *rapid* flow of the river runs the mill.

speedy characterized by rapid motion. She got a *speedy* little motorbike.

swift moving with great speed, often said of animals or people. Carl Lewis is a *swift* runner.

antonym: slow

funny *adj.* causing laughter. Aunt Jo told us a *funny* story.

amusing causing smiles of enjoyment or laughter. She drew an *amusing* picture of me.

comical causing laughter through actions. The dancing bear was *comical* to watch.

hilarious very funny and usually noisy. The new play at the theater is *hilarious*.

humorous funny in a mild or regular way. Eddie is often *humorous* at the wrong time.

G

get *v.* to go for and return with. Please *get* me some scissors.

acquire to come into possession of through effort. Mrs. Cohen has *acquired* many paintings.

earn to gain through effort. How much did you *earn* by baby-sitting?.

obtain to get as one's own, often with some difficulty. Lisa *obtained* a copy of the map.

procure to get hold of through effort. The captain *procured* enough supplies for two weeks.

give *v.* to turn over possession or control of; to make a present of. I will *give* you my old skates.

confer to give an honor. The principal *conferred* awards on several honors students.

contribute to give or supply in common with others. Would you like to *contribute* to the Heart Fund?

grant to give in response to a request. The IRS *granted* him an extension to pay his taxes.

present to give in a formal way, usually something of value. Minnie will *present* the award.

antonyms: *See* take.

good *adj.* above average in quality; not bad. These are *good* photographs.

excellent extremely good. He makes an *excellent* omelet.

fair somewhat good; slightly better than average. He did a *fair* job but not a great one.

fine of high quality; very good. We took out our *fine* silver.

antonyms: bad, poor

See also great.

great *adj.* of unusual quality or ability. Van Cliburn is a *great* pianist.

remarkable having unusual qualities. What a *remarkable* building!

superb of greater quality than most. The lobster was *superb*.

wonderful very good; excellent. Greg made a *wonderful* speech. *See also* good.

H

happy *adj.* having, showing, or bringing pleasure. Rover is always *happy* to see me come home.

gay full of joy and fun. The king's party was a *gay* affair.

glad feeling or expressing joy or pleasure. "Boy, am I *glad* to see you," said John.

joyful very happy; filled with joy. Ana was *joyful* at her wedding.

merry happy and cheerful. Leon has such a *merry* way about him.

pleased satisfied or content. I am *pleased* with her progress.

antonyms: *See* sad.

Other synonyms: delighted, contented, ecstatic, elated, jubilant, overjoyed

hard *adj.* not easy to do or deal with. This book is *hard* to read.

difficult hard to do; requiring effort. Preparing the garden soil is a *difficult* job.

severe difficult or trying; strict. The 26-mile marathon is the most *severe* of all races.

strenuous requiring great effort. Miko followed a *strenuous* training program before running the race.

tough difficult to do, often in a physical sense. We had a *tough* time digging holes for the posts.

antonym: easy

help *v.* to provide with support; to be of service to. Please *help* me lift this crate.

aid to give help to (someone in trouble). The nurse tried to *aid* all of the victims at once.

assist to help, often in a cooperative way. The government can *assist* small businesses.

relieve to take over a post or duty. The night watchman will *relieve* the guard at 10:00 P.M.

remedy to cause to heal or improve. Raising the taxes will not *remedy* the situation.

succor to give help, assistance, or relief to. The doctor gave what little help she could to *succor* the drought victims.

high *adj.* located or extending a great distance above the ground. The roof has a *high* peak.
elevated raised; high. Cars enter the garage on an *elevated* ramp.
lofty very high; of grand or inspiring height. The sailors stared up at the *lofty* cliffs.
tall having a height greater than average but with a relatively narrow width. Poplars are *tall*, but apple trees are short.
towering of great or imposing height. The top of the *towering* skyscraper reached the clouds.
antonyms: low, short

hot *adj.* having a high temperature; having much heat. Be careful, this plate is *hot*.
fiery as hot as fire; burning. He threw water on the *fiery* coals.
scalding hot enough to burn, often said of liquids. Timmy got quite a burn from a pot of *scalding* water.
scorching intensely hot, enough to cause burning or drying. She could barely stand in the *scorching* heat of the desert.
tepid slightly warm; lukewarm. *Tepid* milk tastes strange.
torrid extremely hot, often said of weather. In North Africa the *torrid* summer lasts for months.
antonym: See cold.
Other synonyms: blistering, blazing, sweltering

hurt *v.* to cause pain or damage. The sun *hurt* my eyes.
bruise to cause a bruise on the surface of; to injure or hurt slightly. He *bruised* his knee when he fell on the ice.
damage to injure or harm in a way that causes loss. Cutting the roots will *damage* the tree.
harm to do damage to. That horse is too gentle to *harm* the children.
injure to cause physical damage. Meredith *injured* her wrist.

I

important *adj.* having special value, meaning, authority, or influence. We attended an *important* meeting of the board.
consequential important, usually because of an actual or expected outcome. This will prove to be a *consequential* book on economics.
noteworthy worthy of special notice or attention. She has invented two *noteworthy* products.
prominent well-known or important. Mr. Liu is a *prominent* businessman.
significant having special meaning or importance that may not be immediately apparent. This will be his most *significant* work.
antonyms: insignificant, unimportant, trivial
Other synonyms: momentous, crucial, critical

information *n.* knowledge or facts. Do you have any *information* about the stock market crash?
data information from which conclusions can be drawn; facts and figures. The doctor used

data in his research study.
facts information known to be true or real. The detective set out to learn the *facts*.
statistics numerical data. We have no *statistics* on farming.

interesting *adj.* arousing or holding interest or attention. I found an *interesting* article.
captivating capturing and holding attention by beauty or excellence. We found a *captivating* photograph of the movie star.
fascinating causing and holding interest through a special quality or charm. Stamp collecting is a *fascinating* hobby.
inspiring having a rousing effect; arousing interest. His presentation of the play was *inspiring*.
antonyms: dull, boring
Other synonyms: intriguing, engrossing, gripping, absorbing, thought-provoking

L

large See **big**.

laugh *v.* to make the sounds and facial movements that show amusement. Cheryl loves to *laugh* at a pun.
chortle to chuckle gleefully. Dennis *chortled* at the idea that Barry could beat him at chess.
chuckle to laugh softly, especially to oneself. Several people *chuckled* at his remarks.
giggle to laugh in a silly, high-pitched, or nervous way. Danny *giggled* when he met her.
guffaw to laugh loudly. Penny

guffawed when she saw my costume.
snicker to laugh slyly, in a disrespectful way. Kay *snickered* at her brother's clumsiness.
antonyms: *See* cry.
Other synonyms: titter, crow, cackle, whoop

let *v.* to give permission to. If you're good, I'll *let* you go.
allow to grant permission to or for, usually in relation to rules. Dogs are not *allowed* in school.
concede to grant or yield; to give in. The champion has never *conceded* a match to any opponent.
permit to allow (a person) to do something. We do not *permit* loud talking in the library.
antonyms: deny, refuse, forbid

like *v.* to take pleasure in (something); to feel affection for (someone). I *like* flowers.
admire to have affection and respect for (someone). Karen *admires* her father.
enjoy to take pleasure in (something). Mom *enjoys* reading the newspaper on Sunday.
love to like (something) a lot; to feel great affection for (someone or something). She *loves* the beach.
antonyms: dislike, hate
Other synonyms: relish, savor, cherish, appreciate, approve

little *adj.* small in size; not big. Donald is still a *little* boy.
small not large. The nest held two *small* birds.
tiny extremely small. Young

kangaroos are *tiny* creatures.
wee very small. I remember
when you were a *wee* child.
antonyms: *See* big.
Other synonyms: puny, minute,
minuscule

look *v.* to see with one's eyes.
They *looked* at the house.
glance to look quickly. She
glanced at us from her desk.
peer to look closely. Toni
peered at the strange markings.
stare to look at for a long time
with eyes wide open. Mike
stared at the sign in disbelief.
Other synonyms: behold, perceive, discern, inspect, scan
See also see.

loud *adj.* having a strong sound.
The vase fell with a *loud* crash.
deafening loud enough to make
one deaf. The noise from the
jackhammer was *deafening*.
noisy full of sounds, often unpleasant. The bargain basement
is always a *noisy* place.
raucous loud and rowdy. A
raucous mob marched out of
the stadium.
vociferous characterized by a
loud outcry. The demonstrators
protested with *vociferous* cries.
antonyms: *See* quiet.

M
mad *See* angry; *see* crazy.

many *adj.* consisting of a large
number. He has so *many* books.
myriad of indefinitely large
number; countless. The air
buzzed with *myriad* kinds of
insects.
numerous a great many. There

are *numerous* ways to get there.
plenty (of) enough or more than
enough, suggesting a larger
number. There are *plenty* of
seats left.
several more than a few but
less than many. Cheryl has
played in *several* games.
antonym: few

mean *adj.* lacking in kindness or
understanding. Jackie was *mean*
to his little sister.
cruel willing to cause pain or
suffering to others. *Cruel* soldiers burned the village.
malicious desiring to cause
pain, injury, or misfortune to
another. Leona played a *malicious* trick on her former
boyfriend.
nasty resulting from hate. Why
do you have to be so *nasty*?
selfish concerned only about
oneself. Jon is too *selfish* to buy
anyone a present.
spiteful filled with ill feelings
toward others. Max felt *spiteful*
when he did not win a prize.
antonyms: *See* nice.

N
neat *adj.* clean and orderly. Let's
try to keep the cafeteria *neat*.
meticulous extremely concerned about details. Mr. Morgan
is *meticulous* about his car.
tidy neat and clean, often said
of a place. She usually keeps
her kitchen *tidy*.
well-groomed carefully dressed
and groomed. James has always
been a *well-groomed* boy.
antonyms: messy, untidy,
sloppy, disorderly

new *adj.* having just come into being, use, or possession. It's time to buy a *new* rake.
fresh new or seeming new and unaffected by time or use. I think that we need a *fresh* tablecloth.
innovative newly introduced or changed. This *innovative* device makes cleaning easier.
modern having to do with the present time; up-to-date. This house has *modern* fixtures.
novel new and unusual. What a *novel* idea for a costume!
recent referring to a time just before the present. Have you seen the most *recent* edition?
antonym: old

nice *adj.* agreeable or pleasing. What a *nice* little park!
agreeable to one's liking; pleasant. We found an *agreeable* room in Saco Bay.
gentle mild and kindly in manner. Robb is such a *gentle* man.
kind/kindly gentle and friendly; good-hearted. Nancy has always been *kind* to me.
pleasant agreeable; giving pleasure to. We spent a *pleasant* afternoon by the lake.
sweet having or marked by agreeable or pleasing qualities. It was *sweet* of her to remember my birthday.
antonyms: See mean.

O

often *adv.* many times; again and again. She *often* takes the bus.
frequently happening often on a regular basis. He visits the bookstore *frequently*.

regularly happening at fixed times. Do you write *regularly*?
repeatedly over and over again. I have warned him *repeatedly*.
antonyms: seldom, rarely

old *adj.* having lived or existed for a long time. That *old* tree has survived many storms.
aged having grown old. Her *aged* father still walks a mile every morning.
ancient of great age; very old; of times long past. She took pictures of the *ancient* ruins.
hoary white or gray with age; very old. The ancient man rested his *hoary* head on his hands.
antonym: young
Other synonyms: archaic, elder, venerable, senior, antique

P

particular *adj.* separate or distinct from any other; of or for a single definite person, group, or thing. Was there a *particular* reason why you called me?
certain definite but not named; agreed upon or determined. We have *certain* rules around here.
specific distinctly or explicitly named. He has no *specific* destination.

plain *adj.* not distinguished from others in any way. Kate looks rather *plain* in that gray coat.
common average or standard; not distinguished. These are nothing but *common* weeds.
homely of a familiar or everyday nature. He sat down and read the paper in his *homely* easy chair.

ordinary plain; average; everyday. It's just an *ordinary* shoe.
antonym: special
See also unusual.

possible *adj.* capable of existing, happening, being done, or being proven true. Anything is *possible* with enough hard work.
feasible capable of being done or carried out. This schedule is just not *feasible*.
imaginable capable of being imagined. She tried every *imaginable* way to convince us.
plausible apparently true or acceptable; likely. There is no *plausible* explanation for UFOs.
potential capable of being or becoming; possible but not actual. I found seven *potential* jobs in the newspaper.
antonym: impossible

proud *adj.* having a sense of one's own worth, usually in a positive way. I am *proud* of my art.
conceited having too high an opinion of oneself, in a negative way. He's so *conceited* that he carries a mirror in his pocket.
haughty having or showing much pride in oneself. I've had enough of his *haughty* talk.
immodest boastful; taking too much praise or credit. John's *immodest* speech was offensive.
vain overly concerned with or proud of oneself. She's so *vain* that she thinks the sun revolves around her.
antonym: humble

Q
quiet *adj.* with little or no noise. The classroom was *quiet*.

calm free of excitement or strong feeling; quiet. Mrs. Cole was *calm* during the crisis.
peaceful calm; undisturbed. Cats look so *peaceful* when they sleep.
serene not disturbed or troubled. Many young brides are nervous, but Millie remained *serene*.
silent completely quiet; without noise. As the storm approached, the forest became *silent*.
still without sound; silent. Underwater, everything was *still*.
tranquil of a calm or peaceful nature. The canoe floated across the *tranquil* lake.
antonyms: loud, noisy

R
ready *adj.* fit for use or action. "Are you *ready* yet?" called Mom.
alert watchful and ready. Border guards must always stay *alert*.
handy nearby; ready for use. I like to keep my pencil *handy*.
prepared ready or fit for a particular purpose. The work crews are *prepared* for any emergency.
set ready or prepared to do something. Everything is *set* for the town meeting.

really *adv.* in fact. Did you *really* say that?
actually in fact; really. My name is *actually* Malcolm.
indeed really; truly. Vanna did *indeed* go on a safari in Africa.
truly in fact; really. I am *truly* sorry that this has happened.

rich *adj.* having great wealth. His father is a very *rich* man.
affluent wealthy; prosperous. The mayor lives in an *affluent* neighborhood.
opulent showing wealth or affluence. The mansion was furnished with *opulent* antique sofas and chairs.
wealthy having many material goods or riches. The diamond trade has made my uncle a *wealthy* man.
antonym: poor

right *adj.* free from error; true. Were the directions *right*?
accurate without errors or mistakes. Is this report *accurate*?
correct agreeing with fact or truth. Is this the *correct* way to do this?
exact very accurate; completely correct. What is the *exact* time?
precise strictly accurate; clearly defined. Every detail in the design must be *precise*.
antonyms: wrong, mistaken
Other synonyms: just, fit, fitting, appropriate, apt

rude *adj.* not polite; ill-mannered. It's *rude* to talk with your mouth full.
discourteous without good manners. She was *discourteous* enough to ignore my invitation.
impolite not showing good manners. It is *impolite* to interrupt a conversation.
insolent offensively rude or arrogant. The salesclerk was fired for being *insolent* to customers.
uncouth lacking social polish or culture. Pedro's *uncouth* manner is embarrassing to his friends.
antonyms: polite, courteous

run *v.* to go quickly on foot. You didn't have to *run* all the way.
dash to go very fast; to run with sudden speed. Manny *dashed* across the street.
race to run very fast; to run in competition with. I'll *race* you to the corner!
scurry to move hurriedly. Mrs. Penn *scurried* up and down the aisles.
sprint to run at top speed for a short distance. The older boys ran off, and Lou *sprinted* after them.
Other synonyms: bolt, lope, trot, gallop, scamper, streak, scuttle

S

sad *adj.* feeling or showing unhappiness or sorrow. Carrie cried when she heard the *sad* news.
depressed feeling low; sad. Lyn always feels *depressed* in May.
downcast low in spirits; sad. Donna was *downcast* when she lost her dog.
miserable extremely unhappy. Sara was *miserable* at camp.
wretched very unhappy; deeply distressed. Lonnie felt *wretched* when she finally got home.
antonyms: See happy.

same *adj.* being just like something else in kind, quantity, or degree. Art and Dan are on the *same* team.
alike similar, showing a resemblance. Those houses are *alike*.

equal the same in size, amount, quality, or value. She cut the pie into *equal* portions.

equivalent equal in value, effect, or meaning. A mile is *equivalent* to 5280 feet.

identical the same in every detail. Paul and Dave are *identical* twins.

antonym: different

say *v.* to make known or express in words. *Say* what you think.

declare to make known publicly or formally. Mr. Braun *declared* that he would be a candidate.

pronounce to say formally or officially that something is so. When the trial ended, Ms. Perry *pronounced* the ruling unfair.

speak to express an idea, fact, or feeling. If you want some advice, *speak* to Mrs. Evans.

state to express or explain fully in words. Please *state* the facts in simple language.

talk to express ideas or information by means of speech; to speak. I can't *talk* with you now.

See also tell.

Other synonyms: proclaim, exclaim

scared *adj.* afraid; alarmed. Jenny was *scared* by heights.

afraid feeling fear, often in a continuing way or for a long time. Are you *afraid* of snakes?

fearful filled with fear. "Is that you?" said a *fearful* voice.

frightened scared suddenly or for a short time. When the lights went out, the *frightened* boy cried.

terrified extremely scared; filled with terror. Cal is *terrified* of losing his job.

Other synonyms: petrified, aghast, awestruck

see *v.* to receive information, impressions, etc., through use of the eyes. Can you *see* him?

observe to notice. Lawrence *observed* that the first leaves had fallen.

perceive to become aware of through sight or other senses. She *perceived* a change in hue.

view to see or look at, usually for some purpose. We will *view* the movie at two o'clock.

See also look.

shy *adj.* uncomfortable in the presence of others. Paul was always *shy* as a boy.

bashful easily embarrassed; very shy. Norman was too *bashful* to ask her for a date.

demure quiet and modest, often in an artificial way. Zola's white dresses make her look so *demure*.

reticent restrained or reserved, especially in speech. Writers are often *reticent* about discussing their own lives.

retiring avoiding society or publicity. Benny, a *retiring* man, always stays in the background.

timid showing a lack of courage; easily frightened. The boy felt *timid* standing near so many bulls.

antonym: bold

sick *adj.* having poor health. Lina felt *sick* this morning.

ailing in poor health, especially over a period of time. Mrs. Cole has been *ailing* for three weeks.
ill not healthy; sick. I missed school because I was *ill*.
infirm physically weak, especially from old age. Grampa has been *infirm* since his operation.
nauseated feeling sick to one's stomach. Riding in an elevator makes me feel *nauseated*.
unwell not feeling well. Nancy left because she was *unwell*.
antonyms: well, healthy

small *See* little.

smart *adj.* intelligent; bright; having learned a lot. Dolphins are very *smart* mammals.
clever mentally sharp; quick-witted. Keith always has a *clever* response to everything.
intelligent able to learn, understand, and reason. The ancient cave dwellers were less *intelligent* than we are now.
shrewd clever or sharp in practical matters. Mr. Peters has proven to be a *shrewd* manager.
sly clever about tricky or secret matters. Gary came up with a *sly* plan to deceive the coach.
wise able to know or judge what is right, good, or true, often describing a person with good sense rather than one who knows a lot of facts. My father is a *wise* judge of character.
antonym: stupid

smile *v.* to have, show, or give a smile in a happy or friendly way. Frank *smiled* at his sister.
beam to smile joyfully. Martina *beamed* as she yelled, "Bingo!"
grin to smile broadly, with great happiness or amusement. Larry *grinned* when he recognized me.
simper to smile in a silly, artificial way. Vanna *simpered* at my answer.
smirk to smile in a silly or self-satisfied way. Katie *smirked* when her sister was punished for not washing the dishes.
antonyms: frown, scowl

strange *adj.* differing from the usual or the ordinary. Lemmings are *strange* animals.
bizarre strikingly out of the ordinary; startlingly odd. Brenda likes to dress in *bizarre* clothes.
odd not ordinary. You have an *odd* way of looking at things.
peculiar strange or odd, but in an interesting or curious way. Uncle Pat has some *peculiar* friends.
weird strange or odd, in a frightening or mysterious way. We heard a *weird* screech.
See also unusual.

strong *adj.* having great strength or physical power. Are you *strong* enough to lift this box?
brawny strong and muscular. Both of the young farmers were big and *brawny*.
muscular having well-developed muscles; strong. She has become more *muscular* through exercise.
powerful having great strength, influence, or authority. Many dinosaurs had *powerful* tails.
stalwart morally or physically

strong. The *stalwart* troops withstood a 12-hour attack.
antonym: weak
Other synonyms: hardy, vigorous, mighty, potent, irresistible

sure *adj.* firmly believing in something. Henry was *sure* that his answer was right.
certain free from doubt; very sure. Are you *certain* of that address?
confident firmly trusting; sure of oneself or of another. Meryl felt *confident* that she'd win.
definite positive or certain, often in a factual way. Is that decision *definite*?
antonyms: doubtful, unsure

surprised *adj.* feeling sudden wonder. Were you *surprised* to see me?
amazed overwhelmed with wonder or surprise. Luis was *amazed* by the height of the cliffs.
astonished greatly surprised; shocked. Tina was *astonished* when I walked in the door.
astounded greatly surprised; stunned. Deke was *astounded* to hear that he had won an award.
awestruck filled with awe or wonder. George was *awestruck* by the power of the tornado.

T

take *v.* to get into one's hands or possession; to obtain. Did you *take* my baseball glove?
grab to take roughly or rudely. The thief *grabbed* her purse.
seize to take suddenly and by

force. Officer Holmes *seized* the suitcase and opened it.
snatch to take suddenly and quickly, often in secret. Okay, who *snatched* my money?
antonyms: *See* give.

talk *See* say.

tell *v.* to put or express in written or spoken words. I can't *tell* you where I've been.
announce to state or make known publicly. Ms. Price will *announce* the finalists in the contest tomorrow.
narrate to tell about events, especially a story. Chief Cloud *narrated* the tribe's history.
recount to tell in detail; to narrate. Kenneth *recounts* that story every time I see him.
relate to tell or report events or details. Leo sat down and *related* what had happened.
See also say.

thin *adj.* not fat. Denise has gotten *thin* since her illness.
lean with little or no fat but often strong. The tall, *lean* runners lined up at the start.
skinny very thin, in a way that suggests poor health. I'm so worried about him; he's become so *skinny*.
slim thin, in a good or healthy way. The *slim* girl slipped between the boats.
antonyms: fat, plump, chubby

think *v.* to occupy one's thoughts (with). I'll *think* about it.
contemplate to give long and close attention to. Paul *contemplated* the issues for a long time before he answered.

meditate to think seriously and carefully. Tanya decided to *meditate* on the problem.

muse to think in an idle, unconcerned manner. Mr. Ace sat and *mused* about his childhood.

ponder to consider or think over carefully. *Ponder* it before you act.

U

unusual *adj.* not usual, common, or ordinary. What an *unusual* idea!

exceptional much above average in quality or ability. She makes an *exceptional* lasagna.

extraordinary very unusual; beyond the ordinary. Crossing the ocean was an *extraordinary* act of daring.

rare seldom happening, seen, or found. I found a *rare* gem in her jewelry box.

uncommon rare or unusual. In this region, antelopes are *uncommon*.

unique having no equal or match; one of a kind. Jimbo has a *unique* view of the world. *See also* strange.

antonyms: usual, common *See also* plain.

Other synonyms: abnormal, queer, singular, irregular

upset *adj.* feeling uneasy; distressed. Bob was *upset* when Jules refused to answer him.

anxious uneasy or fearful of what may happen. Terry was *anxious* about her ability.

concerned troubled or worried. I get *concerned* about you when you come home so late.

disturbed in an unsettled state of mind. Cory was *disturbed* by Bill's lack of emotion.

nervous emotionally tense or restless; apprehensive or fearful. Patty felt *nervous* as she stepped onto the stage.

worried uneasy or troubled about something. We were so *worried* about your health.

antonym: calm

Other synonyms: agitated, distraught

V

very *adv.* to a great extent. It was *very* hot all morning.

considerably to a large or important degree. Your health is *considerably* more important than having fun.

extremely greatly or intensely. He reads *extremely* fast.

somewhat a little, to some extent. I am still *somewhat* unsure of what you really want.

W

walk *v.* to move or travel on foot. Will you *walk* home with me?

march to walk with regular steps. Will you *march* in the parade?

stride to walk with long steps, usually with a purpose. The boxers *stride* toward the ring.

stroll to walk in a relaxed or leisurely manner. Would you like to *stroll* through the park?

strut to walk in a vain or very proud way. He loves to *strut* around in his leather jacket.

want *v.* to have a desire or wish for. Do you *want* to go home?

crave to want badly, often in an

uncontrollable way. Mom *craved* pickles when she was pregnant.

desire to have a strong wish for. Just give me a chance; that's all I *desire.*

wish to have a longing or strong need for. Laurie *wished* she would grow a little faster.

yearn to feel a strong and deep desire. After three weeks at camp, I *yearned* for home.

wet *adj.* covered or soaked with water or other liquid. How did this rug get so *wet?*

damp slightly wet. After the rain, everything was *damp.*

moist slightly wet; damp. Make sure you keep the soil *moist.*

soggy damp and heavy. The book was *soggy* when we fished it out.

sopping extremely wet; dripping. Gene was *sopping* as he climbed out of the pool.

antonyms: See dry.

Other synonyms: drenched, dank

whole *adj.* made up of the entire amount, quantity, or number. Did you mow the *whole* yard?

complete having all its parts. Is this a *complete* set of glasses?

entire whole; having all its parts. I read the *entire* book.

total whole, full, or entire, often referring to numbers. The *total* cost was $53.20.

Y

yell *v.* to call or cry out loudly. Please don't *yell* at me.

bellow to cry out in a loud, deep voice. The bear *bellowed* in pain.

holler to yell, especially in a rough-sounding way. Everyone in the gym started *hollering.*

scream to cry out in a loud, shrill, piercing way. Have you ever heard an eagle *scream?*

shout to cry out loudly. "Watch out!" *shouted* Boris.

LETTER MODELS

A Friendly Letter

Letters are frequently the best way to communicate with friends. Writing allows you time to say exactly what you mean. Also, a letter can be read over to keep thoughts fresh. Letters written to friends and family are called friendly letters. Invitations and thank-you letters are also often in the form of a friendly letter.

Friendly letters use **informal** language. They may contain contractions, sentence fragments, and the "latest expressions," depending on your purpose and audience.

Read the following friendly letter.

Heading	114 E. Franklin Street Chapel Hill, NC 27504 June 15, 19--
Greeting Body	Dear Aunt Jeannette, Well, graduation is finally over, and next year I will move on to high school. I can hardly picture myself up there with the "big guys." It's all very exciting. Thank you for remembering the day of my big move. Your note was very sweet and helped make the day special. Now I have the whole summer to spend doing all those things that school never seems to leave time for. I will start by going to Raleigh for a special course for students interested in journalism. I know I will learn much. After that the family will head down your way, so practice up on making hot biscuits.
Closing	Much love,
Signature	*Warren*

A Business Letter

Sometimes you want to obtain information, make a complaint, or place an order. You might perform these tasks by phone. However, it is usually better to write a business letter. First, your letter is a written record of your business transaction. Also, a letter gives you time to express yourself clearly and politely.

The style of a business letter is a little different from the style of a friendly letter. A business letter is more direct and more **formal.** The letter should include all the necessary information.

Read the following business letter.

Heading	1502 Pine Street San Francisco, CA 94110 November 4, 19--
Inside Address	Video Visions P.O. Box 837 Chicago, Illinois 60645
Greeting	Dear Sir:
Body	I recently read in *Video News* that your company is planning to start a video tape club for fans of the music of the "Big Band" era. I am very interested in learning of your plans and what I have to do to join this club. Would you please send me any information you may have about this project. I am also anxious to know if your tapes will be taken from films of the original performers or whether you plan to film new material with the bands on the soundtrack. I look forward to hearing about this very exciting project.
Closing Signature	Yours truly, *Rosemarie Wagner* Rosemarie Wagner

SPELLING STRATEGIES

In your writing it is very important to spell every word correctly. Otherwise, the meaning of what you write may not be clear to your reader. Follow the listed steps below to help you to improve your spelling.

1. Learn some basic spelling rules.
2. Learn to spell some commonly misspelled words.
3. Learn to spell words by syllable.
4. Check your work carefully when you have finished writing.
5. Whenever you have a question about how a word should be spelled, use a dictionary to check the spelling.

Spelling Rules

Here are some rules to help you spell certain kinds of words correctly.

Words with *ie* and *ei*

Spell the word with *ie* when the sound is *ē*, except after *c*.

Examples: relief, believe, shield; deceit, perceive, ceiling

Spell the word with *ei* when the sound is not *ē*, especially if the sound is *ā*.

Examples: neigh, weight, eighty, sleigh

There are some exceptions to this rule.

Exceptions: either, seize, weird, friend

Words with *cede*, *ceed*, and *sede*

There are three words in English that end with *ceed* (*proceed*, *succeed*, and *exceed*). There is only one that ends with *sede* (*supersede*). All other words with a similar-sounding ending are spelled *cede*.

Examples: precede, concede, secede, recede

Making Nouns Plural

The plural of most nouns is formed by adding *s* to the singular. Sometimes when you make a noun plural, the spelling of the word changes. Here are some rules to help you spell these words correctly.

Adding *s* and *es*	In most cases, *s* can be added to a noun without changing the spelling.

Examples: trick + s = tricks
lamp + s = lamps

If a word ends in *ch, s, sh, x,* or *z,* add *es.*

Examples: wrench/wrenches, genius/geniuses,
clash/clashes, suffix/suffixes

Changing *f* to *v*	For most nouns ending in *f* or *fe,* change the *f* to *v* when adding *s* or *es.*

Examples: sheaf/sheaves, scarf/scarves,
self/selves

There are some exceptions to this rule.

Exceptions: roof/roofs, chief/chiefs

Words ending in *o*	For most nouns that end in *o* following a vowel, add *s* to form the plural. studio + s = studios, cameo + s = cameos. For most words that end in *o* following a consonant, add *es*: hero + es = heroes, potato + es = potatoes, echo + es = echoes. For words from the Italian language that refer to music, add *s*: pianos, solos.

Irregular nouns	Some nouns become plural in irregular ways. You must learn their plural forms.

Examples: ox/oxen, child/children,
mouse/mice, tooth/teeth,
goose/geese

Some words stay the same when singular or plural.

Examples: sheep, deer, series

Compound nouns	To form the plural of a compound noun written as one word, add *s* or *es*: leftovers, spoonfuls, stopwatches. If the compound is made up of a noun and modifiers, usually joined by hyphens, make the noun plural: editors-in-chief, presidents-elect, attorneys general. The plural forms of some compound nouns are irregular: ten-year-olds, drive-ins.

Foreign words	For some words taken from foreign languages, the plural in English is the same as the plural in the original language.

Examples: datum/data, alumnus/alumni, alumna/alumnae, crisis/crises

For other foreign words, the plural form from either the foreign language or English would be correct: index/indexes or indices, chateau/chateaus or chateaux.

Numbers, letters, signs, and words	To form the plural of a number, letter, sign, or word considered as a word, add an apostrophe and *s*.

Examples: 7's, two *x*'s, several #'s, too many *dear*'s

Adding Endings

With some words, if you add an ending such as *es*, *ed*, *ing*, *er*, or *est*, the spelling of the word may change. Here are some rules.

Changing *y* to *i*	If the word ends in a consonant and *y*, change the *y* to *i* before any ending that does not begin with *i*.

Examples: tally + es = tallies, hurry + ed = hurried, skinny + est = skinniest

However, for most words that end in a vowel and *y*, keep the *y* when adding an ending.

Examples: overjoy + ed = overjoyed, delay + ing = delaying

Doubling the final consonant	In most cases, if a one-syllable word ends in one vowel and one consonant, double the consonant when adding an ending that begins with a vowel.

Examples: skip + ed = skipped, grim + er = grimmer, chop + ing = chopping, thin + est = thinnest

For most two-syllables words ending in one vowel and one consonant, double the consonant if the accent is on the second syllable.

Examples: prefer + ed = preferred, compel + ing = compelling

Silent e If the word ends in a silent e, drop the e when adding an ending that begins with a vowel.

> **Examples:** sure + er = surer, strive + ing = striving, lame + est = lamest, graze + ed = grazed

Adding Prefixes and Suffixes

When a prefix is added to a word, the spelling of the word stays the same: bi + weekly = biweekly, sub + marine = submarine, fore + warn = forewarn.

When a suffix is added to a word, the spelling of the word may change. If the word ends in a silent e, drop the e when adding a suffix that begins with a vowel, as in: reptile + ian = reptilian, future + ist = futurist.

However, for most words ending in silent e, keep the e when adding a suffix that begins with a consonant.

> **Examples:** shame + less = shameless, side + ward = sideward, prince + ly = princely

> **Exceptions:** true + ly = truly, judge + ment = judgment

When adding the suffix *ness* or *ly*, the spelling of the word usually does not change, as in: ripe + ness = ripeness, cruel + ly = cruelly. However, if the word ends in y and has more than one syllable, change the y to i.

> **Examples:** gloomy + ness = gloominess, sneaky + ly = sneakily

Words Often Confused

There are many pairs of words that sound alike, or similar, but are spelled differently and have different meanings. Knowing what these words mean will help you choose—and spell—the correct word when you use it in your writing. Here are some examples. If you do not know what these words mean, look them up in the dictionary.

affect/effect	formerly/formally
accept/except	loose/lose
beside/besides	principal/principle
capital/capitol	quiet/quite
choose/chose	stationary/stationery
complement/compliment	to/too/two
council/counsel	weather/whether

OVERVIEW OF THE WRITING PROCESS

In this book you have learned that writing is a process. When you write, you follow certain steps. Sometimes you move back and forth between steps, but basically you proceed from the beginning to the end of the process.

Prewrite

- Decide on a purpose and an audience for your writing.
- Choose a topic that would be suitable for your purpose and audience.
- Explore ideas about your topic. You could brainstorm, make a cluster, or make a list.
- Narrow your topic if it is too broad to cover adequately.

Write a First Draft

- Use your prewriting ideas when writing your draft.
- Do not worry too much about making errors. Your goal is to get your ideas on paper.

Revise

- Read your draft. Share it with someone else to get a response.
- Ask yourself these questions about your draft.
  What else will my audience want to know? What details can I add?
  How can I make my purpose clearer?
  How can I make my writing easier to understand?
  How can I improve the organization of my writing?

Proofread

- Read your revised draft.
- Ask yourself these questions about your revised draft.
  Have I followed correct paragraph form?
  Have I used complete sentences?
  Have I used capitalization and punctuation correctly?
  Have I spelled all words correctly?

Publish

- Make a clean copy of your revised and proofread draft.
- Share your writing with the audience for whom you wrote it.

WRITER'S RESOURCES

STUDY STRATEGIES

Whenever you study, you should plan your time carefully. Keep a list of assignments. Decide how much time to spend on each task. Find a quiet, comfortable place to work. Make sure you have study materials handy—paper, pens and pencils, and reference works. Keep your work area clean and neat.

The SQ3R Method

There are many different ways to study. One method is called "SQ3R." The name stands for the five steps you should follow. These steps are summarized below.

1. **Survey**. Survey or scan the whole chapter or article you are going to read to get a general idea of what it covers.
2. **Question**. Prepare questions to help you understand the work. Use the title and any important headings to make up questions.
3. **Read**. Read the chapter or article. Look for answers to the questions you made up and look for important points in what you read.
4. **Record**. Write down the answers to the questions and important points.
5. **Review**. Look back over the article and the notes you have written.

The PROTO Method

The SQ3R Method is most useful for reading a chapter or an article. The PROTO Method can be used in studying all kinds of material. The PROTO Method includes five steps: Preview, Read, Organize, Take Notes, and Overview. Each step is described here.

1. **Preview**. First, preview the material to identify the general idea. Look at the title of the selection. Look at the major headings.
2. **Read**. Second, read the material. Read each part carefully and look at the headings again before you read each part. Identify the most important points in each section. If you don't understand part of what you read, look for clues in the headings and read the material again.

3. **Organize**. After you have read the material once, figure out how the important points should be organized. Important information may be organized by sequential order, classification, cause-effect, or comparison-contrast.
4. **Take notes**. Use the method of organization to take notes. Write down the important points in what you have read. You may want to write down each major idea or title, and then write notes under each idea. Or you may want to use an outline, a time line, or a flow chart.
5. **Overview**. Finally, read through your notes and the list of important ideas again to form an overview or summary of what you have read.

The PROTO Method can help you to study just about any kind of material.

Here are some additional skills that will help you use the PROTO Method.

Special Study Tips

Following Directions
For many assignments, your teacher will give you directions before you begin. Sometimes the directions will be spoken, sometimes written. Pay close attention to the directions.
1. Identify the steps you should follow.
2. Ask questions about any steps you are not sure you understand.
3. Collect the materials you will need for the assignment.
4. Follow the directions step by step.

Setting a Purpose
Before you begin studying, identify the purpose of your work. Your goal might be to identify the causes of an event, to find examples to support a theory, or to contrast two events or documents. Use the directions to help you identify the purpose of your study. Then stick to that purpose as you work.

Outlining
One way to organize your work and take notes about the material is to use an outline. An outline helps you decide what is most important and helps you put each important note in the right place. You can organize an outline by sequential order, classification, cause-effect, or comparison-contrast.

Mapping

Mapping is similar to outlining, but it uses a diagram or picture to organize ideas. You may choose to outline the information in an article by using a map, a time line (listing things in the order in which they happened), a diagram (a picture of how all the parts work together), or a flow chart (a diagram showing how each event leads to the next one).

Using Graphic Aids

Many selections include graphic aids such as maps, charts, tables, graphs, and diagrams. In many cases, the graphic aid provides a summary of important points in the selection. Look at the graphic aid carefully to figure out what it means, how the information relates to the selection, and why this information is important.

Memorizing

When you study something, you want to remember it. Here are some ways to help you memorize important information.

1. **Speak and write**

   First, say it aloud. Then write it down. Hearing and seeing what you want to remember will help you to memorize it more easily.

2. **Classify ideas**

   Think of a way to classify the information you want to remember. For example, you might list important events in chronological order. You might list important facts in alphabetical order or in groups related to categories such as "Causes" and "Effects."

3. **Invent memory joggers**

   A "memory jogger" might be a word or a funny sentence that helps you to remember things. For example, in chemistry there are six important inert gases: Helium, Neon, Argon, Krypton, Xenon, and Radon. You can remember them by making up a name, such as "HaNA KiXeR," or a silly sentence: "Have Now Acquired King's Xylophone Recordings." The first letter in each word of the sentence is the first letter in the name of each gas.

4. **Repeat**

   Repeat things as many times as you can. Repeating information often will help you to remember it.

Taking Tests

Taking tests is an important part of your schoolwork. You can use many of the study skills you have learned to make test-taking easier.

1. **Preview the test**. Look through the test quickly to see what it covers and how long it is.

2. **Plan your time**. Your teacher will tell you how much time you have to finish the test. Decide how much time to spend on each part of the test. Some parts may take longer than others. Reading stories, for example, will usually take longer than answering vocabulary questions. Keep track of the time as you work.

3. **Follow directions**. Listen to any directions your teacher gives you. Then read the test directions carefully before you begin the test. As you work through the test, read any directions you see at the beginning of each new section.

4. **Read questions carefully**. Read each test question carefully. Figure out exactly what the question means. Use key words to figure out what kind of answer is required. (Key words might include "why," "when," "who," "because," "after," and "what.") Then decide on your answer.

5. **Complete easy questions first**. Work through the test and finish every question for which you know the answer. Leave the difficult questions for last. Then go back and work on each difficult question.

6. **Mark your answers carefully**. If you are taking a multiple-choice test, fill in only one bubble for each question and fill it in completely. If you are writing your answers, write each one clearly and neatly so that the teacher can read it.

7. **Check your work**. When you have answered all the questions, use the time you have left to go back and check your work. Make sure that you have answered each question.

USING THE PARTS OF A TEXTBOOK

1. To get a general idea of what the book covers and how it is organized, examine the **table of contents** near the front. The table of contents lists the book's units or chapters and the pages on which they begin; it will also list any special sections found at the back of the book.

2. As you read a textbook chapter or unit, pay careful attention to any **opening or closing features** that identify or summarize key points. Textbook chapters often begin with objectives that tell you what you are about to learn; they often end with a list or paragraph that sums up the main points.

3. Pay careful attention to **highlighted features** within the chapter or unit. Textbooks often highlight key terms, definitions, and other important information by using headings and subheadings, bold (dark) or italic (slanted) print, special boxes, or special colors.

4. Make use of **handbooks, glossaries,** or any other **special features** at the back of the textbook. A **glossary** is an alphabetical list of words and their meanings; a **handbook** lists important facts or rules.

5. To find specific information in a textbook, consult its **index** at the back. The index is an alphabetical list of all the topics discussed in the book, along with their page numbers.

Practice Answer the following questions about *this* textbook.

1. What area of English is covered in all the odd-numbered units of the book? the even-numbered units?
2. What topic is covered in Unit 3? What more specific topic is covered in lesson 2 of Unit 3?
3. On what page does Unit 8 begin?
4. What special section appears near the end of every unit? In addition to the index, what special sections does the back of the book contain?
5. On what pages will you find a story by I.B. Singer?

WRITING APPLICATION A List

Choose another of your school textbooks. Briefly explain how the body of the book is organized. List any special features found at the beginnings or ends of chapters or units. Also list any special sections found at the back of the book.

USING A DICTIONARY

A **dictionary** is a book containing an alphabetical list of words and their definitions. Each listed word is called an **entry word**. Words with the same spellings but different meanings and origins—known as **homographs**—are listed as separate entry words, each followed by a small raised number called a super-script. **Guide words** at the top of each page show the first and last entry word on that page. The following sample dictionary entries appeared on a page with the guide words *gaunt/genius*. *Gauntlet*[1] and *gauntlet*[2] are homographs.

---

gaunt·let[1] (gônt′lit) *also,* **gant·let.** *n.* **1.** a heavy glove made of leather covered with armor plate or mail, used in medieval times to protect the hand. **2.** a glove having a long, flaring cuff. [Old French *gantelet.*] •**to take up the gauntlet.** to accept a challenge. •**to throw down the gauntlet.** to challenge.

gaunt·let[2] (gônt′lit) *also,* **gant·let.** *n.* a form of punishment in which the offender must run between two rows of people who strike him as he passes. [From earlier *gantelope,* from Swedish *gatlopp,* from *gata* lane + *lopp* running.] —**to run the gauntlet.** to be subject to a series of difficulties or severe opposition or criticism.

gawk (gôk) *v.i. Informal.* to stare stupidly; gape.

gawk·y (gô′ke) *adj.* **gawk·i·er, gawk·i·est.** awkward; clumsy. —**gawk′i·ly,** *adv.* —**gawk′i·ness,** *n.*

ga·zelle (gə zel′) *n. pl.,* **ga·zelles** or **ga·zelle.** any or various antelopes found in hot, dry regions of Africa and Asia. [French *gazelle,* from Arabic *ghazāl.*]

gen·e·sis (jen′ə sis) *n. pl.,* **gen·e·ses** (jen′ə sez′). the coming into being of anything; beginning; origin: *The tale had its genesis in a dream.* [Latin *genesis,* from Greek *genesis* origin, creation.]

ge·nie (jē′nē) *also,* **jin·ni.** *n.* in Arabic folklore, a spirit having magic powers.

---

at; āpe; fär; câre; end; mē; it; īce; pîerce; hot; ōld; sông; fôrk; oil; out; up; ūse; rüle; pull; tûrn; chin; sing; shop; thin; this; hw in white; zh in treasure. The symbol ə stands for the unstressed vowel sound heard in about, taken, pencil, lemon, and circus.

Dictionary entries offer the following information.

1. The entry word is broken into **syllables** separated by dots, dashes, or spaces; in the sample entries, dots are used. The syllable divisions show where you can divide a word if you need to break it at the end of a line. One-syllable words such as *gawk* cannot be divided.

2. The entry word also shows the correct **spelling**. If a word has more than one correct spelling—such as *gauntlet*, which is also spelled *gantlet*—the most common spelling is given first. Plural, past tense, and past participle forms are shown only if they need to be clarified, as in the case of the word *gazelle*. Also shown are the comparative and superlative adjective forms that end in *er* and *est*, such as the *gawkier* and *gawkiest* forms of *gawky*.

3. The **pronunciation** appears just after the entry word, usually in parentheses. Accents (′) show which syllables to stress; other symbols are part of the phonetic alphabet and are explained in the dictionary's **pronunciation key**. A short form of the key generally appears on each right-hand page; in the sample, it is at the bottom.

4. The word's **part of speech** is abbreviated; for example, *gawk* is an intransitive verb (*v.i.*). All of a dictionary's abbreviations are explained in a **key to abbreviations** in the front or back of the book.

5. The word's **definition** follows its part of speech; multiple definitions are numbered. Definitions are sometimes clarified with **examples** that show the meaning in context. The entry for *genesis* contains such an example.

6. **Usage labels** indicate definitions with limited or special usage. For example, the definition of *gawk* is labeled *Informal*, as it is used only in informal English.

7. The word's **etymology,** or history, often appears in brackets or parentheses near the start or end of the entry. In the sample entries, etymologies appear in brackets near the ends of entries.

8. Some entries show **additional forms** of the entry word, such as the adverb form *gawkily* in the entry for *gawky*. Entries also list and define **idioms** in which the entry word appears. An idiom is an expression that uses words in a sense different from their usual meaning. The entry for *gauntlet*[2] includes the idiom *to run the gauntlet.*

Practice Answer these questions by using the sample entries and pronunciation key on page 558.

1. How many syllables does *genesis* have?
2. What is the less common spelling of *genie*?
3. What is the plural of *genesis*?
4. Does the g in *genie* sound like the g in *good* or the g in *gesture*?
5. In pronouncing *genesis*, which syllable is stressed?
6. As what part of speech is *genesis* used?
7. Which sentence uses *gawk* correctly?
   (a) He gawked the queen.
   (b) He gawked at the queen.
   (c) Your Highness, I apologize for the gawk look.
8. Is a person who *throws down the gauntlet* most likely (a) defiant, (b) cowardly, or (c) skilled in leather making?
9. From what language does *gazelle* originally come?
10. What is the noun form of *gawky*?
11. From what language does *genesis* originally come?
12. What is the preferred plural form of *gazelle*?
13. What part of speech are *gawkier* and *gawkiest*?
14. Why would you not use *gawk* in a business letter?
15. What would you experience if you "ran the gauntlet"?

WRITING APPLICATION Dictionary Entry

Using the style of the sample entries, create a dictionary entry for an imaginary word. Show the word's syllables, pronunciation, and part of speech as well as its definition(s). Also include other dictionary features, such as a usage label or a made-up etymology.

USING THE LIBRARY

The library offers a wealth of material for research or reading pleasure. To help you find books in a library, every book is cataloged. The library catalog may consist of index cards filed in drawers or of computer printouts in booklets or on microfilm. Although catalog systems vary, every system presents similar information. Nonfiction books are listed by author, title, and subject; fiction, by author and title. Listings are alphabetical: authors are alphabetized by last name; titles, by first word, excluding *A, An,* and *The.* The library's three-way catalog system allows you to find a book when you know only its author or only its title, or to locate nonfiction books on a particular subject when you do not know their authors or titles. Here are three sample catalog listings for the same nonfiction book.

Author Card

973.73	McPherson, James M.
M	Battle Cry of Freedom: The Civil War Era
	New York: Oxford University Press, c. 1988
	904 p.: illus., maps

Title Card

	Battle Cry of Freedom: The Civil War Era
973.73	McPherson, James M.
M	New York: Oxford University Press, c. 1988
	904 p.: illus., maps

Subject Card

UNITED STATES HISTORY--CIVIL WAR

973.73   McPherson, James M.
M   Battle Cry of Freedom: The Civil War Era
             New York: Oxford University Press, c. 1988
             904 p.: illus., maps

Most libraries use the Dewey decimal system to catalog books; others use the Library of Congress system. In each system, non-fiction books are assigned **call numbers** according to their subject. (The book in the sample listings has been assigned a call number in the Dewey decimal system.) On the library shelves, books are arranged by their call numbers, which are printed on the books' spines. Thus, once you learn a book's call number from one of its catalog listings, you can locate the book on the library shelves by following the sequence of call numbers.

Libraries often keep reference books in a special section; their call numbers are usually preceded by *R* or *Ref.* Fiction books are not assigned call numbers; instead they are kept in a special fiction section arranged alphabetically by authors' last names. Biographies are often kept in a special section arranged alphabet-ically by the last names of their subjects.

Practice **A.** Answer these questions about finding library books.

1. In which catalog listing (author, title, or subject) and under what letter would you look to find names and call numbers of science books by Isaac Asimov?
2. In which catalog listing (author, title, or subject) and under what letter would you look to find out who wrote *The New Universe*?
3. In which catalog listing (author, title, or subject) and under what letter would you look to find names and call numbers of books about the sun?
4. How many catalog listings would Isaac Asimov's science-fiction novel *I, Robot* have?
5. Under what letter would *The Pearl* by John Steinbeck be alphabet-ized in the library's fiction section?
6. Under what letter would Samuel Eliot Morison's biography of Columbus be found in the library's biography section?

B. Use this catalog listing to answer questions 7–15.

```
                        Arctic Dreams

508.98                  Lopez, Barry H.
L                       New York: Scribner's, c. 1986
                        496 p.
```

7. Is this an author, title, or subject listing?
8. Who wrote the book?
9. What is the book's title?
10. In what year was the book published?
11. Who published the book?
12. In what city was the book published?
13. How long is the book?
14. What is the book's call number?
15. Is this book fiction or nonfiction? How do you know?

Reference Works

The books in a library's reference section are a good starting point for research. To get an overview of a research topic, you can consult an **encyclopedia**, a multivolume reference work with articles arranged alphabetically by subject. To find out which articles cover the topic you are researching, look up the topic in the encyclopedia's index, which is usually the last volume.

In addition to books, most libraries offer other print media— such as newspapers and magazines—as well as nonprint materials, such as records and videocassettes. Magazines and newspapers—called **periodicals**—can be a valuable source of up-to-date information. Most libraries keep recent issues of periodicals in a special reading area. Older issues are stored in bound volumes or on space-saving microfilm.

To find out which periodical contains an article on a particular topic, you need to consult a **periodical index** at the library. The most widely used periodical index is the *Readers' Guide to Periodical Literature*, which lists magazine articles alphabetically by subject (and sometimes also by author). Each volume of the *Readers' Guide* covers articles published in a specific time period; thus, to find information on recent articles, you should consult a recent volume of the guide. A sample *Readers' Guide* entry appears below.

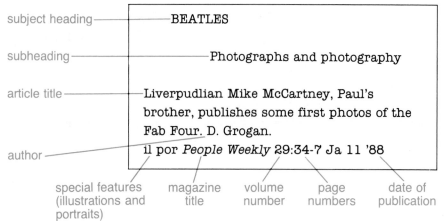

subject heading ——— BEATLES

subheading ——————————— Photographs and photography

article title ——————— Liverpudlian Mike McCartney, Paul's
brother, publishes some first photos of the
Fab Four. D. Grogan.

author ——————— il por *People Weekly* 29:34-7 Ja 11 '88

special features   magazine   volume   page   date of
(illustrations and   title   number   numbers   publication
portraits)

Practice

Use the *Readers' Guide* entry below to answer the questions that follow it.

BASEBALL PLAYERS

Retirement

Last goodbye to glory. T. Callahan. il *Time*
131:63 Ja 4 '88.

---

16. What is the subject heading for this entry?
17. Under what subheading does the entry appear?
18. In what magazine does the article appear?
19. What is the volume number of the magazine?
20. What was the date of publication?
21. On what page or pages does the article appear?
22. What is the title of the article?
23. Who wrote the article?
24. What special feature does the article contain?
25. Under what letter was this entry alphabetized in the *Readers' Guide*?

WRITING APPLICATION A List

Choose a research topic. Then use the library catalog, the *Readers' Guide*, and the library reference section to prepare bibliography cards for five nonfiction books, three magazine articles, and two encyclopedia articles that could help you research the topic.

SKIMMING AND SCANNING

When you are studying or doing research, skimming and scanning can help you use your time efficiently. **Skimming** is the process of glancing quickly at written material to discover its general content. For example, you might skim a book's table of contents to get an idea of what the book treats and how it is organized, or you might skim a magazine article or book chapter to see if it covers information that could be useful in your research.

Scanning is the process of reading quickly to find a specific item of information. For example, to find the page on which your biology textbook discusses photosynthesis, you would scan the *P* section of the book's index until you located the listing for *photosynthesis*. If you then wanted to find the definition of *photosynthesis*, you would scan the page on which photosynthesis is discussed until you came to the term's definition.

Practice   **A.** Skim this table of contents. Then cover it with a sheet of paper and answer the questions below it.

Contents

Part I. Early Detective Fiction

Part II. Twentieth-Century Detective Fiction

---

1. What general subject is the book about?
2. Into how many parts is the body of the book divided?
3. In addition to the index, what special section does the back of the book contain?

4. If you were researching Sherlock Holmes, would this book probably be useful? If you were researching mystery writers before Poe, would it be useful?
5. Which of these research topics does the book cover?
   (a) female writers of detective fiction
   (b) TV and movie detectives
   (c) real-life police investigations

B. Scan the index below to find answers to the questions.

6. On what page is Ross MacDonald discussed?
7. On what page is Sir Arthur Conan Doyle discussed?
8. Where would you find information about British whodunits?
9. Where would you find information about American armchair detectives?

Index

armchair detectives
   in American fiction, 205, 217
   in British fiction, 103–5
Brown, Father, 118, 121
Chandler, Raymond, 169–71
Chesterton, G. K. 118, 121
Christie, Agatha 101–10, 153
Conan Doyle—*see* Doyle
Daughter of Time, The, 208
Doyle, Arthur Conan, 27–58, 59
Hammett, Dashiell, 171–3
Holmes, Sherlock, 27–58, 59
Hound of the Baskervilles, The,
   35–37
James, P. D., 207, 211
MacDonald, John D., 175–6
MacDonald, Ross, 178

Marlowe, Philip, 169–71
Marple, Jane, 101, 103–4, 108
Marsh, Ngaio, 119–21
McBain, Ed, 173
McGee, Travis, 175–6
Murders in the Rue Morgue, The,
   4–7
Poe, Edgar Allan, 3–26, 29
Poirot, Hercule, 101, 103, 105
Queen, Ellery, 217
Sayers, Dorothy L., 111–18
Scotland Yard, 36, 103, 164, 215
Study in Scarlet, A, 27–30, 33, 39
Tey, Josephine, 208
Victorian detective fiction, 59–100
   see also Doyle
whodunits, British, 102–5, 111, 167

WRITING APPLICATION Questions

Cut out an informational article from a newspaper or magazine. Write five questions about its general content—questions that could be answered by skimming the article. Also write five questions about specific information in the article—questions that could be answered by scanning the article. Exchange articles and questions with a classmate. Skim and then scan your classmate's article to answer his or her questions.

TAKING NOTES

Whether you are learning information in class or from your textbooks, taking notes will help you get the most out of the learning experience. Writing information down helps you remember it, and your notes will be a valuable aid when you study for tests. You will also need to take notes for research reports or similar projects.

Guidelines for Taking Notes

1. Label your notes.   For class notes, include the date and the class or subject; in fact, it is a good idea to organize your notebook into sections by subject. For notes from your textbooks, identify chapter and page numbers as well as the subject. For library books, list the title, author, editor (if any), publisher, city of publication, publication date, and page numbers.

2. Paraphrase and summarize most of the notes you take.
Paraphrasing means rewriting ideas in your own words, a process that will help you remember and understand the information. **Summarizing** means writing only the main ideas and important details, a process that saves time and helps you focus on what you most need to know. Since you cannot possibly write down everything your teacher says in class, summarizing enables you to take the most effective notes you can.

3. Use key terms.   Be aware of the means by which your teachers and textbooks highlight the important information that you should include in your notes. Most teachers highlight key terms, definitions, and other important information by speaking more slowly or by writing them on the chalkboard. Textbooks highlight important information by using headings and subheadings, bold (dark) or italic (slanted) print, special colors or boxes, or illustrations such as maps and tables; they may also include special sections that summarize key information in a chapter.

4. Use words and phrases.   To save time, take notes in words and phrases rather than full sentences. You can also use abbreviations and symbols, but be sure you will understand them later.

5. Organize your notes.   You can organize your notes by putting related ideas together and by listing specific details under the main points that they illustrate or support. If necessary, rewrite your notes to organize them so they are clear.

Practice   Take notes on the textbook passages below.

Photosynthesis
Unlike people, who must obtain their food from outside sources, plants make their own food. The process by which plants make their food is called **photosynthesis**. As the word suggests, light (the Greek root *photo*) plays an important role in the process.

In photosynthesis, plants take *carbon dioxide* and *water* from the air and ground and, in the presence of *light*, turn them into *glucose* (sugar) and *oxygen*. They then use the glucose for food. The process is carried on in plant cells called *chloroplasts*, which contain a green substance called *chlorophyll* that captures the sunlight needed for the process to take place. Every green part of a plant contains chlorophyll and is thus capable of photosynthesis.

In effect, photosynthesis converts light energy into chemical energy. It uses sunlight (light energy) to create glucose, which is burned as food (chemical energy) so that the plant can function and grow.

Figure 5-1. *Photosynthesis*

$$\text{carbon dioxide} + \text{water} \xrightarrow[\text{of light}]{\text{in the presence}} \text{glucose} + \text{oxygen}$$

A plant's ability to capture light energy is truly remarkable. Each chloroplast is like a tiny solar energy system. Moreover, the workings of this system support all life on our planet. After all, plants provide all living creatures with food, either directly or indirectly. In addition, oxygen is a byproduct of photosynthesis. Thus plants also help supply the oxygen we breathe.

from *Biology*, Chapter V, p. 68

WRITING APPLICATION A Speech

Research a topic of your choice, taking notes from library books and other sources. Then use your notes to create a ten-minute speech on the topic. As you speak, use the chalkboard to highlight some of the important information. Have your classmates take notes about your speech.

OUTLINING

One of the clearest ways to list information on a subject is to use an outline. An outline has a special visual pattern that instantly shows how items of information are related. A **formal outline** uses a standard pattern of indents, numbers, and letters. Main topics or ideas are listed with Roman numerals (I, II, etc.). Subtopics or supporting ideas are indented and listed with capital letters. Details that give further support are indented further and listed with Arabic numerals (1, 2, etc.). Details that support those details are indented further and listed with small letters.

The Works of Sir Arthur Conan Doyle

I. Fiction
   A. Detective fiction
      1. Sherlock Holmes novels
         a. A Study in Scarlet
         b. The Sign of Four
         c. The Hound of the Baskervilles
         d. The Valley of Fear
      2. Sherlock Holmes stories
   B. Other fiction
      1. Professor Challenger tales
      2. Historical romances
II. Other works
   A. Histories
      1. Military histories
      2. Studies of Napoleonic times
   B. Stage dramas

Notice that the title of the outline is centered at the top; the first word of each listing begins with a capital letter; and the Roman-numeral listings align on the periods after the numerals. In addition, a formal outline must have at least two items at each level—that is, you cannot have a *I* without a *II*, an *A* without a *B*, and so on. Finally, items at the same level should use similar grammatical structures. In a **topic outline**, like the one above, words and phrases list topic, subtopics, and supporting details. In the **sentence outline** that follows, full sentences are used.

The Federal Government
I. The legislative branch, or Congress, makes the laws.
   A. The Senate is the senior house of Congress.
   B. The House of Representatives is the junior house.
II. The executive branch carries out the laws.
   A. The president is the chief executive.
   B. The vice-president assists the president.
   C. Cabinet members run various executive departments.
III. The judicial branch interprets the laws.
   A. Federal courts hear cases in different districts.
   B. The Supreme Court is the nation's highest court.
      1. Cases can be appealed to the Supreme Court.
      2. The Supreme Court interprets the Constitution.

You should follow formal outline style when you prepare an outline for your teacher or someone else to read. However, you will also find it valuable to outline information for your own use only. For instance, you can use an outline to organize your notes or to organize your thoughts before writing a paper or answering an essay question. In such cases, you can modify formal outline style, although you should still use indents to show how the information is related.

Practice Rearrange these items into a formal outline with the title Popular Sports.

Snow and ice sports	Alpine skiing
Basketball	Team ball games
Ball games	Golf
Other sports	Ice hockey
Cross-country skiing	Water sports
Individual ball games	Football
Baseball	Tennis
Swimming	Skiing
Rowing	Surfing

WRITING APPLICATION An Outline

Write a formal sentence outline for a subject you recently studied in science, social studies, or English.

ATLASES AND ALMANACS

Atlases and almanacs are valuable reference books. An **atlas** is a book of **maps**, drawings that show an area of the earth's surface. By providing an accurate picture of an area, a map helps you understand the locations of features and the relationships between them.

Some maps give a general picture of an area; others focus on specific features. For example, *topographical maps* focus on physical surface features, such as mountains and canyons; *road maps* focus on highways and other features important to travelers; and *historical maps* show places as they were at a certain time in history. Usually a map has a title that clarifies what it shows. The map below is a general map of Alaska.

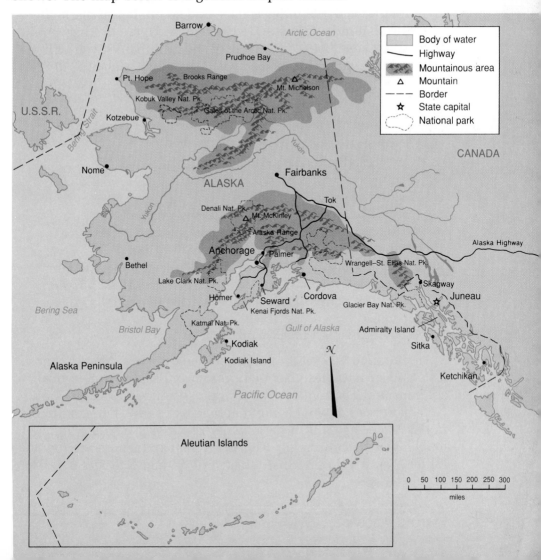

Most maps include a **key** or **legend** that explains the colors and symbols used. On the map of Alaska, the key is in the upper right corner; in some atlases, a general key appears in the front of the book. Maps also include a **north indicator** or a **direction indicator** that clarifies directions on the map. Traditionally, most maps are made with north at the top of the map and south at the bottom. If this varies, the direction indicator will be most useful. The map of Alaska has a north indicator. Once you know north, you can readily determine the other directions: east is to the right of north; south is directly opposite; and so on.

Maps are usually drawn to *scale*; that is, the actual size of the area they show and actual distances between points are scaled down proportionally. Most maps show the scale that was used. On the map of Alaska, the **scale of miles** in the lower right corner shows what 50 miles equals on the map (about a quarter of an inch), what 100 miles equals, and so on. If you mark off the scale's 50-mile points on the edge of a paper and then put the marked edge between Anchorage and Fairbanks, you will find that the actual distance between the cities is about 250 miles.

Practice   Use the map of Alaska to answer these questions.
1. What is the capital of Alaska?
2. What ocean lies to the north of Alaska?
3. What nation borders Alaska on the east?
4. What large river cuts through Alaska?
5. What major roadway heads northwest to Fairbanks?
6. Which city is further south, Seward or Juneau?
7. Of what mountain range is Mt. McKinley a part?
8. In what national park is Mt. McKinley located?
9. At their closest points, is the distance between Alaska and the U.S.S.R. (a) under 100 miles, (b) about 350 miles, or (c) just over 500 miles?
10. About how far is Fairbanks from Nome?

An **almanac** is a yearly published book of facts. Many of those facts appear in **tables**, lists that present information in vertical columns and horizontal rows. To find specific information on a table, you read down a column and across a row. For example, in the following table of national parks in Alaska, you would look down the column for Area (in Acres) and across the row for Katmai Nat. Pk. to find that the area of Katmai National Park is 3,716,000 acres.

National Parks in Alaska	Year Established	Area (in Acres)
Denali Nat. Pk.	1917	4,700,000
Gates of the Arctic Nat. Pk.	1978	7,500,000
Glacier Bay Nat. Pk.	1925	3,225,000
Katmai Nat. Pk.	1918	3,716,000
Kenai Fjords Nat. Pk.	1978	670,000
Kobuk Valley Nat. Pk.	1978	1,750,000
Lake Clark Nat. Pk.	1978	2,874,000
Wrangell–St. Elias Nat. Pk.	1978	8,945,000

Practice   Use the preceding table to answer these questions.

11. Which is the largest of Alaska's national parks?

12. Which is the smallest of Alaska's national parks?

13. In what year was Katmai National Park established?

14. Which of Alaska's national parks was established first?

15. What is the area of Lake Clark National Park?

In addition to tables, almanacs may use graphs to present numerical information. A **bar graph** uses bars to relate the information on its horizontal axis to the information on its vertical axis. For example, in the following bar graph of normal monthly temperatures in Fairbanks, Alaska, the horizontal axis lists the months of the year and the vertical axis lists temperatures in degrees Fahrenheit (from −20 to 70 degrees). Since the bar for April ends at the 30 point of the vertical axis, Fairbanks's normal temperature in April is 30 degrees Fahrenheit.

Normal Monthly Temperatures in Fairbanks, Alaska

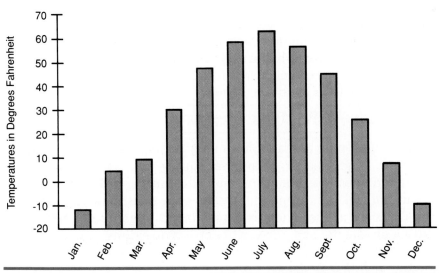

A **circle graph** shows the parts of a whole. For example, in the circle graph of Employment in Alaska, the whole circle is divided into parts that show the fraction or percentage of Alaskans working in various labeled fields. Since a bit more than one fourth, or 25 percent, of the circle is labeled *government*, you know that a bit more than one fourth, or 25 percent, of employed Alaskans work for the government.

Employment in Alaska

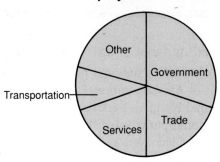

Practice   Use the two graphs to answer these questions.

16. What is the normal December temperature in Fairbanks?
17. What is normally the warmest month in Fairbanks?
18. What is normally the coldest month in Fairbanks?
19. Is Fairbanks normally colder in May or September?
20. In Fairbanks, is there normally a greater temperature drop from October to November or November to December?
21. In which three consecutive months does Fairbanks's temperature normally change the least?
22. Is the fraction of Alaskans employed in transportation (a) under one tenth, (b) about one fourth, or (c) over one third?
23. Is the percentage of Alaskans employed in trade (a) a bit less than 25 percent, (b) a bit more than 25 percent, or (c) about 50 percent?
24. Do more Alaskans work in services or transportation?
25. Who is the biggest employer in Alaska?

WRITING APPLICATION Questions

Find a map and a table in an atlas, an almanac, a tourist brochure, a newspaper, or another source you can bring to class. Write ten questions about the map's features and five questions about the table's information; model your questions on those in the Practices above. Then exchange maps, tables, and questions with a classmate, and answer his or her questions.

DI~

A sentence ~
sentence are relate~
horizontal line called ~
ing only the most importa~
learn to diagram every word i~

Simple Subjects and Simple P~

The two most important parts of any sen~
and the predicate. These sentence parts are diag~
simple subject and simple predicate are written on ~
A vertical line intersects the base line and separates the subject
and the verb.

My family is planning another vacation.

family	is planning

Often the subject of an imperative sentence does not appear in
the sentence. The subject is understood to be *you*. See how the
subject of an imperative sentence is diagramed.

Keep the maps and pamphlets.

(you)	Keep

Practice   Diagram the simple subject and simple predicate.

1. Mother prefers an automobile trip.
2. Dad would like a vacation spot on the beach.
3. I am hoping for some good photographs.
4. Our last vacation was too short.
5. Come with us.

Compound Subjects and Compound Predicates (pp. 8–9)

A compound subject or predicate has two or more parts. Each
part is written on a separate horizontal line. The conjunction
that connects the parts is written on a dotted line.

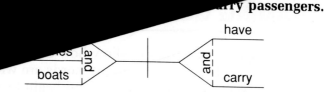

Practice Diagram the simple or compound subject and the simple or compound predicate in each of these sentences.

1. Cars and planes may have gasoline engines.
2. Boats use engines or depend on the wind.
3. Sailors, drivers, and pilots need skills and must like travel.
4. Men, women, and children travel and learn.
5. Stop, think, and decide for yourself.

Predicate Nouns (pp. 138–139)

A predicate noun is written on the base line and is separated from the verb by a slanted line. Remember that a pronoun can take the place of a noun, so that some predicate nouns are actually pronouns.

My favorite game is checkers.

Practice Diagram the subjects, verbs, and predicate nouns or pronouns in these sentences.

1. My family are constant players.
2. Dedicated students are we.
3. Checkers became a challenge to us.
4. Our games are family events.
5. The winner and new champion is she.

Predicate Adjectives (pp. 138–139)

A predicate adjective modifies the subject of a sentence. The predicate adjective is written on the base line. It is separated from the verb by a slanted line, just as a predicate noun is.

Many fads seem silly.

fads | seem \ silly

DIAGRAMING GUIDE

A sentence diagram uses lines to show how all the words in a sentence are related. The most important words are written on a horizontal line called the **base line.** You will begin by diagraming only the most important words. In later lessons you will learn to diagram every word in a sentence.

Simple Subjects and Simple Predicates (pp. 6–7)

The two most important parts of any sentence are the subject and the predicate. These sentence parts are diagramed first. The simple subject and simple predicate are written on the base line. A vertical line intersects the base line and separates the subject and the verb.

My family is planning another vacation.

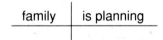

Often the subject of an imperative sentence does not appear in the sentence. The subject is understood to be you. See how the subject of an imperative sentence is diagramed.

Keep the maps and pamphlets.

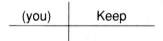

Practice   Diagram the simple subject and simple predicate.

1. Mother prefers an automobile trip.
2. Dad would like a vacation spot on the beach.
3. I am hoping for some good photographs.
4. Our last vacation was too short.
5. Come with us.

Compound Subjects and Compound Predicates (pp. 8–9)

A compound subject or predicate has two or more parts. Each part is written on a separate horizontal line. The conjunction that connects the parts is written on a dotted line.

Cars, planes, and boats have engines and carry passengers.

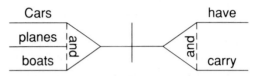

Practice   Diagram the simple or compound subject and the simple or compound predicate in each of these sentences.

1. Cars and planes may have gasoline engines.
2. Boats use engines or depend on the wind.
3. Sailors, drivers, and pilots need skills and must like travel.
4. Men, women, and children travel and learn.
5. Stop, think, and decide for yourself.

Predicate Nouns (pp. 138–139)

A predicate noun is written on the base line and is separated from the verb by a slanted line. Remember that a pronoun can take the place of a noun, so that some predicate nouns are actually pronouns.

My favorite game is checkers.

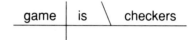

Practice   Diagram the subjects, verbs, and predicate nouns or pronouns in these sentences.

1. My family are constant players.
2. Dedicated students are we.
3. Checkers became a challenge to us.
4. Our games are family events.
5. The winner and new champion is she.

Predicate Adjectives (pp. 138–139)

A predicate adjective modifies the subject of a sentence. The predicate adjective is written on the base line. It is separated from the verb by a slanted line, just as a predicate noun is.

Many fads seem silly.

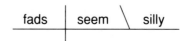

Practice Diagram the subjects, verbs, and predicate adjectives in these sentences.

1. These strange fads seem endless.
2. Small dolls or figures became popular for a while.
3. Pet rocks are more recent and less rare.
4. Some fad items become valuable later.
5. An original hula hoop would be quite rare now.

Direct Objects (pp. 134–135)

A direct object is written on the base line after the verb. A vertical line separates the verb from the direct object. The vertical line does not go below the base line.

Hans Christian Andersen wrote many wonderful stories.

Hans Christian Andersen	wrote	stories

Some sentences may have more than one direct object.

He created poems, plays, and tales.

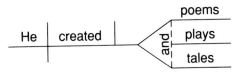

Practice Diagram subjects, verbs, and direct objects in these sentences.

1. His stories have many wonderful characters.
2. In one, a lead soldier loves a beautiful dancer.
3. He described emperors, nightingales, and magic.
4. Children love his tales and read them again and again.
5. Children and adults enjoy films, plays, and ballets of his stories.

Indirect Objects (pp. 136–137)

The indirect object is placed on a line under the base line. A slanting line connects the indirect object to the verb in the sentence diagram.

The teacher gave us a difficult quiz.

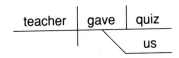

Practice Diagram the subjects, verbs, direct objects, and indirect objects in these sentences.

1. Most students handed her their finished papers.
2. She always gave them a smile.
3. She offered my friend and me a little more time.
4. We gave her our tests, too.
5. She gave me a star and promised him extra help.

Adjectives (pp. 284–285)

Adjectives are diagramed on a slanting line below the word they modify. A series of adjectives is joined by a dotted line. The word *and* or *or* is written on the dotted line.

A spring garden may contain yellow, white, or pink tulips.

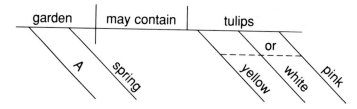

Practice Diagram every word in these sentences.

1. Older tulips won high prices.
2. Many Dutch buyers preferred beautiful and unusual tulips.
3. People sought rare, unusual, or popular bulbs.
4. Such high prices consumed many great fortunes.
5. Several proud families lost great estates.

Adverbs (pp. 294–295)

An adverb that modifies a verb is written on a slanting line below the verb. An adverb that modifies an adjective or another adverb is written on a line parallel to the word that it modifies and is connected to it by a line. Conjunctions that connect two or more adverbs are written on a dotted line.

The very elaborate program ran smoothly and quite easily.

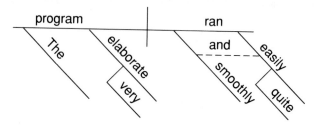

Practice Diagram every word in these sentences.

1. The rather long first act went well.
2. The very fine actors spoke softly but quite movingly.
3. My very first costume looked quite nice.
4. Some older actors smiled encouragingly.
5. A very good director and a rather fine writer work here often.

Prepositional Phrases (pp. 358–359)

A prepositional phrase is added below the base line. The preposition is written on a slanted line below the word it modifies. The object of the preposition is written on a line parallel to the base line. Diagram modifiers in the usual way.

The story of the rabbit in the hat is one of my favorites.

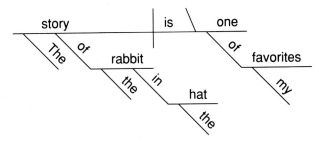

Practice Diagram every word in these sentences.

1. The man in the story meets a friend on the street.
2. The man tips his hat and reveals a rabbit on his head.
3. His friend requests an explanation from him.
4. The man with the hat is silent for a long time.
5. Then the rabbit removes the man under him.

Appositives (pp. 74–75)

In a diagram an appositive appears in parentheses after the noun or pronoun it explains. Modifiers of appositives are written in the usual way.

Jumbo, the famous elephant, was a huge animal.

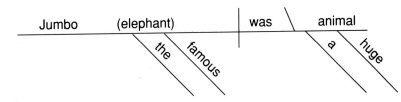

Practice Diagram every word in these sentences.

1. Jumbo arrived in London, England's capital, in 1865.
2. Children rode in a howdah, a covered seat, on his back.
3. P.T. Barnum, an American showman, bought Jumbo in 1881.
4. Jumbo, a gigantic elephant, was used for publicity.

Participles and Participial Phrases (pp. 440–441)

A participial phrase is diagramed like a prepositional phrase. The participle is written on a slanting line connected to a horizontal line. If the participle has an object, it is written on the horizontal line.

Wearing a grin, the boy asked the desired questions.

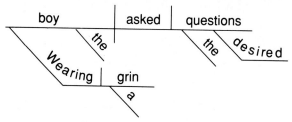

Practice Diagram every word in these sentences.

1. Knowing my answer, the boy read the next typed card.
2. Anticipating my reply, he tapped his toe on the floor.
3. Finally I remembered the needed information.
4. Taking my time, I spoke with increasing excitement.
5. The requested answer was correct, winning the game.

Gerunds and Gerund Phrases (pp. 442–443)

A special line called a **standard** is used for gerunds. The standard is placed where it belongs in the diagram. Then the gerund is written in a curve on the "steps" of the standard.

Good gardening means good planning and hard work.

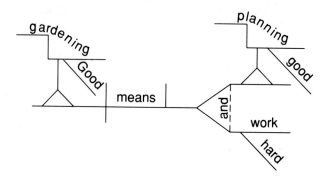

Practice Diagram every word in these sentences.

1. Planting must be done in the fall.
2. Beautiful gardens need digging and working with the dirt.
3. Weeding and watering are necessary and important steps.
4. Trimming of some plants makes flowers larger.
5. Waiting and wondering are the hardest parts of gardening.

Infinitives and Infinitive Phrases (pp. 444–445)

A diagram puts an infinitive used as a subject, a direct object, or a predicate noun on a standard. The object of the infinitive is placed on the horizontal line and set off by a vertical bar, just as a direct object is.

To play baseball well is difficult.

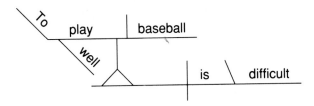

Practice Diagram every word in these sentences.

1. To practice means to improve your skills.
2. The challenge is to play well.
3. To be the best player is a common desire.
4. Many players want to succeed but fail to practice.
5. You must want to do your best and to play your best.

Compound Sentences (pp. 10–11)

Each independent clause of a compound sentence is diagramed as a separate sentence. The conjunction is written on a horizontal line betwen the two clauses. A dotted line connects the conjunction to the verb in each clause.

Hobbies are fun, but a workplace can be a problem.

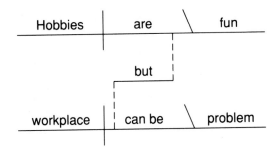

Practice   Diagram every word in these sentences.

1. I can happily make models, but my family complains about the mess.
2. Often I work on a small table, and my brother helps me.
3. We work together, or I work alone.
4. My mother and father give me advice, but I do most of the building alone.
5. I prefer company, but I often sit for hours by myself.

Adverb Clauses (pp. 436–437)

An adverb clause is diagramed as if it were an independent clause, but it is placed below the independent clause. The subordinating conjunction is written on a vertical dotted line between the verbs of both clauses. See how the adverb clause is diagramed below.

After I jog, I swim laps in the pool.

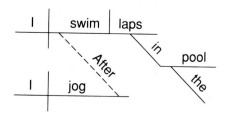

Practice   Diagram every word in these sentences.

1. I breathe carefully when I start my run in the morning.
2. If you forget your breathing, a pain can develop quickly.
3. I prefer a run before the laps in the pool cool me.
4. Until I have my own pool, I will use the city pool.
5. I will own a pool after I am very successful.

Adjective Clauses (pp. 432–433)

An adjective clause is diagramed as if it were an independent clause, but it is placed below the independent clause. Place the adjective clause under the word it modifies. A dotted line connects the word in the independent clause that is modified to the relative pronoun in the adjective clause. Diagram the relative pronoun according to its function in its own clause. See how the adjective clause is diagramed.

A book that I read often is the biography of Martin Luther King, Jr.

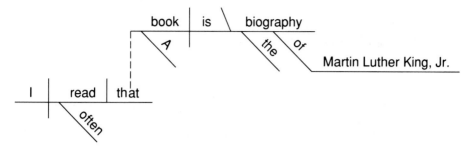

Practice Diagram every word in these sentences.

1. The book describes the circumstances that shaped his life.
2. The people whom he helped recognized his leadership.
3. There were many speeches that made him famous.
4. This man who worked so hard rarely rested or complained.
5. His biography, which I own, is complete in its details.

Noun Clauses (pp. 438–439)

A noun clause uses a standard. It is placed above the base line. When noun clauses begin with the word *that*, write *that* on a horizontal line connected by a dotted line to the verb in its clause. The regular rules of diagraming apply to noun clauses that do not begin with *that*.

What we wanted was that our request should be heard.

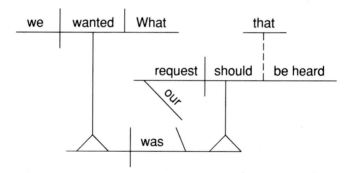

Practice Diagram every word in these sentences.

1. We did not know what the answer would be.
2. We hoped that our listeners would be very sympathetic.
3. Inform whoever is listening about our needs.
4. We mentioned what the plan required from others.
5. Often our listeners agree with whatever we say.

G L O S S A R Y

OF WRITING, GRAMMAR, AND LITERARY TERMS

WRITING TERMS

audience	the reader or readers for whom a composition is written
bibliography	a list of books, articles, and other sources used in writing a research report
brainstorm	to list any thoughts—words, phrases, questions—that come to mind about a writing topic
chronological order	the arrangement of events in the order in which they happen in time
first draft	the first version of a composition, in which the writer gets his or her basic ideas down on paper
overall impression	the general idea or feeling expressed in a description
personal narrative	a piece of writing in which the writer tells about something that has happened in his or her life
prewriting	the stage in the writing process in which the writer chooses a topic, explores ideas, gathers information, and organizes his or her material before writing a first draft
prewriting strategies	particular ways of gathering, exploring, planning, and organizing ideas before writing the first draft of a composition

- **charting** a way to gather ideas under different headings—
especially useful when comparing and contrasting

	Similarities	Differences
Purpose:	produce food	—early farming: mostly for personal use, some sales —modern farm: mostly commercial
Size:		—early farm: small —modern farm: large
Methods:		—early farm: horse and plow, manual —modern farm: huge machines, including tractors
Requirements:	love of nature, physical strength	—modern farming: understanding of business, chemistry, agriculture, mechanics

- **clustering** a way to explore ideas by gathering details
related to the writing topic

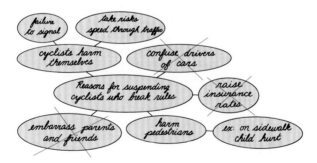

- **freewriting** a way to generate ideas by writing continuously
about thoughts and feelings for a specified time

School play ... which one? How about the first one. Oh, do
I remember that one! It was a musical—Guys and Dolls.
But there's so much that happened. Okay, I'll write about
how I tried out for it and rehearsals and those three
wonderful preformances. I was scared. It was the first
musical I had ever been in. I had a math test that day and
was late for try-outs. Then I forgot part of my monologue.

- **outline**

  a way to organize topic-related ideas in the order in which they will be discussed—especially useful in drafting a research report

The Works of Sir Arthur Conan Doyle
I. Fiction
  A. Detective fiction
    1. Sherlock Holmes novels
      a. A Study in Scarlet
      b. The Sign of Four
      c. The Hound of the Baskervilles
      d. The Valley of Fear
    2. Sherlock Holmes stories
  B. Other fiction
    1. Professor Challenger tales
    2. Historical romances
II. Other works
  A. Histories
    1. Military histories
    2. Studies of Napoleonic times
  B. Stage dramas

- **story outline**

  a way to organize story ideas and details in the order in which they will be treated

I. Beginning
  A. Introduce the main character. Parents? Sister?
  B. Describe the setting and the central problem.
    Should the story begin in the car? In town?
  C. Present the first event of the plot—the new job.
    Introduce conflict—Jason upset.

II. Middle
  A. Describe sequence of events.
    Pack up the house. Say good-bye to friends.
    Drive to new home. Or should they fly?
    See city for the first time—reactions?

- **time line**

  a way to arrange events in time order

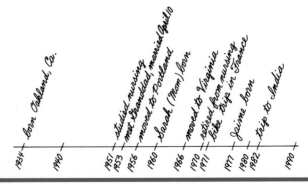

proofread	to correct errors in punctuation, capitalization, spelling, and grammar in a writing draft
publish	to share a composition with an audience
purpose	the writer's reason for writing a composition—for example, to explain, to entertain, or to persuade
revise	to improve the first draft of a composition by adding or taking out information, rearranging sentences, or changing word choice according to one's purpose and audience
supporting details	facts, examples, or sensory details that give more information about the main idea of a paragraph
topic sentence	sentence that states the main idea of a paragraph
transition words	words or phrases that link sentences in a paragraph, such as *next* and *for example*
writing conference	a meeting in which a writer discusses his or her writing with the purpose of improving it
writing process	the steps for writing a composition, including prewriting, writing a first draft, revising, proofreading, and publishing

GRAMMAR TERMS

action verb	a word that expresses action The carpenter *hit* the nail.
adjective	a word that describes a noun or a pronoun A *lazy* cat rested in the sunshine.
adverb	a word that modifies a verb, an adjective, or another adverb We *slowly* ate our picnic lunch.

antecedent	a word or group of words to which a pronoun refers *Aretha* came to the party, but *she* didn't stay.
appositive	a word or group of words that follows and identifies a noun Frank, *our neighbor*, helped start the car.
article	the special adjective *a, an,* or *the* *The* restaurant is *a* popular place.
common noun	a noun that names any person, place, thing, or idea Have you seen any good *movies* lately?
complete predicate	all the words that tell what the subject of a sentence does or is Charles *made the model ship from a kit.*
complete subject	all the words that tell whom or what a sentence is about *The first flight of stairs* is the longest.
complex sentence	a sentence that contains an independent clause and one or more subordinate clauses *Before you sit down, please close the window.*
compound sentence	a sentence that contains two or more simple sentences (independent clauses) *I am tired, but I will go with you anyway.*
conjunction	a word or words that join other words or groups of words in a sentence We were wet *but* happy.
direct object	a word that receives the action of a verb My sister ate the *grapes.*
gerund	a verb form that ends in *ing* and is used as a noun *Singing* in harmony takes practice.
indefinite pronoun	a pronoun that does not refer to a particular person, place, or thing *Someone* borrowed my pencil.
independent clause	a group of words that contains one complete subject and one complete predicate, and that can stand alone as a sentence *I will wait* until you decide.

indirect object	a noun or pronoun that answers *to whom? for whom? to what?* or *for what?* after an action verb Sarah gave *me* a book of puzzles.
infinitive	the base form of a verb preceded by the word *to*, often used as a noun *To begin* is often the hardest part.
interjection	a word or group of words that expresses strong feeling *Oops!* Be careful not to fall.
intransitive verb	a verb that does not take a direct object During the play we all *laughed* loudly.
irregular verb	a verb that does not form either the past tense or the past participle by adding *d* or *ed* I *drew* a diagram of how the gear functions.
linking verb	a word that connects the subject of a sentence to a noun or an adjective in the predicate The sequel to the movie *was* tiresome.
noun	a word that names a person, place, thing, or idea Describe the *story* for me.
object of a preposition	the noun or pronoun that follows the preposition in a prepositional phrase What is the name of your *dog*?
object pronoun	a pronoun that is used as the object of an action verb or as the object of a preposition The last scene in the movie scared *them*.
participial phrase	a group of words that includes a participle and other words that complete its meaning, all acting together as an adjective *Feeling lonely*, I called my friend.
participle	a verb form used as an adjective He drank some *bottled* water.
possessive noun	a noun that shows ownership The *student's* dictionary was always handy.
possessive pronoun	a pronoun that shows who or what owns something *Your* skateboard is wider than *mine*.

preposition	a word that relates a noun or pronoun to another word in a sentence The answer is printed *on* the card.
prepositional phrase	a group of words that begins with a preposition and ends with a noun or pronoun Carlos is the brother *of my best friend.*
pronoun	a word that takes the place of one or more nouns and the words that go with the nouns Drivers change gears as *they* come to a hill.
proper adjective	an adjective formed from a proper noun *African* art interests many collectors.
proper noun	a noun that names a particular person, place, thing, or idea *Cincinnati* is in southern *Ohio.*
run-on sentence	two or more sentences that have been joined together incorrectly *The team members on the bench were nervous they watched the game intently.*
sentence	a group of words that expresses a complete thought *The novel is very descriptive.*
sentence fragment	a group of words that does not express a complete thought *The entrance to the train station.*
simple predicate	the main word or words in the complete predicate Hanya *had read* many of Verne's novels.
simple subject	the main word or words in the complete subject of a sentence The *diving board* was very flexible.
subject pronoun	a pronoun that is used as the subject of a sentence *He* presided over the meeting with ease.
subordinate clause	a group of words that has a subject and a predicate but cannot stand alone as a complete sentence We waited *because we were hungry.*
transitive verb	a verb that takes a direct object Roberto *hit* the ball out of the field.

LITERARY TERMS

alliteration	the repetition of the same first letter or initial sound in a series of words—for example, "Sam saw six sisters smiling."
conflict	the central problem in the plot of a story
dialogue	the conversations in a story, poem, or play
haiku	a poem that has three lines and usually seventeen syllables, and that frequently describes something in nature
idiom	an expression whose meaning is different from the individual words composing it—for example, "Mr. Wilson is all tied up at the moment."
metaphor	a figure of speech in which a comparison is made without using the word *like* or *as*—for example, "The road was a ribbon of light."
meter	the systematic pattern of beats in a poem
mood	the particular feeling suggested by a description
onomatopoeia	the use of a word that imitates the natural sound of the thing described—for example, "The *mooing* of the cow woke us."
personification	a description in which human qualities are given to something that is not human—for example, "The soft wind caressed her cheek."
plot	the sequence of events in a story
point of view	the position from which a story is told
resolution	in a story, the working out of the problem presented in the plot
setting	the time and place in which a story occurs
simile	a figure of speech in which a comparison is made using the word *like* or *as*—for example, "The forest loomed ahead of us like a wall."

INDEX

adjectives, 288-291
added to form comparatives of
adverbs, 296-297
avoiding, with *more*, 296-297
Essays, 392-419
Essential clauses, 434-435
est
added to form superlatives of
adjectives, 288-291
added to form superlatives of
adverbs, 296-297
avoiding, with *most*, 296-297
Exclamation marks
ending sentences, 2-3, 14-15
after interjections, 370-371
Exclamatory sentences, 2-3, 14-15
Explanations, 190-209
writing, 196-203
Explanatory paragraphs
elements of, 190-193
putting together, 192-193
Extra Practice, 24-33, 88-97,
146-177, 236-245, 312-323,
382-391, 456-467

F

Facts, 406
cluster of, 412-413
opinions and, 406-407
slanted, 410
**Family relationships, capital-
izing words showing,** 76-77
Faulty methods of persuasion,
410-411
Figurative language, 338
First-person point of view,
114-115
Formal discussions, 124-125
Fragments, sentence, 12-13
Freewriting, 50-51
Friendly letters
commas after closings of,
302-303
commas after salutations of,
302-303
form of, 546

Future perfect tenses of verbs,
148-149
Future tenses of verbs, 142-143

G

Gender, agreement in, 214-215,
218-219
Gerund phrases, 442-443
Gerunds, 442-443

H

Handbook, Language Study
511-527
Helping verbs, 140-141, 144-153
Homophones and homographs,
228-229
**Hours, colons separating
minutes and,** 372-373
Hyphens
compound words, in, 80-81
syllables, between, 558
Hypotheses, writing, 206

I

Idioms, 22, 381
Imagery, 87, 381
Imperative sentences, 2-3, 4, 6,
14-15
Importance, order of, 191-192,
407
Impression, overall, 336-337
Incidents, telling about, 58-59
Indefinite articles, 286-287
Indefinite pronouns, 220-221
Independent clauses, 428-429
Independent Writing
biographical sketches, 268-275
descriptions, 342-349
editorials, 412-419
explanations, 196-203
personal narratives, 50-57
research reports, 494-503
short stories, 116-123

Mechanics
  capitalizing proper nouns, 76-77
  forming possessive nouns, 78-79
  punctuating sentences, 14-15
  using abbreviations, 226-227
  using commas to separate parts of sentences, 154-155
  using commas with addresses, dates, and names, 302-303
  using commas with clauses, 446-447
  using semicolons and colons, 372-373
Metaphors, 338
Minutes, colons separating hours and, 372-373
Misplaced modifiers, 362, 440
Months
  abbreviations for, 226-227
  using commas with, 302-303
Mood, 282
more and *most*
  in adjective comparison, 288-291
  in adverb comparison, 296-297
much, more, most, 290-291

N

Names, using commas with, 302-303
Narratives, 110
  personal. *See* Personal narratives
Narrators, 114-115
Narrowing topics, 51
Negative words, 298-299
Negatives, avoiding double, 298-299
Newspapers, capitalizing titles of, 76-77
Nominative case for pronouns, 216-217
Nonessential clauses, 434-435
Note cards, 58-59, 350-351
Notes, 204-205

taking, 486-488, 566-567
Noun clauses, 438-439
Noun-forming suffixes, 448
Nouns, 66-67
  abstract, 66-67
  collective, 72-73
  common, 66-67
  compound, 80-81
  concrete, 66-67
  of direct address, commas setting off, 154-155
  kinds of, 66-67
  plural. *See* Plural nouns
  possessive. *See* Possessive nouns
  possessive pronouns used before, 218-219
  predicate. *See* Predicate nouns
  proper. *See* Proper nouns
  showing number, 68-69
  singular, 68-69
Number
  agreement in, 214-215, 218-219
  nouns showing, 68-69
Numerals
  Arabic, to add details under subtopics, 496-497
  Roman, for main outline topics, 489

O

Object pronouns, 212-213, 216-217, 360-361
Objective case for pronouns, 216-217
Objects
  compound. *See* Compound objects
  direct. *See* Direct objects
  indirect, 136-137
Objects of prepositions, 358-359, 360-361
  compound, 364-365
  gerunds as, 442-443
  noun clauses as, 438-439
Omniscient point of view, 115

Quotation marks
in dialogues, 112
for exact words, 277, 488

R

Readers' Guide to Periodical Literature, 486, 563-564
Reasons, order of, 407
Rebuttals in debates, 420
Reference section, library, 486, 563-564
Reflexive pronouns, 222-223, 360-361
Relationships
cause-and-effect, 493-493
family, capitalizing words showing, 76-77
Relative pronouns, 432-433
Reports
book, 127
oral, effective, 504-505
paragraphs in, 489-490
research. See Research reports
Research reports, 486-509
elements of, 486-491
putting together, 491
writing, 494-503
Resolutions in stories, 110-111
Responding to Literature, 41, 107, 187, 259, 333, 403, 483
Revising, 53-54, 119-120, 199-200, 271-272, 345-346, 415-416, 499-500
Revising sentences, 450-451
Rhyme, 454
Rhythm, 454
Roman numerals for main outline topics, 489
Run-on sentences, 12-13

S

Salutations
of business letters, colons after, 372-373
of friendly letters, commas after, 302-303

Scanning and skimming, 564-565
Secondary characters in stories, 111
Semicolons, 372
in compound sentences, 10-11, 12, 14-15, 428-429
before conjunctive adverbs, 368-369
using, 372-373
Sensory details, 337-338
Sentence fragments, 12-13
Sentence outlines, 489
Sentences, 2-33
beginning, 44-45
clauses and, 428-429
colons introducing lists of items ending, 372-373
combining. See Combining sentences
commas separating parts of, 154-155
complete, 2-13
complex, 430-439
compound, 10-11, 364-365, 428-429
concluding, 192
declarative, 2-3, 14-15
diagraming, 574-582
exclamatory, 2-3, 14-15
imperative, 2-3, 4, 6, 14-15
interrogative, 2-3, 4, 6, 14-15
kinds of, 2-3
punctuating, 14-15
reviewing structure, 574-582
run-on, 12-13
simple, 10-11, 428-429
topic, 190-191, 340
Sequence, understanding, 266-267
Series, commas separating items in, 154-155
Settings for stories, 111
Sharing, 57, 123, 203, 275, 349, 419, 503
Short stories, 110-129
elements of, 110-113
putting together, 112-113
writing, 116-123

Brief quotation by James Michener from *Writers on Writing* published by Running Press. Copyright 1986 by Jon Winokur. Used by permission.

"When I Was Young" from *Report of the Fifth Thule Expedition* transcribed by Knud J. Rasmussen. By permission of Rudolf Sand & William Bentzen, Copenhagen.

Brief quotation by Isaac Bashevis Singer from "Profile Isaac Bashevis Singer: Good Luck for Children!" by Roy Eugene Toothaker in *Language Arts.* April 1978. Copyright © 1978 by the National Council of Teachers of English and used with their permission.

Excerpt from "Nightfall" from *Juan Ramon Jimenez: Three Hundred Poems, 1903-1953,* translated by Eloise Roach. English version reprinted by permission of the University of Texas Press.

Maya Angelou quotation is from *Something About the Author:* Volume 49. Edited by Anne Commire. Copyright © 1987 by Gale Research Company. All rights reserved. Reprinted by permission of the publisher.

"Late Starting Dawn" is from *Rommel Drives on Deep into Egypt* by Richard Brautigan. Copyright © 1970 by Richard Brautigan.

Reprinted by permission of The Helen Brann Agency, Inc.

"Reward for a Thing Well Done" is excerpted from *Famous Men of Science* by Sarah K. Bolton, revised by Barbara Lovett Cline. (Thomas Y. Crowell) Copyright © 1960 by Thomas Y. Crowell Company. Used by permission of Harper & Row, Publishers, Inc.

"Thoughts on Modern Painting" is excerpted from *Jackson Pollock: Energy Made Visible* by B. H. Friedman. Copyright © 1972 by B. H. Friedman. All rights reserved. Reprinted by permission of the Author's Representative, Gunther Stuhlman.

Brief quotation by Margaret Atwood is from *Barnes & Noble Book of Quotations*, edited by Robert I. Fitzhenry. Copyright © 1987 by Fitzhenry & Whiteside Limited. All rights reserved. Reprinted by permission of Harper & Row, Publishers, Inc.

Egmont Arens quotation is from W. G. Briggs, *The Camera in Advertising and Industry*, London, 1939, p. 5.

"The Lone Eagle Arrives in Paris" is from *We* by Charles A. Lindbergh. Copyright 1927 G. P. Putnam's Sons, New York, and used with their permission.

"Future Robots" is excerpted from "Hans on Robots" by Fred D'Ignazio. © 1990 Children's Television Workshop. Used by permission of Children's Television Workshop.

"Cells and Circuits" is excerpted from "Nerves of Silicon" by T. A. Hepperheimer. © 1988 Discover Publications, Inc. Used by permission of the publisher.

Excerpt from "Adman's Nightmare: Is the Prune a Witch?" by Robert Graham, from *The Reporter*, October 13, 1953. This has been retitled "The Point of Advertising" and is used by permission of Richard Curtis Associates, Inc. on behalf of the author.

ILLUSTRATION CREDITS: Dan Bridy, 252–259; Bill Cleaver, 22–23, 86, 162, 234, 310, 380–381, 454–455; Eva Vagreti-Cockrille, 63, 129, 209, 281, 355, 425, 509; Marcus Hamilton, 326–333; Mary Haverfield, 102–107; Ketti Kupper, 394–403; Ondre Pettingill, 476–483; Jan Pyk, 42, 60, 108, 126, 188, 206, 260, 278, 334, 352, 404, 422, 484, 506; Mel Wilgiles, 36–41.

PHOTO CREDITS: ALASKAPHOTO: Tom Bean, 65. AMERICAN MUSEUM OF NATURAL HISTORY: Art work by Helmut Wimmer, courtesy, Department of Library Services, 428. APERTURE PHOTOBANK: John Feingersh, 42B; Marty Loken, 369; Tom Tracy, 445. ARCHIVES OF 76, BAY VILLAGE, OH: *Drafting the Declaration of Independence*, © J.L.G. Ferris, 132. ART RESOURCE: Giraudon (Bayeux Tapesty detail, Musee del'Eveche), 450; Scala ("Poseidon" detail, Athens National Museum), 284. THE BETTMAN ARCHIVE: 75. BLACK STAR: NASA, 447. BROWN BROTHERS: 213. BRUCE COLEMAN: Melinda Berge, 131; Pat Canova, 42TR; Robert Carr, 335TR; Larry Ditto, 87; D.P. Hershkowitz, 282; Wendell Metzen, 179; David deVries, 64. CAPITOL CITIES/ABC, INC.: 405T. COLUMBIA UNIVERSITY (Rare Book and Manuscript Division): Original watercolor drawing by Arthur Rackman for the book jacket of *The Legend of Sleepy Hollow*, 67. CULVER PICTURES: 141, 425. GEORGE FISTROVICH: 393. FOCUS ON SPORTS: 163, 260, 297, 363, 405. FOUR BY FIVE: 45. EDUARDO FUSS: 283. THE GRANGER COLLECTION: 143, 191. H. ARMSTRONG ROBERTS: 189T; W. Free, 108L. MICHAL HERON: 301, 404T. HIRSHHORN MUSEUM AND SCULPTURE GARDEN, SMITHSONIAN INSTITUTION: Jackson Pollock, *Number 3, 1949: Tiger*, © ARS (gift of Joseph H. Hirshhorn, 1966), 353. RICHARD HUTCHINGS 231TL, 375. THE IMAGE BANK: Murray Alcosser, 7; Mel DiGiacomo, 392; C.D. Geissler, 356; Jeff Hunter, 427; Don Landwehrle, 101; Patti McConville, 109T; Co Renmeester, 83R; Chris Alan Wilton, 100. KEN KARP: 34, 47, 53, 57, 59, 113, 119, 122, 123, 124, 158, 159L, 193, 199, 202, 203, 209, 265, 271, 275, 276, 339, 345, 348, 349, 350, 409, 415, 419, 426, 503. KING FEATURES SYNDICATE, INC. (Reprinted with special permission): 493. PAUL KOLNIK/SCHOOL OF AMERICAN BALLET: 147. © NICK KOUDIS, COURTESY, VICTOR GIORDANO: 35. © GARY LADD 1972: 451L. © 1980 LUCASFILM, LTD. (all rights reserved, courtesy of Lucasfilm, Ltd.): 507. MAGNUM PHOTOS: 261. MARCH OF DIMES BIRTH DEFECT FOUNDATION: 279. MONKMEYER PRESS: Leonard Lee Rue III, 357. MUSEUM OF FINE ARTS, BOSTON, MA: Mary Cassatt, *The Letter*, Hayden Fund, 219. MUSEUM OF MODERN ART FILE STILLS ARCHIVE: 225. NASA: 377, 449, 474. THE NEW YORK TIMES: 61. PARAMOUNT/THE KOBAL COLLECTION: 509. PETER ARNOLD: Mike Phillips, 377R. PHOTOEDIT: Robert Brenner, 292; Myrlene Ferguson, 18. PHOTOFEST: 129. PHOTO RESEARCHERS: Archiv, 435; Linda Bartlett, 306; Wesley Boxce, 178; Carl Frank, 42TL; F.B. Grunzweig (*Family Group* by Henry Moore, 1948–49. Bronze, cast 1950. A. Conger Goodyear Fund), 335TL; Tom Hollyman (Exhibit, Smithsonian Institution), 423; Anthony Howath, 484T; Andrea Krause, 82; Chris Luneski, 324; NASA, 485B; Joseph Nettis, 108R, 159R; Science Photo Library/Fred Espanak, 438; Science Source/Hale Laboratories, 484B; Soames Summerhays, 334; Wasyl Szkodskinsky, 321R; Vandystadt/Jean-Marc Loubat, 260TR. Jim Zipp, 305. ROBERT QUACKENBUSH (Woodcut for *The Open Boat* by Stephen Crane. Property of the artist.): 71. RAINBOW: Dan McCoy, 207. Printed by permission of the ESTATE OF NORMAN ROCKWELL: *Freedom of Speech*, Copyright © 1943 Estate of Norman Rockwell, 149; Air and Space Museum, Smithsonian Institution, Copyright © 1967, Estate of Norman Rockwell, 451R. SHASHINKA PHOTO LIBRARY: 15. SIPA: Dan Wagner, 3. SPORTS ILLUSTRATED: Mark Pearlstein, 252, 253, 257. STOCK BOSTON: Bob Daemmrich, 19L, 251; Owen Franken, 188B, 189B, 359, 366; Spencer Grant, 485T; Ellis Herwig, 188T; Richard Pasley, 376; Stacy Pick, 335B; Cary Wolinsky, 217. THE STOCK MARKET: Luis S. Giner, 155; Richard Gross, 210; Karen Leeds, xii, 1; Harvey Lloyd, 235, 289; Kunio Owaki, 475; Jim Raycroft, 17; R.B. Sanchez, 109B; Richard Steedman, 83L. ERIKA STONE: 260BR. SUPERSTOCK/SHOSTAL: Ed Cooper, 43; S. Maeda, 311; NASA, 431. MARTHA SWOPE: 137, 211, 307L. TAURUS: Philip Jon Bailey, 307R. MICHAEL TEDESCO: 127. STACK & ASSOCIATES: Ed Robinson, 11; Tom Stack, 404B. TSW-CLICK/CHICAGO: David Austen, 81; Terry Farmer, 355; Chuck Keeler, 250. UPI/BETTMAN NEWSPHOTO: 229. WOODFIN CAMP & ASSOCIATES: Jacques Chenet, 281; Julie Habel, 325; Michael Heron, 19R; Momatiuk/Eastcott, 281.